THE NEW
PALGRAVE

UTILITY
AND PROBABILITY

THE NEW PALGRAVE

UTILITY AND PROBABILITY

EDITED BY

JOHN EATWELL · MURRAY MILGATE · PETER NEWMAN

W. W. NORTON & COMPANY

NEW YORK · LONDON

© The Macmillan Press Limited, 1987, 1990

First published in
The New Palgrave: A Dictionary of Economics
Edited by John Eatwell, Murray Milgate and Peter Newman
in four volumes, 1987

The New Palgrave is a trademark of
The Macmillan Press Limited

First American Edition, 1990
ISBN 0-393-02738-4

ISBN 0-393-95863-9   PBK.

W. W. Norton & Company, Inc.
500 Fifth Avenue
New York, NY 10110

W. W. Norton & Company, Ltd.
37 Great Russell Street
London WC1B 3NU

Printed in Hong Kong

1   2   3   4   5   6   7   8   9   0

Contents

Acknowledgements		vi
General Preface		vii
Preface		xi
Acyclicity	Douglas Blair	1
Allais paradox	Maurice Allais	3
Thomas Bayes	D.V. Lindley	10
Daniel Bernoulli	S.L. Zabell	12
Bounded rationality	Herbert A. Simon	15
Certainty equivalent	Xavier Freixas	19
Contingent commodities	Zvi Safra	22
Economic theory and the hypothesis of rationality	Kenneth J. Arrow	25
Francis Ysidro Edgeworth	Peter Newman	38
Expected utility and mathematical expectation	David Schmeidler and Peter Wakker	70
Expected utility hypothesis	Mark J. Machina	79
Bruno de Finetti	Giancarlo Gandolfo	96
Herman Heinrich Gossen	Jurg Niehans	99
Impatience	Larry G. Epstein	108
Induction	Paul W. Humphreys	116
Interdependent preferences	Peter C. Fishburn	121
Interpersonal utility comparisons	John C. Harsanyi	128
Lexicographic orderings	C. Blackorby	134
Myopic decision rules	Mordecai Kurz	136
Orderings	C. Blackorby	142
Perfect foresight	Margaret Bray	144
Preferences	Georg Henrik von Wright	149

Contents

Preference reversals	Edi Karni	157
Preordering	C. Blackorby	161
Probability	Ian Hacking	163
Psychology and economics	Charles R. Plott	178
Frank Plumpton Ramsey	Peter Newman	186
Rational behaviour	Amartya Sen	198
Representation of preferences	Peter C. Fishburn	217
Risk	Mark J. Machina and Michael Rothschild	227
Leonard J. Savage	I. Richard Savage	240
State-dependent preferences	Edi Karni	242
State preference approach	H.M. Polemarchakis	248
Stochastic dominance	Haim Levy	251
Subjective probability	I.J. Good	255
Time preference	Murray N. Rothbard	270
Transitivity	Wayne Shafer	276
Uncertainty	Peter J. Hammond	280
Utility	R.D. Collison Black	295
Utility theory and decision theory	Peter C. Fishburn	303
Contributors		313

Acknowledgements

The following contributor (article shown in parenthesis) acknowledges support from public bodies and permission to reprint copyright material:

Kenneth J. Arrow (Economic Theory and the Hypothesis of Rationality), support from the Office of Naval Research, originally published as 'Rationality of Self and Others in an Economic System' in the *Journal of Business*, 1986, Vol. 59, No. 4, pt. 2. Reproduced with permission of the University of Chicago Press.

General Preface

The books in this series are the offspring of *The New Palgrave: A Dictionary of Economics*. Published in late 1987, the *Dictionary* has rapidly become a standard reference work in economics. However, its four heavy tomes containing over four million words on the whole range of economic thought is not a form convenient to every potential user. For many students and teachers it is simply too bulky, too comprehensive and too expensive for everyday use.

By developing the present series of compact volumes of reprints from the original work, we hope that some of the intellectual wealth of *The New Palgrave* will become accessible to much wider groups of readers. Each of the volumes is devoted to a particular branch of economics, such as econometrics or general equilibrium or money, with a scope corresponding roughly to a university course on that subject. Apart from correction of misprints, etc. the content of each of its reprinted articles is exactly the same as that of the original. In addition, a few brand new entries have been commissioned especially for the series, either to fill an apparent gap or more commonly to include topics that have risen to prominence since the dictionary was originally commissioned.

As *The New Palgrave* is the sole parent of the present series, it may be helpful to explain that it is the modern successor to the excellent *Dictionary of Political Economy* edited by R.H. Inglis Palgrave and published in three volumes in 1894, 1896 and 1899. A second and slightly modified version, edited by Henry Higgs, appeared during the mid-1920s. These two editions each contained almost 4,000 entries, but many of those were simply brief definitions and many of the others were devoted to peripheral topics such as foreign coinage, maritime commerce, and Scottish law. To make room for the spectacular growth in economics over the last 60 years while keeping still to a manageable length, *The New Palgrave* concentrated instead on economic theory, its originators, and its closely cognate disciplines. Its nearly 2,000 entries (commissioned from over 900 scholars) are all self-contained essays, sometimes brief but never mere definitions.

Apart from its biographical entries, *The New Palgrave* is concerned chiefly with theory rather than fact, doctrine rather than data; and it is not at all clear how theory and doctrine, as distinct from facts and figures, *should* be treated in an encyclopaedia. One way is to treat everything from a particular point of view. Broadly speaking, that was the way of Diderot's classic *Encyclopédie raisonée* (1751–1772), as it was also of Léon Say's *Nouveau dictionnaire d'économie politique* (1891–2). Sometimes, as in articles by Quesnay and Turgot in the *Encyclopédie*, this approach has yielded entries of surpassing brilliance. Too often, however, both the range of subjects covered and the quality of the coverage itself are seriously reduced by such a self-limiting perspective. Thus the entry called '*Méthode*' in the first edition of Say's *Dictionnaire* asserted that the use of mathematics in economics 'will only ever be in the hands of a few', and the dictionary backed up that claim by choosing not to have any entry on Cournot.

Another approach is to have each entry take care to reflect within itself varying points of view. This may help the student temporarily, as when preparing for an examination. But in a subject like economics, the Olympian detachment which this approach requires often places a heavy burden on the author, asking for a scrupulous account of doctrines he or she believes to be at best wrong-headed. Even when an especially able author does produce a judicious survey article, it is surely too much to ask that it also convey just as much enthusiasm for those theories thought misguided as for those found congenial. Lacking an enthusiastic exposition, however, the disfavoured theories may then be studied less closely than they deserve.

The New Palgrave did not ask its authors to treat economic theory from any particular point of view, except in one respect to be discussed below. Nor did it call for surveys. Instead, each author was asked to make clear his or her own views of the subject under discussion, and for the rest to be as fair and accurate as possible, without striving to be 'judicious'. A balanced perspective on each topic was always the aim, the ideal. But it was to be sought not *internally*, within each article, but *externally*, between articles, with the reader rather than the writer handed the task of achieving a personal balance between differing views.

For a controversial topic, a set of several more or less synonymous headwords, matched by a broad diversity of contributors, was designed to produce enough variety of opinion to help form the reader's own synthesis; indeed, such diversity will be found in most of the individual volumes in this series.

This approach was not without its problems. Thus, the prevalence of uncertainty in the process of commissioning entries sometimes produced a less diverse outcome than we had planned. 'I can call spirits from the vasty deep,' said Owen Glendower. 'Why, so can I,' replied Hotspur, 'or so can any man;/ But will they come when you do call for them?' In our experience, not quite as often as we would have liked.

The one point of view we did urge upon every one of *Palgrave*'s authors was to write from an historical perspective. For each subject its contributor was asked to discuss not only present problems but also past growth and future prospects. This request was made in the belief that knowledge of the historical development of any theory enriches our present understanding of it, and so helps to construct better theories for the future. The authors' response to the request was generally so positive that, as the reader of any of these volumes will discover, the resulting contributions amply justified that belief.

John Eatwell
Murray Milgate
Peter Newman

Preface

In the eighteenth and nineteenth centuries, economists and others began to formulate concepts of what is now called rational behaviour. What exactly such behaviour means is not easy to define. John Harsanyi, for example, has said that 'rational behaviour is simply behaviour consistently pursuing some well defined goals, and pursuing them according to some well defined set of preferences or priorities' (*Social Research*, 1977). Put like that, rational behaviour is clearly neither good nor bad in any ethical sense. Even though modern economists fully realise the ethical neutrality of rational behaviour so defined, still they tend to look upon it with approval, preferring to formulate models of economies whose constituent individuals are 'rational agents'. Their reason is simple. To quote Harsanyi again, 'in many fields of human endeavour ... human behaviour does show sufficiently high degrees of rationality as to give a surprising amount of explanatory and predictive power to some analytical models postulating full rationality'.

Models of individual rational behaviour are of two types. The first is that of choice under certainty, where once a person chooses an action (such as to buy a bottle of milk), what he receives will be what he expected. The second is choice under uncertainty, where even though a choice is made (such as to rent a videotape), the outcome may turn out different from expectations. Theories of rational choice under certainty are organised around the two concepts of the individual's preferences and the opportunities open to her, while theories of rational action under uncertainty add to these two notions the probabilities that are attached to those opportunities. The essays in this volume discuss the present and a past nature of such theories of rational behaviour.

In standard models of behaviour under certainty each person is assumed to have consistent preferences over the relevant set of alternatives, and a numerical value is attached to each alternative. As Pareto was the first to emphasize, this value indicates but does not measure how highly that alternative ranks in the person's preferences. Any rule that assigns numerical values to alternatives in a consistent way is thus a real-valued function which *represents* the underlying preferences. The origins of these Paretean representations (or indicators) may be traced back to the 'utility functions' of Gossen, Jevons and Walras, and indeed that older term is still used. Hence, rather than speaking of preferences and probability, it is more customary to talk of utility and probability.

Some of the most prominent members of the marginal utility revolution, such as Sidgwick and Edgeworth, were utilitarians. But this fact does not imply that there is any logical connection between, on the one hand, the ethical doctrines usually designated as Utilitarianism and, on the other, the idea that meaningful predictions of an agent's behaviour can be derived from the postulate that she tries to maximise her utility indicator. Almost a century ago, Alfred Marshall was well aware of the misunderstandings which can arise:

'It has however unfortunately happened that the customary uses of economic terms have sometimes suggested the belief that economists are adherents of the philosophical system of Hedonism or of Utilitarianism ... since there is a general agreement that all incentives to action, in so far as they are conscious desires at all, may without impropriety be spoken of shortly as desired for "satisfaction," it may perhaps be well to use this word instead of "pleasure," (*Principles of Economics*, 4th edition, 1898, 77–78n).

Ever since Gossen's book in 1854, utility functions have played two distinguishable roles. Perhaps the more important for economists was their role in the theory of value. Relative prices were determined by supply and demand, and it was utility, or more precisely marginal utility, which determined demand. The development and refinement of that 'marginalist' story, with the crucial application of utility analysis to the determination of supply that went along with it, is well known to every student of economics. But another strand in Gossen's thought was the much more ambitious role of utility functions as the ground for rational choice in *any* line of human activity. After all his book was called not 'The Principles of Economics (or Political Economy)' but *The Laws of Human Relations*, his preface claiming that: 'I believe I have accomplished for the explanation of the relations among humans what a Copernicus was able to accomplish for the explanation of the relations of heavenly bodies.'

This view, that utility and probability analysis is simply the analysis of choice and action in general, stakes out a much wider claim for economics as a discipline than the mere study of economies. As the comparison with Copernicus implies, economics becomes to the social sciences what physics is to the natural sciences. Whether economics can bear such a burden is an interesting question, but one that is beyond the scope of the present volume. In any event, economists will continue to study the implications of the maximisation of utility, or of expected utility, or of some nonlinear function of utility and probability. What this work is called, whether economics, decision theory, or philosophy, matters less than that it be well done.

The Editors

Acyclicity

DOUGLAS BLAIR

Acyclicity is a consistency property of preferences and other binary relations. It requires that the asymmetric part P of the relation (e.g. the subrelation of strict preference) contain no cycles; that is, for no sequence of alternatives $x_1, x_2, \ldots, x_n$ is it true that $x_1 P x_2, x_2 P x_3, \ldots, x_{n-1} P x_n$, and $x_n P x_1$. The study of cyclic preferences dates at least to Condorcet's (1785) treatment of the paradox of voting, in which transitive individual voters generate cyclic majority preferences.

Whenever a feasible set S contains more than two alternatives, some principle is needed to generate choices $C(S)$ from the pairwise comparisons summarized by the preference relation; one natural candidate is the set of undominated alternatives. Acyclicity is necessary and sufficient for the existence of a non-empty set of undominated elements in any finite feasible subset S of the universal set of alternatives. In addition, defining the choice set as the undominated alternatives according to an acyclic relation guarantees that choices will exhibit a desirable consistency property: if S is a subset of T and if x belongs both to S and to $C(T)$, then x must belong to $C(S)$. In Sen's (1970) example, if the world champion is a Pakistani, then he must be champion of Pakistan as well. This property is attractive in piecemeal decision mechanisms in which choices are made from unions of choices over subsets. If an alternative fails to be chosen in some subset, it need not be reconsidered later, since the contrapositive of this property ensures that the alternative will not be among the final choices.

Acyclicity is a significantly weaker consistency property than transitivity; it permits intransitivities both of the strict preference relation P and the symmetric subrelation of indifference I. For example, the preferences xPy, yPz and xIz are acyclic; so too are the preferences xIy, xIz and xPz.

Acyclicity arises in several contexts in economics. Consumer theory's Strong Axiom of Revealed Preference (see Houthakker, 1950; Ville, 1952), for example, is an axiom asserting that a particular revealed preference relation is acyclic. It arose early in the development of game theory as well; the acyclicity of dominance

1

relations is closely linked to the uniqueness of the von Neumann–Morgenstern (1947, ch. XII) solution.

Acyclicity has been studied most intensively, however, in connection with Arrow's (1951) Impossibility Theorem. This proposition concerns constitutions, which aggregate sets of individuals' preference orderings into social preferences. Arrow showed that the only constitutions satisfying two reasonable axioms and yielding transitive social preferences are dictatorial. Several writers have attempted to circumvent this conclusion by relaxing transitivity to the more defensible requirement of acyclicity. Non-dictatorial acyclic constitutions do exist, but they turn out to be hardly more attractive than dictatorships. Blair and Pollak (1982) review this literature and show that such constitutions must endow at least one voter with extensive veto power over strict social preferences opposite to his or her own. If egalitarian concerns force the vesting of such power in many such voters, the constitution will be highly indecisive, that is, will frequently yield judgements of indifference between alternatives.

BIBLIOGRAPHY

Arrow, K. 1951. *Social Choice and Individual Values.* New York: Wiley.

Blair, D.H. and Pollak, R. 1982. Acyclic collective choice rules. *Econometrica* 50(4), July, 931–43.

Condorcet, Marquis de. 1785. *Essai sur l'application de l'analyse à la probabilité des decisions rendues à la pluralité des voix.* Paris.

Houthakker, H. 1950. Revealed preference and the utility function. *Economica* 17, May, 159–74.

von Neumann, J. and Morgenstern, O. 1947. *Theory of Games and Economic Behavior.* 2nd edn, Princeton: Princeton University Press.

Sen, A. 1970. *Collective Choice and Social Welfare.* San Francisco: Holden-Day.

Ville, J. 1952. The existence conditions of a total utility function. *Review of Economic Studies* 19(2), 123–8.

Allais Paradox

MAURICE ALLAIS

THE ST PETERSBURG PARADOX AND THE BERNOULLIAN FORMULATION. Let there be a random prospect $g_1, \ldots, g_i, \ldots, g_n, \ldots, p_1, \ldots, p_i, \ldots, p_n$ ($\Sigma_i p_i = 1$) giving the probability p_i of positive or negative gains g_i. The early theorists of games of chance considered that a game was advantageous when the mathematical expectation

$$M = \sum_i p_i g_i \qquad (1 \leqslant i \leqslant n) \tag{1}$$

was positive (Allais, 1952b, pp. 68–9).

The principle of the mathematical expectation of monetary gains has proven to be open to question in the case of the *St Petersburg Paradox* outlined by Nicolas Bernoulli. For this game, we have: $g_i = 2^i, p_i = 1/2^i, n = \infty$ so that $M = \infty$. However, if the unit of value is the dollar, it can be seen that for most subjects, the psychological monetary value of the game (that is the price they are ready to pay for this random prospect) is generally lower than 20 dollars. This, at first sight, involves a paradox.

To explain this paradox, Daniel Bernoulli (1738) considered the mathematical expectation of cardinal utilities $u(C + g_i)$ instead of the mathematical expectation of monetary gains, C being the player's capital. Thus the formulation (1) is replaced by the Bernoullian formulation

$$u(C + V) = \sum_i p_i u(C + g_i) \tag{2}$$

in which V is the psychological monetary value of the random prospect. He proposed to take the logarithmic expression $u = \log(C + g)$ as cardinal utility (Bernoulli, 1738; Allais, 1952b, p. 68; 1977, pp. 498–506; 1983, p. 33). It can then be shown that we have approximately $V \sim a + [\log C/\log 2]$ with $a = 0.942$, which yields $V \sim 14$ or 18 US\$ for C equal to 10,000 or 100,000 dollars respectively (Allais, 1977, p. 572).

3

THE NEO-BERNOULLIAN FORMULATION. In order to measure cardinal utility from random choice, von Neumann and Morgenstern demonstrated in the *Theory of Games* (1947), on the basis of a set of more or less appealing postulates, the existence of an index $B(C + g)$, such that

$$B(C + V) = \sum_i p_i B(C + g_i) \tag{3}$$

in which the index $B(C + g)$ is independent of the random prospect considered, but depends on the subject (von Neumann and Morgenstern, 1947, pp. 8–31 and 617–32; Allais, 1952b, p. 74; 1977, pp. 521–3, 591–603; 1983, p. 34).

Using other sets of postulates, Marschak, Friedman and Savage, Samuelson, Savage, etc. (Marschak, 1950 and 1951; Friedman and Savage, 1948; Samuelson, 1952; Savage, 1952 and 1954; Allais, 1952b, pp. 74–5, 88–92, and 99–103; 1977, pp. 464–5, 508–14; 1983, pp. 33–5) came to the same formulation (3), which may be referred to as the neo-Bernoullian formulation, but its interpretation differs depending on the postulates adopted. While von Neumann and Morgenstern believed, at least initially, that $B \equiv u$, the p_i being objective probabilities (Allais, 1952b, p. 74; 1977, pp. 591–2), Savage held that cardinal utility is a myth (Savage, 1954, p. 94), and that the neo-Bernoullian index B alone is real, the p_i being subjective probabilities, the existence of the function B and the p_i being proven on the basis of the axioms considered. Some authors (e.g. de Finetti, Krelle, Harsanyi) admit the existence of cardinal utility u, but they consider that $B \neq u$, and the index B is deemed to take account of the relative propensity for risk corresponding to the distribution of cardinal utility (de Finetti, 1977; Allais, 1952b, pp. 123–4; 1983, pp. 30–31).

Whereas von Neumann's and Morgenstern's opinion, accepted by most authors, is that the crucial axiom of their theory is axiom 3 Cb, I consider that their axioms 3 Ba and 3 Bb are the crucial ones (Allais, 1977, pp. 596–8). However, one way or another, irrespective of the nature of the axioms from which it is derived, the neo-Bernoullian formulation boils down to assuming the independence of the B_i for given values of the p_i. This is the principle of independence (Allais, 1952b, pp. 88–90 and 98–9; 1977, pp. 466–7).

THE ALLAIS PARADOX. When I read the *Theory of Games* in 1948, formulation (3) appeared to me to be totally incompatible with the conclusions I had reached in 1936 attempting to define a reasonable strategy for a repetitive game with a positive mathematical expectation (Allais, 1977, pp. 445–6). Consequently. I viewed the principle of independence as incompatible with the preference for security in the neighbourhood of certainty shown by every subject and which is reflected by the elimination of all strategies implying a non-negligible probability of ruin, and by a preference for security in the neighbourhood of certainty when dealing with sums that are large in relation to the subject's capital (Allais, 1952b, pp. 84–6, 88–90, 92–5; 1977, pp. 451, 466–7, 491–8).

This led me to devise some counter-examples. One of them, formulated in 1952, has become famous as the 'Allais Paradox'. Today, it is as widespread as its real meaning is generally misunderstood.

This counter-example consists of two questions, the gains considered being expressed in (1952) francs [one million (1952) francs is roughly equivalent to 10,000 (1985) dollars].

(1) *Do you prefer Situation A to Situation B?*
Situation A:
– certainty of receiving 100 million.
Situation B:
– a 10 per cent chance of winning 500 million,
– an 89 per cent chance of winning 100 million,
– a 1 per cent chance of winning nothing.

(2) *Do you prefer Situation C to Situation D?*
Situation C:
– an 11 per cent chance of winning 100 million,
– an 89 per cent chance of winning nothing.
Situation D:
– a 10 per cent chance of winning 500 million,
– a 90 per cent chance of winning nothing.

It can be shown that, according to the neo-Bernoullian formulation, the preference $A > B$ should entail the preference $C > D$, and conversely (Allais, 1952b, pp. 88–90; 1977, pp. 533–41).

However, it is observed that for very careful persons, well aware of the probability calculus and considered as rational, and whose capital C is relatively low by comparison with the gains considered, the preference $A > B$ can be observed in parallel to the preference $C < D$. Since the neo-Bernoullians consider the axioms from which they deduce the neo-Bernoullian formulation as evident, they consider this result a paradox.

In 1952, Savage's answers to these two questions contradicted his own axioms. The explanation he gave is somewhat surprising. It boiled down to stating: 'Since my axioms are totally evident, my answers, which are indeed incompatible with my axioms, are explained by the fact that I did not give the matter enough thought' (Savage, 1954, pp. 101–103).

EMPIRICAL RESEARCH. After analysing the answers to the 1952 Questionnaire (Allais, 1952d), I found that the rate of violation of the neo-Bernoullian formulation corresponding to the Allais Paradox was approximately 53 per cent (Allais, 1977, p. 474).

This violation example is not an isolated one (Allais, 1977, pp. 636–6, n. 15). There is even one test for which the rate of violation is 100 per cent. It is based on the comparative analysis of, on the one hand, the monetary value x' attributed to a probability of $1/2$ of winning a sum between 0.0001 and 1000 million, with a probability of $1/2$ of winning nothing at all; and, on the other hand, of the monetary value x'' attributed to a probability p_i between 0.25 and 0.999 of winning

200 million, with a probability $1 - p_i$ of winning nothing at all. The two indexes $B_{1/2}$ and B_{200} deduced from these two series of questions, which according to the neo-Bernoullian formulation should be totally identical up to a linear transformation, in fact are completely different for all the subjects who answered the questions. Such was in particular the case of de Finetti (Allais, 1977, pp. 612–13, 620–31; 1983, pp. 61–2 and 110–11, n. 146).

Much empirical research has been carried out since 1952. It has shown that many subjects who can be viewed as rational may behave in contradiction with the neo-Bernoullian formulations (e.g. MacCrimmon and Larsson, 1975; Allais, 1977, pp. 507–8, pp. 611–54). Confronted with these results, the neo-Bernoullians always explain these violations as 'anomalies', 'errors', 'insufficient thought by the subjects', or 'ill constructed and inconclusive' experiments made by incompetent persons, 'inexperienced in experimental psychology' (e.g. Amihud, 1974 and 1977; Morgenstern, 1976). But these statements do not hold in the face of the very numerous violations observed by the many researchers, following different methods and operating in different countries at different times (Allais, 1977, pp. 541–2; 1983, p. 66).

THE ALLAIS PARADOX: A SIMPLE ILLUSTRATION OF ALLAIS' GENERAL THEORY OF RANDOM CHOICE. These violations can be explained very simply. Limiting consideration to the mathematical expectation of the B_i involves neglecting the basic element characterizing psychology vis-à-vis risk, namely the distribution of cardinal utility about its mathematical expectation (Allais, 1952b, pp. 51–5, 96–7; 1977, pp. 481–2, 520–23, 550–52; 1983, pp. 30–31), and in particular, when very large sums are involved in comparison with the psychological capital of the subject, the strong dependence between the different eventualities (g_i, p_i), and the very strong preference for security in the neighbourhood of certainty.

My 1952 inquiry (Allais, 1952d; 1977, pp. 447–9, 451–4, 604–54; 1983, pp. 28 and 41) showed that all the subjects questioned were able to answer questions on the intensity of their preferences for different possible gains, setting aside any consideration of random choices (only a few neo-Bernoullian authors refused to answer these questions) (Allais, 1943, pp. 156–77; 1952b, pp. 43–6; 1977, pp. 460–61, 475–80, 614–17, 632–3). The analysis of the answers made it possible to design a well defined cardinal utility curve, the structure of which is the same for all the subjects up to a linear transformation. It portrays their answers on average remarkably well (Allais, 1984a and 1984c).

This result is all the more significant in that this expression of cardinal utility shows a very striking similarity to the expression for psychophysiological sensation as a function of luminous stimulus, determined by Weber's and Fechner's successors (Allais, 1984c, §4.3 and Charts III and XXV).

The existence of a cardinal utility $u(C + g)$ being proven and the neo-Bernoullian index $B(C + g)$, if it exists, being defined also up to a linear transformation, it can be shown that the two indexes are necessarily identical up to a linear transformation (Allais, 1952b, pp. 97–8, 103, 128–30; 1977, pp. 465, 483, 604–7; 1983, pp. 29–30; 1985).

As a consequence the neo-Bernoullian formulation reduces to considering the mathematical expectation of cardinal utility alone, neglecting its dispersion about the average. In so doing, it neglects what may be considered as the specific element of risk (Allais, 1952b, pp. 49–56; 1983, pp. 35–41).

In fact the cardinal utility corresponding to a monetary value V of a random prospect should be considered as a function

$$u(C+V) = F[u(C+g_1), \ldots, u(C+g_i), \ldots, u(C+g_n), p_1, \ldots, p_i, \ldots, p_n]$$
$$(4)$$

of cardinal utilities u_i corresponding to the different gains g_i. Since utilities u_i are defined up to a linear transformation, it can be shown that (Allais, 1977, pp. 481–3, 550–52, 607–9; 1985, §12 and 22)

$$u + \Delta = F(u_1 + \Delta, \ldots, u_i + \Delta, \ldots, u_n + \Delta, p_1, \ldots, p_i, \ldots, p_n) \quad (5)$$

in which Δ is any constant (property of cardinal isovariation). Consequently it can be shown that relation (4) can be written

$$u(C+V) = \bar{u} + R(\mu_2, \ldots, \mu_l, \ldots, \mu_{2n-1}) \quad (6)$$

in which $\bar{u}$ represents the mathematical expectation of the u_i and the μ_l represent the moments of order l:

$$\mu_l = \sum_i p_i(u_i - \bar{u})^l. \quad (7)$$

The ratio $\rho = R/\bar{u}$ can be considered as an index of the propensity for risk. For $\rho = 0$, the behaviour is Bernoullian; for $\rho > 0$, there is a propensity for risk; for $\rho < 0$, there is a propensity for security. For a given subject, ρ can be nil, positive or negative, depending on the domain of the field of random choices considered (Allais, 1983, pp. 35–41; 1985).

The mistake made by the proponents of the neo-Bernoullian formulation is to want to impose restrictions on the preference index

$$I = f[g_1, \ldots, g_i, \ldots, g_n, p_1, \ldots, p_i, \ldots, p_n] \quad (8)$$

of any subject other than those corresponding to conditions of rationality, such as the existence of a field of ordered random choice or the axiom of absolute preference. According to this axiom, taking two random prospects g_i, p_i and g_i', p_i such that $g_i > g_i'$ for any p_i, the first is obviously preferable to the second (Allais, 1952b, pp. 38–41; 1977, pp. 457–8, 530–35; 1985, §31.3).

Imposing other restrictions would, in the case of certain goods $(A), (B), \ldots, (C)$, reduce to imposing special restrictions on the preference index $I(A, B, \ldots, C)$ which no author has ever envisaged. In fact, to have a marked preference for security in the neighbourhood of certainty together with a preference for risk far from certainty is not more irrational than preferring roast beef to chicken (Allais, 1952b, pp. 65–7; 1977, pp. 527–33; 1983, pp. 39–40; §31.3).

FROM THE ST PETERSBURG PARADOX TO THE ALLAIS PARADOX. In sum, just as the St Petersburg Paradox led Daniel Bernoulli to replace the principle of maximization of the mathematical expectation of monetary values by the Bernoullian principle of maximization of cardinal utilities, the Allais Paradox leads to adding to the Bernoullian formulation a specific term characterizing the propensity to risk which takes account of the distribution as a whole of cardinal utility (Allais, 1978, pp. 4–7; 1977, pp. 548–52; 1983, pp. 35–42).

Neither the St Petersburg nor the Allais Paradox involves a paradox. Both correspond to basic psychological realities: the non-identity of monetary and psychological values and the importance of the distribution of cardinal utility about its average value.

For nearly forty years the supporters of the neo-Bernoullian formulation have exerted a dogmatic and intolerant, powerful and tyrannical domination over the academic world; only in very recent years has a growing reaction begun to appear. This is not the first example of the opposition of the 'establishments' of any kind to scientific progress, nor will it be the last (Allais, 1977, pp. 518–46; 1983, pp. 69–71, 112–14).

The Allais Paradox does not reduce to a mere counter-example of purely anecdotal value based on errors of judgement, as too many authors seem to think without referring to the general theory of random choice which underlies it. It is fundamentally an illustraton of the need to take account not only of the mathematical expectation of cardinal utility, but also of its distribution as a whole about its average, basic elements characterizing the psychology of risk.

BIBLIOGRAPHY

Allais, M. 1943. *A la recherche d'une discipline économique*, Première partie: l'économie pure. Ateliers Industria, 920 pp. Second edition under the title *Traité d'économie pure*, Paris: Imprimerie Nationale, 1952, 5 vols. (The second edition is identical to the first, apart from the addition of a new introduction, 63 pp.)

Allais, M. 1952a. Fondements d'une théorie positive des choix comportant un risque et critique des postulats et axiomes de l'école Américaine. International Conference on Risk, Centre National de la Recherche Scientifique, May 1952. *Colloques Internationaux XL, Econométrie*, Paris, 1953, 257–332.

Allais, M. 1952b. The foundations of a positive theory of choice involving risk and a criticism of the postulates and axioms of the American school. English translation of 1952a. In Allais and Hagen (1979), 27–145.

Allais, M. 1952c. Le comportement de l'homme rationnel devant le risque: critique des postulats et axiomes de l'école Américaine. *Econometrica* 21(4), October 1953, 503–546. This paper corresponds to some parts of Allais, 1952a.

Allais, M. 1952d. La psychologie de l'homme rationnel devant le risque – la théorie et l'expérience. *Journal de la Société de Statistique de Paris*, January–March 1953, 47–73.

Allais, M. 1977. The so-called Allais' Paradox and rational decisions under uncertainty. In Allais and Hagen (1979), 437–699.

Allais, M. 1978. Editorial Introduction, Foreword. In Allais and Hagen (1979), 3–11.

Allais, M. 1983. The foundations of the theory of utility and risk. In *Progress in Decision Theory*, ed. O. Hagen and F. Wenstop, Dordrecht: Reidel, 1984, 3–131.

Allais, M. 1984a. L'utilité cardinale et sa détermination – hypothèses, méthodes et résultats empiriques. Memoir presented to the Second International Conference on Foundations of Utility and Risk Theory, Venice, 5–9 June 1984.

Allais, M. 1984b. The cardinal utility and its determination – hypotheses, methods and empirical results. English version of 1984a, in *Theory and Decision*, 1987.

Allais, M. 1984c. Determination of cardinal utility according to an intrinsic invariant model. Abridged version of 1984a in *Recent Developments in the Foundations of Utility and Risk Theory*, ed. L. Daboni et al., Dordrecht: Reidel, 1985, 83–120.

Allais, M. 1985. Three theorems on the theory of cardinal utility and random choice. In *Essays in Honour of Werner Leinfellner*, ed. H. Berghel, Dordrecht: Reidel, 1986.

Allais, M. and Hagen, O. (eds) 1979. *Expected Utility Hypotheses and the Allais' Paradox; Contemporary Discussions and Rational Decisions under Uncertainty with Allais' Rejoinder*. Dordrecht: Reidel.

Amihud, Y. 1974. Critical examination of the new foundation of utility. In Allais and Hagen (1979), 149–60.

Amihud, Y. 1977. A reply to Allais. In Allais and Hagen (1979), 185–90.

Bernoulli, D. 1738. Specimen theoriae novae de mensura sortis. Trans. as 'Exposition of a new theory on the measurement of risk'. *Econometrica* 22 (1954), 23–36.

de Finetti, B. 1977. A short confirmation of my standpoint. In Allais and Hagen (1979), 161.

Friedman, M. and Savage, J.L. 1948. The utility analysis of choices involving risk. *Journal of Political Economy* 56, August, 279–304.

MacCrimmon, K. and Larsson, S. 1975. Utility theory: axioms versus paradoxes. In Allais and Hagen (1979), 333–409.

Marschak, J. 1950. Rational behavior, uncertain prospects and measurable utility. *Econometrica* 18(2), April, 111–41.

Marschak, J. 1951. Why 'should' statisticians and businessmen maximize moral expectation? In *Proceedings of the Second Berkeley Symposium on Mathematical Statistics and Probability*, Berkeley: University of California Press.

Marschak, J. 1977. Psychological values, and decision makers. In Allais and Hagen (1979), 163–75.

Morgenstern, O. 1976. Some reflections on utility. In Allais and Hagen (1979), 175–83.

Samuelson, P. 1952. Utility, preference and probability. International Conference on Risk, Centre National de la Recherche Scientifique, Paris, May 1952. *Colloques Internationaux XL, Econométrie*, Paris, 1953, 141–50.

Savage, L. 1952. An axiomatization of reasonable behavior in the face of uncertainty. International Conference on Risk, Paris, May 1952. Centre National de la Recherche Scientifique, *Colloques Internationaux XL, Econométrie*, Paris, 1953, 29–33.

Savage, L. 1954. *The Foundations of Statistics*. New York: Wiley.

von Neumann, J. and Morgenstern, O. 1947. *Theory of Games and Economic Behavior*. 2nd edn, Princeton: Princeton University Press.

Thomas Bayes

D.V. LINDLEY

The Rev. Thomas Bayes (1702–1761) was the eldest son of Joshua Bayes, a minister in the Nonconformist church. He was probably educated at Coward's Academy. After assisting his father as pastor in Hatton Garden, London, he became, in 1731, Presbyterian minister at Mount Sion, Tunbridge Wells where he remained until his death on 17 April 1761. His fame today rests entirely on one paper, found by his friend Richard Price amongst Bayes' effects after his death and presented to the Royal Society: Bayes (1763). (A convenient recent reference is Bayes, 1958.) The paper appears to have aroused little interest at the time and a proper appreciation was left to Laplace. Even today there is much discussion over just what Bayes meant, but the fact that so much interest is taken in a paper over 200 years old testifies to the importance of the problem and the brilliance of Bayes' argument.

The problem was this (as stated at the beginning of the paper): '*Given* the number of times in which an unknown event has happened and failed: *Required* the chance that the probability of its happening in a single trial lies somewhere between any two degrees of probability that can be named.'

Bayes' solution depended on two original ideas. The first, in the modern notation where $p(A|B)$ means the probability of A given B, says

$$p(B|A) = p(A|B)p(B)/p(A)$$

and is always known as Bayes' theorem. The second idea is more controversial and open to many interpretations. The question is what 'rule is the proper one to be used in the case of an event concerning the probability of which we absolutely know nothing antecedently to any trials made concerning it'?

To solve the problem Bayes took A to be the event of r happenings and s failures; B to be the unknown value θ of 'its happening in a single trial' so that $p(r, s|\theta) = \theta^r(1-\theta)^s$; and supposed $p(r, s) = (r+s)^{-1}$ as a solution to the second question. This is equivalent to taking $p(\theta)$ constant.

The importance of Bayes' ideas goes beyond the initial problem. Let A be any

10

particular event and *B* some *general* proposition. Then his theorem enables one to pass from the probability of the particular given the general, $p(A\,|\,B)$, which, as above, is often straightforward, to the difficult probability of the general given the particular, $p(B\,|\,A)$. As such it provides a solution to the central problem of induction or inference, enabling us to pass from a particular experience to a general statement. This Bayesian inference applies generally in science, economics and law. A special case with statistical problems is called Bayesian Statistics. It has been shown by Ramsey (1931), de Finetti (1974/5) and others that this is the only coherent form of inference. Despite this, eminent philosophers like Popper (1959) still misunderstand Bayes and deny probabilistic induction.

Bayes' solution to the second question has not been generally accepted and the probability to be assigned to the general proposition before the particular is observed, $p(B)$, has been the subject of much discussion. Solutions by Jeffreys (1985), and by Jaynes (1983) using entropy ideas, have all met with difficulties. The best solution currently available is to accept that *all* probabilities are subjective so that, in particular, $p(B)$ is the subject's probability for the general proposition. This view is primarily due to de Finetti. Enough data (in the form of particular events) enable subjects, despite differences in $p(B)$, to have close agreement on $p(B\,|\,A)$.

An interesting feature of Bayes' approach is that he defines probability in terms of expectation. The amount you would pay for the expectation of one unit of currency were *B* to occur is $p(B)$. Because of its confusion with utility concepts, this approach has not been much used.

It is hard to think of a single paper that contains such important, original ideas as does Bayes'. His theorem must stand with Einstein's $E = mc^2$ as one of the great, simple truths.

BIBLIOGRAPHY

Bayes, T. 1763. An essay towards solving a problem in the doctrine of chances. *Philosophical Transactions of the Royal Society* 53, 370–418.

Bayes, T. 1958. Reprint of the above with biographical note by G.A. Barnard. *Biometrika* 45, 293–315.

De Finetti, B. 1974/5. *Theory of Probability*. 2 vols, New York: Wiley.

Jaynes, E.T. 1983. *Papers on Probability, Statistics and Statistical Physics*. Ed. R.D. Rosenkrantz, Dordrecht: Reidel.

Jeffreys, H. 1985. *Theory of Probability*. Oxford: Clarendon Press.

Popper, K.R. 1959. *The Logic of Scientific Discovery*, London: Hutchinson; New York: Basic Books.

Ramsey, F.P. 1931. *The Foundations of Mathematics and Other Logical Essays*. London: Kegan, Paul, Trench, Trubner.

Daniel Bernoulli

S.L. ZABELL

Swiss mathematician and theoretical physicist; born at Groningen, 8 February 1700; died at Basel, 17 March 1782.

Daniel Bernoulli was a member of a truly remarkable family which produced no fewer than eight mathematicians of ability within three generations, three of whom – James 1 (1654–1705), John 1 (1667–1748) and Daniel – were luminaries of the first magnitude.

Although initially trained in medicine, in 1725 Daniel Bernoulli accepted a position in mathematics at the newly founded Imperial Academy in St Petersburg, but returned to Basel in 1733, holding successively the chairs in anatomy and botany, physiology (1743), and physics (1750–77). He was elected to membership in all of the major European learned societies of his day, including those of London, Paris, Berlin and St Petersburg, and maintained an extensive scientific correspondence which included both Euler and Goldbach.

Original in thought and prolific in output, Bernoulli worked in many areas but his most important contributions were to the fields of mechanics, hydrodynamics and mathematics. He enjoys with Euler, his close friend from childhood, the distinction of having won or shared no fewer than ten times the annual prize of the Paris Academy. His masterpriece, the *Hydrodynamica* (1738), contains a derivation of the *Bernoulli equation* for the steady flow of a non-viscous, incompressible fluid, and the earliest mathematical treatment of the kinetic theory of gases, including a derivation of Boyle's Law.

Bernoulli also made important contributions to probability and statistics, including an early application of the method of maximum likelihood to the theory of errors and an investigation of the efficacy of smallpox inoculation (Todhunter, 1865, ch. 11). Nevertheless, his best-known contribution to this subject is unquestionably his 1738 paper 'Specimen theoriae novae de mensura sortis', which discusses utility, 'moral expectation' and the St Petersburg paradox.

The St Petersburg paradox (so called because Bernoulli's paper appeared in the *Commentarii* of the St Petersburg Academy) concerns a game, first suggested by Nicholas Bernoulli (Daniel's cousin) in correspondence with Montmort: a coin is tossed n times until the first head appears; 2^n ducats are then paid out. Paradoxically, the mathematical expectation of gain is infinite although common sense suggests that the fair price to play the game should be finite.

Bernoulli proposed that the paradox could be resolved by replacing the mathematical expectation by a moral expectation, in which probabilities are multiplied by personal utilities rather than monetary prices. Arguing that incremental utility is inversely proportional to current fortune (and directly proportional to the increment in fortune), Bernoulli concluded that utility is a linear function of the logarithm of monetary price, and showed that in this case the moral expectation of the game is finite.

Strictly speaking, Bernoulli's advocacy of logarithmic utility did not 'solve' the paradox: if utility is unbounded, then it is always possible to find an appropriate divergent series. Nor was he the first to adopt such a line of attack; the Swiss mathematician Gabriel Cramer had earlier written to Nicholas Bernoulli in 1728, noting that if utility were either bounded or proportional to the square root of monetary price, then the moral expectation would be finite. But it was via Bernoulli's paper that the utility solution entered the literature, and despite initial (and eccentric) criticism by D'Alembert, by the 19th century most treatises on probability would contain a section on moral expectation and the paradox.

An English translation of Bernoulli's 1738 paper on the St Petersburg paradox was published in *Econometrica* (1954), and is reprinted in Baumol and Goldfeld (1968, pp. 15–26). An English translation of Bernoulli's paper on maximum likelihood estimation appears in *Biometrika* (1961, pp 1–18).

For further biographical information about Daniel Bernoulli and a detailed scientific assessment of his work, see the article by Hans Straub in *Dictionary of Scientific Biography* (1970). The DSB also contains excellent entries on several other members of the Bernoulli family. Eric Temple Bell's *Men of Mathematics* (1937) contains a spirited, if not necessarily reliable, account of the Bernoullis.

Todhunter (1865, ch. 11) is still valuable as a summary of Bernoulli's work in probability; Todhunter's book is, as Keynes justly remarked, 'a work of true learning, beyond criticism'. For further information on Bernoulli's contributions to probability and statistics, see also Sheynin (1970 and 1972) and Maistrov (1974, pp. 106–7 and 110–18). The dispute with D'Alembert is discussed by Baker, (1975, pp. 172–5); see also Pearson (1978, pp. 543–55 and 560–65) and Daston (1979, pp. 259–79).

Useful discussions of Bernoulli's paper on the St Petersburg paradox include Leonard J. Savage (1954, pp. 91–5) and J.M. Keynes (1921, pp. 316–20). The mathematician Abel once wrote that one should read the masters and not the pupils; those who wish to follow Abel's advice will find challenging but rewarding Laplace's discussion of moral expectation in his *Théorie analytique des probabilités* (1812, ch. 10: 'De l'espérance morale').

The literature on the St Petersburg paradox up to 1934 is surveyed in Karl Menger (1934); an English translation of Menger's paper appears in M. Shubik (ed., 1967). For a discussion of the St Petersburg paradox in the context of an axiomatization of utility and probability other than that of Ramsey and Savage, see Jeffrey (1983, pp. 150–55). The paradox still continues to inspire interest and analysis; a recent example is Martin-Lof (1985).

BIBLIOGRAPHY

Baker, K.M. 1975. *Condorcet: From Natural Philosophy to Social Mathematics*. Chicago: University of Chicago Press.

Baumol, W.J. and Goldfeld, S.M. (eds). 1968. *Precursors in Mathematical Economics: An Anthology*. Series of Reprints of Scarce Works on Political Economy, No. 19, London: London School of Economics and Political Science, 15–26.

Bell, E.T. 1937. *Men of Mathematics*. New York: Simon & Schuster; Harmondsworth: Pelican Books, 1953.

Bernoulli, D. 1738. Specimen theoriae novae de mensara sortis. *Commentarii Academiae Scientiarum Imperialis Petropolitanae* 5, 175–92. Trans. L. Sommer, *Econometrica* 22 (1954), 23–36. (In Baumol and Goldfeld (1968).)

Bernoulli, D. 1777. Diiudicatio maxime probabilis plurium obferuation um difcrepantium atque verificillima inductio inde form anda. *Acta Academiae Scientiarum Imperialis Petropolitanae*. Trans. *Biometrika* 48 (1961), 1–18.

Daston, L.J. 1979. D'Alembert's critique of probability theory. *Historia Mathematica* 6, 259–79.

Jeffrey, R.C. 1983. *The Logic of Decision*. 2nd edn, Chicago: University of Chicago Press.

Keynes, J.M. 1921. *A Treatise on Probability*. London: Macmillan; New York: Harper & Row, 1962.

Laplace, P.S. 1812. *Théorie analytique des probabilités*. Paris. 2nd edn, 1814; 3rd edn, 1820.

Maistrov, L.E. 1974. *Probability Theory: A Historical Sketch*. New York: Academic Press.

Martin-Lof, A. 1985. A limit theorem which clarifies the 'Petersburg paradox'. *Journal of Applied Probability* 22, 634–43.

Menger, K. 1934. Die Unsicherheitsmoment in der Wehrtlehre. *Zeitschrift für Nationalökonomie* 5, 459–85. Trans. in *Essays in Mathematical Economics in Honor of Oskar Morgenstern*, ed. M. Shubik, Princeton: Princeton University Press, 1967.

Pearson, K. 1978. *The History of Statistics in the 17th and 18th Centuries*. New York: Macmillan.

Savage, L.J. 1954. *The Foundations of Statistics*. New York: Wiley.

Sheynin, O.B. 1970. Daniel Bernoulli on the Normal Law. *Biometrika* 57, 99–102.

Sheynin, O.B. 1972. D. Bernoulli's work on probability. *RETE Strukturgeschichte der Naturwissenschaften* 1, 273–300.

Straub, H. 1970. Bernoulli, Daniel. In *Dictionary of Scientific Biography*, ed. C.C. Gillispie, New York: Scribner's, Vol. 2, 136–46.

Todhunter, I. 1865. *A History of the Mathematical Theory of Probability from the Time of Pascal to that of Laplace*. Cambridge: Cambridge University Press, repr. New York: Chelsea, 1961.

Bounded Rationality

HERBERT A. SIMON

The term 'bounded rationality' is used to designate rational choice that takes into account the cognitive limitations of the decision-maker – limitations of both knowledge and computational capacity. Bounded rationality is a central theme in the behavioural approach to economics, which is deeply concerned with the ways in which the actual decision-making process influences the decisions that are reached.

The theory of subjective expected utility (SEU theory) underlying neo-classical economics postulates that choices are made: (1) among a given, fixed set of alternatives; (2) with (subjectively) known probability distributions of outcomes for each; and (3) in such a way as to maximize the expected value of a given utility function (Savage, 1954). These are convenient assumptions, providing the basis for a very rich and elegant body of theory, but they are assumptions that may not fit empirically the situations of economic choice in which we are interested.

Theories of bounded rationality can be generated by relaxing one or more of the assumptions of SEU theory. Instead of assuming a fixed set of alternatives among which the decision-maker chooses, we may postulate a process for generating alternatives. Instead of assuming known probability distributions of outcomes, we may introduce estimating procedures for them, or we may look for strategies for dealing with uncertainty that do not assume knowledge of probabilities. Instead of assuming the maximization of a utility function, we may postulate a satisfying strategy. The particular deviations from the SEU assumptions of global maximization introduced by behaviourally oriented economists are derived from what is known, empirically, about human thought and choice processes, and especially what is known about the limits of human cognitive capacity for discovering alternatives, computing their consequences under certainty or uncertainty, and making comparisons among them.

GENERATION OF ALTERNATIVES. Modern cognitive psychology has studied in considerable depth not only the processes that human subjects use to choose

15

among given alternatives, but also the processes (problem-solving processes) they use to find possible courses of action (i.e., actions that will solve a problem) (Newell and Simon, 1972). If we look at the time allocations of economic actors, say business executives, we find that perhaps the largest fraction of decision-making time is spent in searching for possible courses of action and evaluating them (i.e., estimating their consequences). Much less time and effort is spent in making final choices, once the alternatives have been generated and their consequences examined. The lengthy and crucial processes of generating alternatives, which include all the processes that we ordinarily designate by the word 'design', are left out of the SEU account of economic choice.

Study of the processes for generating alternatives quickly reveals that under most circumstances it is not reasonable to talk about finding 'all the alternatives'. The generation of alternatives is a lengthy and costly process, and one where, in real-world situations, even minimal completeness can seldom be guaranteed. Theories of optimal search can cast some light on such processes, but, because of limits on complexity, human alternative-generating behaviour observed in the laboratory is usually best described as heuristic search aimed at finding satisfactory alternatives, or alternatives that represent an improvement over those previously available (Hogarth, 1980).

EVALUATION OF CONSEQUENCES. Cognitive limits, in this case lack of knowledge and limited ability to forecast the future, also play a central role in the evaluation of alternatives. These cognitive difficulties are seen clearly in decisions that are taken on a national scale: whether to go ahead with the construction of a supersonic transport; the measures to be taken to deal with acid rain; Federal Reserve policies on interest rates; and, of course, the supremely fateful decisions of war and peace.

The cognitive limits are not simply limits on specific information. They are almost always also limits on the adequacy of the scientific theories that can be used to predict the relevant phenomena. For example, available theories of atmospheric chemistry and meteorology leave very wide bands of uncertainty in estimating the environmental or health consequences of given quantities and distributions of air pollutants. Similarly, the accuracy of predictions of the economy by computer models is severely limited by lack of knowledge about fundamental economic mechanisms represented in the models' equations.

CRITERIA OF CHOICE. The assumption of a utility function postulates a consistency of human choice that is not always evidenced in reality. The assumption of maximization may also place a heavy (often unbearable) computational burden on the decision maker. A theory of bounded rationality seeks to identify, in theory and in actual behaviour, procedures for choosing that are computationally simpler, and that can account for observed inconsistencies in human choice patterns.

SUBSTANTIVE AND PROCEDURAL RATIONALITY. Theories of bounded rationality, then, are theories of decision-making and choice that assume that the decision-maker wishes to attain goals, and uses his or her mind as well as possible to that end; but theories that also take into account in describing the decision process the actual capacities of the human mind.

The standard SEU theory is presumably not intended as an account of the process that human beings use to make a decision. Rather, it is an apparatus for predicting choice, assuming it to be an objectively optimal response to the situation presented. Its claim is that people choose as if they were maximizing subjective expected utility. And a strong *a priori* case can be made for the SEU theory when the decision-making takes place in situations so transparent that the optimum can be reasonably approximated by an ordinary human mind.

Theories of bounded rationality are more ambitious, in trying to capture the actual process of decision as well as the substance of the final decision itself. A veridical theory of this kind can only be erected on the basis of empirical knowledge of the capabilities and limitations of the human mind; that is to say, on the basis of psychological research.

The distinction between substantive theories of rationality (like the SEU theory) and behavioural theories is closely analogous to a distinction that has been made in linguistics between theories of linguistic competence and theories of linguistic performance. A theory of competence would characterize the grammar of a language in terms of a system of rules without claiming that persons who speak the language grammatically do so by applying these rules. Performance theories seek to capture the actual processes of speech production and understanding.

The question of the desirability and usefulness of a procedural theory of decision involves at least two separate issues. First, which kind of theory, substantive or procedural, can better predict and explain what decisions are actually reached. Does SEU theory predict, to the desired degree of accuracy, the market decisions of consumers and businessmen, or does such prediction require us to take into account the cognitive limits of the economic actors?

Second, are we interested only in the decisions that are reached, or is the human decision-making process itself one of the objects of our scientific curiosity? In the latter case, a substantive theory of decision cannot meet our needs; only a veridical theory of a procedural kind can satisfy our curiosity.

BOUNDED RATIONALITY IN NEOCLASSICAL ECONOMICS. It should not be supposed that mainstream economic theory has been completely oblivious to human cognitive limits. In fact, some of the most important disputes in macroeconomic theory can be traced to disagreements as to just where the bounds of human rationality are located. For example, one of the two basic mechanisms that accounts for underemployment and business cycles in Keynesian theory is the money illusion suffered by the labour force – a clear case of bounded rationality. In Lucas's rational expectationist theory of the cycle, the corresponding cognitive limitation is the inability of businessmen to discriminate between movements of industry prices and movements of the general price level – another variant of the money illusion. Thus the fundamental differences between these theories do not derive from different inferences drawn from the assumptions of rationality, but from different views as to where and when these assumptions cease to hold – that is, upon differences in their theories of bounded rationality.

What distinguishes contemporary theories of bounded rationality from these ad hoc and casual departures from the SEU model is that the former insist that the model of human rationality must be derived from detailed and systematic empirical study of human decision-maing behaviour in laboratory and real-world situations.

BIBLIOGRAPHY

Cyert, R.M. and March, J.G. 1963. *A Behavioral Theory of the Firm.* Englewood Cliffs, NJ: Prentice-Hall; 2nd edn, 1975.

Hogarth, R.M. 1980. *Judgment and Choice: The Psychology of Decision.* New York: Wiley.

Nelson, R.R. and Winter, S.G. 1982. *An Evolutionary Theory of Economic Change.* Cambridge, Mass.: Harvard University Press.

Newell, A. and Simon, H.A. 1972. *Human Problem Solving.* Englewood Cliffs, NJ: Prentice-Hall.

Savage, L.J. 1954. *The Foundations of Statistics.* New York: Wiley.

Simon, H.A. 1982. *Models of Bounded Rationality.* 2 vols, Cambridge, Mass.: MIT Press (especially Sections VII and VIII).

Williamson, O. 1975. *Markets and Hierarchies.* New York: Free Press.

Certainty Equivalent

XAVIER FREIXAS

In order to take a decision in an uncertainty context, it is necessary, from a theoretical point of view, to build a model and specify all the consequences in every possible state of the world. In applied work this method is much too involved. Consequently, for applied purposes, it would be interesting to have a model where uncertainty is treated in such a way that the decision problems are as simple as the equivalent ones in a certainty framework. The identification of the conditions under which such an isomorphism between the optimal decisions under uncertainty and the optimal decisions in an equivalent certainty context holds is called the certainty equivalent problem.

Theil (1954) has been the first to point out the problem and to suggest a specific model in which the certainty equivalent property holds.

Theil imposes the following two assumptions: (i) the vector x of instruments and the vector y of result variables are related by a simple equation

$$y = g(x) + S \tag{1}$$

where S is a vector of random variables, that we can take to have a zero expected value without loss of generality. (ii) The decision-maker's objective function is quadratic and can be written as

$$u(x, y) = A(x) + \sum_{i=1}^{m} A_i(x)y_i + \frac{1}{2} \sum_{i=1}^{m} \sum_{y=1}^{m} A_{ij}y_iy_j. \tag{2}$$

Using such a model it is straightforward to show that whenever the optimal solution to the problem of maximizing the expected utility under the constraint (1) exists, it is the same as the optimal solution to the equivalent certain problem:

$$\begin{cases} \text{Max } u(x, y) \\ y = g(x) \end{cases}.$$

This result is extended not only to the multiperiod problem but also to the case where the decision-maker receives more and more information as time elapses. The resulting stochastic problem is then more involved, but it is simply solved

19

by use of dynamic programming, the optimal strategy in period t being a function of the previously observed signals η_{t-k}

$$X_t^* = x_t^*(\eta_1, \eta_2, \ldots, \eta_{t-1}).$$

Again, the conditions for the first period solution to this problem being the solution of the equivalent certain problem are very strong. As before, it has to be the case that the objective function is quadratic, but in addition the constraint relating instruments to results is restricted to be of the following type:

$$y = RX + S$$

where R is a matrix with some required specifications (namely, the value of the instrument variables of one period have no effect on the result variables of the preceding periods).

The conditions that guarantee the equivalence between the uncertainty problem and the certainty problem are so restrictive, that an alternative view of the problem has been suggested. Instead of setting restrictions on the parameters of the model, the uncertainty itself is restricted to be 'small'. Formally, this is equivalent to considering an entire class of problems that can be ranked in their uncertainty as measured by a parameter ε and whose limit is the certain problem. The question is then to know under what conditions the solution to the limit of the random problems, that is equal to the one of the certain problem, is independent of ε to the first order, so that

$$\frac{dE[x_t^*(\eta_1, \ldots, \eta_t)\varepsilon]}{d\varepsilon} = 0 \qquad \text{for} \quad \varepsilon = 0.$$

This slightly different point of view is called the 'first order certainty equivalence' problem and has been dealt with by Theil (1957) and Malinvaud (1969).

The very general conditions obtained by Malinvaud for the first order certainty equivalent to hold are (i) that the objective function is twice differentiable and (ii) that the optimal strategy is continuous with respect to the degree of uncertainty. If this condition holds, the optimal values of the instruments at time 1 are, to the first order approximation, independent of the degree of uncertainty.

It is clear that this condition cannot be met if there are constraints on the future instrument variables, since this will bring in a kink. A particular and natural example of a framework where the first order certainty equivalence does not hold is when decisions are irreversible. As pointed out in Henry (1974), it is then the case that the value of the decision in the first period will affect the decision set in the following periods, and consequently, the use of the certainty equivalent would generate a systematic error.

BIBLIOGRAPHY

Henry, C. 1974. Investment decisions under uncertainty: the irreversible effect. *American Economic Review* 64, 1996–2012.

Malinvaud, E. 1969. First order certainty equivalence. *Econometrica* 37, 706–18.

Simon, H. 1956. Dynamic programming under uncertainty with a quadratic criterion function. *Econometrica* 24, 74–81.

Theil, H. 1954. Econometric models and welfare maximization. *Weltwirtschaftigsches Archiv* 72, 60–83.

Theil, H. 1957. A note on certainty equivalence in dynamic planning. *Econometrica* 25, 346–9.

Contingent Commodities

ZVI SAFRA

The theory of general competitive equilibrium was originally developed for environments where no uncertainty prevailed. Everything was certain and phrases like 'it might rain' or 'the weather might be hot' were outside the scope of the theory. The idea of *contingent commodity*, that was introduced by Arrow (1953) and further developed by Debreu (1953), was an ingenious device that enabled the theory to be interpreted to cover the case of uncertainty about the availability of resources and about consumption and production possibilities. Basically, the idea of contingent commodity is to add the environmental event in which the commodity is made available to the other specifications of the commodity. With no uncertainty every commodity is specified by its physical characteristics and by the location and date of its availability. It is fairly clear, however, that such a commodity can be considered to be quite different where two different environmental events have been realised. The following examples clarify this: an umbrella at a particular location and at a given date in case of rain is clearly different from the same umbrella at the same location and date when there is no rain; some ice cream when the weather is hot is clearly different from the same ice cream (and at the same location and date) when the weather is cold; finally, the economic role of wheat with specified physical characteristics available at some location and date clearly depends on the precipitation during its growing season. Thus, specifying commodities by both the standard characteristics and the environmental events seems very natural, whereas the role of the adjective in 'contingent commodities' is simply to make it clear that one is dealing with commodities, the availability of which is contingent on the occurrence of some environmental event. With this specification the model with contingent commodities is very similar to the classical model of general competitive equilibrium, and thus questions like the existence of equilibrium and its optimality (with the additional aspect of efficient allocation of risk bearing) are answered in a similar way. Note that although this model deals with uncertainty, no concept of probabilities is needed for its formal description.

22

To make things more explicit we look at a simple model with contingent commodities. Assume that, without referring to uncertain events, there are $k \geqslant 1$ commodities, indexed by i, and that there are $n > 1$ mutually exclusive and jointly exhaustive events (or states of nature), indexed by s, where k and n are finite. Thus a contingent commodity is denoted by x_{is} and the total number of these commodities is kn, which is greater than k but still finite. Consumption and production sets are thus defined as subsets of the kn-dimensional Euclidean space and the economic behaviour of firms and consumers naturally follow from profit maximization (by firms) and utility maximization (by consumers). The price p_{is} of the contingent commodity x_{is} is the number of units of account that have to be paid in order to have the ith commodity delivered at the sth event. It is assumed that the market is organized before the realization of the possible events. Thus payment for the contingent commodity x_{is} is done at the beginning, while delivery takes place after the realization of events and only in case event s has occurred. Note that the price of the (certain) ith commodity, i.e. the number of units of account that have to be paid in order to have the ith commodity *for sure*, is the sum over s of the prices p_{is}. For example, assume that the price of one quart of ice cream if the weather is hot is $2.00, the price of one quart of the same ice cream if the weather is cold is $1.00 and than $n = 2$ (either it is hot or cold). Thus the price of having one quart of that ice cream for sure is $2.00 + $1.00 = $3.00.

It should be noted that although the probabilities of the possible events do not explicitly enter the model, the attitude toward risk of both consumers and producers is of interest and does play a significant role in this framework. The preference relations of consumers defined on subsets of the kn-dimensional Euclidean space reflect not only their 'tastes' but also their subjective beliefs about the likelihoods of different events as well as their attitude toward risk. Convexity of consumers' preferences, for example, is interpreted as risk-aversion while, in the same spirit, profit maximization of firms is interpreted as risk-neutrality. It should be mentioned that both Arrow and Debreu basically assume expected utility maximizing behaviour, in the sense of the Savage (1954) framework. A more general approach to such preference relations can be found in Yaari (1969), where, again, convexity is taken to mean risk aversion.

A unified and more formal treatment of time and uncertainty using contingent commodities can be found in Debreu (1959, ch. 7). Radner (1968) presents an extension of the above model to the case in which different economic agents have different information.

BIBLIOGRAPHY

Arrow, K.J. 1953. Le rôle de valeurs boursières pour la répartition la meilleure des risques. *Econométrie*, Paris: CNRS. English translation as 'The role of securities in the optimal allocation of risk-bearing' in *Review of Economic Studies* (1964); reprinted in K.J. Arrow, *Essays in the Theory of Risk-Bearing*, Chicago: Markham, 1971.

Debreu, G. 1953. Une économie de l'incertain. Mimeo, Paris: Electricité de France.

Debreu, G. 1959. *Theory of Value*. New York: Wiley.

Radner, R. 1968. Competitive equilibrium under uncertainty. *Econometrica* 36, January, 31–58.

Savage, L.J. 1954. *Foundations of Statistics*. New York: Wiley.

Yaari, M.E. 1969. Some remarks on measures of risk aversion and their uses. *Journal of Economic Theory* 1(3), October, 315–29.

Economic Theory and the Hypothesis of Rationality

KENNETH J. ARROW

In this paper, I want to disentangle some of the senses in which the hypothesis of rationality is used in economic theory. In particular, I want to stress that rationality is not a property of the individual alone, although it is usually presented that way. Rather, it gathers not only its force but also its very meaning from the social context in which it is embedded. It is most plausible under very ideal conditions. When these conditions cease to hold, the rationality assumptions become strained and possibly even self-contradictory. They certainly imply an ability at information processing and calculation that is far beyond the feasible and that cannot well be justified as the result of learning and adaptation.

Let me dismiss a point of view that is perhaps not always articulated but seems implicit in many writings. It seems to be asserted that a theory of the economy must be based on rationality, as a matter of principle. Otherwise, there can be no theory. This position has even been maintained by some who accept that economic behaviour is not completely rational. John Stuart Mill (1848, bk. 2, ch. 4) argued that custom, not competition, governs much of the economic world. But he adds that the only possible theory is that based on competition (which, in his theories, includes certain elements of rationality, particularly shifting capital and labour to activities that yield higher returns); 'Only through the principle of competition has political economy any pretension to the character of science', ([1848] 1909, p. 242).

Certainly, there is no general principle that prevents the creation of an economic theory based on hypotheses other than that of rationality. There are indeed some conditions that must be laid down for an acceptable theoretical analysis of the economy. Most centrally, it must include a theory of market interactions, corresponding to market clearing in the neoclassical general equilibrium theory. But as far as individual behaviour is concerned, any coherent theory of reactions to the stimuli appropriate in an economic context (prices in the simplest case)

25

could in principle lead to a theory of the economy. In the case of consumer demand, the budget constraint must be satisfied but many theories can easily be devised that are quite different from utility maximization. For example, habit formation can be made into a theory; for a given price–income change, choose the bundle that satisfies the budget constraint and that requires the least change (in some suitably defined sense) from the previous consumption bundle. Though there is an optimization in this theory, it is different from utility maximization; for example, if prices and income return to their initial levels after several alterations, the final bundle purchased will not be the same as the initial. This theory would strike many lay observers as plausible, yet it is not rational as economists have used that term. Without belabouring the point, I simply observe that this theory is not only a logically complete explanation of behaviour but one that is more powerful than standard theory and at least as capable of being tested.

Not only is it possible to devise complete models of the economy on hypotheses other than rationality, but in fact virtually every practical theory of macroeconomics is partly so based. The price- and wage-rigidity elements of Keynesian theory are hard to fit into a rational framework, though some valiant efforts have been made. In the original form, the multiplier was derived from a consumption function depending only on current income. Theories more nearly based on rationality make consumption depend on lifetime or 'permanent' income and reduce the magnitude of the multiplier and, with it, the explanatory power of the Keynesian model. But if the Keynesian model is a natural target of criticism by the upholders of universal rationality, it must be added that monetarism is no better. I know of no serious derivation of the demand for money from a rational optimization. The loose arguments that substitute for a true derivation, Friedman's economizing on shoe leather or Tobin's transaction demand based on costs of buying and selling bonds, introduce assumptions incompatible with the costless markets otherwise assumed. The use of rationality in these arguments is ritualistic, not essential. Further, the arguments used would not suggest a very stable relation but rather one that would change quickly with any of the considerable changes in the structure and technology of finance. Yet the stability of the demand function for money must be essential to any form of monetarism, not excluding those rational expectations models in which the quantity theory plays a major role.

I believe that similar observations can be made about a great many other areas of applied economics. Rationality hypotheses are partial and frequently, if not always, supplemented by assumptions of a different character.

So far, I have argued simply that rationality is not in principle essential to a theory of the economy, and, in fact, theories with direct application usually use assumptions of a different nature. This was simply to clear the ground so that we can discuss the role of rationality in economic theory. As remarked earlier, rationality in application is not merely a property of the individual. Its useful and powerful implications derive from the conjunction of individual rationality and the other basic concepts of neoclassical theory – equilibrium, competition and completeness of markets. The importance of all these assumptions was first made explicit by Frank Knight (1921, pp. 76–9). In the terms of Knight's one-time student, Edward Chamberlin (1950, pp. 6–7), we need not merely pure but perfect competition before the rationality hypotheses have their full power.

It is largely this theme on which I will expand. When these assumptions fail, the very concept of rationality becomes threatened, because perceptions of others and, in particular, of their rationality become part of one's own rationality. Even if there is a consistent meaning, it will involve computational and informational demands totally at variance with the traditional economic theorist's view of the decentralized economy.

Let me add one parenthetic remark to this section. Even if we make all the structural assumptions needed for perfect competition (whatever is needed by way of knowledge, concavity in production, absence of sufficient size to create market power, etc.), a question remains. How can equilibrium be established? The attainment of equilibrium requires a disequilibrium process. What does rational behaviour mean in the presence of disequilibrium? Do individuals speculate on the equilibrating process? If they do, can the disequilibrium be regarded as, in some sense, a higher-order equilibrium process? Since no one has market power, no one sets prices; yet they are set and changed. There are no good answers to these questions, and I do not pursue them. But they do illustrate the conceptual difficulties of rationality in a multiperson world.

RATIONALITY AS MAXIMIZATION IN THE HISTORY OF ECONOMIC THOUGHT. Economic theory, since it has been systematic, has been based on some notion of rationality. Among the classical economists, such as Smith and Ricardo, rationality had the limited meaning of preferring more to less; capitalists choose to invest in the industry yielding the highest rate of return, landlords rent their property to the highest bidder, while no one pays for land more than it is worth in product. Scattered remarks about technological substitution, particularly in Ricardo, can be interpreted as taking for granted that, in a competitive environment, firms choose factor proportions, when they are variable, so as to minimize unit costs. To be generous about it, their rationality hypothesis was the maximization of profits by the firm, although this formulation was not explicitly achieved in full generality until the 1880s.

There is no hypothesis of rationality on the side of consumers among the classicists. Not until John Stuart Mill did any of the English classical economists even recognize the idea that demand might depend on price. Cournot had the concept a bit earlier, but neither Mill nor Cournot noticed – although it is obvious from the budget constraint alone – that the demand for any commodity must depend on the price of all commodities. That insight remained for the great pioneers of the marginalist revolution, Jevons, Walras and Menger (anticipated, to be sure, by the Gregor Mendel of economics, H.H. Gossen, whose major work, completely unnoticed at the time of publication (1854), has now been translated into English (1983)). Their rationality hypothesis for the consumer was the maximization of the utility under a budget constraint. With this formulation, the definition of demand as a function of all prices was an immediate implication, and it became possible to formulate the general equilibrium of the economy.

The main points in the further development of the utility theory of the consumer are well known. (1) Rational behaviour is an ordinal property. (2) The assumption that an individual is behaving rationally has indeed some observable implications, the Slutsky relations, but without further assumptions, they are not very strong. (3) In the aggregate, the hypothesis of rational behaviour has in general no implications; that is, for any set of aggregate excess demand functions, there is a choice of preference maps and of initial endowments, one for each individual in the economy, whose maximization implies the given aggregate excess demand functions (Sonnenschein, 1973; Mantel, 1974; Debreu, 1974; for a survey, see Shafer and Sonnenschein, 1982, sec. 4).

The implications of the last two remarks are in contradiction to the very large bodies of empirical and theoretical research, which draw powerful implications from utility maximization for, respectively, the behaviour of individuals, most especially in the field of labour supply, and the performance of the macroeconomy based on 'new classical' or 'rational expectations' models. In both domains, this power is obtained by adding strong supplementary assumptions to the general model of rationality. Most prevalent of all is the assumption that all individuals have the same utility function (or at least that they differ only in broad categories based on observable magnitudes, such as family size). But this postulate leads to curious and, to my mind, serious difficulties in the interpretation of evidence. Consider the simplest models of human capital formation. Cross-sectional evidence shows an increase of wages with education or experience, and this is interpreted as a return on investment in the form of foregone income and other costs. But if all individuals are alike, why do they not make the same choice? Why do we observe a dispersion? In the human capital model (a particular application of the rationality hypothesis), the only explanation must be that individuals are not alike, either in ability or in tastes. But in that case the cross-sectional evidence is telling us about an inextricable mixture of individual differences and productivity effects. Analogously, in macroeconomic models involving durable assets, especially securities, the assumption of homogeneous agents implies that there will never be any trading, though there will be changes in prices.

This dilemma is intrinsic. If agents are all alike, there is really no room for trade. The very basis of economic analysis, from Smith on, is the existence of differences in agents. But if agents are different in unspecifiable ways, then remark (3) above shows that very few, if any, inferences can be made. This problem, incidentally, already exists in Smith's discussion of wage differences. Smith did not believe in intrinsic differences in ability; a porter resembled a philosopher more than a greyhound did a mastiff. Wage differences then depended on the disutilities of different kinds of labour, including the differential riskiness of income. This is fair enough and insightful. But, if taken seriously, it implies that individuals are indifferent among occupations, with wages compensating for other differences. While there is no logical problem, the contradiction to the most obvious evidence is too blatant even for a rough approximation.

I have not carried out a scientific survey of the uses of the rationality hypothesis in particular applications. But I have read enough to be convinced that its apparent force comes only from the addition of supplementary hypotheses. Homogeneity across individual agents is not the only auxiliary assumption, though it is the deepest. Many assumptions of separability are frequently added. Indeed, it has become a working methodology to start with very strong assumptions of additivity and separability, together with a very short list of relevant variables, to add others only as the original hypotheses are shown to be inadequate, and to stop when some kind of satisfactory fit is obtained. A failure of the model is attributed to a hitherto overlooked benefit or cost. From a statistical viewpoint, this stopping rule has obvious biases. I was taught as a graduate student that data mining was a major crime; mortality has changed here as elsewhere in society, but I am not persuaded that all these changes are for the better.

The lesson is that the rationality hypothesis is by itself weak. To make it useful, the researcher is tempted into some strong assumptions. In particular, the homogeneity assumption seems to me to be especially dangerous. It denies the fundamental assumption of the economy, that it is built on gains from trading arising from individual differences. Further, it takes attention away from a very important aspect of the economy, namely, the effects of the distribution of income and of other individual characteristics on the workings of the economy. To take a major example, virtually all of the literature on savings behaviour based on aggregate data assumes homogeneity. Yet there have been repeated studies that suggest that saving is not proportional to income, from which it would follow that distributional considerations matter. (In general, as data have improved, it has become increasingly difficult to find any simple rationally based model that will explain savings, wealth and bequest data.)

The history of economic thought shows some other examples and difficulties with the application of the rationality hypothesis. Smith and the later classicists make repeated but unelaborated references to risk as a component in wage differences and in the rate of return on capital (e.g., Mill, [1848] 1909, pp. 385, 406–407, 409). The English marginalists were aware of Bernoulli's expected-utility theory of behaviour under uncertainty (probably from Todhunter's *History of the Mathematical Theory of Probability*, (1865)) but used it only in a qualitative and gingerly way (Jevons, [1871] 1965, pp. 159–60; Marshall, 1920, pp. 842–3). It was really not until the last 30 years that it has been used systematically as an economic explanation, and indeed its use coincided with the first experimental evidence against it (see Allais, 1979). The expected-utility hypothesis is an interesting transition to the theme of the next section. It is in fact a stronger hypothesis than mere maximization. As such it is more easily tested, and it leads to stronger and more interesting conclusions. So much, however, has already been written about this area that I will not pursue it further here.

RATIONALITY, KNOWLEDGE AND MARKET POWER. It is noteworthy that the everyday usage of the term 'rationality' does not correspond to the economist's definition as transitivity and completeness, that is, maximization of something. The common understanding is instead the complete exploitation of information, sound reasoning and so forth. This theme has been systematically explored in economic analysis, theoretical and empirical, only in the last 35 years or so. An important but neglected predecessor was Holbrook Working's random-walk theory of fluctuations in commodity futures and securities prices (1953). It was based on the hypothesis that individuals would make rational inferences from data and act on them; specifically, predictability of future asset prices would be uncovered and used as a basis for current demands, which would alter current prices until the opportunity for gain was wiped out.

Actually, the classical view had much to say about the role of knowledge, but in a very specific way. It emphasized how a complete price system would require individuals to know very little about the economy other than their own private domain of production and consumption. The profoundest observation of Smith was that the system works behind the backs of the participants; the directing 'hand' is 'invisible'. Implicitly, the acquisition of knowledge was taken to be costly.

Even in a competitive world, the individual agent has to know all (or at least a great many) prices and then perform an optimization based on that knowledge. All knowledge is costly, even the knowledge of prices. Search theory, following Stigler (1961), recognized this problem. But search theory cannot easily be reconciled with equilibrium or even with individual rationality by price setters, for identically situated sellers should set identical prices, in which case there is nothing to search for.

The knowledge requirements of the decision may change radically under monopoly or other forms of imperfect competition. Consider the simplest case, pure monopoly in a cone-commodity partial equilibrium model, as originally studied by Cournot in 1838. The firm has to know not only prices but a demand curve. Whatever definition is given to complexity of knowledge, a demand curve is more complex than a price. It involves knowing about the behaviour of others. Measuring a demand curve is usually thought of as a job for an econometrician. We have the curious situation that scientific analysis imputes scientific behaviour to its subjects. This need not be a contradiction, but it does seem to lead to an infinite regress.

From a general equilibrium point of view, the difficulties are compounded. The demand curve relevant to the monopolist must be understood *mutatis mutandis*, not *ceteris paribus*. A change in the monopolist's price will in general cause a shift in the purchaser's demands for other goods and therefore in the prices of those commodities. These price changes will in turn affect by more than one channel the demand for the monopolist's produce and possibly also the factor prices that the monopolist pays. The monopolist, even in the simple case where there is just one in the entire economy, has to understand all these repercussions. In short, the monopolist has to have a full general equilibrium model of the economy.

The informational and computational demands become much stronger in the case of oligopoly or any other system of economic relations where at least some agents have power against each other. There is a qualitatively new aspect to the nature of knowledge, since each agent is assuming the *rationality* of other agents. Indeed, to construct a rationality-based theory of economic behaviour, even more must be assumed, namely, that the rationality of all agents must be *common knowledge*, to use the term introduced by the philosopher David Lewis (1969). Each agent must not only know that the other agents (at least those with significant power) are rational but know that each other agent knows every other agent is rational, know that every other agent knows that every other agent is rational, and so forth (see also Aumann, 1976). It is in this sense that rationality and the knowledge of rationality is a social and not only an individual phenomenon.

Oligopoly is merely the most conspicuous example. Logically, the same problem arises if there are two monopolies in different markets. From a practical viewpoint, the second case might not offer such difficulties if the links between the markets were sufficiently loose and the monopolies sufficiently small on the scale of the economy that interaction was negligible; but the interaction can never be zero and may be important. As usually presented, bargaining to reach the contract curve would, in the simplest case, require common knowledge of the bargainer's preferences and production functions. It should be obvious how vastly these knowledge requirements exceed those required for the price system. The classic economists were quite right in emphasizing the importance of limited knowledge. If every agent has a complete model of the economy, the hand running the economy is very visible indeed.

Indeed, under these knowledge conditions, the superiority of the market over centralized planning disappears. Each individual agent is in effect using as much information as would be required for a central planner. This argument shows the severe limitations in the argument that property rights suffice for social rationality even in the absence of a competitive system (Coase, 1960).

One can, as many writers have, discuss bargaining when individuals have limited knowledge of each other's utilities (similarly, we can have oligopoly theory with limited knowledge of the cost functions of others: see, e.g., Arrow, 1979). Oddly enough, it is not clear that limited knowledge means a smaller quantity of information than complete knowledge, and optimization under limited knowledge is certainly computationally more difficult. If individuals have private information, the others form some kind of conjecture about it. These conjectures must be common knowledge for there to be a rationality-based hypothesis. This seems to have as much informational content and to be as unlikely as knowing the private information. Further, the optimization problem for each individual based on conjectures (in a rational world, these are probability distributions) on the private information of others is clearly a more difficult and therefore computationally more demanding problem than optimization when there is no private information.

RATIONAL KNOWLEDGE AND INCOMPLETE MARKETS. It may be supposed from the foregoing that informational demands are much less in a competitive world. But

31

now I want to exemplify the theme that perfect, not merely pure, competition is needed for that conclusion and that perfect competition is a stronger criterion than Chamberlin perhaps intended. A complete general equilibrium system, as in Debreu (1959), requires markets for all contingencies in all future periods. Such a system could not exist. First, the number of prices would be so great that search would become an insuperable obstacle; that is, the value of knowing prices of less consequence, those of events remote in time or of low probability, would be less than the cost, so that these markets could not come into being. Second, markets conditional on privately observed events cannot exist by definition.

In any case, we certainly know that many – in fact, most – markets do not exist. When a market does not exist, there is a gap in the information relevant to an individual's decision, and it must be filled by some kind of conjecture, just as in the case of market power. Indeed, there turn out to be strong analogies between market power and incomplete markets, though they seem to be very different phenomena.

Let me illustrate with the rational expectations equilibrium. Because of intertemporal relations in consumption and production, decisions made today have consequences that are anticipated. Marshall (1920, bk 5, chs 3–5) was perhaps the first economist to take this issue seriously. He introduced for this purpose the vague and muddled concepts of the short and long runs, but at least he recognized the difficulties involved, namely, that some of the relevant terms of trade are not observable on the market. (Almost all other accounts implicity or explicitly assumed a stationary state, in which case the relative prices in the future and between present and future are in effect current information. Walras (1874, lessons 23–25) claimed to treat a progressive state with net capital accumulation, but he wound up unwittingly in a contradiction, as John Eatwell has observed in an unpublished dissertation. Walras's arguments can only be rescued by assuming a stationary state.) Marshall in effect made current decisions, including investment and savings, depend on expectations of the future. But the expectations were not completely arbitrary; in the absence of disturbances, they would converge to correct values. Hicks (1946, chs 9–10) made the dependence of current decisions on expectations more explicit, but he had less to say about their ultimate agreement with reality.

As has already been remarked, the full competitive model of general equilibrium includes markets for all future goods and, to take care of uncertainty, for all future contingencies. Not all of these markets exist. The new theoretical paradigm of rational expectations holds that each individual forms expectations of the future on the basis of a correct model of the economy, in fact, the same model that the econometrician is using. In a competitive market-clearing world, the individual agent needs expectations of prices only, not of quantities. (For a convenient compendium of the basic literature on rational expectations, see Lucas and Sargent (1981).) Since the world is uncertain, the expectations take the form of probability distributions, and each agent's expectations are conditional on the information available to him or her.

As can be seen, the knowledge situation is much the same as with market power. Each agent has to have a model of the entire economy to preserve rationality. The cost of knowledge, so emphasized by the defenders of the price system as against centralized planning, has disappeared; each agent is engaged in very extensive information gathering and data processing.

Rational expectations theory is a stochastic form of perfect foresight. Not only the feasibility but even the logical consistency of this hypothesis was attacked long ago by Morgenstern (1935). Similarly, the sociologist Robert K. Merton (1957) argued that forecasts could be self-denying or self-fulfilling; that is, the existence of the forecast would alter behaviour so as to cause the forecast to be false (or possibly to make an otherwise false forecast true). The logical problems were addressed by Grunberg and Modigliani (1954) and by Simon (1957, ch. 5). They argued that, in Merton's terms, there always existed a self-fulfilling prophecy. If behaviour varied continuously with forecasts and the future realization were a continuous function of behaviour, there would exist a forecast that would cause itself to become true. From this argument, it would appear that the possibility of rational expectations cannot be denied. But they require not only extensive first-order knowledge but also common knowledge, since predictions of the future depend on other individuals' predictions of the future. In addition to the information requirements, it must be observed that the computation of fixed points is intrinsically more complex than optimizing.

Consider now the signalling equilibrium originally studied by Spence (1974). We have large numbers of employers and workers with free entry. There is no market power as usually understood. The ability of each worker is private information, known to the worker but not to the employer. Each worker can acquire education, which is publicly observable. However, the cost of acquiring the education is an increasing function of ability. It appears natural to study a competitive equilibrium. This takes the form of a wage for each educational level, taken as given by both employers and workers. The worker, seeing how wages vary with education, chooses the optimal level of education. The employer's optimization leads to an 'informational equilibrium' condition, namely, that employers learn the average productivity of workers with a given educational level. What dynamic process would lead the market to learn these productivities is not clear, when employers are assumed to be unable to observe the productivity of individual workers. There is more than one qualitative possibility for the nature of the equilibrium. One possibility, indeed, is that there is no education, and each worker receives the average productivity of all workers (I am assuming for simplicity that competition among employers produces a zero-profit equilibrium). Another possibility, however, is a dispersion of workers across educational levels; it will be seen that in fact workers of a given ability all choose the same educational level, so the ability of the workers could be deduced from the educational level ex post.

Attractive as this model is for certain circumstances, there are difficulties with its implementation, and at several different levels. (1) It has already been noted that the condition that, for each educational level, wages equal average productivity of workers is informationally severe. (2) Not only is the equilibrium not unique, but there is a continuum of possible equilibria. Roughly speaking, all that matters for the motivation of workers to buy education are the relative wages at different educational levels; hence, different relations between wages and education are equally self-fulfilling. As will be seen below, this phenomenon is not peculiar to this model. On the contrary, the existence of a continuum of equilibria seems to be characteristic of many models with incomplete markets. Extensive non-uniqueness in this sense means that the theory has relatively little power. (3) The competitive equilibrium is fragile with respect to individual actions. That is, even though the data of the problem do not indicate any market power, at equilibrium it will frequently be possible for any firm to profit by departing from the equilibrium.

Specifically, given an equilibrium relation between wages and education, it can pay a firm to offer a different schedule and thereby make a positive profit (Riley, 1979). This is not true in a competitive equilibrium with complete markets, where it would never pay a firm to offer any price or system of prices other than the market's. So far, this instability of competitive equilibrium is a property peculiar to signalling models, but it may be more general.

As remarked above, the existence of a continuum of equilibria is now understood to be a fairly common property of models of rational market behaviour with incomplete information. Thus, if there were only two commodities involved and therefore only one price ratio, a continuum of equilibria would take the form of a whole interval of price ratios. This multiplicity would be nontrivial, in that each different possible equilibrium price ratio would correspond to a different real allocation.

One very interesting case has been discussed recently. Suppose that we have some uncertainty about the future. There are no contingent markets for commodities; they can be purchased on spot markets after the uncertainty is resolved. However, there is a set of financial contingent securities, that is, insurance policies that pay off in money for each contingency. Purchasing power can therefore be reallocated across states of the world. If there are as many independent contingent securities as possible states of the world, the equilibrium is the same as the competitive equilibrium with complete markets, as already noted in Arrow (1953). Suppose there are fewer securities than states of the world. Then some recent and partly still unpublished literature (Duffie, 1985; Werner, 1985; Geanakoplos and Mas-Colell, 1986) shows that the prices of the securities are arbitrary (the spot prices for commodities adjust accordingly). This is not just a numéraire problem; the corresponding set of equilibrium real allocation has a dimensionality equal to the number of states of nature.

A related model with a similar conclusion of a continuum of equilibria is the concept of 'sunspot' equilibria (Cass and Shell, 1983). Suppose there is some uncertainty about an event that has in fact no impact on any of the data of the economy. Suppose there is a market for a complete set of commodity contracts contingent on the possible outcomes of the event, and later there are spot markets. However, some of these who will participate in the spot markets cannot participate in the contingent commodity markets, perhaps because they have not yet been born. Then there is a continuum of equilibria. One is indeed the equilibrium based on 'fundamentals', in which the contingencies are ignored. But there are other equilibria that do depend on the contingency that becomes relevant merely because everyone believes it is relevant. The sunspot equilibria illustrate that Merton's insight was at least partially valid; we can have situations where social truth is essentially a matter of convention, not of underlying realities.

THE ECONOMIC ROLE OF INFORMATIONAL DIFFERENCES. Let me mention briefly still another and counterintuitive implication of thoroughgoing rationality. As I noted earlier, identical individuals do not trade. Models of the securities markets based on homogeneity of individuals would imply zero trade; all changes in information are reflected in price changes that just induce each trader to continue holding the same portfolio. It is a natural hypothesis that one cause of trading is difference of information. If I learn something that affects the price of a stock and others do not, it seems reasonable to postulate that I will have an opportunity to buy or sell it for profit.

A little thought reveals that, if the rationality of all parties is common knowledge, this cannot occur. A sale of existing securities is simply a complicated bet, that is, a zero-sum transaction (between individuals who are identical apart from information). If both are risk averters, they would certainly never bet or, more generally, buy or sell securities to each other if they had the same information. If they have different information, each one will consider that the other has some information that he or she does not possess. An offer to buy or sell itself conveys information. The offer itself says that the offerer is expecting an advantage to himself or herself and therefore a loss to the other party, at least as calculated on the offerer's information. If this analysis is somewhat refined, it is easy to see that no transaction will in fact take place, though there will be some transfer of information as a result of the offer and rejection. The price will adjust to reflect the information of all parties, though not necessarily all the information.

Candidly, this outcome seems most unlikely. It leaves as explanation for trade in securities and commodity futures only the heterogeneity of the participants in matters other than information. However, the respects in which individuals differ change relatively slowly, and the large volume of rapid turnover can hardly be explained on this basis. More generally, the role of speculators and the volume of resources expended on informational services seem to require a subjective belief, at least, that buying and selling are based on changes in information.

SOME CONCLUDING REMARKS. The main implication of this extensive examination of the use of the rationality concept in economic analysis is the extremely severe strain on information-gathering and computing abilities. Behaviour of this kind is incompatible with the limits of the human being, even augmented with artificial aids (which, so far, seem to have had a trivial effect on productivity and the efficiency of decision-making). Obviously, I am accepting the insight of Herbert Simon (1957, chs 14, 15), on the importance of recognizing that rationality is bounded. I am simply trying to illustrate that many of the customary defences that economists use to argue, in effect, that decision problems are relatively simple, break down as soon as market power and the incompleteness of markets are recognized.

But a few more lessons turned up. For one thing, the combination of rationality, incomplete markets and equilibrium in many cases leads to very weak conclusions, in the sense that there are whole continua of equilibria. This, incidentally, is a conclusion that is being found increasingly in the analysis of games with structures extended over time; games are just another example of social interaction, so the common element is not surprising. The implications of this result are not clear. On the one hand, it may be that recognizing the limits on rationality will reduce the number of equilibria. On the other hand, the problem may lie in the concept of equilibrium.

Rationality also seems capable of leading to conclusions flatly contrary to observation. I have cited the implication that there can be no securities transactions due to differences of information. Other similar propositions can be advanced, including the well-known proposition that there cannot be any money lying in the street, because someone else would have picked it up already.

The next step in analysis, I would conjecture, is a more consistent assumption of computability in the formulation of economic hypotheses. This is likely to have its own difficulties because, of course, not everything is computable, and there will be in this sense an inherently unpredictable element in rational behaviour. Some will be glad of such a conclusion.

BIBLIOGRAPHY

Allais, M. 1979. The so-called Allais paradox and rational decisions under uncertainty. In *Expected Utility Hypothesis and the Allais Paradox*, ed. M. Allais and O. Hagen, Boston: Reidel.

Arrow, K.J. 1953. Le rôle des valeurs boursières dans la répartition la meilleure des risques. In *Econométrie*, Paris: Centre National de la Recherche Scientifique.

Arrow, K.J. 1979. The property rights doctrine and demand revelation under incomplete information. In *Economics and Human Welfare*, ed. M.J. Boskin, New York: Academic Press.

Aumann, R.J. 1976. Agreeing to disagree. *Annals of Statistics* 4, 1236–9.

Cass, D. and Shell, K. 1983. Do sunspots matter? *Journal of Political Economy* 91, 193–227.

Chamberlin, E. 1950. *The Theory of Monopolistic Competition*. 6th edn, Cambridge, Mass.: Harvard University Press.

Coase, R. 1960. The problem of social cost. *Journal of Law and Economics* 3, 1–44.

Cournot, A.A. 1838. *Researches into the Mathematical Principles of the Theory of Wealth*. Translated by N.T. Bacon, New York: Macmillan, 1927.

Debreu, G. 1959. *Theory of Value*. New York: Wiley.

Debreu, G. 1974. Excess demand functions. *Journal of Mathematical Economics* 1, 15–23.

Duffie, J.D. 1985. Stochastic equilibria with incomplete financial markets. Research Paper No. 811, Stanford: Stanford University, Graduate School of Business.

Geanakoplos, J. and Mas-Colell, A. 1986. Real indeterminacy with financial assets. Paper No. MSRI 717–86, Berkeley: Mathematical Science Research Institute.

Gossen, H.H. 1983. *The Laws of Human Relations*. Cambridge, Mass.: MIT Press.

Grunberg, E. and Modigliani, F. 1954. The predictability of social events. *Journal of Political Economy* 62, 465–78.

Hicks, H.R. 1946. *Value and Capital*. 2d edn, Oxford: Clarendon.

Jevons, W.S. 1871. *The Theory of Political Economy*. 5th edn; reprinted, New York: Kelley, 1965.

Knight, F. 1921. *Risk, Uncertainty, and Profit*. Boston: Houghton Mifflin.

Lewis, D. 1969. *Convention*. Cambridge, Mass.: Harvard University Press.

Lucas, R. and Sargent, T. 1981. *Rational Expectations and Econometric Practice*. 2 vols, Minneapolis: University of Minnesota Press.

Mantel, R. 1974. On the characterization of excess demand. *Journal of Economic Theory* 6, 345–54.

Marshall, A. 1920. *Principles of Economics*. 8th edn; reprinted, New York: Macmillan, 1948.

Merton, R.K. 1957. The self-fulfilling prophecy. In R.K. Merton, *Social Theory and Social Structure*, revised and enlarged edn, Glencoe, Ill.: Free Press.

Mill, J.S. 1848. *Principles of Political Economy*. London: Longmans, Green, 1909; New York: A.M. Kelley, 1965.

Morgenstern, O. 1935. Volkommene Voraussicht und wirtschaftliches Gleichgewicht. *Zeitschrift für Nationalökonomie* 6, 337–57.

Riley, J.G. 1979. Informational equilibrium. *Econometrica* 47, 331–60.

Shafer, W. and Sonnenschein, H. 1982. Market demand and excess demand functions. In *Handbook of Mathematical Economics*. Vol. 2, ed. K.J. Arrow and M. Intriligator, Amsterdam: North-Holland.

Simon, H. 1957. *Models of Man*. New York: Wiley.

Sonnenschein, H. 1973. Do Walras's identity and continuity characterize the class of community excess demand functions? *Journal of Economic Theory* 6, 345–54.

Spence, A.M. 1974. *Market Signaling*. Cambridge, Mass.: Harvard University Press.

Stigler, G.J. 1961. The economics of information. *Journal of Political Economy* 69, 213–25.

Todhunter, I. 1865. *A History of the Mathematical Theory of Probability from the Time of Pascal to that of Laplace*. Cambridge: Cambridge University Press, repr. New York: Chelsea, 1961.

Walras, L. 1874. *Elements of Pure Economics*. Translated by W. Jaffé, London: Allen & Unwin, 1954; Homewood, Ill.: R.D. Irwin.

Werner, J. 1985. Equilibrium in economies with incomplete financial markets. *Journal of Economic Theory* 36, 110–19.

Working, H. 1953. Futures trading and hedging. *American Economic Review* 43, 314–43.

Francis Ysidro Edgeworth

PETER NEWMAN

Giving the Sidney Ball Lecture in May 1929, A.C. Pigou remarked that 'During some thirty years until their recent deaths in honoured age, the two outstanding names in English economics were Marshall at Cambridge and Edgeworth here in Oxford' (Pigou and Robertson, 1931, p. 3). That the names were presented in that non-alphabetical order was not just Cambridge insularity but a universal perception. In a letter to Edgeworth from Bari in November 1890, Pantaleoni wrote that '... you are the closest approximation of a match for Marshall in England. You know that to my mind, Marshall is simply a new Ricardo who has appeared in the field – and to be second to him is as great an honour as a scientific man can wish for, in our time.' The modest Edgeworth would have concurred: 'Marshall was at the Council to-day; it was as if Achilles had come back,' (reported by Bonar, 1926, p. 650).

In our time the issue of the relative merit of these two great scientists is not so clear cut. 'Edgeworth, the tool-maker, gloried in his tools' (Pigou, ibid.). The general form of the utility function, indifference curves, the convexity of those curves, Pareto optimality, the contract curve; where would we be without them? But Marshall too forged some powerful and durable tools: the three-fold division of time for adjustment (market, short and long periods), consumer's surplus, elasticity, they are all now second nature to us. On tools, it is a tie.

The universal use of mathematics in economics and the necessity of statistical inference in econometrics clearly tell against Marshall and for Edgeworth. The relative shift of interest from the partial to the general equilibrium of competitive markets has also been unkind to Marshallian analysis, though marking only a marginal gain for Edgeworth, who clearly never understood such important aspects of Walrasian thought as the capital theory.

But it is above all Edgeworth's profound analysis of the relation between non-market and market forms of economic organization, with its emphasis on contract and the core, that resonates in the modern mind in a way that Marshallian ideas do not. This very modern-seeming aspect of Edgeworth's work may of course be a temporary phenomenon, simply a reflection of currently fashionable preoccupations with contract theory and game theory. But that seems unlikely. It took almost 80 years for the profession to grasp the meaning and significance of the core, Edgeworth's greatest invention, and we are not going to let go now.

Edgeworth was a prolific writer, but regrettably there has never been a complete bibliography of his work. An incomplete and slightly inaccurate compilation was made under Harry Johnson's direction in 1953–4 but was never published, although a mimeographed version was circulated from Chicago sometime after 1960. A partial enlargement and correction of this yields four books; 172 articles, pamphlets and notes, several of them in multiple parts; at least 173 book reviews; and 132 entries in Palgrave's original *Dictionary of Political Economy*, with 77 in Volume I, 38 in II, 17 in III, plus 4 new items in Higgs's second edition (1925).

One of the books and 89 of the articles were on probability and statistics and have not been reprinted. Of the rest, 32 were reprinted in whole or in part in Edgeworth (1925), as were 69 distinct review essays. Some 41 of his non-statistical articles appeared in the *Economic Journal*, of which he was editor for so long, as did 132 of his book reviews. The reader should be warned that the aged Edgeworth severely edited many of the items appearing in his collected *Papers*, so that to avoid error one must refer to the article as originally published.

Each quotation from Edgeworth given here is intended to be exact; in particular, all italicizing of words and sentences is his not mine.

With such profusion in his publications, this relatively short essay cannot begin to do justice to the variety and subtlety of Edgeworth's work. However, references to and discussions of his seminal contributions to the theory of monopoly and duopoly, of international trade, of taxation and public utility pricing of index numbers and of distribution will be found throughout *The New Palgrave*, under the appropriate headings. Rather than attempt any wide coverage (which would at best be merely an annotated bibliography) this essay concentrates instead on his biography and on two early works, *New and Old Methods of Ethics* (1877) and *Mathematical Psychics* (1881). Since the first of these has never been reprinted and seems almost never to have been read, disproportionate attention is quite deliberately paid to it here; but it is of course the better-known Economic Calculus in *Mathematical Psychics* which decisively changed economic theory, albeit some 80 years later.

I. LIFE

Edgeworth's remark that 'The life of Jevons was not eventful' (1886, p. 355) applies just as well to his own. He was born at Edgeworthstown, Co. Longford in Ireland on 8 February 1845 and actually named Ysidro Francis (Butler and Butler, 1928, Dedication and p. 244; Kendall, 1968, p. 269). Educated at home by tutors (and so avoiding the rigours of Victorian public school life) he entered Trinity College, Dublin in 1862 and specialized in classics. There he earned the highest honours and great praise from his teachers, among whom was J.K. Ingram. In 1867 he moved from Dublin to Oxford, without a degree but still reading classics and ancient philosophy, and as a student of Balliol achieved in

1869 a First Class in *Literae Humaniores*, the degree itself not being awarded until 1873 (Bowley, 1934, p. 113).

In his successful application for the Drummond Professorship in Political Economy at Oxford in 1890, Edgeworth recalled that 'After leaving Oxford, I studied mathematics for some years', apparently on his own in Hampstead and living obscurely on a modest private income. Either then or soon after he read law as well and was called to the Bar by the Inner Temple in 1877, a year which also saw his first substantial publication (at his own expense), *New and Old Methods of Ethics*, and apparently his first regular (if temporary) academic appointment as teacher of Greek at Bedford College for Women in London. Like his grandfather R.L. Edgeworth, he never practised the law. Instead, struggling through many unsuccessful applications for teaching posts in classics and 'moral science', he gradually made his way up through the margins of Victorian academic life, helped along by an increasing stream of publications.

The benchmarks of success were a lectureship in logic in 1880, a professorship in political economy in 1888 and the Tooke Professorship of Economic Science and Statistics in 1890, all at King's College, London and all badly paid. In the Tooke Chair he succeeded the economic historian Thorold Rogers and did so again in 1891 with the Drummond Chair at Oxford, since Rogers had held both posts simultaneously. With the latter appointment Edgeworth was elected a Fellow of All Souls which 'became his home for the rest of his life' (Keynes, 1926, p. 143), although he continued to rent the two small rooms near Hampstead Heath that he had taken when first in London.

Edgeworth received many academic honours: twice President of Section F of the British Association (1889 and 1922), President of the Royal Statistical Society (1912), Vice-President of the Royal Economic Society, and one of the original Fellows of the British Academy (1903). One valued prize escaped him: although his case was often urged by his strong admirer Francis Galton, Edgeworth was never elected a Fellow of the Royal Society (Stephen Sitgler, 1978, p. 309), mainly because, as John Venn wrote to Galton in 1896, 'it is difficult to point to any single essay of his which, ... , is decisive at once in the way of power and originality' – this of the author of *Mathematical Psychics*, which Venn certainly read! He became emeritus at Oxford in 1922.

The most important honour was his Editorship of the *Economic Journal*, offered to him after J.N. Keynes declined appointment as its first editor. Edgeworth served from 1890 until 1911, when he resigned to make way for J.M. Keynes and became Chairman of the Editorial Board (Harrod, 1951, pp. 158–9). At Versailles in 1919 Maynard Keynes found himself more than usually busy and so Edgeworth became active again as Joint Editor with Keynes, continuing until the day he died, 13 February 1926, at the age of 81. Keynes 'received a final letter from him about its business after the news of his death' (1926, p. 140).

Family background. Edgeworth cannot be understood apart from his extraordinary family. The tradition in that family was that its Irish branch came originally from Edgeworth in Middlesex (now Edgeware, a London suburb). R.L. Edgeworth alleged that it descended from a monk named Roger Edgeworth, who sermonizing against Henry the Eighth fell in love 'with the bright eyes of beauty' and like Henry changed his faith in order to marry (1820, I, p. 5; this story should however be taken 'with a grain of salt', Butler and Butler, 1928; p. 7fn). Roger's two sons Edward and Francis crossed to Ireland in 1583, probably under the auspices of the Earl of Essex, and successfully sought their fortune. Edward became Bishop of Down and Connor, and Francis married into the Irish squirearchy.

For the next 250 years the family prospered as part of the Protestant Ascendancy, their proclivity for gambling and conspicuous consumption sufficiently balanced by talents for marrying wealthy wives and widows and for obtaining the favours offered by a place-seeking society. Edgeworth's grandfather Richard Lovell Edgeworth (1744–1817) was an eccentric in the grand tradition, inventor of many odd mechanical devices and a devoted member of the Lichfield circle of savants around Erasmus Darwin (the grandfather of Charles), which included such luminaries of the Industrial Revolution as Boulton, Watt and Wedgwood. Enthusiastic in all things, Richard raised his eldest son by the precepts of *Emile* and in Paris had the boy inspected by Rousseau himself (1820, I, pp. 177–9, 258–9). Energetic in all things, he married four times and had 22 children over a span of 48 years, of whom seven sons and eight daughters survived him; the last of these 'died at the age of 92 in 1897, a hundred and fiftythree years after her father's birth' (Butler and Butler, 1928, p. 250).

His chief favourite was his second child and eldest daughter Maria (1767–1849), with whom he collaborated in works on education and who became a celebrated and pioneering novelist in her own right. Father and daughter travelled widely and made many friends, among them David Ricardo and Dugald Stewart, Jeremy Bentham and his early disciple and translator Etienne Dumont (1820, II, pp. 275–6). With such friends, and visitors like Sir Walter Scott, Edgeworthstown became 'the most illustrious of all the country houses' (H. Butler, *Social Life in Ireland, 1800–1845*, quoted in Hankins, 1980, p. 404, n. 52). In 1824, when her father was dead and the glory years past, still Maria and her Edgeworthstown could so impress the 19 year-old William Rowan Hamilton (already acclaimed as a second Newton and forever commemorated in the word 'Hamiltonian') that the rest of his life became interwoven with theirs. It was 'a house full of "children" of all ages. Maria lived in the midst of constant commotion, writing her books in the drawing room with the rest of the family about her' (Hankins, 1980, p. 35).

Edgeworth's father Francis Beaufort Edgeworth (1809–1846) was Richard's sixth son, by his last wife Anne Beaufort. She was of Huguenot extraction and eldest sister of the man who invented the Beaufort Wind Scale. Francis was an engaging child, a favourite both of his elderly father and his half-sister Maria (R.L. Edgeworth, 1820, II, p. 359; Graves, 1882, pp. 330–31). Sardonic and sensible and his senior by 42 years, Maria was more Wodehousian Aunt than sister and took a genuine though clear-eyed interest in his education (Graves, 1882, pp. 287–94) and marriage (Hankins, 1980, p. 414, n. 56). The contrary assertion by Mozley (quoted by Keynes) seems mainly to reflect that author's Tory prejudice against Maria and her 'sensational novels, ..., written to damage

41

the character of the statesmen, the aristocracy, and the Church of this country' (1882, pp. 41–2).

Francis grew to be an affectionate though ineffectual man with many friends, living the kind of nomadic literary life common among those with some talent and less money. Unusual for an Edgeworth in being educated at Cambridge, he wilted in the dry cool atmosphere of Trinity College's mathematics and science, subjects for which he had no aptitude at all. While Keynes (1926, p. 146n) was perhaps mistaken in citing a partial passage from Mozley to imply that the boy Francis believed in perpetual motion – the full passage making more sense if the credulity was that of his friend David Reid – the adult Francis was just as credulous, and on the same subject (Hankins, 1980, pp. 411–12, n. 3). Hamilton lamented this lack of scientific judgement but shared his friend's passion for Plato and Kant and lengthy philosophical and poetical discussion.

Failing with a private tutoring establishment at Eltham near London, Francis returned home some time after 1836 to help manage the family estate, a task at which – if the sneering Carlyle is to be believed – 'it was said he shone ... and had become a taciturn grim landmanager' (1851, p. 173). After a long illness he died at the age of 37 on 12 October 1846, in the worst season of the Irish Famine (Graves, 1882, p. 331n).

The most decisive act in his life was his marriage. In 1831, aged 22 and in matrimonial mood made possible by a private income, he seriously considered two of Hamilton's sisters as possible partners. He wrote poetry for the elder and in Dublin came within 'one quarter of an inch' of proposing to her. However, much to Maria's relief – 'I ... did not feel that I could have *loved* either of these sisters' – he fled instead to London and his former lodgings near the British Museum, where quite by accident he soon met a beautiful Catalan refugee, Rosa Florentina Eroles. She was quite poor and only 16, from a family that apparently was well-educated and whose precise identity is the subject of some speculation by Hicks (1984, pp. 160–62). Like so many of his ancestors Francis fell in love at once, writing to her 'a poem of remarkable beauty' (Graves, 1882, p. 510) and to his mother a letter describing Rosa as 'fat, voluptuous and made for love' (Hankins, p. 414, n. 56). Within three weeks she was married and carried off to Florence, where the young couple were reported to be 'very happy' (Graves 1882, p. 558). Meeting her in Dublin three years later, Hamilton wrote of his liking for Francis's 'foreign wife' who 'has conquered ... his dislike to learning modern languages' (Graves, 1885, p. 93).

Ysidro Francis was the couple's fifth and last son, born just 18 months before his father died. Rosa continued to live at Edgeworthstown and survived only until 1864, outlasted by her mother-in-law who died the next year aged 96. Death and emigration (Keynes, 1951, p. 218, n. 3) took a quite remarkable toll of Richard Edgeworth's numerous progeny, so much so that Francis Ysidro's death in 1926 marked the end of the male line in Europe. He inherited Edgeworthstown in 1911 but never lived there.

Character and style. Edgeworth's character was elusive and contradictory. 'On

42

anyone who knew Edgeworth he must have made a strong individual impression as a person. But it is scarcely possible to portray him to those who did not' (Keynes, 1926, p. 156). Nevertheless Keynes made a wonderful try, his vivid impressionistic skill bringing the old gentleman marvellously alive, in a way reminiscent of his sketches of Lloyd George and other protagonists at Versailles (Keynes, 1933). Sparkling as it was, however, his memoir remains a portrait of the economist as an old man.

Indeed, none of Edgeworth's biographers actually met him before 1888, by which time he was 43 and well on his way to becoming (at least on the surface) almost a caricature of the popular idea of an unworldly professor. He had in abundance all the usual traits of that stereotype. He was extraordinarily absent-minded, in New York in 1902 quite literally missing the boat back to Britain (Fisher, 1956, p. 92) – although, because he 'was a bad sailor even on Swiss lakes' (Bonar, 1926, p. 647), that may simply have been a subconscious protest. He was an incoherent lecturer, hilariously described as such by several witnesses; 'when, after many hours ... he at last made the supply curve intersect the demand curve ... One knew it was a great moment. He wagged his beard and muttered inaudible things into it. He seemed to be in a kind of ectasy' (Harrod, 1951, p. 373). He was adept at 'avoiding conversational English' (Graves, 1958, p. 267) using instead the long Latinate words that he loved. 'Was it very caliginous in the Metropolis?' he once asked T.E. Lawrence at All Souls' Gate, receiving the grave reply: 'Somewhat caliginous but not altogether inspissated.'

He was both diffident and a pickfault: a maddening combination. L.L. Price catches well if haltingly a reaction shared by anyone who knows his work:

> hesitating and tentative, [he] was always seeking shelter behind deference to multiplied authority, and yet was not displeased to find, and was punctilious in exhibiting, minute discrepancies in the numerous texts consulted, ending, as a result, to all appearance, in more, rather than less, unstable ambiguity than that with which he started (1926, pp. 371–2).

The diffidence was chronic. 'Edgeworth lacked the force that produces impressive treatises and assembles adherents ... unleaderly is, I think, the word' (Schumpeter, 1954, p. 831). A sadder and more personal consequence was his lifelong bachelorhood. Himself just married, Keynes wrote that Edgeworth 'did not have as much happiness as he might have had' although 'it was not for want of susceptibility' that he did not marry. Indeed, in June 1889 Beatrice Potter (passionately in love a year earlier with Joseph Chamberlain and to be married three years later to Sidney Webb) was being 'halfheartedly courted by a middle-aged economist named Edgeworth' and 'shamefacedly observed [to her diary] that "relations with men stimulate and excite one's lower nature" and that "that part of a woman's nature dies hard"' (N. and J. MacKenzie, 1977, p. 134). Later, Edgeworth 'collected his friends' opinions on the subject of matrimony and told me he was disappointed: "They were all so happily married"' (Bonar, 1926, p. 649). Remembering his father's urgent courtship of Rosa, such wretched diffidence!

43

To set against these infirmities were many positive qualities. 'The kindest and most courteous of men' (Butler and Butler, 1928, p. 244, n. 1), 'with a natural inclination to encourage the youthful and the unknown' (Keynes, 1926, p. 152). Sanguine by nature, 'few visitors were so beloved as he' (Bonar, 1926, p. 652). His enormous scientific productivity bears witness that he worked very hard, being physically strong and mentally alert well into his seventies, 'his iron frame' fond of walking, cycling, golfing, boating, swimming and mountaineering. Rather surprisingly, in the administration of the *Economic Journal* this archetypal abstracted academic displayed that 'great practical sense of the Edgeworth kind' for which his Aunt Maria had been famous (Mill, 1873, p. 56).

Few economists have read so widely, not only economics and philosophy but also science and mathematics and the literature of many languages alive and dead. He reviewed for the *Economic Journal* books in French, Italian, German, Dutch and modern Greek, and 'appears to have looked critically at every book that reached the *Journal's* office' (Bowley, 1934, p. 123). Like his fellow Irish outsiders and younger contemporaries Shaw and Wilde he was cosmopolitan in outlook, warmly hospitable to visiting foreign scholars and 'the most accessible of the English economists' (ibid., p. 122), a marked contrast to the insularity that prevailed elsewhere. His sense of humour was no less acute for being expressed often by apt quotation from foreign languages ancient and modern, or by allusion to dry donnish English prose and poetry.

Which brings us to his literary style, the most searching appraisal of which may be found in Stephen Stigler (1978, pp. 292–3); see, for example, his enlightening analysis of Edgeworth's constant recourse to 'authority'. He justly remarks that 'investigators of Edgeworth's work must at some point come to grips with his unique style of writing' and means precisely that – one of a kind. Especially idiosyncratic in his early writings, with their abundance of free and apposite quotation from the classics so that one 'can scarcely tell whether it is a line of Homer or a mathematical abstraction which is in course of integration' (Keynes, 1926, p. 145), there is nothing like Edgeworth's style in the entire literature of economics and statistics, nor scarcely in general literature. To some people (Keynes, Schumpeter, Stigler *père et fils*) that style is charming and addictive, to many others the reverse.

Only Stephen Stigler seems to have observed how appropriate was Edgeworth's peculiar style to his peculiar purposes. Particularly in those early works, the extravagant and sustained metaphors were clearly meant to help the reader grasp ideas whose depth and originality required that hardest response of all, a wrenching of the mind from its old familiar routines. While his success in this was at best partial (the rediscovery of the core did after all have to wait for almost 80 years) that was probably due as much to the sheer newness and profundity of the ideas as it was to the 'strange but charming amalgam of poetry and pedantry, science and art, wit and learning, of which he had the secret,' (Keynes, 1926, p. 146).

That style was already 'all ... there full-grown' (Keynes again) at the age of 32 in *New and Old Methods of Ethics* and we do not know why. This is just one of the many questions about the young Edgeworth to which there are no clear answers. On the personal side, why did he switch from TCD to Oxford and take so long to graduate; why did he study law and then not practise it; and, to be mundane, what was his income during the many years of study in London? On the intellectual side, what gave rise to his interest in ethics and why did he become so strong a utilitarian; why did he study mathematics to such depth; why was he drawn to economics; and why then to statistics, so soon after the fundamental contributions to economic theory of *Mathematical Psychics*?

Intellectual influences. The interest in ethics is perhaps sufficiently accounted for by his immersion in Plato and Aristotle, caused by *Lit. Hum.* if nothing else; but his passion for utilitarianism is not so readily explained. The early Edgeworth was the most exact of utilitarians, utility itself being for him a stuff 'as real as his morning jam' (Samuelson, 1947, p. 206, who however later referred to Edgeworth's All Souls' breakfasts of pheasant and champagne: 1951, p. 53n). While it was reported that his father 'showed an early and strong revolt against the hollowness, callousness and deadness of utilitarianism' (Mozley, 1882, p. 41), that may again speak more to the reporter's prejudices than to the facts; and the youthful revolt may not have lasted. Keynes suggests that in 'his early adherence to Utilitarianism Edgeworth reacted back from his father's reaction against Maria Edgeworth's philosophy in these matters' (1926, p. 148n), a Bloomsbury-like speculation which seems to ignore how little direct intellectual influence either of them could have had on the infant Edgeworth.

It is almost as hard to explain his longer-lasting attachment to mathematics, though perhaps here the speculation can be more solidly based. We have already seen that William Rowan Hamilton was for decades a close and affectionate friend to both Edgeworth's aunt and father. Writing to the widowed Rosa Edgeworth early in 1847 Hamilton referred to 'our lost Francis' (Graves, 1885, p. 554) and in a letter to his Scottish disciple Peter Tait, to 'Francis Edgeworth ... who was during his life a great friend of mine, and for whose memory I retain respect and love' (Graves, 1889, p. 188). In 1858 he was invited to Edgeworthstown to take part in a tenants' festival honouring the return of one of Francis's sons, William Edgeworth, from army service in India. This retying of old bonds so overcame Hamilton that he was moved to write in Maria's memory what is apparently his last poem extant, a sonnet of superb Victorian sentimentality, and to present it on the spot to Edgeworth's sister Mary (Graves, 1889, pp. 102–3).

'One would guess' says Hicks (1984, p. 162) 'that when the boy went to Trinity, he would have been given an introduction to Hamilton.' There is no need to guess. Writing from Dunsink Observatory in Dublin on 6 December 1864, nine months before he died at the age of 60, Hamilton wrote to a correspondent that 'We all enjoyed much a recent visit from Francis Edgeworth – who permits me in conversation to call him "Frank" – for to me there can be no second "Francis"' (Graves, 1889, p. 168). That Edgeworth knew Hamilton is confirmed by his review of the third volume of Graves's biography (Edgeworth, 1889), which also makes clear his unbounded admiration and respect for Hamilton, 'not merely the Irish

Lagrange ... [but] ... the Pascal or Descartes of his country. What Leibnitz said of himself, that his mind could not be satisfied by one species of study, may be said with equal truth of the Irish polymath.'

Given this evidence it seems reasonable to speculate that the young fatherless Edgeworth, discovering in himself both a comparative lessening of interest in the classics (Stephen Stigler, 1978, p. 289) and an increasing enthusiasm for mathematics, should have taken as model and inspiration this close family friend, only four years older than his father, who as an undergraduate had gained a rare *optime* in both mathematics and Greek, and who happened to be one of the greatest men of science of his or any other age. If true, this hypothesis would explain not only the fact but also the direction of his studies in mathematics, which is otherwise rather puzzling. 'His first substantial effort, *New and Old Methods of Ethics*, ... already showed a confident and creative mastery of the calculus of variations, not to mention some knowledge of mathematical physics' (ibid. p. 290). Playing as it did so essential a role in Hamilton's path-breaking work on dynamics and optics, it would then not be surprising that 'the wily charms of the calculus of variations', 'the most sublime branch of analysis' (Edgeworth 1881, pp. 93, 109), became the focus of Edgeworth's mathematical studies.

It would also help to explain Edgeworth's delight in the aesthetic aspects of mathematics, a response so depressingly missing in Marshall. Hamilton's masters were Lagrange and Laplace, 'the mathematics of the Ecole Polytechnique', and for him Lagrange's *Mécanique analytique* was quite literally a 'scientific poem', a point of view 'that Hamilton had worked out in his discussions with [FYE's father] Francis Edgeworth' (Hankins, 1980, pp. 23 and 104–5). Contrast this with the system that produced Marshall, the Cambridge Mathematical Tripos of the 19th century, when 'True to their sporting instincts the English had contrived to turn even the university examinations into an athletic contest' (Annan, 1952, p. 24).

> It was an examination in which the questions were usually of considerable mechanical difficulty – but unfortunately did not give any opportunity for the candidate to show mathematical imagination or insight or any quality that a creative mathematician needs (Snow, 1967, p. 22).

The result was a system that according to G.H. Hardy effectively ruined serious mathematics in England for a hundred years, so that when in 1908 he came to write an elementary text on analysis it was like 'a missionary talking to cannibals' (Hardy, 1938, Preface).

Edgeworth's passionate vision of 'the double-sided height of one maximum principle, the supreme pinnacle of moral as of physical science' (1881, p. 12) is also traceable to Hamilton, since it is to him we owe 'the most general energetical principle governing all dynamical motions' (Lindsay and Margenau, 1957, p. 195), and 'the cornerstone of modern physics' (Erwin Schrodinger, quoted in Hankins, 1980, p. 64). The striking combination of scientific power and aesthetic appeal in Hamilton's mathematics must have made it impossible for Edgeworth to resist.

'Clearly, the superior genius who reduced the general dynamical problem to the discovery of a single action-function was as much affected by the ideal beauty of "one central idea," as by the practical consequences of his discovery' (1881, p. 94; see also p. 11); a footnote here cites Hamilton's two great papers on dynamics in the *Philosophical Transactions* of the Royal Society of 1834 and 1835.

Edgeworth's attraction to economics was almost certainly due to Jevons alone. In the mid-1870s Edgeworth became friends with the psychologist James Sully (1842–1923), a fellow member of the recently founded Savile Club (Sully, 1918, p. 164). Their common interest in the 'psychophysics' of Weber and Fechner and in moral science was reflected in *New and Old Methods of Ethics*, whose only acknowledgement was to Sully. At about that time the latter moved to Hampstead, in part to be near his 'bachelor chum' (ibid., pp. 177–9; Howey, 1960, pp. 98–100). Although Sully coyly does not identify this chum, his detailed description fits Edgeworth like a glove, even down to Edgeworth's love (reported also by Keynes) of swimming in ice-cold water.

Sully was also a neighbour and great friend of Jevons (Black, 1977, Vol. IV, p. 239 n. 2), and 'A common interest drew him and my chum together, and so we made a trio in many a pleasant walk and skating excursion' (Sully, 1918, p. 181). We also know from a perceptive testimonial written for Edgeworth by H.S. Foxwell on 6 October 1881, in connection with an unsuccessful application for a professorship at Liverpool, that

> Between the publication of these brilliant and suggestive papers [Edgeworth (1879) and (1881)], I had the pleasure of making the acquaintance of Mr. Edgeworth, through our common friend Professor Jevons, at whose house and elsewhere we have had many discussions, chiefly upon economics, but frequently also upon ethical and philosophical subjects ... [in] these conversations ... he showed great speculative ability, singularly wide and various acquirements, and marked originality and vigour of expression.

Edgeworth's article 'Hedonical Calculus' in *Mind*, July 1879 was reprinted essentially unchanged as pages 56 to 82 of *Mathematical Psychics* and is itself almost free of economics. It seems likely, then, that at least until 1879 he had learned very little of the subject. If so, the appearance of *Mathematical Psychics* in the middle of 1881 was a truly stunning performance (to use a favourite word of Schumpeter). The economics of the book are strongly Jevonian rather than Classical, with very few references to Smith, Ricardo or Malthus, some to Mill, and many to Cournot, Jevons, Marshall and Walras.

Perhaps because his father died so young, Edgeworth seems always to have had a need for heroes. Hamilton was probably one such, Jevons certainly another. In an affecting letter to Jevons' widow written three days after her husband had drowned in August 1882, Edgeworth lamented

> the loss of my venerated friend ... and a peculiar intellectual sympathy which he extended ... It is difficult to realize that I shall never more meet Mr. Jevons on the ice or heath, be fascinated by his philosophic smile and drink in his

words. I shall always regard it as one of the privileges of my life to have come under the influence of his serene and lofty intellect (Black, 1977, V, pp. 201–2).

This severe intellectual loss could help to account for his lack of research in economics in the years after *Mathematical Physics*, although a possible further explanation is a perceived need for more reading in the subject, especially in classical economics.

With the loss of Jevons a new hero was needed. Sidgwick was an obvious candidate, since *New and Old Methods of Ethics* had been variations on a theme in that author's *Methods of Ethics*. Moreover, 'Partly ... from his strong sense of humour, Sidgwick came near to rivalling Marshall for first place in Edgeworth's admiration' (Bonar, 1926, pp. 649–50). But 'on the whole Marshall was the great Apollo, oracle, or highest authority' (ibid.). The change from Jevons to Marshall was in fact soon made, perhaps accelerated by Marshall's review of *Mathematical Psychics* (Marshall, 1881), which was marginally less uncomprehending than that of Jevons (1881). As early as September 1882 Marshall was writing to 'My dear Edgeworth' and ending 'Yours very sincerely', while Mary Marshall sent her 'very kind regards'.

In spite of some strains such as that over barter (recorded in Marshall, 1961, II, pp. 791–8) the closeness thus established between Edgeworth and Marshall was not broken until the latter's death in 1924. There was genuine respect and affection on each side, even though 'there can seldom have been a couple whose conversational methods were less suited to one another' (Keynes, 1926, p. 144). The relationship was asymmetric, however. It was understood that Edgeworth was to make strong (and sometimes unsuccessful) efforts to comprehend the other's modes of thought, his 'arms of mathematics ... under the garb of literature' (*Mathematical Psychics*, p. 138; the order is inverted here), but that Marshall need not reciprocate those efforts; for he seems never to have entered seriously into Edgeworth's economics or statistics.

Edgeworth and Hobson. Edgeworth was 'entirely incapable of intentional discourtesy. It was against his nature to inflict an insult' (Bonar, 1926, p. 650). So it is a shock to encounter the allegation that his disapproval of J.A. Hobson's heterodox views led to the latter's exclusion from offering courses in political economy as an Extension Lecturer at London. The allegation appears to originate with Hobson himself (1938, p. 30). 'This was due, I learned, to the intervention of an economic Professor who had read my book [*The Physiology of Industry*] and considered it as equivalent in rationality to an attempt to prove the flatness of the earth.' Hobson did not name the professor, and the connection to Edgeworth appears to have been made first by Hutchison (1953, pp. 118–19), who observed that Edgeworth, then a professor at London, indeed reviewed the book in the journal *Education* in 1890. That seems to be the extent of the proof.

Even if it could be firmly established that it was Edgeworth who was responsible for the refusal to permit Hobson to teach economics, it does not follow that his reason was the latter's heterodoxy – it may have been his ignorance of some important party of economic analysis. Thus in his 1904 paper on Distribution (1925, pp. 19–20, fn. 3), Edgeworth took Hobson severely to task for the latter's lack of understanding of marginal productivity theory in *The Economics of Distribution*, where in effect he confused (according to Edgeworth) Δx or dx with x. Schumpeter said of Hobson (1954, pp. 832–3, fn. 2) that he

> was by no means averse to the comfortable explanation that his Marshallian opponents were actuated by an inquisitional propensity to crush dissent, if not by class interest: the possibility that, owing to his inadequate training, many of his propositions, especially his criticisms, might be provably wrong and due to nothing but failure to understand never entered his head, however often it was pointed out to him.

II. WORKS

A. EXACT UTILITARIANISM. Edgeworth's first known publication was a short note on Matthew Arnold's interpretation of Bishop Butler, in the first volume of *Mind* (1876). His next was *New and Old Methods of Ethics*, a quite extraordinary monograph of 92 pages that remains almost unread to the present day (see however Howey, 1960, ch. XI, and Creedy, 1986, ch. 2). Half of the book (the first 34 pages plus 12 pages of Notes) is concerned with an elaborate philosophical critique of the recently published work of Barratt and Sidgwick on ethics and need not detain us here, except to note Howey's interesting suggestion that Edgeworth's style owed something to 'that of the brilliant and precocious Alfred Barratt, whose writings read quite like Edgeworth's (1960, p. 107).

For the economist the book takes off abruptly on p. 35, which is headed 'Meaning of Utilitarianism'. *Exact utilitarianism* is defined by Edgeworth to be 'The doctrine of Fechner and Sidgwick', which is 'the greatest quantity of happiness of sentients, exclusive of number and distribution – an end to which number and distribution are but means'. He then analyses various mathematical meanings that can be given to the formula 'the greatest happiness of the greatest number', and in so doing uses a Lagrange multiplier for apparently the first time ever in social science, in a variational (rather than finite-dimensional) problem and in very throwaway of-course-everyone-knows-this fashion (p. 38, (4)). He concludes: 'it appears impossible to assign any intelligible or tenable meaning to the formula ... but that of exact utilitarianism' (p. 39).

He next calls upon the work of the psychophysicists, such as Weber, Fechner, Wundt, Delboeuf and Helmholtz (for useful brief accounts of which see Howey, 1960, pp. 95–8 and Stigler, 1965, pp. 113–17). '[A]greeably to the Fechnerian law, the pleasure of each sentient element is represented by $k(\log \gamma - \log \beta)$, where γ is the stimulus, and k and β are constants.' Then 'if a given amount of "stimulus" ... is to be distributed among a given set of sentients, the distribution favourable to the production of the greatest quantity of happiness is equality' (p. 40).

However, this Fechnerian law had been criticized 'by many high authorities' so Edgeworth modifies it to keep its desirable qualitative properties but dispense with its objectionable quantitative aspects. These qualitative properties are 'that the first differential is positive, the second differential negative for values of the variable, or at least all with which we are concerned' (p. 40). In more modern language, he wishes to make the pleasure an increasing *concave* function of the stimulus. (Later, he actually used that language in referring to 'concave functions, as they might be called' in *Mathematical Psychics* (1881, p. 130), which is the more interesting since the perception that separate theory is possible for such functions is quite recent. 'The foundations of the theory of convex functions are due to Jensen [1906]' (Hardy, Littlewood and Polya, 1934, p. 71)). Edgeworth admits that the curve might have an initially convex part, as in the standard Knightian diagram of diminishing returns, and frequently adverts to this possibility; but by reference to second order conditions (a constant preoccupation in all this early work) he argues that 'the *upper* part of the curve is alone that capable of being employed in cases of maximum pleasure, and therefore alone concerning us here' (p. 42).

His generalization is the 'quasi-Fechnerian law $\pi = k|f(y) - f(\beta)|$', where 'π dt represents, or is proportional to, the pleasure of a sentient element during an element of time'; f is any function having the two properties listed above; and β and k are two co-efficients, the former denoting 'the "threshold", the lowest value of stimulus for which the sentient has any pleasure at all', it being understood, with Wundt, that 'The threshold[s] of sensation and pleasure are, ..., identical. It follows that β^{-1} is a measure of the sentient element's 'sensibility'.

The interpretation of the co-efficient k is subtle, and important for later developments. On p. iii of the Contents at the beginning of the book we find an interesting double criterion (reminiscent of topologies on spaces of differentiable functions) for one sentient to be more productive of pleasure than another;

> A sensory element is said to have greater capacity for pleasure, when it not only affords a greater quantity of pleasure, pleasure arising from simple sensations, for the same quantity of stimulus, *ceteris paribus*; but also a greater increment of pleasure for the same increment of stimulus, *ceteris paribus*.

It is immediate from the quasi-Fechnerian formula, with its stimulus function f common to all, that for two elements i and j such that $\beta_i = \beta_j$, both $\pi_i > \pi_j$ and $[d\pi_i(y_i)/dy] > [d\pi_j(y_j)/dy]$ if and only if $k_i > k_j$. Thus 'The co-efficient k in the Fechnerian formula perhaps corresponds to "capacity for pleasure"' (p. iii). In principle, both co-efficients β and k 'vary with different elements' (p. 42).

The Calculus of Hedonics. Edgeworth formulates 'two main problems of the Calculus of Hedonics', the first posed as 'a certain quantity of stimulus to be distributed among a given set of sentients ... to find the law of distribution productive of the greatest quantity of pleasure', subject to the proviso that 'every element is to have *some* stimulus' (p. 43). The second main problem drops this proviso.

He attacks the first problem under the assumption that the set of sentients is finite, which leads at once to a standard Lagrangean problem of finite multidimensional calculus. Assuming that k and β are the same for all sentients, he finds that 'the law of distribution is equality' though he does not interpret the Lagrange multiplier. Allowing β but not k to vary across sentients does not change this conclusion, unlike the converse assumption, which leads to the proposition that 'Unto him that hath greater capacity for pleasure shall be added more of the means of pleasure.' When both k and β vary across sentients, this last conclusion remains unaffected.

In the next step he argues that it is 'more appropriate' to treat each sentient as

infinitesimal with regard to the whole ... since, strictly speaking, each pleasure element consists of the indefinitely small pleasure afforded during a given time, by each indefinitely small element of the whole sensory tract to which the stimulus is applied. (The whole sensory tract is generally considered as made up of tracts belonging to different sentient individuals, e.g. different animals). The latter conception (that of infinitesimals) will therefore generally be adopted in the sequel, ... the conclusions are equally deducible on either supposition [i.e. finite or infinitely many sentients] (p. 44).

This passage seems to be the earliest use of the idea of a continuum of economic actors, which was introduced into the modern literature in the classic paper of Aumann (1964). Moreover, it makes explicit that the units of feeling which he calls sentients (the term seems borrowed from Sidgwick, e.g. 1877, p. 382) comprise more than humankind. In this Edgeworth follows Bentham and Mill, and their practice finds an echo in current arguments concerning animal rights (see e.g. Singer, 1985, pp. 4–6).

To keep the second main problem as simple as possible, Edgeworth first supposes that k and β each depend on the same variable x. Hence if y is the required function that expresses the law of distribution over sentients, the interval $[x_0, x_1]$ the support of this distribution and D the available stimulus, Problem II may be expressed: Find y, x_0 and x_1 to

$$\max \int_{x_0}^{x_1} k\{f(y) - f(\beta)\}\, dx \text{ subject to } \int_{x_0}^{x_1} y\, dx = D. \tag{1}$$

Although Edgeworth's treatment of (1) and similar problems is quite competent and careful by the standards of rigour of English mathematics of the 19th century, and even by the standards of many latter-day economists (for whom simple Euler necessary conditions suffice), still much of his variational analysis is suspect. He was himself far from satisfied with his analysis; for example,

It is not pretended that even the mathematical reasoning of the preceding theory is free from objection. Thus it might be objected that account is taken only of *some* solutions. ... Again, it might be objected that a *maximum* found by the Calculus of Variations ... may not be the *greatest possible* value of a proposed integral (pp. 48–9).

Although that of a self-professed 'amateur' mathematician (1889a, p. 262), his discussion was far from naive.

As with the first problem, he considers four cases: where k and β are constant across sentients; where β alone varies; where k but not β varies; and where they both vary. In the first case the conclusion is that y gives equality of distribution and that $[x_1 - x_0]$ is determinate in length though not position. In the second case, the first two results remain and the indeterminacy as a position is removed, the location comprising 'a region of maximum sensibility'. The solution of the third case results in a law of distribution like that of the corresponding case of the first problem, with a determinate interval $[x_1 - x_0]$ whose location 'corresponds to the greatest capacity for pleasure' (p. 47). The solution of the fourth case is similar.

He next tackles the case where the support of y may not be an interval but instead a disconnected set. The analysis is heuristic rather than formal, 'not mathematically very elegant' (p. 47), and illustrated in typical Edgeworth fashion by a 'snake argument' (pp. 53–4), a 'somewhat amphibious investigation'. This is a long and fanciful (but accurate) story of an unfortunate snake which crawls up a range of mountains, in the process being dismembered and rearranged in order to ensure that it occupies the largest possible total height. It is argued that the basic structure and conclusions of the previous arguments remain in this new, possibly disconnected situation.

Extensions. The argument is then extended in several directions, allegedly all without loss of the main thread of reasoning or conclusion. The first is to the case where k and β are functions of not one but several variables. It is pointed out (p. 52) that the 'sentient elements' of this calculus are not individuals but parts of individuals. One individual may be composed of a small number of elements with high-ranking capacity for pleasure (k) and/or sensibility (β^{-1}) and a large number of low-ranking elements, while another individual may consist entirely of medium-ranking elements and so contribute more pleasure to the social total than the high-variance individual.

The next extension is to where the distribuend D is not a constant but can be written $D = \phi(x_1 - x_0)$, where $d\phi/dx > 0$ and $d^2\phi/dx^2 > 0$.

> To excite interest in this case, it may be well to make the premature remark, that these are precisely the relations which Malthus correctly supposed to exist between the quantity of the food and the number of population, and which he illustrated by the properties of the logarithm (p. 53).

This is the first and essentially the only intrusion of standard political economy into the book.

Another extension, 'an important modification of the preceding theory', is given towards the end of the book but is conveniently treated here, even though that involves the anticipation of some of his later arguments and language. His introduction of the problem is succinct:

Up to this, sentients being regarded as so many lamps of different lighting power, the questions have been what lamps shall be lit, and how much material shall be supplied to each lamp, in order to produce the greatest quantity of light. And the answers, neither unexpected, nor yet distinctly foreshadowed by common sense, are, that a limited number of the best burners are to be lit, and that most material is to be given to the best lamp. But the conception more appropriate to the real phenomena is, that a large portion of the material to be distributed is applied not to be burned by the lamp, but to construct and repair it (p. 74).

The consequences of incorporating these needs for reproduction are straightforward but serious. Because '*minus* pain is sweeter than *plus* pleasure ... where the curve of pain descends to ever lower depths ... if there is not enough for all, no one should get very much ... [so that] ... the very rich will go away sorrowful from utilitarian teaching' (p. 75). In giving an apt example, Edgeworth cannot resist some characteristically donnish humour:

Prior to [this] consideration, it might normally have been argued (p. 48), that out of the same quantity of material a hundred philosophers would elicit more happiness than a hundred capuchin monkeys. But perhaps the material which would keep a hundred little monkeys in health and happiness would not feed twenty philosophers! (p. 76).

Fechner to Bentham to Spencer. Edgeworth's overriding concern is with exact utilitarianism, the allocation of scarce means to secure the maximum of pleasure over all sentients and all time. But, strictly speaking, the conclusions reached so far (i.e. through p. 53) apply only to the psychophysical entities of stimulus and sensation. So two separate amendments need to be made in order to transit from the world of Fechner to that of Bentham, one at each 'end' of the Calculus of Hedonics, as it were. 'Stimulus' must be replaced by 'means to stimulus', and 'sensation' by 'emotion' or 'pleasure', and the wording of the two main problems of the Calculus amended accordingly (no matter that such terms as 'capacity for pleasure' have already been used; 'The reader is requested to make allowances and corrections, if the language has already appeared hovering, preparing for this hypothetical flight above the region of sensation' (p. 54, fn. 1).

In making this change Edgeworth takes the opportunity to generalize the stimulus–sensation function yet further. Pleasure π is a function of β, k and stimulus, as before, but now stimulus σ is a function ϕ of y, the 'share of distribuend'. Hence,

$$\pi = f(\beta, k, \ldots, \phi(y)). \tag{2}$$

He argues that if the following four conditions hold, then 'The preceding conclusions [i.e. those prior to p. 54] are reducible by reasoning analogous to that ... [for] ... the simple cases of isolated sensations; subject to the same mathematical difficulties' (p. 56).

(I) β and k vary with the individual, but ϕ is the same across all individuals.

(II) $\partial^2\pi(\ )/\partial y^2$ is always negative; 'or, at any rate, there must exist satisfactory criteria of a maximum'.

(III) $\partial\phi(\ )/\partial y$ always increases with k.

(IV) If both k and β depend on another variable x, then $\partial\pi(\ )/\partial x$ is always positive.

The next stage is to argue, at some length, that '*None* of these conditions are fulfilled' (p. 57) but that in effect they are a good place from which to start. Thus, he admits that ϕ depends not on y alone, and not even only on y and the individual's characteristics k and β, but also on the y, k and β of 'his fellow-creatures'. He attempts some mathematical analysis of this complicated situation, which leaves the tentative impression that under further plausible assumptions the original conclusions are not much affected.

Rather separable from this discussion of Condition I is an interesting but brief analysis (pp. 63–6) of a society 'homogeneous as to tastes and pleasures' which, to carry out various consumption activities, forms into individuals, couples, triples, ..., such that in each of these groups each individual has the same (partial) utility function for that activity. Not surprisingly, it turns out by the usual Lagrange multiplier analysis that the distribution of this society's means should be equal for each group of a given size:

> on each individual, for his self-regarding pleasures; on each couple, for their *egoisme à deux*; on each triplet, and more numerous association, for their social pleasures. The theory does not pronounce upon the manner in which the distribuend should thus be equally applied; whether, for example, the expenditure of a household should be defrayed directly out of the common store, or should pass through the hands of the members of the household (p. 64).

He also allows for some, rather systematic, heterogeneity in this society of groups.

The case for Condition (II) is simply that if it did not hold then 'the greatest quantity of pleasure is obtained ... by assigning the whole of ... [a] ... given quantity ... [of material] ... to *one* individual' (p. 69). So $\partial^2\pi(\ )/\partial y^2$ 'must be negative for the higher values of y at least'.

The reasonableness of Conditions III and IV really turn on what interpretation is to be given to k, heretofore the 'capacity for pleasure' Sadly, it is here that Edgeworth's analysis begins to slide into Victorian eugenics (a word not coined until 1833), which is so alien in spirit and conclusion to modern readers. Up to now, Edgeworth's exact utilitarianism and its blithe reckoning of the net pleasure of every living being into the accounts of common happiness may have provoked smiles, but after all differ only in shamelessness and universality from such everyday exercises of modern welfare economics as normative growth theory. Now, with k given 'the second intention of order of evolution' (p. 57), his happy utilitarian world switches abruptly to the deadly earnestness of Herbert Spencer and Social Darwinism, of Galton and eugenics. What was before merely a matter of individual differences in capacity for pleasure is transmuted into *systematic* variation of such capacity with the creature's alleged position in the alleged evolutionary order, so that indeed $\partial \pi(\ )/\partial y$ increases with k. In *New and Old Methods of Ethics* the potentially harmful consequences of this new meaning for k are kept in check (as shown by the next two extensive quotations) but in 'The Hedonical Calculus' of 1879 they come perilously close to disaster.

Edgeworth next applies the third of the extensions listed above, where a substantial proportion of available means is devoted to the reproduction of society, to analyse Mill's advocacy of a stationary state. 'To the [reproductive] necessities of the individual must be added his contribution to the necessities of the social state to which he belongs' [public goods?], in order to arrive at the 'threshold' T which 'must be deducted from the individual's share (y) before the quasi-Fechnerian theory can be applied' (p. 76). Next, total happiness being $\Sigma\pi$, the number of the population n, 'the order of evolution' (monkeys, apes, men, etc.) x, and the distributed function ϕ (now dependent on n and x), an implicit definition of F is given by

$$\sum \pi = nF(x, [\phi(n, x)/n - T]) \qquad (3)$$

where $\partial F(\ )/\partial z > 0$. (cf. the deeply interesting discussion by Yaari (1981, pp. 14–21) of the Hedonical Calculus). Edgeworth observes that from this equation,

As long as T does not increase with x, an indefinite progress in evolution is desirable .... . But if the threshold increased with evolution, then we should tend to a 'stationary state', not only wealth and number, but also, what Mill hardly contemplated, cultivation, evolution, stationary (p. 78).

The next quotation shows the Edgeworth of 1877 very far from crasser versions of eugenics, exemplifying as it does, all at once, his style of exposition, subtlety of thought, liberality of spirit, allusiveness of reference and diffidence (not to say slyness) of manner. He first remarks (pp. 75–6), 'Behind the first problem, to distribute over the present generation, looms the second problem, to select from posterity.' This prompts the following footnote:

Not only from the second generation, but from 'the innumerable multitude of living beings present and to come.' This extension of view is not always favourable to privilege. For example, *prima facie*, unequal legislation directed against the influx of Chinese labour might be justified, on the supposition that, if on a large scale Chinese competed successfully with Aryans, an inferior race would inherit the earth. But this *prima facie* correspondence between exact utilitarianism and commercial selfishness would disappear, *if* it were probable that the inferior race, not retarded by unequal laws, would catch up the superior in the race of evolution, and become ultimately as highly civilized,

'as completely so,
As who began a thousand years ago.'
The difference of civilization during a short interval of such pursuit might be neglected, or rather, would be counterbalanced by the invidiousness and deteriorating tendencies of unequal legislation.

Of course, it will be understood that examples are put forward in these pages τνπω [in outline] and παχνλώs [coarsely], and without practical qualifications. It has been sought, not to clothe generality in circumstances, but to exhibit boldly the conception of exact utilitarianism – with a not unfelt sacrifice of delicacy to clearness.

He concludes the whole investigation of the consequences of exact utilitarianism as follows:

With regard to the theory of distribution, there is no indication that, at any rate between classes so nearly in the same order of evolution as the modern Aryan races, a law of distribution other than equality is to be wished . . . . With regard to the theory of population, there should be a limit to the number. As to the quality . . . if number and quality should ultimately come into competition, . . . , then the indefinite improvement of quality is no longer to be wished . . . . Not the most cultivated coterie, not the most numerous proletariate [sic], but a happy middle class shall inherit the earth. – It is submitted that these conclusions are acceptable to common utilitarianism, and, if not to common, at least to good, sense (p. 78).

The Hedonical Calculus. 'The Hedonical Calculus' of 1879, reprinted in *Mathematical Psychics* (whose pagination is used here), has been the primary source for scholarly discussion of Edgeworth's utilitarianism. This is unfortunate, since it is both less subtle and more tarnished with eugenics than the analysis of *New and Old Methods of Ethics*. Since its basic approach is the same as that of the earlier work, however, the discussion here can be brief, concentrating only on points of difference.

(i) Capacity for happiness is defined as before, and a similar double criterion is given for *capacity for work*, 'when for the same amount whatsoever of work done he incurs a less amount of fatigue, *and also* for the same increment (to the same amount) whatsoever of work done a less increment of fatigue' (p. 59; fn. 1 here is *not* in the article). As before, pleasure increases at a diminishing rate with means, and now fatigue increases at an increasing rate with work. It is postulated 'that capacity for pleasure and capacity for work generally speaking go together; that they both rise with evolution' (p. 68). Indeed, these capacities are *identified* with evolution (p. 70). Unsurprisingly, eugenics creeps in fast: 'it is probable that the highest in the order of evolution are most *capable of education* and improvement. In the general advance the most advanced should advance most' (p. 68).

(ii) The variational problem (1) above is generalized to include 'the pains of production' as well as 'the pleasures of consumption' (p. 66), and conclusions similar to those of the earlier work are found. Possibly because of the addition of the capacity for work, it is not made clear that the discussion includes the whole of the animal kingdom and not just humankind; perhaps, in this new version, it does not.

(iii) In exploring the solution for optimal growth of 'sections' of the population, it is assumed 'that the issue of each (supposed endogamous) section ranges on either side of the parental capacity' according to the normal distribution (pp. 69–70). This is apparently Edgeworth's first use of his beloved 'Law of Error'. Consideration of the problem of optimum population structure leads to the following 'outlandish' solution: 'the average issue shall be as large as possible for all sections above a determinate degree of capacity, but zero for all sections below that degree' (p. 70). (Yaari (1981, pp. 18–19) argues that the bizarre aspects of this bang-bang solution to the control problem spring not from Edgeworth's method but from its application to population planning.)

(iv) Edgeworth poses the Rawls-like question: '*What is the fortune of the least favoured class in the Utilitarian community?*' (p. 72), and concludes with relief that '*the condition of the least favoured class is positive happiness*' (p. 73). If nothing else, this shows that not only did he consider utility cardinally measurable, both individually and collectively, but also that for him such measurement does not, like height, temperature and von Neumann–Morgenstern utility, have an arbitrary origin and scale. 'The zero-point of pleasure corresponding to a minimum of means' (p. 72) implies that at most only scale can be arbitrary; and even there, any permitted scale change must be the same for everyone.

(v) *New and Old Methods of Ethics* urged utilitarians to be aware that sentients may differ in capacity for pleasure, before making their felicific calculations. The later conjunction of capacity for pleasure with position in the evolutionary order, however, threatened an unappetising brew of utilitarianism and eugenics. In 'The Hedonical Calculus' the potion turns poisonous.

> But Equality is not the whole of distributive justice ... in the minds of many good men among the moderns and the wisest of the ancients, there appears a deeper sentiment in favour of aristocratical privilege – the privilege of man above brute, of civilised above savage, of birth, of talent, and of the male sex. This sentiment of right has a ground of utilitarianism in supposed differences of *capacity* (p. 77).

Luckily, Edgeworth at last draws back from such sophistry:

> Pending a scientific hedonimetry, the principle 'Every man, and every woman, to count for one,' should be very cautiously applied (p. 81).

(vi) After all is said and done and integrated, 'the Hedonical Calculus supplies less a definite direction than a general bias' (p. 81), though towards what is not clear. Its deductions are 'of a very abstract, perhaps, only negative, character; negativing the assumption that *Equality* is necessarily implied in Utilitarianism' (p. vii). Thus the bright shining stream of *New and Old Methods of Ethics* finally stagnates into the muddy delta of '*Nothing indeed appears to be certain from a quite abstract point of view*' (pp. 74–5).

Such a sad conclusion did not keep the irrepressible Edgeworth down for long. Newly fired by the stimulus of Jevons, his own powerful capacity for work and intellectual pleasure soon produced one of the greatest achievements of all economic theory, the Economical Calculus of *Mathematical Psychics*.

B. MATHEMATICAL PSYCHICS. Short as it is, the book may be divided into three parts:
(A) An account and defence of the role of mathematics in economics [pp. 1–15, plus Appendices I (pp. 83–93), II (pp. 94–8) and VI (pp. 116–25)];
(B) The Economical Calculus [pp. 15–56, plus Appendices V (pp. 104–116) and VII (pp. 126–48)];
(C) The Utilitarian Calculus [pp. 56–82, plus Appendices III (pp. 98–102) and IV (pp. 102–4)].

Part C, which is essentially 'The Hedonical Calculus' of 1879, has already been discussed.

(A) *Mathematical Economics.* Edgeworth's defence of mathematical economics consists of two related lines of argument, buttressed in the three Appendices by some vigorous counter-attacks against the ἀγεωμέτρητοι (a term which Edgeworth uses frequently, and which means literally, 'those who have not studied geometry'; presumably the reference is to the inscription on the door at the entrance to Plato's Academy: 'no one who has not studied geometry may enter').

'*Loose Indefinite Relations*'. In the first line of argument, 'it is attempted to illustrate the possibility of Mathematical reasoning without *numerical* data' (p. v). Keynes observed that it was 'a thesis which at the time it was written was of much orginality and importance' (1926, p. 146) but did not elucidate the nature of its orginality. In fact most of the more obvious points about the non-necessity of actual numerical data and actual functional forms for economic analysis had already been made in 1838 by Cournot, 'the father of Mathematical Economics' (p. 83), and Edgeworth was never one to repeat what was already clear, at least to him. 'We must take for granted that our intelligent inquirer understands what is intelligible to the intelligent' (p. 126).

His new arguments are more subtle. First, it is suggested that indeed

> our social problems ... [have] ... *some* precise data: for example, the property of *uniformity of price* in a market; ... the *fulness* [sic] of the market: that there *continues* to be up to the conclusion of the dealing an indefinite number of dealers; ... the *fluidity* of the market, or infinite dividedness of the dealers' interests (p. 5).

Secondly, although very often we only know 'a certain *loose quantitative relation*, the *decrease-of-the-rate-of-increase* of a quantity' this is often enough, since 'The criterion of a *maximum* turns not upon the *amount* but upon the *sign* of a certain quantity.' It is precisely this quantitative relation that is 'given in such data as the *law of diminishing returns to capital and labour*, the *law of diminishing utility*, the *law of increasing fatigue*: the very same irregular, unsquared material which constitutes the basis of the Economical and the Utilitarian Calculus' (p. 6). For problems of optimum it is 'the loose, indefinite relations of positive and negative, convex or concave' (p. 91) that are important, and it is 'this very relation of concavity, not a whit more indefinite in psychics than in physics, ... [which is]

... quarried from such data as the law of decreasing utility, of increasing fatigue, of diminished returns to capital and labour;' (p. 92).

Nor is the use of such relations confined to economics. 'The great Bertrand–Thompson maximum–minimum principles and their statical analogues present abundant instances of mathematical reasoning about loose, indefinite relations' (pp. 88–90). The constant repetition of the phrase 'loose indefinite [or quantitative] relations'–at least 16 times in these pages and in Appendix I – achieves at last an almost incantatory effect.

'*Mécanique sociale*'. The earlier discussion of Hamilton's possible influences on the young Edgeworth referred to the latter's passionate comparison of Social Mechanics with Celestial Mechanics in *Mathematical Psychics*, in a section which is perhaps that most frequently quoted, possibly because it comes early on in a difficult book, more likely because it inspired his most rhapsodic writing.

> Imagine a material Cosmos, a mechanism as composite as possible, and perplexed with all manner of wheels, pistons, parts, connections, and whose mazy complexity might far transcend in its entanglement the webs of thought and wiles of passion; nevertheless, if any given impulses be imparted ... each part of the great whole will move off with a velocity such that the energy of the whole may be the greatest possible (p. 9).

> 'Mécanique sociale' may one day take her place along with 'Mécanique Celeste', throned each upon the double-sided height of one maximum principle, the supreme pinnacle of moral as of physical science (p. 12).

Such analogies seem to have had an almost mystical significance for Edgeworth, undoubtedly reinforcing his faith in 'the employment of mechanical terms and Mathematical reasoning in social science' (p. 15).

The ἀγεωμετρητοι. Appendix II is chiefly notable for setting a very Oxbridge-like 'examination paper' containing seven tough questions for the mathematically unblessed, such as: '6. It has been said that the *distribution of net produce* between cooperators (labourers and capitalists associated) is arbitrary and *indeterminate*. Discuss this question' (p. 96). It is admitted that some scholars may of course turn 'away contemptuously from such questions', but 'Are they not all quantitative conceptions, best treated by means of the science of quantity?' (p. 98).

Appendix VI carries the attack further, listing mathematical errors by those eminent but ageometrical social scientists Bentham, J.S. Mill, Carines, Spencer and Sidgwick. It is remarkable chiefly for Edgeworth's quite deliberate singling out of Cairnes for a savage attack, apparently provoked by the latter's 'amazing blindness' (p. 119) to Jevons's theory of exchange.

(B) *Economical Calculus*. Edgeworth now enters quite precipitately upon the work on which his main claim to immortality as an economist must rest. It is best told predominantly in his own subtle words.

First (pp. 16–19) come some important definitions and assumptions, which set the table very precisely for what is to follow:

(a) '[E]very agent is actuated only by self-interest', and may act '*without*, or *with*, the consent of others affected by his actions ... the first species of action may be called *war*; the second, *contract*.

(b) '[E]conomic *competition* ... is both, *pax* or *pact* between contractors during contract, *war*, when some of the contractors *without the consent of others recontract*.'

(c) 'The *field of competition* ... consists of all the individuals who are willing and able to recontract about the articles under consideration.'

(d) Any individual may contract or 'recontract with any out of an indefinite number' of agents, 'without the consent being required of, any third party'; 'e.g., any [individual] X (and similarly Y) may deal with any number of Ys.'

(e) '[I]f any X deal with an indefinite number of Ys he must have given each an indefinitely small portion of x', from which there follows 'the indefinite divisibility of each *article* of contract'.

(f) 'A *settlement* is a contract which cannot be varied with the consent of all the parties to it.'

(g) 'A *final settlement* is a settlement which cannot be varied by recontract within the field of competition.'

(h) 'Contract is *indeterminate* when there are an indefinite number of *final settlements*.' (A copy of the book annotated by Edgeworth himself replaces 'are' by 'may be'; I am indebted to Stephen Stigler for this information).

Notice the lawyerly language employed, most probably a consequence of Edgeworth's legal training. In particular, note the stress on the word 'contract', which is used in simple or compound form over 200 times in this Economical Calculus and its two Appendices. As Howey, writing in 1960 (and not today!) pointed out: 'No one had used it in this sense earlier in economics and no one followed Edgeworth in his use' (p. 240, fn. 48).

More importantly, notice the subtlety of (f) and (g). If a contract cannot be varied by the consent of *all* parties to it, then that must be because at least one will be hurt by a given change and would therefore block any such proposed move. Hence, a settlement is *precisely* a Pareto-optimal point for the parties to the contract; and this many years before Pareto considered the matter. Moreover, a *final* settlement is one which cannot be varied, even by negotiation with any or all of the parties outside the contract. Taken in conjunction with (d), this implies that a final settlement is *precisely* one that, as we would now say, lies in the core.

The indeterminacy of contract. Most probably inspired by Cournot's passage from monopoly to pure competition (1838, ch. VII), and 'Going beyond ... [him] ..., not without trembling' (p. 47), Edgeworth at once raises the question: '*How far contract is indeterminate?*' (p. 20). He begins its answer by considering first two individuals X and Y, exchanging two goods in the amounts x and y from initial holdings $(a, 0)$ and $(0, b)$, respectively. Hence the post-trade amounts held are $(a - x, y)$ and $(x, b - y)$. At first he assumes additive Jevonian utility functions but immediately switches, 'more generally' to the form $P = F(x, y)$ and $\Pi = \Phi(x, y)$ for X and Y, respectively—the first use of this general form in economics, unless one includes his formulations in *New and Old Methods of Ethics*.

We now have to find 'To what *settlement* they [i.e. X and Y] will consent; the answer is in general that contract by itself does not supply sufficient conditions to determinate the solution;' (p. 20), but 'will supply only *one* condition (for the two variables), namely' (p. 21)

$$F_x(x, y)\phi_y(x, y) - F_y(x, y)\phi_x(x, y) = 0 \qquad (4)$$

where $F_x(x, y) = \partial F(x, y)/\partial x$, etc. The locus of points (x, y) which satisfy (4) 'it is proposed here to call the *contract-curve*' (p. 21), 'along which the pleasure-forces of the contractors are mutually antagonistic' (p. 29).

Edgeworth arrives at (4) by several different routes. First, 'X will step only on one side of a certain line, the *line of indifference*, as it might be called;' (p. 21). (The name probably comes not from Jevons's Law of Indifference but from *New and Old Methods of Ethics* (p. 9, fn. 1), where 'indifferent actions' are 'those which are supposed equally to end to the general good', and/or from Sidgwick (e.g. 1877, p. 125): 'a scale of desirability, measured positively and negatively from a zero of perfect indifference').

And ... X will *prefer* to move ... perpendicular to the line of indifference ... X and Y will consent to move together ... in any direction between their respective lines of indifference ... they will refuse to move at all ... When their *lines of indifference* are coincident ... whereof the *necessary* (but not *sufficient*) condition is [(4)] (p. 22).

The second route is via consideration of the total differential of F, expressed in polar form, but a more interesting route is the third:

motion is possible so long as, one party not losing, the other gains. The point of equilibrium, therefore, may be described as a *relative maximum*, the point at which e.g. Π being constant, P is a maximum. Put $P = P - c(\Pi - \Pi')$, where c is a constant [i.e. a Lagrange multiplier] and Π' is the supposed given value of Π (p. 23).

Eliminating c leads to (4) again.

The interest of this third route is of course that Edgeworth, giving here the standard alternative definition of a Pareto-optimal point, is making it quite clear exactly what a settlement means, namely, an efficient allocation for the parties to the contract.

The argument is then 'extended to several persons and several variables' (pp. 26–8). Pages 28–9 illustrate the two-person two-good case by a diagram (*not* a box, the usual historical ascription being inaccurate) which measures along the abscissa the wages paid by Crusoe and along the ordinate the labour given up by Friday. Because of this the indifference curves run from southwest to northeast, and the contract curve from northwest to southeast, the reverse of the usual box diagram.

> [S]ettlements are represented by an *indefinite number of points*, a locus, the *contract-curve* CC', or rather, a certain portion of it which ... lies between two points ... which are respectively the intersections with the contract-curve of the *curves of indifference* [the first such naming for each party drawn through the [no-trade] origin (p. 29).

Perfect and imperfect competition.

> With this clogged and underground procedure [of bilateral exchange] is contrasted ... the smooth machinery of the open market ... . You might suppose each dealer to write down[3] [the reference is to Walras, 1874, Article 50; see Walras, 1954, p. 93] his *demand*, how much of an article he would take at each price, without attempting to conceal his requirements; and these data having been furnished to a sort of market-machine, the *price* to be passionlessly evaluated. That contract in a state of perfect competition is determined by demand and supply is generally accepted, but is hardly to be fully understood without mathematics. ... [t]he familiar pair of equations is [i.e. will be] deduced by the present writer from the first principle: Equilibrium is attained when the existing contracts can neither be varied without recontract with the consent of the existing parties, nor by contract within the field of competition. The advantage of this general method is that it is applicable to the particular cases of imperfect competition; where the conceptions of *demand and supply at a price* are no longer appropriate (pp. 30–31).

In other words, equilibrium of perfect competition is *defined* to be attained when the contract is in the core.

Edgeworth starts the analysis of 'imperfect competition', the 'limitation of numbers' (p. 42), by supposing that there is introduced a second *X* and a second *Y*, each of them with 'the same requirements, the same nature as the old' *X* and *Y*, respectively (p. 35). For this four-member economy,

> there cannot be an equilibrium unless (1) all the field is collected at one point; (2) that point is on the *contract-curve*. For (1) if possible let one couple be at one point, and another couple at another point. It will generally be the interest of the *X* of one couple and the *Y* of the other to rush together, leaving their partners in the lurch. And (2) if the common point is not on the contract-curve, it will be the interest of *all parties* to descend to the contract-curve.

However, the contract-curve appropriate to the new, quadrilateral situation is *not* that belonging to the old, but a strict subset of it. In particular, the end-points of the old bilateral contract-curve, determined by the respective indifference curves through the initial no-trade point, will no longer be sustainable. Take either such end-point, say that closer to the *X*-origin. Then 'it will in general be possible for *one* of the *Y*s (without the consent of the other) to *recontract* with the two *X*s, so that for all those three parties the recontract is more advantageous than the previously existing contract' (p. 35), i.e. than that which was at the X-end of the original contract-curve. The detailed geometric argument that establishes this is presented in pp. 35–7 (for a somewhat simpler discussion see Newman, 1965, pp. 111–15), and depends crucially on the property that the indifference curves of each agent are strictly convex.

It is sometimes said (e.g. by Stigler, 1965, p. 103) that Edgeworth assumed this property of convex indifference curves, but in fact he *proves* it on the basis of earlier assumptions, viz: that $F_x < 0$, $F_y > 0$, $F_{xx} < 0$, $F_{yy} < 0$ and $F_{xy} < 0$. From these it readily follows that the standard sufficient conditions for indifference curves to be convex (as given for example in Allen (1938, p. 375)) are satisfied, and that in fact they are equivalent to the conditions presented by Edgeworth on page 36. Note that $F_x < 0$ because x is the amount of good given up by X, while F_{xx} and F_{yy} are both negative by the law of diminishing marginal utility. The unusual assumption is $F_{xy} < 0$, which in the later definition of Auspitz and Lieben (1889, p. 482; 1914, Texte, p. 318) would imply that x and y are substitutes. Edgeworth chooses to be coy about this: 'Attention is solicited to the interpretation of the third condition [i.e. $F_{xy} < 0$]' (p. 34), and so almost deliberately loses the chance for yet another explicit first, a formal definition of substitutes and complements; but he is quite clear about its role in establishing convexity.

'If now a *third X* and third Y (still equal-natured) be introduced into the field' (p. 37) then the original bilateral contract-curve shrinks yet further, as now $2Y$s can recontract with $3X$s, and so on.

> [I]n general for any number short of the *practically infinite* (if such a term be allowed) there is a finite length of contract-curve, ..., at any point of which if the system is placed, it cannot by contract or recontract be displaced; ... there are *an indefinite number of final settlements*, a quantity continually diminishing as we approach a perfect market (p. 39),

since competitive allocations always remain in that finite length (p. 37).

There seems to be no warrant for the claim (e.g. in Creedy, 1986, pp. 65, 69) that Edgeworth considered competitive equilibrium to be unique. Indeed, speaking of one application (to personal service) he says that 'there is no *determinate*, and very generally[1] *unique*, arrangement towards which the system tends' (p. 46), the footnote referring explicitly to Marshall and Walras on multiple equilibria. Elsewhere in the book he makes frequent and delighted reference to the (very different) demonstrations by Walras and Marshall of the possibility of such multiple equilibria.

Finally, even a passing remark sounds startlingly modern, especially in the example given,

> [D]ifferent final settlements would be reached if the system should run down from different *initial positions* or contracts. The sort of difference which exists between[1] Dutch and English auction, theoretically unimportant in *perfect competition*, does correspond to different results, *different final settlements* in imperfect competition. And in general, and in the absence of imposed

conditions, the said final settlements are not on the demand-curve, but on the contract-curve (pp. 37–8),

i.e. they are core allocations but not competitive allocations. The footnote mentions (but does not give a reference to) W.T. Thornton, who first pointed to the possibility of such a discrepancy between the results of English and Dutch auctions (see 1870, pp. 56ff): 'Now we believe', Edgeworth remarks acidly, 'but not because that unmathematical writer has told us.' Down with the ἀγεωμέτρητοι!

Determinateness and arbitration. Towards the end of the Economical Calculus there is an indictment of competition as sharp as any penned by an anti-neoclassical, and more powerful than most since it is based on exact analysis.

> To impair, it may be conjectured, the reverence paid to *competition*; in whose results – as if worked out by a play of physical forces, impersonal, impartial – economists have complacently acquiesced. Of justice and humanity there was no pretence; but there seemed to command respect the majestic neutrality of Nature. But if it should appear that the field of competition is deficient in that *continuity of fluid*, that *multiety of atoms* which constitute the foundations of the uniformities of Physics; if competition is found wanting, not only the regularity of low, but even the impartiality of chance – the throw of a die loaded with villainy – economics would be indeed a 'dismal science', and the reverence for competition would be more no more.
>
> There would arise a general demand for a *principle of arbitration* (pp. 50–51).

Edgeworth is ready to hand with just the right principle for the occasion.

> *Equity* and 'fairness of division' are charming ... but how would they be applicable to the distribution of a joint product between cooperators? ... *Justice* requires to be informed by some more definite principle (p. 51).

This principle is – exact utilitarianism.

> Now, it is a circumstance of momentous interest ... that *one* of the in general indefinitely numerous *settlements*[1] between contractors is ... the contract tending to the greatest possible utility of the contractors. In this direction ... is to be sought the required principle (p. 53).

The footnote first offers a proof of the proposition in the text, a proof which is incomplete since it shows neither the uniqueness of the utilitarian point nor that it is on the contract-curve, a settlement, and not merely on the (larger) efficiency-locus. It then goes on to consider the case of altruistic agents, Xs whose utility functions are not F but $F + \lambda\phi$, 'where λ is a *coefficient of effective sympathy*' and similarly for any Y, whose utility is now given by $\phi + \mu F$. For these 'modified contractors', it turns out that their contract-curve is '*The old contract-curve between narrower limits* ... As the coefficients of sympathy increase, utilitarianism becomes more *pure*, ... the *contract-curve narrows down to the utilitarian point*.'

The argument has come, designedly, full circle. After the Utopias of *New and Old Methods of Ethics* and 'The Hedonical Calculus', the positive economics of the Economical Calculus leads us after all back to Utilitarianism, considered now as a practical way of overcoming the evils of imperfect competition and indeterminacy. But, to paraphrase a harsh (though just) remark the Edgeworth once made (1889a, p. 435) about Walras' *tâtonnement*, this utilitarian principle of arbitration 'indicate[s] *a* way, not the *way*', to justice. Moreover, it is 'not a very good [way]' (ibid.) since not only does it require cardinality of utility measurement (as does, for example, the bargaining solution of Nash, 1950), but its cardinality is quite strict, not allowing (as does Nash) independent changes of origin and scale in each of the agents' utility functions. Edgeworth's attempt to move from his 'weak' bargaining solution, the contract-curve, to a 'strong' solution, the utilitarian point, cannot be judged a success. But what a road he travelled before arriving at this Oz-like destination!

AFTER MATHEMATICAL PSYCHICS

It must have been deeply disappointing to Edgeworth that in their reviews of his book neither of his two great heroes, Jevons and Marshall, displayed the slightest understanding of his profound analysis of contract and its indeterminacy. Both were quite laudatory in general terms, but both were patronizing, Jevons in his criticism of the difficulty of Edgeworth's style – 'an uncouth and even clumsy piece of literary work' (1881, p. 583), Marshall in his worry 'to see how far he succeeds in preventing his mathematics from running away with him, ... out of sight of the actual facts of economics' (1881, p. 457).

However, it was some consolation to Edgeworth to receive a very encouraging letter from Galton (see Stephen Stigler, 1978, pp. 290–91), who strongly disagreed with Jevons. From the narrow point of view of economics, encouragement from such a quarter was perhaps not to be wished, for it may have confirmed Edgeworth's attraction to eugenics. More probably and more usefully, it may well have helped to set him on the road to his distinguished contributions to probability and statistics, which began in 1883 (see the companion entry on his contributions to this subject).

Apart from a brief note (1884), in which he drew a rather forced analogy between the limit processes that lead to competitive allocations and the limiting processes that lead to the Central Limit Theorem, Edgeworth never again returned to the theory of contract. Why this should be so is a puzzle. The unperceptive reviews must have been a factor, and so perhaps was his consciousness that his 'proofs' of the main results were '*Conclusions*, rather, the mathematical demonstration of which is not fully exhibited' (1881, p. 20, fn. 1). Perhaps the failure to return was fortuitous. It is not uncommon for a scholar, on completion of a major work, to turn to something quite different. So Edgeworth, tempted by statistics, may have found its attractions overwhelming, to the exclusion not only of the theory of contract but of all other work in economics. Between 1881 and 1888 he published essentially nothing in economics, apart from the note already alluded to, during a period for which over 30 publications in statistics and probability are recorded.

65

It is clear that he must have continued to read widely and deeply in economics during this time – those 77 entries in the first volume of Palgrave's *Dictionary* did not come out of the air. Moreover, he took an active part in economic discussions, not only in such formal settings as the British Association but also in informal clubs like those in intellectual Hampstead that were frequented by Wicksteed, Shaw and Webb. With his election to the Drummond Chair at Oxford in 1890, Edgeworth settled down to that 'long stream of splinters ... split off from his bright mind to illumine (and obscure) the pages of the *Statistical* and *Economic Journals*' (Keynes, 1926, p. 149).

If its creator did not languish, the theory of contract certainly did. The silence was extraordinary. Keynes's biography was superb about the man but again rather patronizing about his work, especially about 'Mathematical Psychics [which] has not ... fulfilled its early promise' (1926, p. 149). It cannot be said that Keynes's criticism was very acute, being mainly of that kind of Platonist pseudo-profundity which can be gained by capitalizing such words as 'Organic Unity, ... Discrete-ness, ... Discontinuity' (p. 150).

A faint rustle stirred the silence in an article by the young Hicks (1930; see also 1932; p. 26), while Stigler (1942, p. 81) observed that 'It can be demonstrated that the length of the contract curve decreases as the number of bargainers increases', though without direct reference to *Mathematical Psychics*. That was apparently the entire literature on the subject. I remember vividly a conversation in 1952–3 with a distinguished economic theorist, subsequently a Nobel Prize winner, in which he (and I, come to that) expressed puzzlement about what this passage of Stigler's could possibly mean.

The silence was broken by Martin Shubik (1959), who made the essential connection between Edgeworth's contract theory, coalitions and game theory. After nearly 80 years in the wilderness Edgeworth's theory finally moved, all at once, on to centre stage. Thereafter progress was rapid, with the theorems of Scarf (1962), Scarf and Debreu (1963), Aumann (1964) and many others. Edgeworth's faith in the importance of the theory of contract has been triumphantly vindicated.

ENVOI. Following the strategy of this essay, which has been to let Edgeworth speak for himself, let the final word concerning the significance of his work be left to him. If this eloquent passage is reminiscent of another and much better known peroration (Keynes, 1936, pp. 383–4), remember that Edgeworth was always ahead of his time.

Considerations so abstract it would of course be ridiculous to fling upon the flood-tide of practical points. But they are not perhaps out of place when we remount to the little rills of sentiment and secret springs of motive where every course of action must be originated. It is at a height of abstraction in the rarefied atmosphere of speculation that the secret springs of action take their rise, and a direction is imparted to the pure fountains of youthful enthusiasm whose influence will ultimately affect the broad current of events (1881, Appendix VII, 'On the Present Crisis in Ireland', pp. 128–9).

SELECTED WORKS

Books

1877. *New and Old Methods of Ethics.* Oxford: James Parker & Co.
1881. *Mathematical Psychics.* London: C. Kegan Paul & Co; New York: A.M. Kelley, 1967.
1887. *Metretike.* London: The Temple Company.
1925. *Papers Relating to Political Economy.* 3 vols, London: Macmillan for the Royal Economic Society; New York: B. Franklin, 1963.

Articles

1876. Mr Matthew Arnold on Bishop Butler's Doctrine of Self-Love. *Mind* I, 570–71 (signed T.Y. Edgeworth).
1879. The Hedonical Calculus. *Mind* IV, 349–409.
1884. The rationale of exchange. *Journal of the Statistical Society* 47, 164–6.

Reviews

1886. Journal and Letters of W. Stanley Jevons, edited by his Wife. *The Academy*, 22 May, No. 733, 355–6.
1889. (Review of) L. Walras: *Eléments d'économie politique pure*, 2nd edition. *Nature* 40, 434–36.

BIBLIOGRAPHY

Works referring to the life of Edgeworth and his family

Black, R.D.C. 1977. *Papers and Correspondence of William Stanley Jevons*, Vols. IV and V. London: Macmillan, in association with the Royal Economic Society.
Bonar, J. 1926. Memories of F.Y. Edgeworth. *Economic Journal* 36, 647–53.
Bowley, A.L. 1934. Francis Ysidro Edgeworth. *Econometrica* 2, 113–24.
Butler, H.J. and H. E. 1928. *The Black Book of Edgeworthstown and other Edgeworth Memories 1585–1817.* London: Faber & Gwyer.
Carlyle, T. 1851. *The Life of John Sterling.* Boston: Phillips, Sampson.
Creedy, J. 1986. *Edgeworth and the Development of Neoclassical Economics.* Oxford: Basil Blackwell.
Edgeworth, R.L. 1820. *Memories of Richard Lovell Edgeworth, Esq.; begun by himself and concluded by his daughter Marias Edgeworth.* 2 vols, London: R. Hunter and Baldwin, Cradock and Joy.
Fisher, I.N. 1956. *My Father Irving Fisher.* New York: Comet Press.
Graves, R. 1958. *Goodbye to All That.* New edn, revised, London: Cassell & Co. Originally published in England in 1929; the first American edition (1930) omitted the Edgeworth–Lawrence anecdote.
Graves, R.P. 1882, 1885, 1889. *Life of Sir William Rowan Hamilton.* Vol. I (1882), Vol. II (1885) and Vol. III (1889), Dublin: Hodges, Figgis.
Hankins, T.L. 1980. *Sir William Rowan Hamilton.* Baltimore: Johns Hopkins Press. (Contains portraits of Edgeworthstown House and Francis Beaufort Edgeworth.)
Harrod, R.F. 1951. *The Life of John Maynard Keynes.* London: Macmillan; New York: St Martin's Press, 1963.

Hicks, J.R. 1984. Francis Ysidro Edgeworth. In *Economists and the Irish Economy: from the Eighteenth Century to the Present Day*, ed. Dublin: Irish Academic Press in association with *Hermathena* Trinity College Dublin, 157–74.

Hildreth, C. 1968. Edgeworth, Francis Ysidro. In *International Encyclopaedia of the Social Sciences*, ed. D.E. Sills, New York: Macmillan and Free Press, Vol. 4, 506–9.

Hobson, J.A. 1938. *Confessions of an Economic Heretic*. London: Allen & Unwin. Reprinted Brighton: Harvester Press, 1976.

Howey, R.S. 1960. *The Rise of the Marginal Utility School 1870–1889*. Lawrence: University of Kansas Press.

Hutchison, T.W. 1953. *A Review of Economic Doctrines 1870–1929*. Oxford: Clarendon Press.

Kendall, M.G. 1968. Francis Ysidro Edgeworth, 1845–1926. *Economic Journal* 36, March, 140–53.

Keynes, J.M. 1933. *Essays in Biography*. London; Macmillan. New edn, ed. Geoffrey Keynes, London; Rupert Hart-Davis, 1951. Reprinted as Vol. X of *The Collected Writings of John Maynard Keynes*, London: Macmillan for the Royal Economic Society, 1972. (The footnote referred to was in neither the 1926 nor (the first printing of) the 1933 version of Keynes's essay.) New York: St Martin's Press, 1972.

MacKenzie, N. and MacKenzie, J. 1977. *The Fabians*: New York; Simon & Schuster.

Marshall, A. 1961. *Principles of Economics*. 9th (Variorum) edn, ed. C.W. Guillebaud, 2 vols, London and New York: Macmillan.

Mill, J.S. 1873. *Autobiography*. London: Longmans, Green, Reader & Dyer; New York: Oxford University Press, 1944.

Mozley, T. 1882. *Reminiscences, chiefly of Oriel College and the Oxford Movement*. 2 vols, Boston: Houghton Mifflin.

Pigou, A.C. and Robertson, D.H. 1931. *Economic Essays and Addresses*. London: P.S. King & Son.

Price, L.L. 1926. Francis Ysidro Edgeworth. *Journal of the Royal Statistical Society* 89, March, 371–7.

Samuelson, P.A. 1947. *Foundations of Economic Analysis*. Cambridge, Mass.: Harvard University Press.

Samuelson, P.A. 1951. Schumpeter as a teacher and economic theorist. In *Schumpeter: Social Scientist*, ed. S.E. Harris, Cambridge, Mass.: Harvard University Press.

Schumpeter, J.A. 1954. *History of Economic Analysis*. New York: Oxford University Press.

Stigler, S. 1978. Francis Ysidro Edgeworth, statistician. *Journal of the Royal Statistical Society*, Series A 141(3), 287–322.

Sully, J. 1918. *My Life and Friends*. New York: E.P. Dutton & Co.

Other references

Allen, R.G.D. 1938. *Mathematical Analysis for Economists*. London: Macmillan.

Annan, N. 1952. *Leslie Stephen*. Cambridge, Mass.: Harvard University Press.

Aumann, R. 1964. Markets with a continuum of traders *Econometrica* 32, 39–50.

Auspitz, R. and Lieben, R. 1889. *Untersuchungen über die Theorie des Preises*. Leipzig; Duncker & Humblot, French trans. in 2 vols (Texte and Album), Paris: Giard, 1914.

Cournot, A.A. 1838. *Recherches sur les principes mathématiques de la théorie des richesses*. Paris: Hachette. New edn., ed. G. Lutfalla, Paris: Rivière, 1938.

Hardy, G.H. 1938. *Pure Mathematics*. 7th edn, Cambridge: Cambridge University Press.

Hardy, G.H., Littlewood, J.E. and Polya, G. 1934. *Inequalities*. Cambridge: Cambridge University Press.

Hicks, J.R. 1930. Edgeworth, Marshall, and the indeterminateness of wages. *Economic Journal* 40, 215–31.

Hicks, J.R. 1932. *The Theory of Wages*. London: Macmillan; New York: St. Martin's Press, 1963.

Jensen, J.L.W.V. 1906, Sur les fonctions convexes et les inégalités entre les valeurs moyennes. *Acta Mathematica* 30, 175–93.

Jevons, W.S. 1881. Review of *Mathematical Psychics*. *Mind* 6, 581–3.

Keynes, J.M. 1936. *The General Theory of Employment, Interest and Money*. London: Macmillan; New York: Harcourt, Brace & World, 1965.

Lindsay, R.B. and Margenau, H. 1957. *Foundations of Physics*. New York: Dover.

Marshall, A. 1881. Review of *Mathematical Psychics*. *Academy* 476, June, 457.

Nash, J.F. 1950. The bargaining problem. *Econometrica* 18, 155–62.

Newman, P. 1965. *The Theory of Exchange*. Englewood Cliffs, NJ: Prentice-Hall.

Scarf, H. 1962. An analysis of a market with a large number of participants. In H. Scarf, *Recent Advances in Game Theory*, Princeton; Princeton University Press.

Scarf, H. and Debreu, G. 1963. A limit theorem on the core of an economy. *International Economic Review* 4, 235–47.

Shubik, M. 1959. Edgeworth market games. In *Contributions to the Theory of Games*, Vol IV, ed. A.W. Tucker and R.D. Luce, Annals of Mathematics Studies No. 40, Princeton: Princeton University Press.

Sidgwick, H. 1874. *The Methods of Ethics*. London: Macmillan. 2nd edn, 1877.

Singer, P. (ed.) 1985. *In Defence of Animals*. Oxford: Basil Blackwell.

Snow, C.P. 1967. Foreword to new edition of G.H. Hardy: *A Mathematician's Apology*. Cambridge: Cambridge University Press.

Stigler, G.J. 1942. *The Theory of Competitive Price*. New York: Macmillan.

Stigler, G.J. 1965. *Essays in the History of Economics*. Chicago: University of Chicago Press.

Thornton, W.T. 1870. *On Labour*. 2nd edn, London: Macmillan. Rome: Edizioni Bizzarri, 1969.

Walras, L. 1874. *Eléments d'économie politique pure*. Lausanne: L. Corbaz. English translation by W. Jaffé of the Edition Definitive (1926), London: Allen & Unwin, 1954; Homewood, Ill.: R.D. Irwin.

Yaari, M.E. 1981. Rawls, Edgeworth, Shapley and Nash: theories of distributive justice re-examined. *Journal of Economic Theory* 24, 1–39.

Expected Utility and Mathematical Expectation

DAVID SCHMEIDLER AND PETER WAKKER

1. Expected utility theory deals with choosing among acts where the decision-maker does not know for sure which consequence will result from a chosen act. When faced with several acts, the decision-maker will choose the one with the highest 'expected utility', where the expected utility of an act is the sum of the products of probability and utility over all possible consequences.

The introduction of the concept of expected utility is usually attributed to Daniel Bernoulli (1738). He arrived at this concept as a resolution of the so-called St Petersburg paradox. It involves the following gamble: A 'fair' coin is flipped until the first time heads up. If this is at the kth flip, then the gambler receives $\$2^k$. The question arose how much to pay for participation in this gamble. Since the probability that heads will occur for the first time in the kth flip is 2^{-k} (assuming independence of the flips), and the gain then is $\$2^k$, the 'expected value' (i.e. the *mathematical expectation* of the gain) of the gamble is infinite. It has been observed though that gamblers were not willing to pay more then $\$2$ to $\$4$ to participate in such a gamble. Hence the 'paradox' between the mathematical expectation of the gain, and the observed willingness to pay.

Bernoulli suggested that the gambler's goal is not to maximize his expected gain, but to maximize the expectation of the logarithm of the gain which is $\Sigma_{j=1}^{\infty}$ $2^{-j} \log 2^j$, i.e. $2 \log 2 (= \log 4)$. Then the gambler is willing to pay $\$4$ for the gamble. The idea that *homo economicus* considers the expected utility of the gamble, and not the expected value, is a cornerstone of expected utility theory.

In the next section the approach of Savage to decisions under uncertainty is presented. In section 3 the von Neumann–Morgenstern characterization of expected utility maximization for the context of decisions under risk is given. Section 4 briefly mentions same related approaches. Section 5, the Appendix, defines (mathematical) expectation.

2. EXPECTED UTILITY WHEN APPLIED TO DECISIONS UNDER UNCERTAINTY; SAVAGE'S APPROACH

2.1 The main ingredients of a decision problem under uncertainty are acts consequences' and states of nature. Suppose that a decision-maker has to choose one of three feasible acts f, g, h. Act f leads to one (only) of the two consequences a and b. Act g leads to a or c, act h to b or d. Thus the set of consequences, C, is in this example $\{a, b, c, d\}$.

The matching of feasible acts to consequences is expressed by the concept of 'state of nature', or 'state' for short. More precisely, a given state of nature indicates for each feasible act what the resulting consequence will be. In the above example, there are three feasible acts f, g, h, each leading to one of two possible consequences. See Table 2.1.

A state of nature completely resolves the uncertainty relating acts to consequences. If the decision-maker would know for sure which state of nature is the true one, then he would choose an act which results in the most desirable consequence. The desirability of a consequence neither depends on the act nor on the state of nature leading to it.

In constructing a table like Table 2.1 some of the states of nature may be deleted if the decision-maker is certain that they cannot occur.

TABLE 2.1 The eight logically possible matchings of feasible acts to consequences

Acts				States				
	s_1	s_2	s_3	s_4	s_5	s_6	s_7	s_8
f	a	a	a	a	b	b	b	b
g	a	a	c	c	a	a	c	c
h	b	d	b	d	b	d	b	d

The next step in the process of selecting the best act is to construct 'conceivable' acts, which are not feasible. Thus the set of acts, F, in Savage's set-up consists of all functions from the set of states of nature, S, to the set C of consequences. In our example there are 4^8 acts. Of these, three acts f, g and h are actually feasible: The additional 65533 acts are only conceivable. The construction of the conceivable acts and the possibility of all acts of F is a basic assumption of the present approach. For the sake of presentation we will in the next subsection assume the validity of the expected utility theory and then we will return to the rationale of our construction.

2.2 Suppose for the present that the decision-maker, in choosing between acts, indeed computes the expected utility of each act, and selects a feasible act with the highest expected utility. Thus we are assuming that he has assigned probability $P(s)$ to every state of nature s in S, and the utility $U(c)$ to every consequence c in C. So, given an act f in F, the expected utility $EU(f)$ of f equals $\Sigma_{s \in S} P(s) U[f(s)]$. More generally, if the set S is infinite, then P is a finitely additive probability measure defined on all events (i.e. subsets of S), and $EU(f)$ equals $\int U[f(s)] \, dP(s)$ (assuming the integral to exist; say U is bounded; see the Appendix, on Mathematical Expectation, section 5). So in fact in this case the decision-maker has a well-defined 'preference relation' (i.e. binary relation) $\geqslant$ on the set of acts F, with, for all f, g in F:

(2.3) $f \gtrsim g$ iff $EU(f) \geqslant EU(g)$.

It is easily seen that the preference relation, defined in (2.3), is not affected when the utility function $U : C \mapsto R$ is replaced by any positive linear transformation of it (say $\bar{U} : c \mapsto \alpha U(c) + \beta$, for some real β and positive α).

2.4 If a preference relation, $\gtrsim$, over acts is derived from comparisons of expected utility as in (2.3), then it must satisfy several properties. We follow the terminology and order of Savage (1954). He listed seven postulates, five of which (P1 up to P4, and P7) are implied by (2.3). Postulate P1 says that the preference relation is complete ($f \gtrsim g$ or $g \gtrsim f$ for all acts f, g) and transitive. Postulate P2 is referred to as the sure-thing principle. It says that, when comparing two acts, only those states of nature matter, on which these acts differ. In other words, for the comparison between two acts, if they coincide on an event A, it really does not matter what actually the consequence is for each state in A. Thus P2 makes it possible to derive a preference relation over acts, conditioned on the event A^c; this for any event A.

Postulate P3 entails that the desirability of a consequence does not depend on the combination of state and act that lead to it; hence the desirability of consequences can be expressed by a utility function on C.

P4 guarantees that the preference relation over acts induces a qualitative probability relation ('at least as probable as') over events, which is transitive and complete. P7 is a technical monotonicity condition.

P5 and P6 are Savage's only postulates which are not a necessary implication of (2.3). P5 simply serves to exclude the trivial case where the decision-maker is indifferent between any two acts. P6 implies some sort of continuity of the preference relation, and non-atomicity of the probability measure; the last term means that any non-impossible event can be partitioned into two non-impossible events. Hence there must be an infinite number of states.

Savage's great achievement was not to *assume* (2.3), but to show that his list of postulates P1–P7 *implies* that the preference relation over acts has an expected utility representation as in (2.3). Savage argued compellingly for the appropriateness of his postulates. Furthermore, Savage showed that the probability measure in (2.3) is uniquely determined by the preference relation $\geqslant$, and that the utility function is unique up to a positive linear transformation.

2.5 The significance of Savage's achievement is that it gives the first, and until today most complete, conceptual foundation to expected utility. Savage's conclusion, to use expected utility for the selection of optimal acts, can be used even if we do not have the structure and the seven postulates of Savage. Indeed, the assumption needed on consequences, states, acts and preferences, is that they can be extended so as to satisfy all requirements of Savage's model. Also other models, as mentioned in section 4, can be used to obtain expected utility representations.

Given a decision problem under uncertainty, if we assume that it can be embedded in Savage's framework, then it is not necessary to actually carry out this embedding. In other words, if the decision-maker is convinced that in principle it is possible to construct the conceivable acts as in subsection 2.1 and the ranking of all acts in accordance with the postulates, then this construction does not have to be made. Instead one can directly try to assess probabilities and utilities, and apply the expected utility criterion. As an example, suppose a market-vendor has to decide whether to order 50 portions of ice-cream (f), or not (g). One portion costs \$1, and is sold for \$2. If the weather will be nice the next day, the school nearby will allow the children to go to the market, and all 50 portions, if ordered, will be sold, yielding a profit of \$50. If the weather is not nice, no portion will be sold. We assume that the ice-cream cannot be kept in stock and hence bad weather will yield a 'gain' of \$$-50$ if the portions have been ordered.

Instead of embedding the above example into Savage's framework, the market salesman may immediately assess P_1 (or $1 - P_1$), the probability for good (bad) weather; next assess the utilities of gaining \$50, \$0 and $-$\$50; finally order the 50 portions if $P_1 U(\$50) + (1 - P_1)U(-\$50) > U(\$0)$.

Theoretical conclusions can be derived from the mere assumption of expected utility maximization, without an actual assessment of the probabilities and utilities. Examples are the theories of attitudes towards risk, with applications to insurance, portfolio choice, etc. The validity of these applications depends on expected utility theory, which in turn depends on the plausibility of Savage's model (or other derivations of expected utility).

Another important theoretical application of Savage's model is to neo-Bayesian statistics. For applied statistics, in this vein, the availability of a 'prior distribution', as proved by Savage's approach, is essential.

3. EXPECTED UTILITY WHEN APPLIED TO DECISIONS UNDER RISKS; THE VON NEUMANN–MORGENSTERN APPROACH

Special and extreme cases of decisions under uncertainty are decisions in 'risky' situations. In decisions under uncertainty, as exposited in the previous section, the decision-maker who follows the dictum of expected utility has to assign utilities to the consequences and probabilities to the states. He can do it by mimicking the proof of Savage's theorem, or more directly by organizing his information, as the case may be.

Decision-making under risk considers the special case where the formulation of the problem for the decision-maker includes probabilities for the events, so that he only has to derive the utilities of consequences. As an example, consider a gambler in a casino who assumes that the roulette is really unbiased, so that each number has probability $1/37$ (or $1/38$). Another example is the St Petersburg paradox, described in subsection 1.2.

Within the framework of expected utility theory, for the evaluation of an act, only its probability distribution over the consequences has to be taken into account. Thus, for decision-making under risk, with probabilities known in advance, one may just as well describe acts as probability distributions over consequences instead of as functions from the states to the consequences.

3.1 Let us denote by L the set of probability distributions over C with finite support. We refer to them as lotteries. Von Neumann and Morgenstern (1947, Appendix) suggested conditions on a preference relation $\gtrsim$ between lotteries, necessary and sufficient for the existence of a real-valued utility function U on C, such that for any two lotteries P and Q in L:

$$(3.2) \qquad P \geqslant Q \qquad \text{iff} \quad \sum_{c \in C} P(c)U(c) \geqslant \sum_{c \in C} Q(c)U(c).$$

It is easy to see that the utility function, U, is unique up to positive linear transformations. Before we present a version of von Neumann–Morgenstern's theorem, recall that for any $0 \leqslant \alpha \leqslant 1$, and for any two lotteries P and W, $R := \alpha P + (1 - \alpha)Q$ is again a lottery, assigning probability $R(c) = \alpha P(c) + (1 - \alpha)Q(c)$ to any c in C. Also note that the assumption that all lotteries are given is sometimes as heroic as Savage's assumption that all functions from S to C are conceivable acts.

The first axiom of von Neumann–Morgenstern, NM1, says that the preference relation over the lotteries is complete and transitive. NM2, the continuity axiom, says that, if $P \succ Q \succ R$, then there are α, β in $]0, 1[$, such that $\alpha R + (1 - \alpha)P \succ Q \succ \beta P + (1 - \beta)R$. Here the strict preference relation $\succ$ is derived from $\gtrsim$ in the usual way: $P \succ Q$ if $P \gtrsim Q$ and not $Q \gtrsim P$.

The third axiom NM3 is the independence axiom. It says that for α in $[0, 1]$, P is preferred to Q iff $\alpha P + (1 - \alpha)R$ is preferred to $\alpha Q + (1 - \alpha)R$. This condition is the antecedent of Savage's sure-thing principle, and is the most important innovation of the above axioms.

3.3 Von Neumann and Morgenstern originally stated their theorem for more general sets than L. They did it for so-called mixture spaces, i.e. spaces endowed with some sort of convex combination operation. This has been done more precisely by Herstein and Milnor (1953).

Von Neumann and Morgenstern introduced their theory of decision-making under risk as a normative tool for playing zero-sum games in strategic form. There the 'player' (i.e. decision-maker) can actually construct any lottery he wishes over his pure-strategies (but not over his consequences).

The theorem of von Neumann and Morgenstern, stated above, is a major step in the proof of Savage's theorem.

Recently there has been much research on decision-making under risk for its own end. Some of this research is experimental; subjects are asked to express their preferences between lotteries. These experiments, or polls, reveal violations of most of the axioms. They lead to representations different from expected utility.

4. OTHER APPROACHES AND BIBLIOGRAPHICAL REMARKS

The first suggestion for expected utility theory in decision-making under uncertainty in the vein of Savage was Ramsey's (1931). His model was not completely formalized. The work of Savage was influenced by de Finetti's approach to probabilities, as in de Finetti (1931, 1937). The decision-theoretic framework to which Savage's expected utility model owes much is that of Wald (1951), who regards a statistician as a decision-maker.

A model which can be considered intermediate between those of Savage and von Neumann and Morgenstern is that considered by Anscombe and Aumann (1963). Formally it is a special case of a mixture set, but like Savage it introduces states of nature, and gives a simultaneous derivation of probabilities for the states, and of utilities for the consequences. A consequence in this model consists of a lottery over deterministic outcomes; this involves probabilities known in advance, as in the approach of von Neumann and Morgenstern. The Anscombe and Aumann theory, as well as most of the technical results up to 1970, are presented in detail in Fishburn (1970).

In the expected utility theory, described above, the desirability (utility) of consequences does not depend on acts or states of nature. This is a restriction in many applications. For example the desirability of family income may depend on whether the state of nature is 'head of family alive' or 'head of family deceased'. Karni (1985) summarized and developed the expected utility theory without the restrictive assumption of state-independent preferences over consequences.

Ellsberg (1961) argued against the expected utility approach of Savage by proposing an example, inconsistent with it. A way of resolving the inconsistency is to relax the additivity property of the involved probability measures. Schmeidler (1984) formulated expected utility theory with non-additive probabilities for the framework of Anscombe and Aumann (1963). Gilboa (1986) did the same for the original framework of Savage. Wakker (1986) obtained expected utility representation, including the non-additive case, for a finite number of states of nature and non-linear utility.

5. APPENDIX: MATHEMATICAL EXPECTATION

5.1 *Expectation with respect to finitely additive probability.* A non-empty collection Σ of subsets (called events) of a non-empty set S is said to be an algebra if it contains the complement of each set belonging to it, and it contains the union of any two sets belonging to it. A (finitely additive) probability P on Σ assigns to every event in Σ a number between 0 and 1 such that $P(S) = 1$ and for any two *disjoint* events A and B, $P(A \cup B) = P(A) + P(B)$.

A random variable X is a real-valued function on S such that, for any open or closed (bounded or unbounded) interval I, $\{s \in S \mid X(s) \in I\}$ (or $[X \in I]$ for short) is an event i.e., in Σ. Given such a random variable X, its (mathematical) expectation is:

$$(5.2) \qquad E(X) = \int_0^\infty P[X \geqslant \alpha] \, d\alpha - \int_{-\infty}^0 (1 - P[X \geqslant \alpha]) \, d\alpha,$$

where the integration above is Riemann-integration and it is assumed that the integral exist. The integrands in (5.2) are monotonic, so $E(X)$ exist if X is bounded. If the random variable X has finitely many values, say $x_1, \ldots, x_n$ then (5.2) reduces to

$$(5.3) \qquad E(X) = \sum_{i=1}^n P(X = x_i) x_i.$$

However, an equation like that above may not hold if the random variable obtains countably many different values. An example will be provided in subsection 5.7.

5.4 *σ-additive probability.* Kolmogorov (1933) imposed an additional continuity assumption on probability P on Σ: To simplify presentation he first assumed that Σ is a σ-algebra, i.e., an algebra such that for every sequence of events $(A_i)_{i=1}^\infty$ it contains its union $\cup_{i=1}^\infty A_i$. He then required that $P(\cup_{i=1}^\infty A_i) = \Sigma_{i=1}^\infty P(A_i)$ if the A_i's are pairwise disjoint.

This last property is referred to as σ-additivity of the probability P. In this way Kolmogorov transformed large parts of probability theory into (a special case of) measure theory. Thus an expectation of a random variable X is

$$(5.5) \qquad E(X) = \int_S X(s) \, dP(s)$$

where the right side is a Lebesgue integral (if it exists...), defined as a limit of integrals of random variables with countably many values. Let Y be such a random variable with values $(y_i)_{i=1}^\infty$, then

$$(5.6) \qquad E(Y) = \sum_{i=1}^\infty P(Y = y_i) y_i$$

if the right side is absolutely convergent.

5.7 *An example* will now be introduced of a finitely additive probability, i.e. a probability for which (5.3) holds but (5.6) does not hold. Let S be the set of rational numbers in the interval $[0, 1]$ and let Σ be the algebra of all subsets of S. (It is in fact a σ-algebra.) For $0 \leqslant \alpha \leqslant \beta \leqslant 1$ define $P(S \cap [\alpha, \beta]) = \beta - \alpha$ and extend P to all subsets of Σ. For each s in S, $P(s) = 0$. Since S is countable we can write $S = \{s_1, s_2, \ldots\}$ and $1 = P(S) > \Sigma_{i=1}^{\infty} P(s_i) = 0$. Defining $Y(s_i) = 1/i$ for all i, we get a contradiction to (5.6). The finitely additive probability P has also the property implied by Savage's P6 (see 2.4): If $P(A) > 0$ then there is an event $B \subset A$ such that $0 < P(B) < P(A)$.

5.8 *Distributions.* A non-decreasing right continuous function on the extended real line is called a distribution function if $F(-\infty) = 0$ and $F(\infty) = 1$. Given a random variable X, its distribution function F_X is defined by $F_X(\alpha) = P(X \leq \alpha)$ for all real α. Then

$$(5.9) \qquad E(X) = \int_0^{\infty} [1 - F_X(\alpha)] \, d\alpha - \int_{-\infty}^0 F(\alpha) \, d\alpha$$

which is the dual formula (5.2). If the distribution F_X is smooth we say that the random variable X has a density $f_X : R \to R$, which is the derivative of F_X. In this case

$$(5.10) \qquad E(X) = \int_{-\infty}^{\infty} \alpha f(\alpha) \, d\alpha.$$

5.11 *Non-additive probability.* A function $P : \Sigma \to [0, 1]$ is said to be a *non-additive* probability (or capacity) if $P(S) = 1$, $P(\phi) = 0$ and for $A \subset B$, $P(A) \leq P(B)$. Choquet (1953–4) suggested integrating a random variable with respect to non-additive probability for formula (5.2).

BIBLIOGRAPHY

Anscombe, F.J. and Aumann, R.J. 1963. A definition of subjective probability. *Annals of Mathematical Statistics* 34, 199–205.

Bernoulli, D. 1738. Specimen theoriae novae de mensura sortis. *Commentarii Academiae Scientiarum Imperialis Petropolitanae* 5, 175–92. Translated into English by L. Sommer (1954) as: Exposition of a new theory on the measurement of risk, *Econometrica* 12, 23–36; or in *Utility Theory: A Book of Readings*, ed. A.N. Page, New York: Wiley, 1986.

Choquet, G. 1953–4. Theory of capacities. *Annales de l'Institut Fourier* (Grenoble), 131–295.

de Finetti, B. 1931. Sul significato soggettivo della probabilita. *Fundamenta Mathematicae* 17, 298–329.

de Finetti, B. 1937. La prévision: ses lois logiques, ses sources subjectives. *Annales de l'Institut Henri Poincaré* 7, 1–68. Translated into English in *Studies in Subjective Probability*, ed. H.E. Kyburg and H.E. Smokler, 1964, New York: Wiley.

Ellsberg, D. 1961. Risk, ambiguity, and the Savage axioms. *Quarterly Journal of Economics* 75, 643–69.

Fishburn, P.C. 1970. *Utility Theory for Decision Making.* New York: Wiley.

Gilboa, I. 1986. Non-additive probability measures and their applications in expected utility theory. PhD Thesis submitted to Tel Aviv University.

Herstein, I.N. and Milnor, J. 1953. An axiomatic approach to measurable utility. *Econometrica* 21, 291–7.

Karni, E. 1985. *Decision-Making under Uncertainty: The Case of State-Dependent Preferences*. Cambridge, Mass.: Harvard University Press.

Kolmogorov, A.N. 1933. *Grundbegriffe der Wahrscheinlichkeitrechnung*. Berlin. Translated into English by Nathan Morrison (1950, 2nd edn, 1956), New York: Chelsea Publishing Company.

Loeve, M. 1963. *Probability Theory*. 3rd edn, Princeton: Van Nostrand.

Ramsey, F.P. 1931. Truth and probability. In *The Foundations of Mathematics and Other Logical Essays*, ed. R.B. Braithwaite, New York: Harcourt, Brace.

Savage, L.J. 1954. *The Foundations of Statistics*. New York: Wiley, 2nd edn, 1972.

Schmeidler, D. 1984. Subjective probability and expected utility without additivity. CARESS, University of Pennsylvania and IMA University of Minnesota, mimeo.

Wald, A. 1951. *Statistical Decision Functions*. New York: Wiley.

Wakker, P.P. 1986. Representations of choice situations. PhD thesis, University of Tilburg, Department of Economics.

von Neumann, J. and Morgenstern, O. 1947. *Theory of Games and Economic Behavior*. 2nd edn, Princeton: Princeton University Press.

Expected Utility Hypothesis

MARK J. MACHINA

The expected utility hypothesis of behaviour towards risk is essentially the hypothesis that the individual decision-maker possesses (or acts as if possessing) a 'von Neumann–Morgenstern utility function' $U(\cdot)$ or 'von Neumann–Morgenstern utility index' $\{U_i\}$ defined over some set of outcomes, and when faced with alternative risky prospects or 'lotteries' over these outcomes, will choose that prospect which maximizes the expected value of $U(\cdot)$ or $\{U_i\}$. Since the outcomes could represent alternative wealth levels, multidimensional commodity bundles, time streams of consumption, or even non-numerical consequences (e.g. a trip to Paris), this approach can be applied to a tremendous variety of situations, and most theoretical research in the economics of uncertainty, as well as virtually all applied work in the field (e.g. optimal trade, investment or search under uncertainty) is undertaken in the expected utility framework.

As a branch of modern consumer theory (e.g. Debreu, 1959, ch. 4), the expected utility model proceeds by specifying a set of objects of choice and assuming that the individual possesses a preference ordering over these objects which may be represented by a real-valued maximand or 'preference function' $V(\cdot)$, in the sense that one object is preferred to another if and only if it is assigned a higher value by this preference function. However, the expected utility model differs from the theory of choice over non-stochastic commodity bundles in two important respects. The first is that since it is a theory of choice under uncertainty, the objects of choice are not deterministic outcomes but rather probability distributions over these outcomes. The second difference is that, unlike in the non-stochastic case, the expected utility model imposes a very specific restriction on the functional form of the preference function $V(\cdot)$.

The formal representation of the objects of choice, and hence of the expected utility preference function, depends upon the structure of the set of possible outcomes. When there are a finite number of outcomes $\{x_1, \ldots, x_n\}$, we can represent any probability distribution over this set by its vector of probabilities $P = (p_1, \ldots, p_n)$ (where $p_i = \text{prob}(\tilde{x} = x_i)$), and the preference function takes the

79

form

$$V(P) = V(p_1, \ldots, p_n) \equiv \Sigma U_i p_i.$$

When the outcome set consists of the real line or some subset of it, probability distributions are represented by their cumulative distribution functions $F'(\cdot)$ (where $F(x) = \text{prob}(\tilde{x} \leqslant x)$), and the expected utility preference function takes the form $V(F) \equiv \int U(x)\,dF(x)$. (When $F(\cdot)$ possesses a density function $f(\cdot) \equiv F'(\cdot)$ this integral can be equivalently written as $\int U(x)f(x)\,dx$.) When the outcomes are multivariate commodity bundles of the form $(z_1, \ldots, z_n)$, $V(\cdot)$ takes the form $\int \ldots \int U(z_1, \ldots, z_n)\,dF(z_1, \ldots, z_n)$ over multivariate cumulative distribution functions $F(\cdot, \ldots, \cdot)$. The expected utility model derives its name from the fact that in each case, the preference function $V(\cdot)$ consists of the mathematical expectation of the von Neumann–Morgenstern utility function $U(\cdot)$, $U(\cdot, \ldots, \cdot)$, or utility index $\{U_i\}$ with respect to the probability distribution $F(\cdot)$, $F(\cdot, \ldots, \cdot)$, or P.

Mathematically, the hypothesis that the preference function $V(\cdot)$ takes the form of a statistical expectation is equivalent to the condition that it be 'linear in the probabilities'; that is, either a weighted sum of the components of P (i.e. $\Sigma U_i p_i$) or else a weighted integral of the functions $F(\cdot)$ or $f(\cdot)[\int U(x)\,dF(x)$ or $\int U(x)f(x)\,dx]$. Although this still allows for a wide variety of attitudes towards risk, depending upon the shape of the von Neumann–Morgenstern utility function $U(\cdot)$ or index $\{U_i\}$, the restriction that $V(\cdot)$ be linear in the probabilities is the primary empirical feature of the expected utility model and provides the basis for many of its observable implications and predictions.

It is important to distinguish between the preference function $V(\cdot)$ and the von Neumann–Morgenstern utility function $U(\cdot)$ (or index $\{U_i\}$) of an expected utility maximizer, in particular with regard to the prevalent though mistaken belief that expected utility preferences are somehow 'cardinal' in a sense which is not exhibited by preferences over non-stochastic commodity bundles. As with any real-valued representation of a preference ordering, an expected utility preference function $V(\cdot)$ is 'ordinal' in that it may be subject to any increasing transformation without affecting the validity of the representation; thus, for example, if $V(F) \equiv \int U(x)\,dF(x)$ represents the preferences of some expected utility maximizer, so will the (nonlinear) preference function $Y(F) \equiv [\int U(x)\,dF(x)]^3$. On the other hand, the von Neumann–Morgenstern utility functions which generate these preference functions are 'cardinal' in the sense that a function $U^*(\cdot)$ will generate an ordinally equivalent linear preference function $V^*(F) \equiv \int U^*(x)\,dF(x)$ if and only if it satisfies the cardinal relationship $U^*(x) \equiv a \cdot U(x) + b$ for some $a > 0$ (in which case $V^*(\cdot) = a \cdot V(\cdot) + b$). However, such situations also occur in the theory of preferences over non-stochastic commodity bundles: the Cobb–Douglas preference function $\alpha \cdot \ln(x) + \beta \cdot \ln(y) + \gamma \cdot \text{lin}(z)$ (written here in its additive form) can be subject to any increasing transformation and is clearly ordinal, even though a vector of parameters $(\alpha^*, \beta^*, \gamma^*)$ will generate an ordinally equivalent additive form $\alpha^* \cdot \ln(x) + \beta^* \cdot \ln(y) + \gamma^* \cdot \ln(z)$ if and only if it satisfies the cardinal relationship $(\alpha^*, \beta^*, \gamma^*) = \lambda \cdot (\alpha, \beta, \gamma)$ for some $\lambda > 0$.

In the case of a simple outcome set of the form $\{x_1, x_2, x_3\}$, it is possible to illustrate the 'linearity in the probabilities' property of an expected utility maximizer's preferences over lotteries. Since every probability distribution (p_1, p_2, p_3) over this set must satisfy the condition $\Sigma p_i = 1$, we may represent each such distribution by a point in the unit triangle in the (p_1, p_3) plane, with p_2 given by $p_2 = 1 - p_1 - p_3$ (Figures 1 and 2). Since they represent the loci of solutions to the equations

$$U_1 p_1 + U_2 p_2 + U_3 p_3 = U_2 - [U_2 - U_1] \cdot p_1 + [U_3 - U_2] \cdot p_3$$

$$= \text{constant}$$

for the fixed utility indices $\{U_1, U_2, U_3\}$, the indifference curves of an expected utility maximizer consist of parallel straight lines in the triangle of slope $[U_2 - U_1]/[U_3 - U_2]$, as illustrated by the solid lines in Figure 1. An example of indifference curves which do *not* satisfy the expected utility hypothesis (i.e. are not linear in the probabilities) is given by the solid curves in Figure 2.

When the outcomes $\{x_1, x_1, x_3\}$ represent different levels of wealth with $x_1 < x_2 < x_3$, this diagram can be used to illustrate other possible aspects of an expected utility maximizer's attitudes toward risk. On the general principle that more wealth is better, it is typically postulated that any change in a distribution (p_1, p_2, p_3) which increases p_3 at the expense of p_2, increases p_2 at the expense of p_1, or both, will be preferred by the individual: this property is known as 'first-order stochastic dominance preference'. Since such shifts of probability mass are represented by north, west or north-west movements in the diagram, first-order

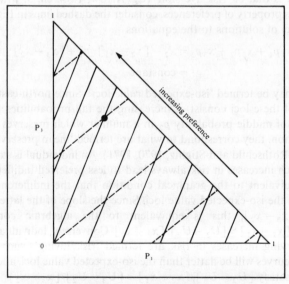

Figure 1 Expected utility indifference curves

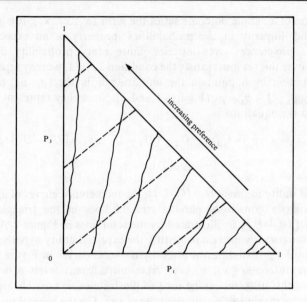

Figure 2 Non-expected utility indifference curves

stochastic dominance preference is equivalent to the condition that indifference curves are upward sloping, with more preferred indifference curves lying to the north-west. Algebraically, this is equivalent to the condition $U_1 < U_2 < U_3$.

Another widely, though not universally hypothesized aspect of attitudes towards risk is that of 'risk aversion' (e.g. Arrow, 1974, ch. 3; Pratt, 1964). To illustrate this property of preferences, consider the dashed lines in Figure 1, which represent loci of solutions to the equations

$$x_1 p_1 + x_2 p_2 + x_3 p_3 = x_2 - [x_2 - x_1] \cdot p_1 + [x_3 - x_2] \cdot p_3$$

$$= \text{constant}$$

and hence may be termed 'iso-expected *value* loci'. Since north-east movements along any of these loci consist of increasing the tail probabilities p_1 and p_3 at the expense of middle probability p_2 in a manner which preserves the mean of the distribution, they correspond to what are termed 'mean preserving increases in risk' (e.g. Rothschild and Stiglitz, 1970, 1971). An individual is said to be 'risk averse' if such increases in risk always lead to less preferred indifference curves, which is equivalent to the graphical condition that the indifference curves be steeper than the iso-expected value loci. Since the slope of the latter is given by $[x_2 - x_1]/[x_3 - x_2]$, this is equivalent to the algebraic condition that $[U_2 - U_1]/[x_2 - x_1] > [U_3 - U_2]/[x_3 - x_2]$. Conversely, individuals who *prefer* mean preserving increases in risk are termed 'risk loving': such individuals' indifference curves will be flatter than the iso-expected value loci, and their utility indices will satisfy $[U_2 - U_1]/[x_2 - x_1] < [U_3 - U_2]/[x_3 - x_2]$.

Note finally that the indifference map in Figure 1 indicates that the lottery P^*

is indifferent to the origin, which represents the degenerate lottery yielding x_2 with certainty. In such a case the amount x_2 is said to be the 'certainty equivalent' of the lottery P^*. The fact that the origin lies on a lower iso-expected value locus than P^* reflects a general property of risk averse preferences, namely that the certainty equivalent of any lottery will always be less than its mean. (For risk lovers, the opposite is always the case.)

When the outcomes are elements of the real line, it is possible to represent the above (as well as other) aspects of preferences in terms of the shape of the von Neumann–Morgenstern utility function $U(\cdot)$, as seen in Figures 3 and 4. In each figure, consider the lottery which assigns the probabilities $2/3 : 1/3$ to the outcome levels x' and x'', respectively. The expected value of this lottery (i.e. the value $\bar{x} = 2/3 \cdot x' + 1/3 \cdot x''$) is seen to lie between these two values, two-thirds of the way towards x'. The expected *utility* of this lottery – i.e. the value $\bar{u} = 2/3 \cdot U(x') + 1/3 \cdot U(x'')$ – is similarly seen to lie between $U(x')$ and $U(x'')$ on the vertical axis, two-thirds of the way towards $U(x')$. The point $(\bar{x}, \bar{u})$ will accordingly lie on the line segment connecting the points $(x', U(x'))$ and $(x'', U(x''))$, two-thirds of the way towards the former. In each figure, the certainty equivalent of this lottery is given by that sure outcome c which also yields a utility level of $\bar{u}$.

It is clear from our definition of first-order stochastic dominance preference above that this property of preferences can be extended to the case of density functions $f(\cdot)$ or cumulative distribution functions $F(\cdot)$ over the real line (e.g. Quirk and Saposnik, 1962), and that it is equivalent to the condition that $U(x)$ be an increasing function of x, as in Figures 3 and 4. It is also possible to generalize

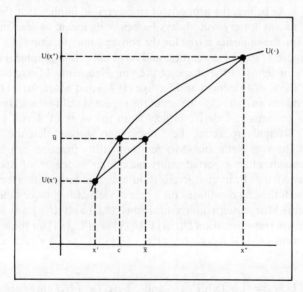

Figure 3　Von Neumann–Morgenstern utility function of a risk averse individual

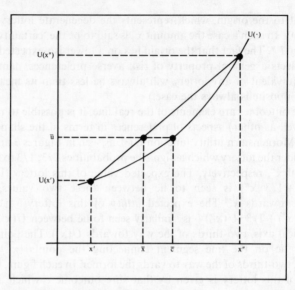

Figure 4 Von Neumann–Morgenstern utility function of a risk loving individual

the notion of a mean preserving increase in risk to density functions or cumulative distribution functions (e.g. Rothschild and Stiglitz, 1970, 1971), and our earlier algebraic condition for risk aversion generalizes to the condition that $U''(x) < 0$ for all x, i.e. that the von Neumann–Morgenstern utility function $U(\cdot)$ be concave, as in Figure 3. As before, the property of risk aversion implies that the certainty equivalent c of any lottery will always lie below its mean, as seen in Figure 3. and once again, the opposite is true for the convex utility function of a risk lover, as seen in Figure 4. Two of the earliest and most important graphical analyses of risk attitudes in terms of the shape of the von Neumann–Morgenstern utility function are those of Friedman and Savage (1948) and Markowitz (1952).

The tremendous analytic capabilities of the expected utility model for the study of behaviour towards risk derive largely from the work of Arrow (1974) and Pratt (1964). Roughly speaking, these researchers showed that the 'degree' of concavity of the von Neumann–Morgenstern utility function can be used to provide a measure of an expected utility maximizer's 'degree' of risk aversion. Formally, the Arrow–Pratt characterization of comparative risk aversion is the result that the following conditions on a pair of (increasing, twice differentiable) von Neumann–Morgenstern utility functions $U_a(\cdot)$ and $U_b(\cdot)$ are equivalent: $U_a(\cdot)$ is a concave transformation $U_b(\cdot)$ (i.e. $U_a(x) \equiv \rho[U_b(x)]$ for some increasing concave function $\rho(\cdot)$), $-U_a''(x)/U_a'(x) \geqslant -U_b''(x)/U_b'(x)$, for each x, and if c_a and c_b solve

$$U_a(c_a) = \int U_a(x)dF(x) \quad \text{and} \quad U_b(c_b) = \int U_b(x)dF(x)$$

for some distribution $F(\cdot)$, then $c_a \leqslant c_b$, and if $U_a(\cdot)$ and $U_b(\cdot)$ are both concave, these conditions are in turn equivalent to: if $r > 0$, $E[\tilde{z}] > r$, and α_a and α_b maximize

$$\int U_a[(I - \alpha)r + \alpha z]\mathrm{d}F(z) \quad \text{and} \quad \int U_b[(I - \alpha)r + \alpha z]\mathrm{d}F(z)$$

respectively, then $\alpha_a \leqslant \alpha_b$.

The first two of these conditions provide equivalent formulations of the notion that $U_a(\cdot)$ is a more concave function than $U_b(\cdot)$. In particular, the curvature measure $R(x) \equiv -U''(x)/U'(x)$ is known as the 'Arrow–Pratt index of (absolute) risk aversion', and plays a key role in the analytics of the expected utility model. The third condition states that the more risk averse utility function $U_a(\cdot)$ will never assign a higher certainty equivalent to any lottery $F(\cdot)$ than will $U_b(\cdot)$. The final condition pertains to the individuals' respective demands for risky assets. Specifically, assume that each of them must allocate \$$I$ between two assets, one yielding a riskless (gross) return of r per dollar, and the other yielding a risky return $\tilde{z}$ with a higher expected value. This condition thus says that the less risk averse utility function $U_b(\cdot)$ will generate at least as great a demand for the risky asset than the more risk averse utility function $U_a(\cdot)$. It is important to note that it is the *equivalence* of the above certainty equivalent and asset demand conditions which makes the Arrow–Pratt characterization such an important result in expected utility theory. (See Ross, 1981, however, for an alternative and stronger characterization of comparative risk aversion.)

Although the applications of the expected utility model extend to virtually all branches of economic theory (e.g. Hey, 1979), much of the flavour of these analyses can be gleaned from Arrow's (1974, ch. 3) analysis of the portfolio problem of the previous paragraph: rewriting $(Ir - \alpha)r + \alpha z$ as $Ir + \alpha \cdot (z - r)$, the first-order condition for this problem can be expressed as:

$$\int z \cdot U'[Ir + \alpha \cdot (z - r)]\mathrm{d}F(z) - r \cdot \int U'[Ir + \alpha \cdot (z - r)]\mathrm{d}F(z) = 0,$$

that is, the marginal *expected* utility of the last dollar allocated to each asset is the same. The second-order condition can be written as:

$$\int (z - r)^2 \cdot U''[Ir + \alpha \cdot (z - r)]\mathrm{d}F(z) < 0$$

and is ensured by the property of risk aversion [i.e. $U''(\cdot) < 0$].

As usual, we may differentiate the first-order condition to obtain the effect of a change in some parameter, say initial wealth I, on the optimal level of investment in the risky asset (i.e. on the optimal value of α). Differentiating the first-order condition (including α) with respect to I, solving for $\mathrm{d}\alpha/\mathrm{d}I$, and invoking the second-order condition and the positivity of r yields that this effect possesses the same sign as:

$$\int (z-r)\cdot U''[Ir + \alpha\cdot(z-r)]\,dF(z).$$

Making the substitution $U''(\cdot) \equiv -R(\cdot)\cdot U'(\cdot)$ and subtracting $R(Ir)$ times the first-order condition yields that this term is equal to:

$$-\int (z-r)\cdot\{R[Ir + \alpha\cdot(z-r)] - R(I)\}U'[Ir + \alpha\cdot(z-r)]\,dF(z).$$

On the assumption that α is positive and $R(\cdot)$ is monotonic, the expression $(z-r)\cdot[R(Ir + \alpha\cdot(z-r)) - R(Ir)]$ will possess the same sign as $R'(\cdot)$. This implies that the derivative $d\alpha/dI$ will always be positive (negative) whenever the Arrow–Pratt index $R(x)$ is a decreasing (increasing) function of the individual's wealth level x. In other words, an increase in initial wealth will always increase (decrease) the demand for the risky asset if and only if $U(\cdot)$ exhibits decreasing (increasing) absolute risk aversion in wealth. Further examples of the analytics of risk and risk aversion in the expected utility model may be found in the above references as well as the surveys of Hirshleifer and Riley (1979), Lippman and McCall (1981) and Machina (1983b)

Finally, in addition to the case of preferences over probability distributions, it is also possible to refer to expected utility preferences over alternative 'state-payoff bundles' (e.g. Hirshleifer, 1965, 1966). This approach postulates a (typically finite) set of 'states of nature' (i.e. a mutually exclusive and exhaustive partition of the set of observable occurrences) and the objects of choice consist of state-payoff bundles of the form $(x_1,\dots,x_n)$, where x_i denotes the outcome the individual will receive should state i occur. An expected utility maximizer whose subjective probabilities of the n states are given by the values $(\bar{p}_1,\dots,\bar{p}_n)$ will rank such bundles according to the preference function $V(x_1,\dots,x_n) \equiv \Sigma U(x_i)\bar{p}_i$, or in the event that the utility of wealth function $U_i(\cdot)$ itself depends upon the state of nature, according to the 'state-dependent' preference function $V(x_1,\dots,x_n) \equiv \Sigma U_i(x_i)\bar{p}_i$ (e.g. Karni, 1985). One of the advantages of the general 'state-preference' approach is that it does not require that we be able to observe the individual's probabilistic beliefs, or that different individuals share the same probabilistic beliefs.

AXIOMATIC DEVELOPMENT. Although there exist dozens of formal axiomatizations of the expected utility model in its different contexts, most proceed by specifying an outcome space and postulating that the individual's preferences over probability distributions on this outcome space satisfy the following four axioms: completeness, transitivity, continuity and the independence axiom. Although it is beyond the scope of this essay to provide a rigorous derivation of the expected utility model in its most general setting, it is possible to illustrate the meaning of the axioms and sketch a proof of the expected utility representation theorem in the simple case of a finite outcome set of the form $\{x_1,\dots,x_n\}$.

Recall that in such a case the objects of choice consist of all probability distributions $P = (p_1, \ldots, p_n)$ over $\{x_1, \ldots, x_n\}$, so that the following axioms refer to the individuals' weak preference relation $\succsim$ over this set, where $P^* \succsim P$ is read 'P^* is weakly preferred (i.e. preferred or indifferent) to P' (the associated strict preference relation $\succ$ and indifference relation $\sim$ are defined in the usual manner):

Completeness: For any two distributions P and P^* either $P^* \succsim P$, $P \succsim P^*$, or both,

Transitivity: If $P^{**} \succsim P^*$ and $P^* \succsim P$, then $P^{**} \succsim P$,

Mixture Continuity: If $P^{**} \succsim P^* \succsim P$, then there exists some $\lambda \in [0, 1]$ such that $P^* \sim \lambda P^{**} + (1 - \lambda)P$, and

Independence: For any two distributions P and P^*, $P^* \succsim P$ if and only if $\lambda P^* + (1 - \lambda)P^{**} \succsim \lambda P + (1 - \lambda)P^{**}$ for all $\lambda \in (0, 1]$ and all P^{**}, where $\lambda P + (1 - \lambda)P^*$ denotes the 'probability mixture' of P and P^*, i.e., the lottery with probabilities

$$(\lambda p_1) + (1 - \lambda)p_1^*, \ldots, \lambda p_n + (1 - \lambda)p_n^*).$$

The notion of a probability mixture is closely related (though not identical) to that of a 'compound lottery', in the sense that the probability mixture $\lambda P + (1 - \lambda)P^*$ yields the same probabilities of ultimately obtaining the outcomes $\{x_1, \ldots, x_n\}$ as would a compound lottery yielding a $\lambda:(1 - \lambda)$ chance of obtaining the respective lotteries P or P^*.

The completeness and transitivity axioms are completely analogous to their counterparts in the standard theory of the consumer (in particular, transitivity of $\succsim$ can be shown to imply transitivity of both $\succ$ and $\sim$). Mixture continuity states that if the lottery P^{**} is weakly preferred to P^*, and P^* is weakly preferred to P, then there will exist some probability mixture of the most and least preferred lotteries which is indifferent to the intermediate one.

As in standard consumer theory, completeness, transitivity and continuity serve essentially to establish the existence of a real-valued preference function $V(p_1, \ldots, p_n)$, which represents the relation $\succsim$, in the sense that $P^* \succsim P$ if and only if $V(p_1^*, \ldots, p_n^*) \geq V(p_1, \ldots, p_n)$. It is the independence axiom which, besides forming the basis of its widespread normative appeal, gives the theory its primary empirical content by implying that the preference function must take the linear form $V(p_1, \ldots, p_n) \equiv \Sigma U_i p_i$. To see the meaning of this axiom, assume that one is always indifferent between a compound lottery and its probabilistically equivalent single-stage lottery, and that P^* happens to be weakly preferred to P. In that case, the choice between the mixtures $\lambda P^* + (1 - \lambda)P^{**}$ and $\lambda P^* + (1 - \lambda)P^{**}$ is equivalent to being presented with a coin that has a $(1 - \lambda)$ chance of landing tails (in which case the prize will be P^{**}) and being asked *before the flip* whether one would rather win P or P^* in the event of a head. The normative argument for the independence axiom is that either the coin will land tails, in which case the choice would not have mattered, or it will land heads, in which case one is 'in effect' back to a choice between P and P^* and one 'ought' to have the same preferences as before. Note finally that the above statement of the axiom in terms of the weak preference relation $\succsim$ also implies its counterparts in terms of strict preference and indifference.

In the following sketch of the expected utility representation theorem, expressions such as '$x_i \succsim x_j$' should be read as saying that the individual weakly prefers the degenerate lottery yielding x_i with certainty to that yielding x_j with certainty, and '$\lambda x_i + (1 - \lambda)x_j$' will be used to denote the $\lambda:(1 - \lambda)$ probability mixture between these two degenerate lotteries, and so on.

The first step in the argument is to define the von Neumann–Morgenstern utility index $\{U_i\}$ and the expected utility preference function $V(\cdot)$. Without loss of generality, we may reorder the outcomes so that $x_n \succsim x_{n-1} \succsim \cdots \succsim x_2 \succsim x_1$. Since $x_n \succsim x_i \succsim x_1$ for each outcome x_i, we have by mixture continuity that there will exist scalars $\{U_i\} \subset [0, 1]$ such that $x_i \sim U_i x_n + (1 - U_i)x_i$ for each i (note that we can define $U_1 = 0$ and $U_n = 1$). Given this, define $V(P)$ to equal $\Sigma U_i p_i$ for all P.

The second step is to show that each lottery $P = (p_1, \ldots, p_n)$ is indifferent to the mixture $\lambda x_n + (1 - \lambda)x_1$ where $\lambda = \Sigma U_i p_i$. Since $(p_1, \ldots, p_n)$ can be written as the n-fold probability mixture $p_1 \cdot x_1 + p_2 \cdot x_2 + \cdots + p_n \cdot x_n$ and each outcome x_i is indifferent to the mixture $U_i x_n + (1 - U_i)x_i$, an n-fold application of the independence axiom yields that $(p_1, \ldots, p_n)$ is indifferent to the mixture

$$p_1 \cdot [U_1 x_n + (1 - U_1)x_1] + p_2 \cdot [U_2 x_n + (1 - U_2)x_1] + \cdots$$
$$+ p_n \cdot [U_n x_n + (1 - U_n)x_1],$$

which is equal to $(\Sigma U_i p_i) \cdot x_n + (1 - \Sigma U_i p_i) \cdot x_1$.

The third step is to demonstrate that the mixture $\lambda x_n + (1 - \lambda)x_1$ is weakly preferred to the mixture $\gamma x_n + (1 - \gamma)x_1$ if and only if $\lambda \geqslant \gamma$. This follows immediately from the independence axiom and the fact that $\lambda \geqslant \gamma$ implies that these two lotteries may be expressed as the respective mixtures

$$(\lambda - \gamma) \cdot x_n + (1 - \lambda + \gamma) \cdot Q$$

and

$$(\lambda - \gamma) \cdot x_1 + (1 - \lambda + \gamma) \cdot Q,$$

where Q is defined as the mixture

$$[\gamma/(1 - \lambda + \gamma)] \cdot x_n + [(1 - \lambda)/(1 - \lambda + \gamma)] \cdot x_1.$$

The completion of the proof is now simple. For any two distributions P^* and P, we have by transitivity and the second step that $P^* \succsim P$ if and only if

$$(\Sigma U_i p_i^*) \cdot x_n + (1 - \Sigma U_i p_i^*) \cdot x_1 \succsim (\Sigma U_i p_i) \cdot x_n + (1 - \Sigma U_i p_i) \cdot x_1,$$

which by the third step is equivalent to the condition that $\Sigma U_i p_i^* \geqslant \Sigma U_i p_i$, or in other words, that $V(P^*) \geqslant V(P)$.

As mentioned, the expected utility model has been axiomatized many times and in many contexts. The most comprehensive account of the axiomatics of the model is undoubtedly Fishburn (1982).

HISTORY. The hypothesis that individuals might maximize the expectation of 'utility' rather than of monetary value was first proposed independently by the mathematicians Gabriel Cramer and Daniel Bernoulli, in each case as the solution to a problem posed by Daniel's cousin Nicholas Bernoulli (see Bernoulli, 1738). This problem, which has since come to be known as the 'St Petersburg Paradox', considers the gamble which offers a $1/2$ chance of $1.00, a $1/4$ chance of $2.00, a $1/8$ chance of $4.00, and so on. Although the expected value of this prospect is

$$(1/2)\cdot\$1.00 + (1/4)\cdot(\$2.00) + (1/8)\cdot(\$4.00) + \cdots$$
$$= \$0.50 + \$0.50 + \$0.50 + \cdots = \$\infty,$$

common sense suggests that no one would be willing to forgo a very substantial certain payment in order to play it. Cramer and Bernoulli proposed that instead of looking at expected value, individuals might evaluate this and other lotteries by their 'expected utility', with utility given by a function such as the natural logarithm or the square root of wealth, in which case the certainty equivalent of the St Petersburg gamble becomes a moderate (and plausible) amount.

Two hundred years later, the St Petersburg Paradox was generalized by Karl Menger (1934) who noted that whenever the utility of wealth function was unbounded (as with the natural logarithm or square root functions), it would be possible to construct similar examples with infinite expected utility and hence infinite certainty equivalents (replace the payoffs $1.00, $2.00, $4.00,... in the above example by $x_1, x_2, x_3,...$ where $U(x_i) = 2^i$ for each i). In light of this, von Neumann–Morgenstern utility functions are typically (though not universally) postulated to be bounded functions of wealth.

The earliest formal axiomatic treatment of the expected utility hypothesis was developed by Frank Ramsey (1926) as part of his theory of subjective probability or individuals' 'degrees of belief' in the truth of various alternative propositions. Starting from the premise that there exists an 'ethically neutral' proposition whose degree of belief is $1/2$ and whose validity or invalidity is of no independent value, Ramsey proposed a set of axioms on how the individual would be willing to stake prizes on its truth or falsity in a manner which allowed for the derivation of the 'utilities' of these prizes. He then used these utility values and betting preferences to determine the individual's degrees of belief in other propositions. Perhaps because it was intended as a contribution to the philosophy of belief rather than the theory of risk bearing. Ramsey's analysis did not have the impact upon the economics literature that it deserved.

The first axiomatization of the expected utility model to receive widespread attention was that of John von Neumann and Oskar Morgenstern, which was presented in connection with their formulation of the theory of games (von Neumann and Morgenstern, 1944). Although both these developments were recognized as breakthroughs, the mistaken belief that von Neumann and Morgenstern had somehow mathematically overthrown the Hicks–Allen 'ordinal revolution' led to some confusion until the difference between 'utility in the von Neumann–Morgenstern and ordinal (i.e. non-stochastic) senses was illuminated by writers such as Ellsberg (1954) and Baumol (1958).

Another factor which delayed the acceptance of the theory was the lack of recognition of the role played by the independence axiom, which did not explicitly appear in the von Neumann–Morgenstern formulation. In fact, the initial reaction of researchers such as Baumol (1951) and Samuelson (1950) was that there was no reason why preferences over probability distributions must *necessarily* be linear in the probabilities. However the independent discovery of the independence axiom by Marschak (1950), Samuelson (1952) and others, and Malinvaud's (1952) observation that it had been implicitly invoked by von Neumann and Morgenstern, led to an almost universal acceptance of the expected utility hypothesis as both a normative and positive theory of behaviour toward risk. Practically the only dissenting voice was that of Maurice Allais, whose famous paradox (see below) and other empirical and theoretical work (e.g. Allais, 1952) has provided the basis for the resurgence of interest in alternatives to expected utility in the late 1970s and 1980s. This period also saw the development of the elegant axiomatization of Herstein and Milnor (1953) as well as Savage's (1954) joint axiomatization of utility and subjective probability, which formed the basis of the state-preference approach described above.

While the 1950s essentially saw the completion of foundational work on the expected utility model, the 1960s and 1970s saw the flowering of its analytic capabilities and its application to fields such as portfolio selection (Merton, 1969), optimal savings (Levhari and Srinivasan, 1969), international trade (Batra, 1975), and even the measurement of inequality (Atkinson, 1970). This movement was spearheaded by the development of the Arrow–Pratt characterization of risk aversion (see above) and the characterization, by Rothschild–Stiglitz (1970, 1971) and others, of the notion of 'increasing risk'. This latter work in turn led to the development of a general theory of 'stochastic dominance' (e.g. Whitmore and Findlay, 1978), which further expanded the analytical powers of the model.

Although the expected utility model received a small amount of experimental testing by economists in the early 1950s (e.g. Mosteller and Nogee, 1951; Allais, 1952) and continued to be examined by psychologists, interest in the empirical validity of the model waned from the mid-1950s through the mid-1970s, no doubt due to both the normative appeal of the independence axiom and the model's analytical successes. However, the late 1970s and 1980s have witnessed a revival of interest in the testing of the expected utility model; a growing body of evidence that individuals' preferences *systematically* depart from linearity in the probabilities; and the development, analysis and application of alternative models of choice under risk (see below). It is fair to say that today the debate over the descriptive (and even normative) validity of the expected utility hypothesis is more extensive than it has been in 30 years, and the outcome of this debate will have important implications for the direction of research in the economic theory of individual behaviour towards risk.

EVIDENCE AND ALTERNATIVE HYPOTHESES. As mentioned above, the current body of experimental evidence suggests that individual preferences over lotteries are typically *not* linear in the probabilities, but rather depart systematically from this property. The earliest, and undoubtedly best-known, example of this is the so-called 'Allais paradox' (Allais, 1952), in which the individual is asked to rank each of the following pairs of prospects (where $1M = $1,000,000):

$$a_1: \{1.00 \text{ chance of } \$1M \quad \text{versus} \quad a_2: \begin{cases} 0.10 \text{ chance of } \$5M \\ 0.89 \text{ chance of } \$1M \\ 0.01 \text{ chance of } \$0, \end{cases}$$

and:

$$a_3: \begin{cases} 0.10 \text{ chance of } \$5M \\ 0.90 \text{ chance of } \$0 \end{cases} \quad \text{versus} \quad a_4: \begin{cases} 0.11 \text{ chance of } \$1M \\ 0.89 \text{ chance of } \$0. \end{cases}$$

Since each of these lotteries involves outcomes in the set $\{x_1, x_2, x_3\}$ = $\{\$0, \$1M, \$5M\}$, they may be plotted in the (p_1, p_3) triangle diagram, as illustrated in Figures 5 and 6. The fact that the four prospects form a parallelogram in this triangle makes this problem a useful test of linearity (i.e. the expected utility hypothesis), since it implies that an expected utility maximizer will prefer a_1 to a_2 if and only if he or she prefers a_4 to a_3 (algebraically, this is in turn equivalent to the inequality $(0.10 \cdot U(\$5M) - 0.11 \cdot U(\$1M) + 0.01 \cdot U\$(0) < 0)$.

However, experimenters such as Allais (1952), Morrison (1967), Moskowitz (1974), Raiffa (1968), Slovic and Tversky (1974) and others, have found that the modal if not majority choice was for a_1 in the first pair and a_3 in the second pair, as would be chosen by an individual whose indifference curves 'fanned out'

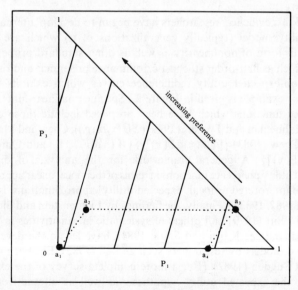

Figure 5   Allais Paradox with expected utility indifference curves

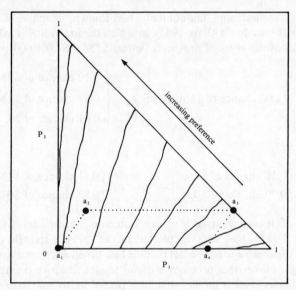

Figure 6 Allais Paradox with non-expected utility indifference curves that 'fan out'

as in Figure 6. Subsequent studies by Hagen (1979), Karmarkar (1974), MacCrimmon and Larsson (1979), McCord and de Neufville (1983) and others, using both similar and qualitatively different types of examples, have also revealed systematic departures from linearity in the direction of 'fanning out' (see Machina, 1983a, 1983b).

In light of this evidence, researchers have begun to develop alternatives to the expected utility model (typically generalizations of it) which are capable of exhibiting this form of nonlinearity as well as other standard properties of risk preferences such as first-order stochastic dominance preference and risk aversion. (A set of non-expected utility indifference curves which exhibits these three properties, for example is given in Figure 2.) Specific nonlinear functional forms for preference functions which have been proposed include those of Edwards (1955) and Kahneman and Tversky (1979) $(\Sigma U(x_i)\pi(p_i))$; Chew and MacCrimmon (1979) and Chew (1983) $\{[\int U(x)\mathrm{d}F(x)]/[\int W(x)\mathrm{d}F(x)]\}$; and Quiggin (1982) $\{\int U(x)\mathrm{d}G[F(x)]\}$. A general framework for the analysis of differentiable non-expected utility preference functions in terms of their local linear approximations, which can be interpreted as local 'expected utility' approximations, is developed in Machina (1982, 1983a). Finally, the findings by Lichtenstein and Slovic (1971), Grether and Plott (1979) and others of systematic intransitivities in preferences over lotteries (but see Karni and Safra, 1984), have led to the development of non-transitive models by researchers such as Bell (1982), Fishburn (1983), and Loomes and Sugden (1982). (For a more complete survey of the experimental evidence on the expected utility hypothesis as well as alternative models of behaviour towards risk, see Machina, 1983b.)

BIBLIOGRAPHY

Allais, M. 1952. Fondements d'une théorie positive des choix comportant un risque et critique des postulats et axiomes de l'école Américaine. *Colloques Internationaux du Centre National de la Recherche Scientifique* 40 (1953), 257–332. Trans. as: The foundations of a positive theory of choice involving risk and a criticism of the postulates and axioms of the American School, in Allais and Hagen (1979).

Allais, M. and Hagen, O. (eds) 1979. *Expected Utility Hypotheses and the Allais Paradox.* Dordrecht: D. Reidel.

Arrow, K. 1974. *Essays in the Theory of Risk-Bearing.* Amsterdam: North-Holland.

Atkinson, A. 1970. On the measurement of inequality. *Journal of Economic Theory* 2(3), September, 244–63.

Batra, R. 1975. *The Pure Theory of International Trade under Uncertainty.* London: Macmillan; New York: Halsted Press.

Baumol, W. 1951. The Neumann–Morgenstern utility index: an ordinalist view. *Journal of Political Economy* 59(1), February, 61–6.

Baumol, W. 1958. The cardinal utility which is ordinal. *Economic Journal* 68, December, 665–72.

Bell, D. 1982. Regret in decision making under uncertainty. *Operations Research* 30, September–October, 961–81.

Bernoulli, D. 1738. Specimen theoriae novae de mensura sortis. *Commentarii Academiae Scientiarum Imperialis Petropolitanae.* Trans. as: Exposition of a new theory on the measurement of risk, *Econometrica* 22, January 1954, 23–36.

Chew, S.H. 1983. A generalization of the quasilinear mean with applications to the measurement of income inequality and decision theory resolving the Allais paradox. *Econometrica* 51(4), July, 1065–92.

Chew, S. and MacCrimmon, K. 1979. Alpha–Nu choice theory: a generalization of expected utility theory. University of British Columbia Faculty of Commerce and Business Administration Working Paper No. 669, July.

Debreu, G. 1959. *Theory of Value: An Axiomatic Analysis of Economic Equilibrium.* New Haven: Yale University Press.

Edwards, W. 1955. The prediction of decisions among bets. *Journal of Experimental Psychology* 50(3), September, 201–14.

Ellsberg, D. 1954. Classical and current notions of 'measurable utility'. *Economic Journal* 64, September, 528–56.

Fishburn, P. 1982. *The Foundations of Expected Utility.* Dordrecht: D. Reidel.

Fishburn, P. 1983. Nontransitive measurable utility. *Journal of Mathematical Psychology* 26(1), August, 31–67.

Friedman, M. and Savage, L. 1948. The utility analysis of choices involving risk. *Journal of Political Economy* 56, August, 279–304. Reprinted in *Readings in Price Theory*, ed. G. Stigler and K. Boulding, London: George Allen & Unwin, 1953; Chicago: R.D. Irwin, 1952.

Grether, D. and Plott, C. 1979. Economic theory of choice and the preference reversal phenomenon. *American Economic Review* 69(4), September, 623–38.

Hagen, O. 1979. Towards a positive theory of preferences under risk. In Allais and Hagen (1979).

Herstein, I. and Milnor, J. 1953. An axiomatic approach to measurable utility. *Econometrica* 21, April, 291–7.

Hey, J. 1979. *Uncertainty in Microeconomics.* Oxford: Martin Robinson; New York: New York University Press.

Hirshleifer, J. 1965. Investment decision under uncertainty: choice theoretic approaches. *Quarterly Journal of Economics* 79, November, 509–36.

Hirshleifer, J. 1966. Investment decision under uncertainty: applications of the state-preference approach. *Quarterly Journal of Economics* 80, May, 252–77.

Hirshleifer, J. and Riley, J. 1979. The analytics of uncertainty and information – an expository survey. *Journal of Economic Literature* 17(4), December, 1375–421.

Kahneman, D. and Tversky, A. 1979. Prospect theory: an analysis of decision under risk. *Econometrica* 47(2), March, 263–91.

Karmarkar, U. 1974. The effect of probabilities on the subjective evaluation of lotteries. Massachusetts Institute of Technology Sloan School of Management Working Paper No. 698–74, February.

Karni, E. 1985. *Decision Making under Uncertainty: the Case of State-Dependent Preferences.* Cambridge, Mass.: Harvard University Press.

Karni, E. 1985. Increasing risk with state dependent preferences. *Journal of Economic Theory* 35(1), 172–7.

Karni, E. and Safra, Z. 1984. 'Preference reversal' and the theory of choice under risk. Johns Hopkins University Working Papers in Economics No. 141.

Levhari, D. and Srinivasan, T.N. 1969. Optimal savings under uncertainty. *Review of Economic Studies* 36–2, April, 153–64.

Lichtenstein, S. and Slovic, P. 1971. Reversals of preferences between bids and choices in gambling decisions. *Journal of Experimental Psychology* 89(1), July, 46–55.

Lippman, S. and McCall, J. 1981. The economics of uncertainty: selected topics and probabilistic methods. In *Handbook of Mathematical Economics*, ed. K. Arrow and M. Intriligator, Vol. 1, Amsterdam: North-Holland.

Loomes, G. and Sugden, R. 1982. Regret theory: an alternative theory of rational choice under uncertainty. *Economic Journal* 92 (368), December, 805–24.

McCord, M. and de Neufville, R. 1983. Empirical demonstration that expected utility analysis is not operational. In Stigum and Wenstøp (1983).

MacCrimmon, K. and Larsson, S. 1979. Utility theory: axioms versus 'paradoxes'. In Allais and Hagen (1979).

Machina, M. 1982. 'Expected utility' analysis without the independence axiom. *Econometrica* 50(2), March, 277–323.

Machina, M. 1983a. Generalized expected utility analysis and the nature of observed violations of the independence axiom. In Stigum and Wenstøp (1983).

Machina, M. 1983b. The economic theory of individual behavior toward risk: theory, evidence and new directions. Institute for Mathematical Studies in the Social Sciences Technical Report No. 433, Stanford University, October.

Malinvaud, E. 1952. Note on von Neumann–Morgenstern's strong independence axiom. *Econometrica* 20(4), October, 679.

Markowitz, H. 1952. The utility of wealth. *Journal of Political Economy* 60, April, 151–8.

Marschak, J. 1950. Rational behavior, uncertain prospects and measurable utility. *Econometrica* 18, April, 111–41 (Errata, July 1950).

Menger, K. 1934. Das Unsicherheitsmoment in der Wertlehre. *Zeitschrift für Nationalökonomie.* Trans. as: The role of uncertainty in economics, in *Essays in Mathematical Economics in Honor of Oskar Morgenstern*, ed. M. Shubik, Princeton: Princeton University Press, 1967.

Merton, R. 1969. Lifetime portfolio selection under uncertainty: the continuous time case. *Review of Economics and Statistics* 51(3), August, 247–57.

Morrison, D. 1967. On the consistency of preferences in Allais' paradox. *Behavioral Science* 12(5), September, 373–83.

Moskowitz, H. 1974. Effects of problem representation and feedback on rational behavior in Allais and Morlat-type problems. *Decision Sciences* 2.

Mosteller, F. and Nogee, P. 1951. An experimental measurement of utility. *Journal of Political Economy* 59, October, 371–404.

Pratt, J. 1964. Risk aversion in the small and in the large. *Econometrica* 32, January–April, 122–36.

Quiggin, J. 1982. A theory of anticipated utility. *Journal of Economic Behavior and Organization* 3(4), December, 323–43.

Quirk, J. and Saposnick, R. 1962. Admissibility and measurable utility functions. *Review of Economic Studies* 29, February, 140–46.

Raiffa, H. 1968. *Decision Analysis: Introductory Lectures on Choice under Uncertainty.* Reading, Mass.: Addison Wesley.

Ramsey, F. 1926. Truth and probability. In *The Foundations of Mathematics and Other Logical Essays*, ed. R. Braithwaite, New York: Harcourt, Brace and Co., 1931. Reprinted in *Foundations: Essays in Philosophy, Logic, Mathematics and Economics*, ed. D. Mellor, New Jersey: Humanities Press, 1978.

Ross, S. 1981. Some stronger measures of risk aversion in the small and in the large, with applications. *Econometrica* 49(3), May, 621–38.

Rothschild, M. and Stiglitz, J. 1970. Increasing risk I: a definition. *Journal of Economic Theory* 2(3), September, 225–43.

Rothschild, M. and Stiglitz, J. 1971. Increasing risk II: its economic consequences. *Journal of Economic Theory* 3(1), March, 66–84.

Safra, Z. 1985. Existence of equilibrium for Walrasian endowment games. *Journal of Economic Theory* 37(2), 366–78.

Samuelson, P. 1950. Probability and attempts to measure utility. *Economic Review* 1, July, 167–73. Reprinted in Stiglitz (1965).

Samuelson, P. 1952. Probability, utility, and the independence axiom. *Econometrica* 20, October, 670–78. Reprinted in Stiglitz (1965).

Savage, L. 1954. *The Foundations of Statistics.* New York: John Wiley & Sons. Enlarged and revised edn, New York: Dover, 1972.

Slovic, P. and Tversky, A. 1974. Who accepts Savage's Axiom? *Behavioral Science* 19(6), November, 368–73.

Stiglitz, J. (ed.) 1965. *Collected Scientific Papers of Paul A. Samuelson*, Vol. 1. Cambridge, Mass.: MIT Press.

Stigum, B. and Wenstøp, F. (eds) 1983. *Foundations of Utility and Risk Theory with Applications.* Dordrecht: D. Reidel.

von Neumann, J. and Morgenstern, O. 1944. *Theory of Games and Economic Behavior.* Princeton: Princeton University Press. 2nd edn, 1947; 3rd edn, 1953.

Whitmore, G. and Findlay, M. (eds) 1978. *Stochastic Dominance: An Approach to Decision Making Under Risk.* Lexington, Mass.: D.C. Heath.

Bruno de Finetti

GIANCARLO GANDOLFO

De Finetti was born in Innsbruck, Austria in 1906, and died in Rome in 1985. After a degree in mathematics at Milan University, he chose practical activities rather than an academic career, and worked at the Istituto Centrale di Statistica (1927–31) and then at the Assicurazioni Generali (1931–46). Only later did he turn to an academic career and win a chair in Financial Mathematics at Trieste University (1939); from 1954 to 1961 he held the chair in the same subject at the University of Rome and from 1961 to 1976 the chair of Calculus of Probabilities at the same university. He was a member of the Accademia Nazionale dei Lincei and Fellow of the International Institute of Mathematical Statistics.

De Finetti's fame rests on his contributions to probability and to decision theory, but he also worked in descriptive statistics, mathematics and economics.

Together with Ramsey and Savage, de Finetti is one of the founders of the subjectivist approach to probability theory. The first illustrations (in non-technical terms) of his conception are in (1930a) and (1931b). He considers probability as a purely subjective entity 'as it is conceived by all of us in everyday life'. The probability that a person attributes to the occurrence of an event is nothing more nor less than the measure of the person's degree of confidence (hope, fear, . . .) in this event actually taking place. This can be interpreted as the amount (say, 0.72) that the person deems it fair to pay (or receive) in order to receive (or pay) the amount 1 if the event in question occurs. The mathematical theory was presented in his 1935 lectures at the Institut Poincaré (1937); see also (1970) and (1972).

De Finetti also introduced the important concept of *exchangeability* in probability (1929, 1930b, 1937, 1938) and proved the theorem on exchangeable variables named after him. Exchangeability is a weaker concept than independence and has been receiving increasing attention in probability theory (in fact, the natural assumption for a Bayesian inference is not independence, but exchangeability). In his 1935 Poincaré lectures (1937) he also treated the relations between the subjectivist point of view and the concept of exchangeability, which in his view are at the basis of sound inductive reasoning and behaviour and, hence, of (statistical) decision theory (1959, 1961). It goes without saying that his position on the subject of statistical inference is fundamentally Bayesian.

In descriptive statistics he adhered to the functional concept according to which a statistic is an index selected on the basis of the single case (the aspects that one wants to stress, the aim of the statistical investigation, etc.); in (1931a) he stressed the importance of means which are associative.

Among his mathematical contributions the (1949) paper is especially interesting for economists. Here de Finetti investigates the conditions under which a concave function can be associated with a given 'convex stratification' (i.e. a one-parameter family of convex sets, one interior to the other as the parameter varies). The author also discusses the conditions for a quasi-concave function to be transformed into a concave one by means of an increasing function. This paper started the literature on the 'concavification' of quasi-concave functions. As the author pointed out, these investigations also bear on consumer theory – where the convex stratification is the indifference map and the associated function is the utility function.

De Finetti also wrote on economic problems, where he stressed the importance of rigorous reasoning and verification, and emphasized the idea that the scope of economics, freed from the tangle of individual and corporative interests, should always and only be that of realizing a collective optimum (in Pareto's sense) inspired by criteria of equity (1969). An important initiative of his for the diffusion and correct application of mathematical and econometric methods in economics was the annual CIME (Centro Internazionale Matematico Estivo) seminar that he organized from 1965 to 1975; this enabled young Italian economists to benefit from courses given by Frisch, Koopmans, Malinvaud, Morishima, Zellner, to mention only a few of the lecturers.

SELECTED WORKS

A full bibliography of de Finetti's works up to 1980 is contained in B. de Finetti, *Scritti (1926–1980)*, ed. L. Daboni et al., Padua: Cedam, 1981, with an autobiographical note.

1929. Funzione caratteristica di un fenomeno aleatorio. In *Atti del Congresso Internazionale dei Matematici* (1928), Bologna: Zanichelli, 179–90.

1930a. Fondamenti logici del ragionamento probabilistico. *Bollettino dell'Unione Matematica Italiana* 9, December, 258–61.

1930b. Funzione caratteristica di un fenomeno aleatorio. *Memorie della Reale Accademia dei Lincei*, Classe di scienze fisiche, matematiche e naturali, Vol. IV, fasc. 5.

1931a. Sul concetto di media. *Giornale dell'Istituto Italiano degli Attuari* 2, 369–96.

1931b. *Probabilismo. Saggio critico sulla teoria delle probabilità e sul valore della scienza.* Naples: Perrella; also in *Logos*, 1931, 163–219.

1937. La prévision: ses lois logiques, ses sources subjectives. *Annales de l'Institut Henri Poincaré*, vol. VII, fasc. I. Trans. as 'Foresight: its logical laws, its subjective sources', in *Studies in Subjective Probability*, ed. H.E. Kyburg Jr. and H.E. Smokler, New York: Wiley, 1964.

1938. Sur la condition de 'équivalence partielle'. (Conférence au Colloque consacré à la théorie des probabilités, University of Geneva, 1937.) In *Actualités Scientifiques et Industrielles*, no. 739, Paris: Herman.

1949. Sulle stratificazioni convesse. *Annali di matematica pura e applicata*, Series IV, Vol. XXX, 173–83.

1959. La probabilità e la statistica nei rapporti con l'induzione, secondo i diversi punti di vista. In *Atti corso CIME su Induzione e Statistica* (Varenna), Rome: Cremonese, 1–115.

1961. Dans quel sens la théorie de la décision est-elle et doit-elle être 'normative'. In *Colloques internatonaux du Centre National de la Recherche Scientifique*, Paris: CNRS, 159–69.

1969. *Un matematico e l'economia*. Milan: F. Angeli (anthology of previously published papers).

1970. *Teoria delle probabilità. Sintesi introduttiva con appendice critica*. Turin: Einaudi, 2 vols. Trans. as *Theory of Probability*, 2 vols, New York: Wiley, 1974–5.

1972. *Probability, Induction and Statistics*. New York: Wiley (anthology of writings).

Hermann Heinrich Gossen

JÜRG NIEHANS

Gossen was born in Düren (between Aachen and Cologne) on 7 September 1810; he died in Cologne on 13 February 1858. Little is known about his life, partly because the inconspicuous bachelor did not attract attention, partly because most of those who had known him were dead by the time he became famous, partly also because his literary remains, scant as they must have been, are lost. The principal biographical source is the essay by Walras (1885). The available facts are admirably surveyed by Georgescu-Roegen (1983), on whose masterly introduction to the English translation of Gossen's book the following life sketch is mostly based.

Gossen's father was a tax collector under Napoleon and subsequently the Prussian administration; later he managed his wife's estate near Godesberg. Hermann obtained a good high school education, showing ability in 'elementary mathematics', but his mathematical training never went beyond that level. Since his father insisted on a government career in the tradition of his forebears, his university studies in Bonn and Berlin concentrated on law and government.

In 1834, Gossen entered the civil service as a 'Referendar' (junior law clerk) in Cologne. While he seems to have been a well-mannered young man, the performance of his duties left much to be desired. He simply had no interest in a government career and loved the good things in life. There were complaints and reprimands, and the promotion to the rank of 'Regierungsassessor' came rather later than usual. Finally, in 1847, though his superiors seem to have shown considerable sympathy, he had no choice but to resign.

The transition to a new career was perhaps eased by his father's death, which spared him recriminations about his failure and provided him with the means for a new start. Gossen went to Berlin, where he seems to have sympathized with the liberal revolution, and then returned to Cologne as a partner in a new accident insurance firm. He soon withdrew from the firm, but continued to devise grandiose insurance projects.

Living with his two sisters, Gossen now devoted most of his energies to developing the unorthodox ideas he had expressed in his civil service examination papers into his *magnum opus*. The preface suggests that he hoped this would not only make him the Copernicus of the social universe but also open the door to an academic career. In 1853 an attack of typhoid fever undermined his health, and the disappointment about the fate of his book depressed him. Death came from pulmonary tuberculosis. He seems to have been an amiable, sincere and idealistic human being with broad interests, including music and painting. Brought up a Catholic, he developed into an enthusiastic hedonist. Dreaming of reforming the world, he lacked the force to conquer it.

The *Entwicklung der Gesetze des menschlichen Verkehrs* was published in 1854 at Gossen's expense by the publisher Vieweg in Brunswick. Very few copies were sold and the book remained unnoticed for years. Shortly before his death, Gossen withdrew it from circulation and the unsold copies were returned to him. After the author had become famous, Vieweg's successor, Prager, bought this stock from Gossen's nephew, a professor of mathematics by the name of Hermann Kortum, and put it on the market again with a new title page, as a 'second edition', in 1889. There is an Italian translation by Tullio Bagiotti and there is now, since 1983, a careful English translation by Rudolph C. Blitz, nicely divided into chapters. The manuscript of a French translation by Walras was apparently lost.

The first known references to Gossen's book were by Julius Kautz (1858/60), but they only show that their author did not understand the problems Gossen had solved. Slightly more understanding was shown by F.A. Lange, but again in no more than a footnote. Fortunately, Kautz's reference was seen by Robert Adamson, who was able to get hold of a copy and reported its content to Jevons. In the second edition of *The Theory of Political Economy* Jevons included a generous acknowledgement of Gossen's priority 'as regards the general principles and method of the theory of Economics', which became the ignition point of Gossen's posthumous fame.

Though Gossen's name became famous, his book remains largely unread to this day. Pantaleoni ([1889] 1898) was the only notable economist who based his own work on it. This has inspired many disparaging remarks about the 'immaturity' of economic science and the like. The simple fact is that the book, even for a German-speaking economic theorist, is very hard to read. It is true that the reasoning is precise and the material reasonably well organized, but there are no chapter headings, the style is involved, the copious algebra is inelegant, the numerical examples are tedious, and the sermonizing is often disconcerting. Gossen had brilliant thoughts, but he never learnt to communicate them effectively. Sombart's often-quoted description of him reflects sadly on the style of academic discourse in Imperial Germany, but if it is modified to 'idiosyncratic genius' it becomes a fitting epitome of Gossen's tragedy.

At the level of individual behaviour, Gossen's basic theoretical problem concerns optimization with limited resources (references are to the 1889 edition; they are followed by the corresponding references to the English translation, marked T). Resources are first visualized as time (p. 1f.; T ch. 1), thus foreshadowing an approach recently developed by Gary Becker. The given life-time, $\bar{E}$, has to be allocated to enjoyable activities $l \dots i \dots m$ in such a way that life-time enjoyment or, in modern terminology, utility, U, is maximized. In symbols,

$$\max U = \Sigma U_i(e_i), \qquad \text{s.t. } \Sigma e_i = \bar{E}.$$

For a given activity, marginal utility, u_i, is assumed to be a declining function of the time spent on it, e_i. In Gossen's words, 'The magnitude of a given pleasure decreases continuously if we continue to satisfy this pleasure without interruption until satiety is ultimately reached' (p. 4f.; T p. 6). This is the postulate Wilhelm Lexis (1895) christened 'Gossen's First Law'. *In itself*, it was neither new nor profound. W.F. Lloyd had expressed it twenty years earlier just as clearly, it had a long ancestry reaching back to Bentham, the French 'subjectivists', Daniel Bernoulli, and the scholastics, and it is essentially commonplace. To simplify, Gossen assumes the marginal utility curves to be linear, as drawn in Figure 1. It is important to note that Gossen's curves do *not* describe the decline in the marginal utility of a good as its quantity increases, but the decline in the utility from the marginal unit of resources as the quantity of resources is increased. While this facilitated the analysis in some respects, it became a crucial handicap in others.

Gossen realized that each of these marginal utility functions must be thought of as being derived by solving a suboptimization problem, inasmuch as time allocated to activity i must be spent in the most enjoyable way, probably with interruptions. However, his analysis of this difficult subproblem, though original and suggestive, remained incomplete and unsatisfactory, leaving much to do for future research on the allocation of time.

Gossen recognized at once that a necessary condition for the optimal allocation of resources is the equality of the marginal utilities in different activities. This is 'Gossen's Second Law', which he had printed in heavy type: 'The magnitude of each single pleasure at the moment when its enjoyment is broken off shall be the same for all pleasures' (p. 12; T p. 14). This theorem is Gossen's principal claim

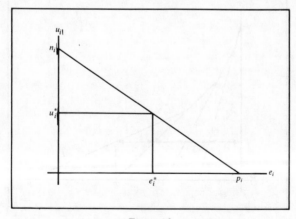

Figure 1

to fame. In it he had no forerunners. It was the key that opened the door to a fruitful analytical use of the First Law and thus initiated the 'marginal revolution' in the theory of value.

The resulting allocation of resources was summarized in a brilliantly constructed graph by the horizontal addition of the marginal-utility curves (Figure 2). The resulting solid line represents the marginal utility of resources, u, as a function of total resources. Its level at the point $E = \bar{E}, u^*$, is the marginal utility of resources in the optimal plan. The resources allocated to each activity, e_i^*, can simply be read off the horizontal distances between the individual marginal-utility curves at the level of u^*.

Gossen also succeeds in determining u^* algebraically by starting from a simple tautology,

$$u^* = u^* \frac{\sum p_i - \sum e_i^*}{\sum(p_i - e_i^*)} = \frac{P - \bar{E}}{\sum \dfrac{p_i - e_i^*}{u^*}} = \frac{P - \bar{E}}{\sum \dfrac{p_i}{n_i}},$$

where P is the sum of the horizontal intercepts. The non-tautological step is the last one, where Gossen recognizes that the ratio $(p_i - e_i^*)/u^*$ for each activity corresponds to the slope of the respective marginal utility curve.

Once u^* is known, it is easy to determine total utility as the sum of the triangular areas under the marginal utility curves minus the sum of the triangles with bases $p_i - e_i^*$ and height u^*. These results are derived without the use of calculus. The latter is used, however, to show that u^* corresponds to the increase in total utility obtainable from a relaxation of the resources constraint, namely to $dU/d\bar{E}$.

In a second step, the model is extended to include production (p. 34f.; T ch. 2). This is achieved by reinterpreting activities as products and resources as 'effort', where total effort can be varied. This requires a transformation of utility curves, each of which now shows the marginal utility resulting from the effort spent on

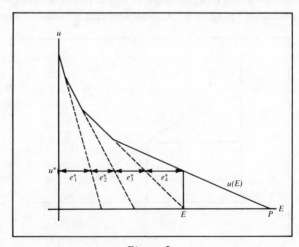

Figure 2

a certain product, taking into account the required amount of effort per unit of product. The time constraint is now replaced by a linear function representing the marginal utility of effort. A small amount of effort is assumed to be pleasurable, but after a point diminishing marginal utility changes into growing marginal disutility. As Georgescu-Roegen has noted, an analysis of leisure is lacking. In Figure 3, the marginal utility of effort, v, is measured downward, positive values thus expressing marginal disutilities. The remainder of the graph corresponds to Figure 2.

The optimal input of effort, E^*, is characterized by the equality between the utility of the marginal effort spent on each product and the marginal disutility of effort. Total utility is then described by the curved triangle between the two marginal curves. Again Gossen is able to describe the optimal solution algebraically in terms of the intercepts of the individual marginal curves and he also determines the comparative-static effects on this solution of various changes in the underlying parameters (p. 48f.; T chs 4–6).

The third stage is reached with the introduction of exchange (p. 80f.; T ch. 7). Gossen begins with the bilateral case. He immediately perceives that there are many different opportunities for mutually beneficial exchange, but his discussion of these possibilities is, understandably, inconclusive. As a necessary condition for optimal exchange he postulates that the marginal utilities must be equalized between individuals for each product. While this formulation requires both cardinality and interpersonal comparability of utility, its economic substance, since it can be expressed in terms of marginal rates of substitution, is independent of these assumptions. The concept of a 'contract curve', however, is not used. The statement that each individual would usually be willing to forego a portion of what he receives suggests some notion of consumer's surplus.

The analysis is then extended to market exchange, where each individual can exchange goods and effort at parametrically given prices, expressed in a common numéraire called money. This means that E is again reinterpreted, this time in the sense of expenditure or income. The product curves now relate to marginal utility per dollar spent on a given product, the solid convex line relates to the marginal utility of income and the rising line expresses the disutility from earning a marginal dollar of income at the going prices. We thus end up with the optimization problem that became the banner of the 'marginal revolution'. The 'Second Law' can then be expressed by the condition that 'the last atom of money creates the same pleasure in each pleasurable use' (p. 93f.; T p. 109).

The solution to this problem determines the individual's market demand and supply for each product and effort. Gossen also shows how the value of intermediate products can sometimes be derived from that of the final goods, thereby foreshadowing Menger's theory of 'imputation', but he is careful to note that the market mechanism works even where imputation fails (p. 24f.; T p. 28f.). If prices are specified at random, aggregate demand and supply will generally differ. Gossen explains how this exerts pressure on prices until all markets are cleared. Prices are thus endogenously determined by general equilibrium. This argument, though concise, is presented in verbal form only. The mathematical

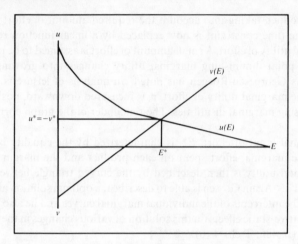

Figure 3

formulation of general equilibrium, foreshadowed by Cournot, had to wait for Walras.

In the fourth stage, Gossen introduces rent (p. 102f.; T chs 8–12). If the profundity of an economist can be gauged by his treatment of rent, Gossen comes out near the top. The worker described by Figure 3 is assumed to own a specific piece of land. Suppose he is now offered the use of land at a superior location, owned by another individual. This does not affect his utility curves, but for the amount of effort for which the marginal utility of effort is just zero he can now earn a higher income. At the same time the marginal disutility curve becomes flatter because the same total enjoyment is now spread over a higher income. In Figure 4 this change is expressed by the dotted line.

In the absence of rent, the superior location would, of course, promise higher income. However, moves to superior locations are not free, but cost rent. This means that at the new location the individual has to earn a certain amount, $\bar{R}$, before he can even begin to buy commodities. The origin of the marginal disutility curve is thus shifted to the left as indicated by the broken line.

What is the maximum rent an individual is willing to pay for a superior location? This 'warranted rent' is reached at the point where total utility at the superior location, measured by the shaded area, is equal to the total utility at the original location, described by the solid triangle. Gossen shows algebraically that with rent at the warranted level, superior locations are associated with higher earned income and higher consumption.

A corresponding experiment can be conducted for a move to an inferior location. In this case, the marginal disutility curve is steeper than the solid line and its origin is shifted to the right, the individual now receiving rent and thus spending more than he earns. Competition in the market for land will see to it that in full equilibrium all rents are at the warranted level.

While Gossen developed a novel and fruitful way to incorporate rent into a

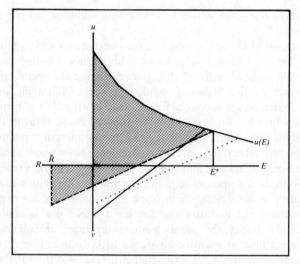

Figure 4

general equilibrium framework, his theory of rent is less rich than von Thünen's, published 28 years before. Gossen was no better in reading his predecessors than the later 'marginalists' were in reading Gossen.

The fifth stage introduces capital and interest (p. 114; T ch. 13). The basic question concerns the highest amount of present utility that could be sacrificed for a piece of land with a given annual rent, continuing into the distant future. Gossen finds the answer by discounting the utility of each future rent payment at the appropriate rate of psychological time preference (as we would call it), reflecting uncertainty of expectations (pp. 30, 115; T pp. 35, 134). This promising idea is not successfully exploited, however, and the adaptation of the land paradigm to capital goods remains sketchy. Gossen thinks in terms of land and labour, while capital goods are played down (p. 172; T p. 194). He also makes an effort to determine the optimal amount of saving by the condition that the highest price the individual is willing to pay for a source of rent should be equal to the market price, but he seems to confuse average and marginal concepts and the sense of his argument remains obscure.

In an effort to interpret everyday observations in the light of his theory, Gossen offers an elaborate discussion of the effect of price changes on demand and expenditure. This discussion anticipates a lot of later work on demand elasticities, but it is also cumbersome. The reason is that Gossen's analytical engine, while permitting a brilliantly simple determination of the optimal budget at given prices, is ill-suited for the analysis of price change. Since Gossen's curves, as observed above, relate the marginal utility of expenditure to expenditure, they have to be redrawn after each price change. The insights which Marshall's apparatus made so easy to communicate, remained virtually incommunicable for Gossen. This may be one of the main reasons why his achievement, though at the highest intellectual level, remained sterile. If he had read Cournot, his fate might have been different.

The second part of Gossen's book is largely devoted to social philosophy and policy. It shows its author as a passionate libertarian. Through free markets, mankind would succeed without effort where all socialist planning must fall, namely in reaching the highest possible happiness. Abhorring all forms of protection. Gossen was in favour of free trade, the protection of property rights and a liberal education for both sexes. To prevent fluctuations in the value of money, he advocated a metallic currency and the abolition of paper money. That he also asked for restrictions on child labour and government sponsorship of credit unions seems to indicate that he knew externalities and market imperfections when he saw them. Competitive equilibrium was for him much more than an economic theory or an ideology; it was the gospel, revealing the perfection of a benevolent creator. For him, the 'invisible hand' was not a didactic metaphor, but religion itself. Today, this apotheosis of competition, in language closer to a revival meeting than to scientific discourse, strikes one as bizarre.

Major sources of inefficiency, Gossen thought, were distortions in the allocation of land, preventing land from actually being used by the potentially most efficient user. To correct this defect, he proposed that the government use borrowed money to buy land on the free market and then lease it to the highest bidder (p. 250f.; T ch. 23). Since governments differ from individuals by (1) being immortal, (2) having a higher credit rating, and (3) a lower time preference, such a scheme, he argued, would actually improve government wealth, and the initial debt could eventually be repaid out of rising rent income. For a given year, the scheme would be viable if the price paid by government for a price of land, A, did not exceed the sum of the rent, a, and the annual increase in the value of land, capitalized at the market rate of interest, z. This led him to the condition

$$A \leqslant \frac{a + \dfrac{z'}{z}a}{z},$$

where z' is the annual rate of rent increase. It is understandable that Walras was attracted to this scheme. It is also evident, however, that Gossen was not a 'land socialist'; he was not concerned about 'land monopoly' and the 'socialization of rent'. His objective was the correction of a market imperfection without any limitation of property rights.

Gossen, though perhaps not quite a genius, had a brilliant, original and precise mind. With his one book, he moved constrained optimization into the centre of the theory of value and allocation, where it has since remained. With respect to economic content, his was probably the greatest single contribution to this theory in the 19th century. He failed, however, to develop the basic principle into a usable analytical engine. As a consequence, the so-called 'founders' of the modern theory of value had to rediscover those principles before they could proceed with their engineering work.

SELECTED WORKS

1854. *Entwicklung der Gesetze des menschlichen Verkehrs, und der daraus fliessenden Regeln für menschliches Handeln.* Braunschweig: Vieweg. Reprinted. Amsterdam: Liberac, 1967. 2nd edn, Berlin: Prager, 1889. 3rd edn (with introduction by F.A. Hayek), Berlin: Prager, 1927. Italian translation by T. Bagiotti as *Ermanno Enrico Gossen, Sviluppo delle leggi del commercio umano.* Padua: CEDAM, 1950. English translation by R.C. Blitz (with introductory essay by N. Georgescu-Roegen) as *The Laws of Human Relations and the Rules of Human Action Derived Therefrom,* Cambridge, Mass.: MIT Press, 1983.

BIBLIOGRAPHY

Bagiotti, T. 1957. Reminiszenzen anlässlich des hundertsten Jahrestages des Erscheinens des Buches von Gossen. *Zeitschrift für Nationalökonomie,* 17.

Bousquet, G.-H. 1958. Un centennaire: l'oeuvre de H.H. Gossen (1810–1858) et sa véritable structure. *Revue d'économie politique* 68.

Edgeworth, F.Y. 1896. Gossen, Hermann Heinrich. In *Dictionary of Political Economy,* ed. R.H. Inglis Palgrave, Vol. 2, London and New York: Macmillan.

Georgescu-Roegen, N. 1983. Introduction to H.H. Gossen, *The Laws of Human Relations and the Rules of Human Action Derived Therefrom,* trans. R.C. Blitz, Cambridge, Mass.: MIT Press.

Jevons, W.S. 1879. *The Theory of Political Economy.* London: Macmillan; 5th edn, New York: A.M. Kelley, 1965.

Kautz, J. 1858, 1860. *Theorie und Geschichte der National-Oekonomik.* 2 vols, Vienna: Gerold.

Krauss, O. 1910. Gossen, Hermann Heinrich. In *Allgemeine Deutsche Biographie,* Vol. 55, Leipzig: Duncker & Humblot.

Lange, F.A. 1875. *Die Arbeiterfrage. Ihre Bedeutung für Gegenwart und Zukunft.* 3rd edn, Winterthur: Bleuler–Hausheer.

Lexis, W. 1895. Art. Grenznutzen. *Handwörterbuch der Staatswissenschaften,* Vol. 1 (Supplement), Jena: Fischer.

Liefmann, R. 1910. Hermann Heinrich Gossen und seine Lehre. Zur hundertsten Wiederkehr seines Geburtstages am 7. September 1910. *Jahrbücher für Nationalökonomie und Statistik* 40.

Neubauer, J. 1931. Die Gossenschen Gesetze. *Zeitschrift für Nationalökonomie* 2.

Pantaleoni, M. 1889. *Principii di economia pura.* Florence: G. Barbèra. Trans. by T.B. Bruce as *Pure Economics,* London: Macmillan, 1898.

Riedle, H. 1953. *Herman Heinrich Gossen 1810–1858. Ein Wegbereiter der modernen ökonomischen Theorie.* Winterthur: Keller.

Walras, L. 1885. Un économiste inconnu: Hermann-Henri Gossen. *Journal des Economistes.* Reprinted in L. Walrus, *Etudes d'économie sociale,* Lausanne: Rouge, 1896, 351–74.

Impatience

LARRY G. EPSTEIN

Impatience refers to the preference for earlier rather than later consumption, an idea which stems from Böhm-Bawerk (1912) and Fisher (1930), among others. Preference orderings that exhibit impatience are also described as being myopic or as embodying discounting. Because in many contexts the future has no natural termination date, an infinite horizon framework is most appropriate and convenient for the analysis of many problems in intertemporal economics. The open-endedness of the future raises several issues surrounding impatience (its presence, degree, and the precise form it takes) which do not arise in finite horizon models.

Consider a world with a countable infinity of time periods or generations, $t = 0, 1, \ldots, T, \ldots$, where there is a single good which can be consumed or accumulated. Let $x = (x_0, \ldots, x_t, \ldots)$ represent a consumption programme where x_t denotes the consumption of the representative consumer for the tth generation. Given an initial (capital) stock k_0 of the good, and a technology that transforms capital into a flow output, the set of feasible consumption programmes, denoted $S(k_0)$, is determined.

At issue is the optimal programme of consumption and accumulation. Suppose it is determined by a central planner who ranks programmes in $S(k_0)$ according to the utility function

$$U(x) = \sum_0^\infty (1 + \rho)^{-1} u(x_t). \tag{1}$$

This is a common specification. For $\rho = 0$ it dates from Ramsey (1928); for the general case see Koopmans (1966). The instantaneous utility function $u(\cdot)$ is increasing and concave (diminishing marginal utility).

The parameter ρ equals the rate of time preference. Impatience (in the sense of any of the precise definitions given below) is present if (and only if) $\rho > 0$. There is a preliminary technical problem with (1) for some values of ρ. When $\rho = 0$, for example, the infinite sum in (1) diverges for many of the paths to be compared. Ramsey provides one device for getting around this difficulty. Another device is von Weizsäcker's (1965) overtaking criterion, according to which x^* is *optimal* in $S(k_0)$ if it is feasible and if for any other feasible path x,

$$\sum_0^T (1+\rho)^{-t} u(x_t^*) \geq \sum_0^T (1+\rho)^{-t} u(x_t),$$

for all sufficiently large T. This notion of optimality is well-defined for any value of ρ, even for negative values; and an optimal x^* maximizes U on $S(k_0)$ if $U(x^*)$ is finite.

The specification of ρ is crucial and presumably reflects the ethical principles of the planner. Ramsey (1928) objects to discounting on ethical grounds and thus assumes $\rho = 0$. But Koopmans (1966, 1967) argues that there are technical limitations on the specification of ρ which are imposed by the requirement that an optimal plan x^* exist for a range of choice environments. The potential difficulty is readily understood: a positive return to saving provides an incentive to postpone consumption. Positive (negative) discounting provides an offsetting (reinforcing) incentive. Finally, diminishing marginal utility and diminishing marginal productivity in production induce a smoothing of consumption over time. For many specifications, the net incentive is to postpone and to do so indefinitely, which is clearly not optimal. Consequently an optimal programme fails to exist. The existence problem is mitigated the larger is ρ, in the sense that if $\rho_1 < \rho_2$ and if an optimum in $S(k_0)$ exists when $\rho = \rho_1$, then it exists also when $\rho = \rho_2$. In particular, in order that an optimum exist in several simplified but commonly specified choice environments, it is necessary that $\rho > 0$ and hence that the future be discounted. (See also von Weizsäcker, 1965.)

The existence of solutions to optimization problems is a basic question in mathematical programming which is most commonly resolved by application of the Weierstrass Theorem (or its many extensions). The Theorem guarantees existence of a solution if the objective function is continuous and the constraint set is compact. It is valid in general topological spaces and so is applicable also to the present setting where the choice variable x lies in an infinite dimensional space. The Theorem is the basis for the proof by Magill (1981) of the existence of an optimum to infinite horizon optimization problems. When specialized to the constant discount rate functional (1), his analysis confirms the consequences for existence of large ρ. Moreover, it shows 'why' a large ρ is beneficial – the larger is ρ, the more stringent the form of continuity satisfied by the utility functional and hence the broader the class of constraint sets to which the Weierstrass Theorem is applicable.

To pursue the link between impatience and continuity, it is necessary to consider the latter more carefully. First, however, restrict attention to bounded consumption profiles, that is, to the set

$$L_+^\infty = \{x = (x_0, \ldots, x_t, \ldots): \quad x_t \geq 0 \quad \text{for all } t \text{ and } \sup x_t < \infty \}.$$

109

Secondly, the existence of a utility function is an unnecessarily restrictive assumption. Thus consider preference relations $\succcurlyeq$ on L_+^∞, with strict preference denoted by $\succ$.

To discuss continuity, we need to specify a topology for L_+^∞; that is, we need to define what it means for two consumption paths to be 'close' to one another. This is most simply done by specifying when a sequence of consumption paths $\{x^n = (x_0^n, x_1^n, \ldots, x_t^n, \ldots)\}_{n=1}^\infty$ *converges* to a path x in L_+^∞. (Strictly speaking, generalized sequences called nets should be used, but the use of sequences is adequate for this informal discussion.) For many topologies that are of interest in economics 'closeness' can be measured by a *metric* or distance function d such that $d(x, y)$ measures the 'distance' between x and y. When such a metric exists, convergence of $\{x^n\}$ to x means simply that $d(x^n, x)$ approaches 0 as $n \to \infty$, in which case we refer to the *d-convergence* of the sequence.

Table 1 defines four topologies by specifying the conditions for convergence imposed by each. When a metric exists, it is also specified. Of course many other plausible topologies could be considered.

Continuity of a preference relation means roughly that consumption paths that are close to one another are ranked similarly vis-à-vis other paths. More formally, say that the relation $\succcurlyeq$ is continuous in the topology Γ (or Γ-continuous) if for each x and y in L_+^∞, and for any sequences $\{x^n\}$ and $\{y^n\}$ that converge to x and y respectively according to Γ, it is the case that

$$x \succ y \Rightarrow x \succ y^n \quad \text{and} \quad x^n \succ y$$

for all sufficiently large values of n.

Which topology should be adopted? The question does not arise in finite dimensional contexts. The reason is simply that all 'natural' topologies on finite dimensional Euclidean spaces are *equivalent* in the sense that the corresponding convergence definitions are logically equivalent to one another. This is the case, for example, with the four topologies in the table if they are adapted in the obvious way to a finite horizon context. In all cases, convergence is identical to the usual notion based on the Euclidean metric. Thus the corresponding notions of continuity are also identical.

In contrast, in the infinite horizon model, the noted equivalence fails. It is easily shown that

$$d_s\text{-convergence} \Rightarrow d_\infty\text{-convergence}$$

$$\Rightarrow \text{Mackey-convergence}$$

$$\Rightarrow d_p\text{-convergence.} \tag{2}$$

But none of the reverse implications is true. For example, define the sequences $\{x^n\}$, $\{y^n\}$ and $\{z^n\}$ as follows:

$$x_t^n = 0 \quad \text{if} \quad 0 \leq t \leq n \quad \text{and} \quad = n \quad \text{if} \quad t > n$$

$$y_t^n = 0 \quad \text{if} \quad 0 \leq t \leq n \quad \text{and} \quad = 1 \quad \text{if} \quad t > n$$

$$z^n = (n^{-1}, n^{-1}, n^{-1}, \ldots).$$

110

Table 1

Topology	Definition of convergence of $\{x^n\}$ to x	Metric
product	$x_t^n \xrightarrow[n \to \infty]{} x_t$ for all t	$d_p(x, y) = \sup_t \dfrac{2^{-t}\|x_t - y_t\|}{\{1 + \|x_t - y_t\|\}}$
Mackey	$\sup_t \|a_t \cdot (x_t^n - x_t)\| \xrightarrow[n \to \infty]{} 0$ for all sequences of real numbers $\{a_t\}_0^\infty$ that converge to 0	—
supremum	$\sup_t \|x_t^n - x_t\| \xrightarrow[n \to \infty]{} 0$	$d_\infty(x, y) = \sup_t \|x_t - y_t\|$
Svensson	$\sum_0^\infty \|x_t^n - x_t\| \xrightarrow[n \to \infty]{} 0$	$d_s(x, y) = \min\left(1, \sum_0^\infty \|x_t - y_t\|\right)$

Then $\{x^n\}$ converges to $(0, 0, \dots)$ in the product topology but not in the Mackey topology. In the former case x^n is viewed as being close to the zero consumption path for large n, because the first n generations all have zero consumption. Thus product topology discounts the fact that in x^n, infinitely many generations enjoy large consumption levels which are unbounded as n grows. It is the latter feature which explains why x^n and $(0, 0, \dots)$ are not viewed as being close to one another by the Mackey topology. (Take $a_t = t^{-1/2}$ in the definition of Mackey convergence.) Thus, for example, in the case of $\{y^n\}$ where the consumption of future generations is bounded in n, the sequence is Mackey-convergent to the zero consumption path. The sequence $\{y^n\}$ is not d_∞-convergent since not all generations have consumption near 0. Finally, $\{z^n\}$ converges to $(0, 0, \dots)$ in the sup topology, but it is not d_s-convergent since the 'aggregate' deviation of consumption levels between the two paths is large (indeed $\Sigma_0^\infty \|z_t^n\| = \infty$).

When topologies are not equivalent continuity of a preference relation has a different meaning, depending upon which topology is adopted. Thus (2) implies immediately that

$$d_p\text{-continuity} \Rightarrow \text{Mackey-continuity}$$

$$\Rightarrow d_\infty\text{-continuity}$$

$$\Rightarrow d_s\text{-continuity}, \qquad (3)$$

111

and none of the reverse implications is valid. In finite dimensional analysis continuity is a purely technical assumption which is innocuous from an economist's point of view. But the discussion of convergence in the above four topologies strongly suggests that in infinite horizon models the specification of a topology and the assumption of continuity can have economic content. Indeed, continuity in some topologies can imply impatience.

One demonstration of the crucial role played by a topology is provided by Diamond (1965) and Svensson (1980). Call a preference relation *equitable* if it provides equal treatment for all generations in the sense that for all x and y in L_+^∞, $x \succcurlyeq y \Leftrightarrow \pi x \succcurlyeq \pi y$, where πx (or πy) is obtained from x (or y) be permuting finitely many of its components. A preference relation is weakly monotonic if $x_t > y_t$ for all $t \Rightarrow x \succ y$. Diamond shows that there does not exist an equitable and weakly monotonic preference relation that is also continuous in the product metric. This preclusion of equity is perhaps not surprising given the discounting of the future that is built into the definition of d_p. But even given the apparently 'time neutral' metric d_∞, the scope for equity is limited. Diamond proves that equity and d_∞-continuity are incompatible given strong monotonicity ($x_t \geqslant y_t$ for all t and $x_\tau > y_\tau$ for some $\tau \Rightarrow x \succ y$). If only weak monotonicity is imposed, then all postulates are satisfied by the maximum ordering, whereby

$$x \succcurlyeq y \Leftrightarrow \inf x_t \geqslant \inf y_t. \tag{4}$$

The view, based on finite dimensional analysis, that continuity is an innocuous technical assumption, would lead one to interpret Diamond's results as demonstrating the non-existence of equitable orderings that satisfy minimal additional regularity conditions. But, the correct interpretation is that Diamond's theorems demonstrate the strong ethical content of d_p-continuity and d_∞-continuity. The latter view is fortified by Svensson (1980). He shows that if the d_s metric is adopted, then there exist equitable and strongly monotonic orderings which are d_s-continuous. Since d_s is a priori plausible, the onus is clearly shifted to the metric. At the extreme, continuity can be imposed with total impunity if the metric d_0 is adopted, where

$$d_0(x, y) = \begin{bmatrix} 0, & \text{if} & x = y \\ 1, & \text{if} & x \neq y \end{bmatrix}.$$

The topology corresponding to d_0 is called the discrete topology. According to this metric distinct consumption paths cannot be close to one another, so continuity is automatic. A natural open question is the characterization of metrics d (and more general topologies) such that d-continuous, equitable and (weakly or strongly) monotonic preference relations exist.

At this point it is worth recalling a principal reason that continuity is of interest – namely that by (an extension of) the Weierstrass Theorem, it will guarantee the existence of optimal elements in compact sets. Given a topology Γ on L_+^∞, a set $K \subset L_+^\infty$ is Γ-compact if every (generalized) sequence of points in K has a (generalized) subsequence that converges according to Γ to a point in K. As the topology changes in such a way as to permit more continuous functions, the family of compact sets shrinks (see (2) and (3)).

Thus as continuity becomes easier to achieve it also becomes less significant. (For example, K is d_0-compact only if it consists of finitely many points; and there exist many economically relevant sets K that are compact in the product topology but not in the sup topology. One example arises in an exhaustible resource model where feasible consumptions plans satisfy $\Sigma_0^\infty x_t \leqslant w$, and w is the initial stock of the good.) If there is a class of constraint sets where the existence of optimal elements is desired, then the 'useful' topologies are those that make each of the constraint sets compact. This approach (emphasized by Campbell, 1985) would remove some of the arbitrariness from the choice of a topology.

Diamond's results suggest that continuity may imply 'some form of impatience', since equity can be viewed as the lack of impatience. A more precise definition of impatience is required for a clearer demonstration of the link between the latter and continuity. For example, impatience could be taken to mean that interchanging the consumption levels of generations 1 and t results in a strictly preferred plan if period t consumption was initially larger. If the preceding statement is valid only for t sufficiently far into the future, then *eventual impatience* could be said to prevail. This latter notion captures not only a preference for the advancement of the timing of satisfaction, but also the idea that the taste for future consumption diminishes as the time of consumption recedes into the future. These and related definitions appear in Koopmans (1960), Koopmans et al. (1964) and Diamond (1965). Their proofs that appropriate continuity implies (eventual) impatience depend, with the single exception of Diamond (p. 174), on maintained separability assumptions on the preference relation. The separability assumptions can be deleted if the existence of a differentiable utility function is assumed (Burness, 1973).

Brown and Lewis (1981) define some notions of asymptotic impatience. For example, they call a preference relation *strongly myopic* if for all x, y and z in L_+^∞, $x \succ y \Rightarrow x \succ y + {}_n z$ for all sufficiently large n, where ${}_n z = (0, \ldots, 0, z_{n+1}, z_{n+2}, \ldots)$. In other words, the preference for x over y is unchanged by an increase in the latter programme in the consumption of infinitely many generations, as long as the increase occurs only for generations that are situated sufficiently far into the future.

Interpret a preference relation as belonging to a consumer rather than to a central planner. Consumption programmes in L_+^∞ describe the consumption of that consumer and his descendants; the latters' consumption levels matter because of intergenerational altruism. This is a common framework in the capital theory literature where the behavioural assumption of impatience is often maintained. This suggests that from the perspective of capital theory, economically interesting topologies are those which (through continuity) imply myopia. For example, any preference relation which is d_p-continuous is necessarily strongly myopic. But the implication is false if the product metric is replaced by d_∞ or d_s. Brown and Lewis show that the Mackey topology bears a special relationship to strong myopia. Mackey-continuity is the weakest continuity requirement (corresponding to topologies in a broad and convenient class) that can be imposed on a preference relation in order that strong myopia be implied. Thus it is a 'natural' topology if strong myopia is desirable.

There is an important link between the Mackey topology and strong myopia on the one hand and general equilibrium analysis in the framework of 'infinitely lived' agents on the other. Bewley (1972) points out that the Mackey topology is particularly appropriate for general equilibrium analysis because continuity requirements weaker than Mackey-continuity do not guarantee the existence of equilibria with price systems that can be represented by absolutely summable sequences $(p_0, \ldots, p_t, \ldots)$, rather than merely for more general mathematical constructs that have no economic interpretation. In light of the relationship between Mackey-continuity and strong myopia, the latter seems necessary for meaningful general equilibrium analysis.

Brown and Lewis sharpen the link between impatience and general equilibrium analysis. They prove that if individual preferences are suitably monotonic, then Mackey-continuity and strong myopia are unnecessarily strong assumptions. But a form of asymptotic impatience is still relevant. Call a preference ordering *weakly myopic* if the implication defining strong myopia is valid for all constant programmes z. Then even if individual preferences are weakly monotonic, the existence of economically interpretable equilibrium price systems as above can be guaranteed only by continuity requirements which imply weak myopia.

Suppose that we are willing to accept more general constructs (linear functionals on L_+^∞) as price systems. Can we then dispense with impatience? Araujo (1985) provides a negative partial answer. He restricts attention to a well-defined subset of those continuity conditions which lie 'between' d_∞-continuity and d_p-continuity. Then he shows that the existence of such general price systems can be guaranteed only if continuity requirements are imposed which imply strong myopia, or, when suitable monotonicity is maintained for preferences, weak myopia. Existence of equilibria cannot be guaranteed in such cases as the maximin ordering (4) exhibits no impatience.

We offer one final comment. In a planning context, continuity of the social preference relation may be desirable not necessarily for its own sake nor because it may imply myopia, but primarily to guarantee that the preference relation be *effective*, that is, that optimal consumption paths exist. From this perspective, it seems more pertinent to investigate the link between effectiveness and impatience directly, without involving continuity which is, after all, at best sufficient and definitely not necessary for the existence of optimal paths. Thus, for example, a pertinent question is whether impatience (in some precise sense) is necessary for effectiveness in a relevant set of choice environments. While this question has been addressed to some extent in the growth theory literature cited earlier based on the additive utility functional (1), an analysis comparable in generality to that of Brown and Lewis or Araujo has yet to be performed.

BIBLIOGRAPHY
Araujo, A. 1985. Lack of Pareto optimal allocations in economies with infinitely many commodities: the need for impatience. *Econometrica* 53(2), March, 455–61.

Bewley, T. 1972. Existence of equilibria in economies with infinitely many commodities. *Journal of Economic Theory* 4(3), June, 514–40.

Böhm-Bawerk, E. von 1912. *Positive Theory of Capital*. South Holland, Ill.: Libertarian Press, 1959.

Brown, D.J. and Lewis, L.M. 1981. Myopic economic agents. *Econometrica* 49(2), March, 359–68.

Burness, H.S. 1973. Impatience and the preference for advancement in the timing of satisfactions. *Journal of Economic Theory* 6(5), October, 495–507.

Diamond, P.A. 1965. The evaluation of infinite utility streams. *Econometrica* 33, January, 170–77.

Fisher, I. 1930. *The Theory of Interest*. New York: Macmillan.

Koopmans, T.C. 1960. Stationary ordinal utility and impatience. *Econometrica* 28, April, 287–309.

Koopmans, T.C. 1966. On the concept of optimal economic growth. In *The Econometric Approach to Development Planning*, Amsterdam: North-Holland.

Koopmans, T.C. 1967. Objectives, constraints, and outcomes in optimal growth models. *Econometrica* 35, January, 1–15.

Koopmans, T.C., Diamond, P.A. and Williamson, R.E. 1964. Stationary utility and time perspective. *Econometrica* 32, January–April, 82–100.

Magill, M.J.P. 1981. Infinite horizon programs. *Econometrica* 49(3), May, 679–711.

Ramsey, F.P. 1928. A mathematical theory of saving. *Economic Journal* 38, December, 543–59.

Svensson, L.G. 1980. Equity among generations. *Econometrica* 48(5), 1251–6.

von Weizsäcker, C.C. 1965. Existence of optimal programs of accumulation for an infinite time horizon. *Review of Economic Studies* 32, April, 85–104.

Induction

PAUL W. HUMPHREYS

Induction, in its most general form, is the making of inferences from the observed to the unobserved. Thus, inferences from the past to the future, from a sample to the population, from data to an hypothesis, and from observed effects to unobserved causes are all aspects of induction, as are arguments from analogy. A successful account of induction is required for a satisfactory theory of causality, scientific laws and predictive applications of economic theory. But induction is a dangerous thing, and especially so for those who lean towards empiricism, the view that only experience can serve as the grounds for genuine knowledge. Because induction, by its very nature, goes beyond the observed, its use is inevitably difficult to justify for the empiricist. In addition, inductive inferences differ from deductive inferences in three crucial respects. First, the conclusion of an inductive inference does not follow with certainty from the premises, but only with some degree of probability. Second, whereas valid deductive inferences retain their validity when extra information is added to the premises, inductive inferences may be seriously weakened. Third, whereas there is widespread agreement upon the correct characterization of deductive validity. there is widespread disagreement about what constitutes a correct inductive argument, and indeed whether induction is a legitimate part of science at all.

Approaches to these issues generally fall into two categories. The older, more philosophical approaches attempt to provide an extremely general justification for the use of inductive methods and to isolate the universal characteristics which make for a correct inductive reference. The second kind of approach focuses on what are called 'local inductions' – analyses of very specific kinds of inferences, applicable in precisely detailed circumstances. With the enormously increased power of statistical methods which is characteristic of this century, the second approach has become more and more the province of theoretical and applied statistics. It would be inappropriate to discuss specifically statistical issues here and the reader is referred to the excellent Barnett (1982). However, it should be recognized that although these detailed mathematical techniques have increased

116

our understanding of induction immensely, they do not by themselves answer all questions about the soundness of inductive procedures. In collecting data, for example, judgements must be made about which situations are similar to one another, and hence a combination of analogical principles and judgements of causal relevance will be needed. The principles of experimental design, not only for field data but also in the growing subject of experimental economics, generally require such judgements. Bayesian statistical methods need principles on which to attribute prior probabilities, and there is an extensive philosophical literature on the acceptability of such principles. Finally, it should be emphasized that most statistical techniques were developed within a climate of extreme empiricism or positivism, and that the application and integration of statistical models to economic systems requires a delicate inductive sensibility that cannot be reduced to algorithmic procedures.

PHILOSOPHICAL APPROACHES. The use of induction as the basis of a general scientific method was first systematically advocated by Francis Bacon. His suggested methods will seem queer to the modern reader, but the importance of his break with the deductive traditions of Greek and medieval thought should not be undervalued. He himself realized this in entitling his principal work *Novum Organum* to mirror Aristotle's *Organum* of logic, and his methods partially anticipate the eliminative methods later championed by J.S. Mill and Popper. Important as Bacon's work was, all modern work on induction lives under the shadow of the later 'problem of induction'.

'The problem of induction' is to state conditions under which an inductive inference can be rationally justified. Ever since its statement in his *Treatise of Human Nature* (1739), it has been associated with the name of the Scots philosopher David Hume. It can be broadly stated in this way: when one infers from the observed O to the unobserved U, O and U are always logically distinct, at least in the sense that one can conceive of O holding, yet U not. So there is no logical necessity for U to follow from O. What then could form the grounds for asserting U, given O? For an empiricist (such as Hume) there was nothing that one could observe which would fit the bill – possible stopgaps such as natural necessity or causal powers were simply metaphysical fictions. There was, in short, merely a succession of events, and nothing we can observe guarantees that the unobserved will continue the pattern of the observed. Furthermore, any attempt to justify induction by a deductive argument would be inappropriate, for induction is essentially ampliative, in that the conclusion goes beyond what is contained in the premises, whereas deductive inferences are always conservative. Conversely, an inductive justification of induction, on the grounds that it has worked well so far, would appear to be circular.

The philosophical responses to this problem can be of two kinds. One response is to acknowledge that inductive inferences are unjustifiable, and that consequently they should play no role in a rational enterprise such as science. Thus many authors have placed great emphasis on eliminative methods, whereby various potential explanations of the inductive evidence are eliminated as impossible or

117

highly improbable, using primarily deductive methods. The best-known modern advocate of this view is Karl Popper, whose *Logic of Scientific Discovery* (1959) is, in part, a sustained defence of a purely deductive scientific methodology. Mill's famous methods of experimental inquity (1843, Book III) are eliminative, as is part of Keynes's (1921) theory of induction, and a large portion of Bacon's approach. It is also possible to view in this way the objectivist statistical methodology of hypothesis testing, where the emphasis is on the rejection of statistical hypotheses. There is serious doubt with all of these approaches, however, as to whether they can function properly without tacitly employing inductive methods at some stage.

The second, and more common response is to provide some reasons why inductive inferences are indeed rationally justifiable. The 'missing premise' approach, for example, suggests that we view inductive arguments as incomplete deductive arguments, or enthymemes. By adding some extra assumption, usually a variant of a uniformity of nature principle, one can convert inductive arguments into deductive ones. Holders of this view have often felt compelled to adopt such a uniformity of nature principle as an a priori truth, one without which science would be impossible. The problems with this approach are many, primarily: what exact form should the uniformity of nature principle take, and how is it to be justified? 'The future resembles the past' is too vague, and almost certainly false, for dissimilarities are at least as common as similarities. 'Every event falls under a law of nature' may be true, but which law for which event? Mill tried to solve the problem by claiming that all inductions were inferences from particulars to particulars, although also asserting that a general uniformity of nature principle could be established inductively using the success of many more specific inductive generalizations.

The pragmatic approach to induction, credited to Hans Reichenbach (1949, pp. 469–82), argues that while induction cannot be guaranteed to work, if any method succeeds then induction will do just as well. Hence one may as well employ what Reichenbach called the 'straight rule' – infer that the relative frequency of observed positive instances of an effect will continue in the future. There is, however, an infinite number of alternative rules that are consistent with Reichenbach's procedure, and hence the vagueness problem is still with him.

Much philosophical work was done in the middle part of this century to construct systems of inductive logic using a logical probability function i.e. a numerical function which attributes a degree of inductive confirmation to an hypothesis, given certain evidence statements. This work, the most developed of which was carried out by Rudolf Carnap (1950), is generally regarded as having failed to achieve its aims. It did, however, produce a number of useful insights into the nature of inductive inferences, among which was the principle of total evidence, which asserts that in applications of inductive logic, no relevant evidence should be omitted.

CONTRIBUTIONS OF ECONOMISTS. Among those who have made important contributions to both economics and the study of induction, we may count primarily J.S. Mill (1843), W.S. Jevons (1874), J.M. Keynes (1921) and R.F. Harrod (1956). Economists who have also written explicitly on induction include A.A. Cournot, F.Y. Edgeworth, F.P. Ramsey, John Hicks, Herbert Simon and F.A. Hayek. (It is worth mentioning that Hume himself made a seminal contribution to economics with his theory of gold-flow equilibrium and defence of free trade.) Mill's views have been described earlier. Jevon's principal work is *The Principles of Science* (1874), within which the use of the hypothetico-deductive method is heavily stressed, as well as the allocation of subjective probabilities to those hypotheses by means of inverse probability methods. Jevons's inductive views are now for the most part regarded as combining exceptional insight with generally fallacious reasoning.

Keynes's only philosophical book, *A Treatise on Probability* (1921), is, like most of his work, of great originality. Here one can find one of the first systematic expositions of logical probability. Keynes is also perhaps the first to have insisted that logical probabilities are relative to evidence and cannot be separated from such. Hence there is no rule of detachment for probabilistic inductive logic, in the sense that evidence premises cannot be detached from the inductively supported conclusion, as is possible in deductive logic. This work on inductive logic was an important precursor of Rudolf Carnap's contributions in this area. Keynes also introduced the Principle of Limited Independent Variety, which essentially asserts that all inductive inferences concern objects with a finite number of independent properties, or, that there cannot be an infinite plurality of causes for an effect. This principle was necessary in order to attribute finite prior probabilities to the hypotheses under consideration. Harrod's (1956) theory cannot be swiftly stated: suffice it to say that he argues for the intrinsic acceptability of certain inductive arguments based on probability without supplementation by additional assumptions. His work has not attracted wide support.

PROSPECTS. Is there a solution to Hume's problem? A characteristic of both kinds of approach discussed above has been their tendency towards an increased level of abstraction, symbolized by increasingly powerful mathematical and logical techniques. Useful as these techniques are, inductive inferences can rarely be made confidently without careful attention to causal relationships. Hume's problem itself arose directly from his argument that there is nothing more to causal connections than the regular succession of temporally ordered contiguous events. Mill gave careful attention to the causal foundations of inductions, but many empiricists are uneasy with causal talk, and the 20th century has largely eschewed causes in favour of mathematics. Because induction, causality and probability are so intimately connected, one may be able to rectify this neglect by making use of a specifically causal concept of probability (e.g. Humphreys, 1985). That is, rather than construing probabilities as logical relations, subjective degrees of belief, or relative frequencies, one may take them to be propensities, i.e. probabilistic dispositions whose concrete structural basis is the economic system under investigation. Indeed, much of the work by Marschak, Hurwicz and by Simon (1977) on identifiability of structural parameters within causally isolated systems lends itself to this kind of approach. Those theories are ultimately reliant upon an understanding of causation which comes from experimental interventions, and since we are undoubtedly acquainted with primitive causal relations in that way, using such relations to justify others will not result in circularity. By localising such inferences, there need be no vagueness about the inductive claims made. This approach does suffer from the extreme difficulty of identifying causal relationships within complex economic systems, and this difficulty is, of course, why one often must replace the experimental controls of simpler physical sciences by statistical surrogates for economic purposes. Complete certainty about inductive inferences is impossible, but the clear and discoverable differences between stable and unstable systems, equilibrium and disequilibrium, and isolated and non-isolated systems lie at the heart of the difference between secure and insecure inductive inferences from the past to the future, and a judicious mixture of statistical techniques with causal models seems to offer a promising alternative to the acausal inductive heritage of Hume.

A comprehensive bibliography up to 1921 may be found in Keynes (1921). More recent work is cited in Swinburne (1974). The best survey is still Kneale (1949) and an elementary source is Skyrms (1986).

BIBLIOGRAPHY

Bacon, F. 1620. *Novum Organum*. Reprinted as *The New Organon*, ed. F.H. Anderson. Indianapolis: Bobbs-Merrill, 1960.

Barnett, V. 1982. *Comparative Statistical Inference*. 2nd edn, Chichester: John Wiley.

Carnap, R. 1950. *Logical Foundations of Probability*. Chicago: University of Chicago Press.

Harrod, R. 1956. *Foundations of Inductive Logic*. New York: Harcourt, Brace.

Hume, D. 1739. *A Treatise of Human Nature*. Ed. L.A. Selby-Bigge, Oxford: Oxford University Press, 1888.

Humphreys, P. 1985. Why propensities cannot be probabilities. *Philosophical Review* 94, 557–70.

Jevons, W.S. 1874. *The Principles of Science*. London: Macmillan.

Keynes, J.M. 1921. *A Treatise on Probability*. London: Macmillan; New York: Harper & Row, 1962.

Kneale, W. 1949. *Probability and Induction*. Oxford: Clarendon Press.

Mill, J.S. 1843. *A System of Logic*. London: J.W. Parker; New York: Longman's Green, 1952.

Popper, K. 1959. *The Logic of Scientific Discovery*. London: Hutchinson; New York: Basic Books.

Reichenbach, H. 1949. *The Theory of Probability*. Berkeley: University of California Press.

Simon, H. 1977. Causal ordering and identifiability. In H. Simon, *Models of Discovery*, Dordrecht: D. Reidel.

Skyrms, B. 1986. *Choice and Chance*. 3rd edn, Belmont: Wadsworth.

Swinburne, R. 1974. *The Justification of Induction*. Oxford and New York: Oxford University Press.

Interdependent Preferences

PETER C. FISHBURN

Interdependent preferences arise in economic theory in the study of both individual decisions and group decisions. We imagine that a decision is required among alternatives in a set X and that the decision will depend on preferences between the elements in X. If the preferences represent different points of view about the relative desirability of the alternatives, or if they are based on multiple criteria that impinge on the decision, then we encounter the possibility of interdependent preferences.

There are two predominant approaches to interdependent preferences, the synthetic and the analytic. The synthetic approach begins with a set of preference relations on X and attempts to aggregate them into a holistic representative preference relation on X. This is done in social choice theory, where each original relation refers to the preferences of an individual in a social group. The aggregate relation is then referred to as a social preference relation. The synthetic approach also appears in studies of individual preferences, as when an individual rank-orders the alternatives for each of a number of criteria and then seeks a holistic ranking that combines the criteria rankings in a reasonable way.

In contrast, the analytic approach begins with a holistic preference relation on X and seeks to analyse its internal structure. This may involve a decomposition into components of preference, or it may concern trade-offs between factors that describe interactive contributions to overall preferences.

The synthetic approach often considers a list $(\gg_1, \gg_2, \dots, \gg_n)$ of preference relations on X, where $x \gg_i y$ could mean that person i prefers x to y, or that an individual prefers x to y on the basis of criterion i. The problem may then be to specify a holistic relation $\gg = f(\gg_1, \gg_2, \dots, \gg_n)$ for each possible n-tuple of individual relations.

The analytic approach often begins with X as a subset of the product $X_1 \times X_2 \times \cdots \times X_n$ of n other sets. It considers a holistic *is preferred to* relation $\gg$ on X and asks how $\gg$ depends on the X_i considered separately or in combination. Under suitably strong *independence* assumptions it may be possible to *define* $\gg_i$

121

for each i in a natural way from $\geqslant$ on X, and perhaps to establish a functional dependence of $\geqslant$ on the $\geqslant_i$. However, interdependencies among the factors will often preclude such a simple resolution.

HISTORICAL REMARKS. During the rise of marginal utility analysis in the latter part of the 19th century (Stigler, 1950), the utility of each commodity bundle in a set $X = X_1 \times X_2 \times \cdots \times X_n$ was thought of as an intuitively measurable quantity. Founders such as Jevons, Menger and Walras regarded x as preferred to y precisely when $u(x)$, the utility of x, is greater than $u(y)$. Their analytic approach ignored interdependencies since they used the independent additive utility form $u(x) = u_1(x_1) + \cdots + u_n(x_n)$.

Later writers such as Edgeworth, Fisher, Pareto and Slutsky discarded the additive decomposition for the general interdependent form $u(x_1, x_2, \ldots, x_n)$. Their ordinalist view of utilities as a mere reflection of a preference ordering remains dominant, and they considered interactive effects among goods, such as complementarities and substitutabilities. A fine example of interdependent analysis appears in Fisher (1892).

Fisher was also one of the first people to mention explicitly the interpersonal effect on individual utility (Stigler, 1950, p. 324). This occurs when one's utility and consequent demand depend on other people's consumption and could generally be expressed by $u_i(x_1, \ldots, x_n)$ as consumer i's utility when x_j denotes the commodity bundle of consumer j. Pigou (1903) considered the interpersonal effect in modest detail, and Duesenberry (1949) explored it in greater depth, but it has never been a prominent concern in economic theory.

Early examples of the synthetic approach in social choice theory come from Borda and Condorcet in the late 1700s. They asked: Given a list of voter preference rankings on a set X of $m \geqslant 3$ nominees, what is the best way of selecting a winner? Borda's answer was to assign $m, m-1, \ldots, 1$ points to each first, second, ..., last place nominee in the rankings and to elect the nominee with the largest point total. Condorcet advocated the election of a nominee who is preferred by a simple majority of voters to each other nominee in pairwise comparisons. Black (1958) contains an excellent review of their work and the proposals of later writers. The debate over good election methods continues today (Brams and Fishburn, 1983).

The turning point for social choice theory was Arrow's (1951) discovery that a few appealing conditions for aggregating individual preference orders on three or more candidates into social preference orders were jointly incompatible. The avalanche of research set off by Arrow's discovery is represented in part by Sen (1970, 1977), Fishburn (1973), Pattanaik (1971) and Kelly (1978).

In the area of risky decision theory, we envision a risky alternative as a probability distribution x on potential outcomes in a set C and observe that such decisions involve multiple factors since they entail both changes and outcomes. Bernoulli (1738) argued that a reasonable person will choose a risky alternative from a set X of distributions that maximizes his expected utility $\Sigma x(c)u(c)$. He proposed that u be assessed without reference to change since he held an intuitive measurability view of utility. Consequently, his approach is wholly synthetic.

Little changed in the foundations of risky decisions during the next two centuries. Then, in a complete turnabout, von Neumann and Morgenstern (1944) introduced the analytic approach by beginning with a preference relation $\gg$ on X. Axioms for $\gg$ on X were shown to imply the existence of a real valued function u on C such that, for all x and y in X, $x \gg y$ precisely when x has greater expected utility than y, and u is to be assessed on the basis of comparisons between distributions. With a few exceptions, most notably Allais (1953), subsequent research has adopted the von Neumann–Morgenstern approach.

In the rest of this essay we comment further on multiattribute preferences under 'certainty', interdependent preferences in risky decisions and social choice theory.

MULTIATTRIBUTE PREFERENCES. We assume throughout this section that $\gg$ is a strict preference relation on $X = X_1 \times X_2 \times \cdots \times X_n$. A given X_i could represent amounts of commodity i, consumption bundles available to person i, levels of income and/or consumption in period i, or values that elements in X might have for criterion i. Also let u on X and u_i denote real valued functions.

A non-empty proper subset N of $\{1, 2, \ldots, n\}$ is defined to be $\gg$-*independent* if, for all x_N and y_N in the product of the X_i over N and for all $z_{(N)}$ in the product of the X_i over i *not* in N,

$$(x_N, z_{(N)}) \gg (y_N, z_{(N)}) \Leftrightarrow (x_N, w_{(N)}) \gg (y_N, w_{(N)}).$$

Most research for $\gg$ on X involves $\gg$-independence for some N, but this need not exclude elementary notions of preference interdependencies. Two models that presume all N to be $\gg$-independent are the additive model (see Krantz, Luce, Suppes and Tversky, 1971)

$$x \gg y \Leftrightarrow u_1(x_1) + \cdots + u_n(x_n) > u_1(y_1) + \cdots + u_n(y_n),$$

and the lexicographic model (Fishburn, 1974a) that places a value hierarchy on the factors.

Relationships between factors in the additive model and the more general model $x \gg y \Leftrightarrow u(x) > u(y)$ with u continuous, are often characterized by indifference maps or iso-utility contours. Interdependence arises in the lexicographic model from the fact that a small change in one factor overwhelms all changes in factors that are lower in the hierarchy.

Situations in which only some of the N are $\gg$-independent are reviewed by Keeney and Raiffa (1976, ch. 3) and Krantz, Luce, Suppes and Tversky (1971, ch. 7). Among other things, these models allow complete reversals in preferences over one factor at different fixed levels of the other factors. This, of course, is a very strong form of interdependence under which all N may fail to be $\gg$-independent.

Other general models for interdependent preferences are discussed by Fishburn

(1972) for finite sets, and by Dyer and Sarin (1979) when u is viewed in the intuitive measurability way.

Models that explicitly incorporate the interpersonal effect in economic analysis have been investigated by Pollak (1976) and Wind (1976), among others. Pollak explores the influence of several versions of interdependence among individuals on short-run and long-run consumption within a group. Using models of demand that are locally linear in others' past consumption, he concludes that the distribution of income need not be a determinant of long-run per capita consumption patterns. Wind's work is representative of empirical approaches to the influence of others on an individual's choice behaviour.

RISKY DECISIONS. Interdependent preferences in risky decisions fall into two categories. The first concerns special forms for $u(c) = u(c_1, c_2, \ldots, c_n)$ in the context of von Neumann–Morgenstern expected utility theory when the outcome set C is a subset of a product set $C_1 \times C_2 \times \cdots \times C_n$. The second focus on changes in the basic model that occur when the independence axiom that gives rise to the expected utility form $\Sigma x(c)u(c)$ is relaxed or dropped.

Decompositions of $u(c_1, c_2, \ldots, c_n)$ in the expected utility model have been axiomatized by various people. Reviews and extensions of much of this work appear in Keeney and Raiffa (1976) and Farquhar (1978). The simplest independent decompositions are the additive form and a multiplicative form. The first of these requires x and y to be indifferent whenever the marginal distributions of x and y on X_i are the same for every i. The multiplicative form arises when, for each non-empty proper subset N of $\{1, \ldots, n\}$, the preference order over marginal distributions on the product of the C_i for i in N, conditioned on fixed values of the other factors, does not depend on those fixed values.

An example of a more involved interdependent decomposition is the two-factor model (Fishburn and Farquhar, 1982) $u(c_1, c_2) = f_1(c_1)g_1(c_2) + \cdots + f_m(c_1)g_m(c_2) + h(c_1)$, which clearly allows a variety of interactive effects.

In the basic formulation for expected utility, assume that X is closed under convex combinations $\lambda x + (1 - \lambda)y$ with $0 < \lambda < 1$ and x and y in X. The *independence axiom* for expected utility asserts that, for all x, y and z in X and all $0 < \lambda < 1$,

$$x \gg y \Rightarrow \lambda x + (1 - \lambda)z \gg \lambda y + (1 - \lambda)z.$$

Systematic violations of this axiom uncovered in experiments by Allais (1953), Kahneman and Tversky (1979) and MacCrimmon and Larsson (1979) among others, have led to new theories of risky decisions (Kahneman and Tversky, 1979; Machina, 1982; Chew, 1983; Fishburn, 1982) that do not assume independence. Machina (1982) proposes a model that approximates expected utility locally but not globally. Fishburn (1982) weakens the usual transitivity and independence assumptions to obtain a non-separable model $x \gg y \Leftrightarrow \phi(x, y) > 0$ that allows preference cycles.

124

Related interdependent generalizations of Savage's subjective expected utility model for decisions under uncertainty are developed by Loomes and Sugden (1982) and Schmeidler (1984).

SOCIAL CHOICE. Many problems in social choice theory are related to Condorcet's phenomenon of cyclical majorities. This phenomenon occurs when voters have transitive preferences yet every nominee is defeated by another nominee under simple majority comparisons. The simplest example has three nominees and three voters with $x \gg_1 y \gg_1 z$, $z \gg_2 x \gg_2 y$ and $y \gg_3 z \gg_3 x$; x beats y, y beats z, and z beats x. Borda's point-summation procedure can fail to satisfy Condorcet's majority-choice principle, and it is notoriously sensitive to strategic voting. Moreover, all summation procedures based on decreasing weights for positions in voters' rankings are sensitive to nominees who have absolutely no chance of winning, but whose presence can affect the outcome.

Various problems and paradoxes for multicandidate elections that arise from combinatorial aspects of synthetic methods are discussed by Fishburn (1974b), Niemi and Riker (1976), Saari (1982) and Fishburn and Brams (1983). Analyses of strategic voting, which suggest that no sensible election method is immune from manipulation by falsification of preferences, are reviewed in Kelly (1978) and Pattanaik (1978).

Arrow's (1951) theorem offers a striking generalization of Condorcet's cyclical majorities phenomenon. Suppose X contains three or more nominees, each of n voters can have any preference ranking on X, and an aggregate ranking $\gg = f(\gg_1, \gg_2, \ldots, \gg_n)$ is desired for each list $(\gg_1, \gg_2, \ldots, \gg_n)$ of individual rankings. The question addressed by Arrow is whether there is any way of doing this that satisfies the following three conditions for all x and y in X:

(1) Pareto optimality: if $x \gg_i y$ for all i, then $x > y$;

(2) Binary independence: the aggregate preference between x and y depends solely on the voters' preferences between x and y;

(3) Non-dictatorship: there is no i such that $x \gg y$ whenever $x \gg_i y$. Arrow's theorem says that it is impossible to satisfy all three conditions.

Several dozen related impossibility theorems have subsequently been developed by others. Many of these are noted in Kelly (1978) and Pattanaik (1978). As well as multi-profile theorems, like Arrow's, that use different lists of preference rankings to demonstrate impossibility, there are single-profile theorems (Roberts, 1980) that use only one list with sufficient variety in the rankings to establish impossibility.

Impossibility theorems, voting paradoxes and results on strategic manipulation highlight the difficulty of designing good election procedures. Recent research to alleviate such problems (Dasgupta, Hammond and Maskin, 1979; Laffont and Moulin, 1982) focuses on the design of preference-revelation mechanisms (generalized ballots) and aggregation procedures that encourage people to vote in such a way that the outcome will agree with some theoretically best decision based on the true but unknown preferences of the voters. Other word, such as that on approval voting (Brams and Fishburn, 1983), continues to search for simple synthetic methods that minimize the problems that beset these methods.

BIBLIOGRAPHY

Allais, M. 1953. Le comportement de l'homme rationnel devant de risque: critique des postulats et axiomes de l'école Américaine. *Econometrica* 21, 503–46.

Arrow, K.J. 1951. *Social Choice and Individual Values.* New York: Wiley. 2nd edn, 1963.

Bernoulli, D. 1738. Specimen theoriae novae de mensura sortis. *Commentarii Academiae Scientarium Imperialis Petropolitanae* 5, 175–92. Trans. by L. Sommer as 'Exposition of a new theory on the measurement of risk', *Econometrica* 22 (1954), 23–36.

Black, D. 1958. *The Theory of Committees and Elections.* Cambridge: Cambridge University Press.

Brams, S.J. and Fishburn, P.C. 1983. *Approval Voting.* Boston: Birkhäuser.

Chew, S.H. 1983. A generalization of the quasilinear mean with applications to the measurement of income inequality and decision theory resolving the Allais paradox. *Econometrica* 51, 1065–92.

Dasgupta, P., Hammond, P. and Maskin, E. 1979. The implementation of social choice rules: some general results on incentive compatibility. *Review of Economic Studies* 46, 185–216.

Duesenberry, J.S. 1949. *Income, Saving, and the Theory of Consumer Behavior.* Cambridge, Mass.: Harvard University Press.

Dyer, J.S. and Sarin, R.K. 1979. Measurable multiattribute value functions. *Operations Research* 27, 810–22.

Farquhar, P.H. 1978. Interdependent criteria in utility analysis. In *Multiple Criteria Problem Solving*, ed. S. Zionts, Berlin: Springer-Verlag, 131–80.

Fishburn, P.C. 1972. Interdependent preferences on finite sets. *Journal of Mathematical Psychology* 9, 225–36.

Fishburn, P.C. 1973. *The Theory of Social Choice.* Princeton: Princeton University Press.

Fishburn, P.C. 1974a. Lexicographic orders, utilities, and decision rules: a survey. *Management Science* 20, 1442–71.

Fishburn, P.C. 1974b. Paradoxes of voting. *American Political Science Review* 68, 537–46.

Fishburn, P.C. 1982. Nontransitive measurable utility. *Journal of Mathematical Psychology* 26, 31–67.

Fishburn, P.C. and Brams, S.J. 1983. Paradoxes of preferential voting. *Mathematics Magazine* 56, 207–14.

Fishburn, P.C. and Farquhar, P.H. 1982. Finite-degree utility independence. *Mathematics of Operations Research* 7, 348–53.

Fisher, I. 1892. Mathematical investigations in the theory of values and prices. *Transactions of the Conneticut Academy of Arts and Sciences* 9, 1–124. Reprinted, New York: Augustus M. Kelley, 1965.

Kahneman, D. and Tversky, A. 1979. Prospect theory: an analysis of decision under risk. *Econometrica* 47, 263–91.

Keeney, R.L. and Raiffa, H. 1976. *Decisions with Multiple Objectives: preferences and value tradeoffs.* New York: Wiley.

Kelly, J.S. 1978. *Arrow Impossibility Theorems.* New York: Academic Press.

Krantz, D.H., Luce, R.D., Suppes, P. and Tversky, A. 1971. *Foundations of Measurement.* Volume I: *Additive and Polynomial Representations.* New York: Academic Press.

Laffont, J.-J. and Moulin, H. (eds) 1982. Special issue on implementation. *Journal of Mathematical Economics* 10(1).

Loomes, G. and Sugden, R. 1982. Regret theory: an alternative theory of rational choice under uncertainty. *Economic Journal* 92, 805–24.

MacCrimmon, K.R. and Larsson, S. 1979. Utility theory: axioms versus 'paradoxes'. In *Expected Utility Hypotheses and the Allais Paradox*, ed. M. Allais and O. Hagen, Dordrecht: Reidel, 333–409.

Machina, M.J. 1982. 'Expected utility' analysis without the independence axiom. *Econometrica* 50, 277–323.

Niemi, R.G. and Riker, W.H. 1976. The choice of voting systems. *Scientific American* 234, 21–7.

Pattanaik, P.K. 1971. *Voting and Collective Choice*. Cambridge and New York: Cambridge University Press.

Pattanaik, P.K. 1978. *Strategy and Group Choice*. Amsterdam: North-Holland.

Pigou, A.C. 1903. Some remarks on utility. *Economic Journal* 13, 58–68.

Pollak, R.A. 1976. Interdependent preferences. *American Economic Review* 66, 309–20.

Roberts, K.W.S. 1980. Social choice theory: the single-profile and multi-profile approaches. *Review of Economic Studies* 47, 441–50.

Saari, D.G. 1982. Inconsistencies of weighted summation voting systems. *Mathematics of Operations Research* 7, 479–90.

Schmeidler, D. 1984. Subjective probability and expected utility without additivity. Preprint # 84, Institute for Mathematics and its Application, University of Minnesota.

Sen, A.K. 1970. *Collective Choice and Social Welfare*. San Francisco: Holden-Day.

Sen, A.K. 1977. Social choice theory: a re-examination. *Econometrica* 45, 53–89.

Stigler, G.J. 1950. The development of utility theory, Part I and II. *Journal of Political Economy* 58, 307–27, 373–96.

von Neumann, J. and Morgenstern, O. 1944. *Theory of Games and Economic Behavior*. Princeton: Princeton University Press. 2nd edn, 1947; 3rd edn, 1953.

Wind, Y. 1976. Preference of relevant others and individual choice models. *Journal of Consumer Research* 3, 50–7.

Interpersonal Utility Comparisons

JOHN C. HARSANYI

Suppose I am left with a ticket to a Mozart concert I am unable to attend and decide to give it to one of my closest friends. Which friend should I actually give it to? One thing I will surely consider in deciding this is which friend of mine would enjoy the concert *most*. More generally, when we decide as private individuals whom to help, or decide as voters or as public officials who are to receive government help, *one* natural criterion we use is who would derive the greatest benefit, that is, who would derive the *highest utility*, from this help. But to answer this last question we must make, or at least attempt to make, *interpersonal utility comparisons*.

At the common-sense level, all of us make such interpersonal comparisons. But philosophical reflection might make us uneasy about their meaning and validity. We have direct introspective access only to our *own* mental processes (such as our preferences and our feelings of satisfaction and dissatisfaction) defining our *own* utility function, but have only very indirect information about other people's mental processes. Many economists and philosophers take the view that our limited information about other people's minds renders it impossible for us to make meaningful interpersonal comparisons of utility.

COMPARISONS OF UTILITY LEVELS VS. COMPARISONS OF UTILITY DIFFERENCES. In any case, if such comparisons are possible at all, then we must distinguish between interpersonal comparisons of utility *levels* and interpersonal comparisons of utility *differences* (i.e. utility increments or decrements).

It is one thing to compare the utility level $U_i(A)$ that individual i enjoys (or would enjoy) in situation A, with utility level $U_j(B)$ that another individual j enjoys (or would enjoy) in situation B (where A and B may or may not refer to the same situation). It is a very different thing to make interpersonal comparisons

128

between utility differences, such as comparing the utility increment

$$\Delta U_i(A, A') = U_i(A') - U_i(A) \tag{1}$$

that individual i would enjoy in moving from situation A to situation A', with the utility increment

$$\Delta U_j(B, B') = U_j(B') - U_j(B) \tag{2}$$

that individual j would enjoy in moving from B to B'. Either kind of interpersonal comparison might be possible without the other kind being possible (Sen, 1970).

Some ethical theories would require one kind of interpersonal comparisons, others would require the other. Thus, *utilitarianism* must assume the interpersonal comparability of utility *differences* because it asks us to maximize a social utility function (social welfare function) defined as the *sum* of all individual utilities. (There are arguments for defining social utility as the *arithmetic mean*, rather than the *sum*, of individual utilities (Harsanyi, 1955). But for most purposes – other than analysing population policies – the two definitions are equivalent because if the number of individuals can be taken for a *constant*, then maximizing the sum of utilities is mathematically equivalent to maximizing their arithmetic mean.) Yet, we cannot add different people's utilities unless all of them are expressed in the same utility units; and in order to decide whether this is the case, we must engage in interpersonal comparisons of utility *differences*. (On the other hand, utilitarianism does not require comparisons of different people's utility *levels* because it does not matter whether their utilities are measured from comparable zero points or not.)

Likewise, the interpersonal utility comparisons we make in everyday life are most of the time comparisons of utility *differences*. For instance, the comparisons made in our example between the utilities that different people would derive from a concert obviously involve comparing utility differences.

In contrast, the utility-based version of Rawls's *Theory of Justice* (1971) does require interpersonal comparisons of utility *levels*, but does not require comparisons of utility *differences*. This is so because his theory uses the *maximin principle* (he calls it the *difference principle*) in evaluating the economic performance of each society, in the sense of using the well-being of the *worst-off* individual (or the worst-off social group) as its principal criterion. But to decide which individuals (or social groups) are worse off then others he must compare different people's utility levels. (In earlier publications, Rawls seemed to define the worst-off individual as one with the lowest utility level. But in later publications, he defined him as one with the smallest amount of 'primary goods'. For a critique of Rawl's theory, see Harsanyi, 1975.)

ORDINALISM, CARDINALISM AND INTERPERSONAL COMPARISONS. In studying comparisons between the utilities enjoyed by *one* particular individual i, we again have to distinguish between comparisons of utility *levels* and comparisons of utility *differences*. The former would involve comparing the utility levels $U_i(A)$ and $U_i(B)$ that i assigns to two different situations A and B. The latter would involve comparing the utility increment

$$\Delta U_i(A, A') = U_i(A') - U_i(A) \tag{3}$$

that i would enjoy in moving from situation A to situation A', with the utility increment

$$\Delta U_i(B, B') = U_i(B') - U_i(B) \tag{4}$$

that he would enjoy in moving from B to B'.

If i has a well-defined utility function U_i at all, then he certainly must be able to compare the utility *levels* he assigns to various situations; and such comparisons will have a clear behavioural meaning because they will correspond to the preference and indifference relations expressed by his choice behaviour. In contrast, it is immediately less obvious whether comparing utility *differences* as defined under (3) and (4) has any economic meaning (but see below).

A utility function U_i permitting meaningful comparisons *only* between i's utility levels, but *not* permitting such comparisons between his utility differences, is called *ordinal*; whereas a utility function permitting meaningful comparisons *both* between his utility levels and his utility differences is called *cardinal*.

As is well known, most branches of economic theory use only ordinal utilities. But, as von Neumann and Morgenstern (1947) have shown, cardinal utility functions can play a very useful role in the theory of risk taking. In fact, utility-difference comparisons based on von Neumann–Morgenstern utility functions turn out to have a direct behavioural meaning. For example, suppose that U_i is such a utility function, and let Δ_i^* and Δ_i^{**} be utility differences defined by (3) and (4). Then, the inequality $\Delta_i^* > \Delta_i^{**}$ will be algebraically equivalent to the inequality

$$\tfrac{1}{2}U_i(A') + \tfrac{1}{2}U_i(B) > \tfrac{1}{2}U_i(B') + \tfrac{1}{2}U_i(A). \tag{5}$$

This inequality in turn will have the behavioural interpretation that i *prefers* an equi-probability mixture of A' and of B to an equi-probability mixture of B' and of A. Of course, once von Neumann–Morgenstern utility functions are used in the theory of risk taking, they become available for possible use also in other branches of economic theory, including welfare economics as well as in ethical investigations. (It has been argued that von Neumann–Morgenstern utility functions have no place in ethics (or in welfare economics) because they merely express people's attitudes toward *gambling*, which has no moral significance (Arrow, 1951, p. 10; and Rawls, 1971, pp. 172 and 323). But see Harsanyi, 1984.)

Note that by taking an ordinalist or a cardinalist position, one restricts the positions one can consistently take as to interpersonal comparability of utilities:

(1) An *ordinalist* is logically free to *reject* both types of interpersonal comparisons. Or he may *admit* comparisons of different people's utility *levels*. But he *cannot* admit the interpersonal comparability of utility differences without becoming a cardinalist. (The reason is this. If the utility differences experienced by one individual i are comparable with those experienced by *another* individual

130

i, this will make the utility differences experienced by *one* individual (say) i, likewise indirectly comparable with one another, which will enable us to construct a *cardinal* utility function for each individual.)

(2) A *cardinalist* is likewise logically free to *reject* both types of interpersonal comparisons. Or he may *admit* both. Or else he may admit interpersonal comparisons only for utility *differences*. (Though it is hard to see why anybody might want to reject interpersonal comparisons for utility levels if he admitted them for utility differences.) But he *cannot* consistently admit interpersonal comparisons for utility *levels* while rejecting them for utility *differences*. (This can be verified as follows. If utility levels are interpersonally comparable, then we can find four situations A, A', B and B' such that $U_i(A) = U_j(B)$ and $U_j(A') = U_j(B')$. But then we can conclude that

$$\Delta_i^* = U_i(A') - U_i(A) = \Delta_j^* = U_j(B') - U_j(B),$$

which means that at least the utility differences Δ_i^* and Δ_j^* are interpersonally comparable. But since U_i and U_j are *cardinal* utility functions, any utility difference Δ_i^{**} experienced by i is comparable with Δ_i^*, and any utility difference Δ_j^{**} experienced by j is comparable with Δ_j^*. Yet this means that *all* utility differences Δ_i^{**} experienced by i are comparable with *all* utility differences Δ_j^{**} experienced by j. Thus, cardinalism together with interpersonal comparability of utility levels *entails* that of utility differences.)

EXTENDED UTILITY FUNCTIONS. In what follows, I will use the symbols $A_i, B_i, \ldots$ to denote the economic and non-economic resources available to individual i in situations $A, B, \ldots$. Moreover, I will use the symbol A_j to denote an arrangement under which j has the same resources available to him as were available to individual i under arrangement A_i. These entities $A_i, B_i, \ldots, A_j, B_j, \ldots$ I will call *positions*.

Interpersonal utility comparisons would pose no problem if all individuals had the *same* utility function. For in this case, any individual j could assume that the utility level $U_i(A_i)$ that another individual i would derive from a given position A_i should be the *same* as he himself would derive from a similar position. Thus, j could write simply

$$U_i(A_i) = U_j(A_j). \tag{6}$$

Of course, in actual fact, the utility of different people are rather *different* because people have different *tastes*, that is, they have different abilities to derive satisfactions from given resource endowments. I will use the symbols $R_i, R_j, \ldots$ to denote the vectors listing the personal psychological characteristics of each individual $i, j, \ldots$ that *explain* the differences among their utility functions $U_i, U_j, \ldots$. Presumably, these vectors summarize the effects that the genetic make-up, the education and the life experience of each individual have on his utility function. This means that any individual j can attempt to assess the utility level $U_i(A_i)$ that another individual j would enjoy in position A_i as

$$U_i(A_i) = V(A_i, R_i) \tag{7}$$

where the function V represents the psychological laws determining the utility functions $U_i, U_j, \ldots$ of the various individuals $i, j, \ldots$ in accordance with their psychological parameters specified by the vectors $R_i, R_j, \ldots$. Since, by assumption, all differences among the various individuals' utility functions $U_i, U_j, \ldots$ are fully explained by the vectors $R_j, R_j, \ldots$, the function V itself will be the same for all individuals. We will call V an *extended utility function*. (See Arrow, 1978; and Harsanyi, 1977, pp. 51–60; though the basic ideas are contained already in Arrow, 1951, pp. 114–15.)

To be sure, we know very little about the psychological laws determining people's utility functions and, therefore, know very little about the true mathematical form of the extended utility function V. This means that, when we try to use equation (7), the best we can do is to use our – surely very imperfect – personal *estimate* of V, rather than V itself. As a result, in trying to make interpersonal utility comparisons, we must expect to make significant errors from time to time – in particular when we are trying to assess the utility functions of people with a very different cultural and social background from our own. But even if our judgements of interpersonal comparisons can easily be *mistaken*, this does not imply that they are *meaningless*.

Ordinalists will interpret both the functions U_i and the function V as *ordinal* utility functions and will interpret (7) merely as a warrant for interpersonal comparisons of utility *levels* (cf. Arrow, 1978). In contrast, cardinalists will interpret all these as *cardinal* utility functions and will interpret (7) as a warrant for *both* kinds of interpersonal comparison (cf. Harsanyi, 1977).

LIMITS TO INTERPERSONAL COMPARISONS. It seems to me that economists and philosophers influenced by *logical positivism* have greatly exaggerated the difficulties we face in making interpersonal utility comparisons with respect to the utilities and the disutilities that people derive from ordinary commodities and, more generally, from the ordinary pleasures and calamities of human life. (A very influential opponent of the possibility of meaningful interpersonal utility comparisons has been Robbins, 1932.) But when we face the problem of judging the utilities and the disutilities that other people derive from various *cultural* activities, we do seem to run into very real, and sometimes perhaps even unsurmountable, difficulties. For example, suppose I observe a group of people who claim to derive great aesthetic enjoyment from a very esoteric form of abstract art, which does not have the slightest appeal to me in spite of my best efforts to understand it. Then, there may be no way for me to decide whether the admirers of this art form *really* derive very great and genuine enjoyment from it, or merely *deceive themselves* by claiming that they do.

Maybe in such cases interpersonal comparisons of utility do reach unsurmountable obstacles. But, fortunately, very few of our personal moral decisions and of our public political decisions depend on such exceptionally difficult interpersonal comparisons of utility. (References additional to those listed below will be found in Hammond, 1977 and in Suppes and Winet, 1955.)

BIBLIOGRAPHY

Arrow, K.J. 1951. *Social Choice and Individual Values.* 2nd edn, New York: Wiley, 1963.

Arrow, K.J. 1978. Extended sympathy and the possibility of social choice. *Philosophia* 7, 223–37.

Hammond, P.J. 1977. Dual interpersonal comparisons of utility and the welfare economics of income distribution. *Journal of Public Economics* 7, 51–71.

Harsanyi, J.C. 1955. Cardinal utility, individualistic ethics, and interpersonal comparisons of utility. *Journal of Political Economy* 63, 309–21. Reprinted as ch. 2 of Harsanyi (1977).

Harsanyi, J.C. 1975. Can the maximin principle serve as a basis for morality? A critique of John Rawls theory. *American Political Science Review* 69, 594–606. Reprinted as ch. 4 of Harsanyi (1977).

Harsanyi, J.C. 1976. *Essays on Ethics, Social Behaviour and Scientific Explanation.* Dordrecht: Reidel.

Harsanyi, J.C. 1977. *Rational Behaviour and Bargaining Equilibrium in Games and Social Situations.* Cambridge and New York: Cambridge University Press.

Harsanyi, J.C. 1984. Von Neumannn–Morgenstern utilities, risk taking, and welfare. In *Arow and the Ascent of Modern Economic Theory*, ed. G.R. Feiwel, New York: New York University Press, 545–58.

Rawls, J. 1971. *A Theory of Justice.* Cambridge, Mass.: Harvard University Press.

Robbins, L. 1932. *An Essay on the Nature and Significance of Economic Science.* London: Macmillan.

Sen, A.K. 1970. *Collective Choice and Social Welfare.* San Francisco: Holden-Day.

Suppes, P. and Winet, M. 1955. An axiomatization of utility based on the notion of utility differences. *Management Science* 1, 259–70.

Von Neumann, J. and Morgenstern, O. 1947. *Theory of Games and Economic Behaviour.* 2nd edn, Princeton: Princeton University Press.

Lexicographic Orderings

C. BLACKORBY

Lexicographic orderings are orderings in which certain elements of the space being ordered have been selected for special treatment. I begin with an example. Suppose an agent has an ordering over commodities a and b. Although he or she likes both a and b, any bundle which has more of a is *preferred* to any bundle which has less of a. Of course among bundles which have the same amount of a, bundles with more b are preferred to those with less. Thus, there are no trade-offs between a and b and each indifference set is a single point. The name 'lexicographic' comes from the way words are ordered in a dictionary, alphabetically by the first letter and then the second and so on.

Lexicographic orderings were known chiefly as simple examples of orderings which *could not* be represented by a continuous real-valued function, see Debreu (1954) for the first discussion of this issue in economics. It is, however, in social choice theory and welfare economics where these orderings have come to prominence. To demonstrate their role a lexicographic maximin rule (leximin) follows. Let $u = (u_1, \ldots, u_N)$ be an element of a Euclidean N-space where u_n is the utility of person n. In each possible state of the world, say $\bar{u}_1 = (\bar{u}_1, \ldots, \bar{u}_N)$, let $r(\bar{u})$ be the person who is the rth best off. For example, if $N = 3$ and $\bar{u} = (2, 7, 3)$, then $1(\bar{u}) = 2$, as person 2 has the highest utility, $2(\bar{u}) = 3$, and $3(u) = 1$; ties are broken arbitrarily. An ordering R is a leximin rule if and only if for all $(u, \bar{u})$, $\bar{u}P\bar{u}$ if and only if there exists a k, $1 \leqslant k \leqslant N$, such that $\bar{u}_{k(u)} > \bar{u}_{k(u)}$ and for all $j > k, \bar{u}_{j(u)} = \bar{u}_{j(u)}$ where P is the strict preference relation, the asymmetric factor of R. That is, if the worst-off $N - k$ people have the same utility levels in $\bar{u}$ and $\bar{u}$ and the next worst-off person, k, is better off in $\bar{u}$ than in $\bar{u}$, then $\bar{u}$ is preferred to $\bar{u}$. Continuing the numerical example above, let $\bar{u} = (2, 7, 2.5)$ so that $1(\bar{u}) = 2$, $2(\bar{u}) = 3$, and $3(\bar{u}) = 1$. Then $k = 2$, $\bar{u}_{2(u)} = 3 > \bar{u}_{2(u)}$ and $\bar{u}_{3(u)} = 2 = \bar{u}_{3(u)}$, hence $\bar{u}P\bar{u}$.

It is important to notice that if each person's utility function were subjected to the same increasing transformation the above ordering would not change. This is a case where utility is ordinally measurable but fully comparable as levels

134

of utility can be compared across individuals. That the leximin rule satisfies all of the original axioms of Arrow (1951) except for the comparability of levels of utility was first worked out by D'Aspremont and Gevers (1977).

Other types of lexicographic orderings appear frequently in social choice theory; see section 6 of Sen (1986).

BIBLIOGRAPHY

Arrow, K.J. 1951. *Social Choice and Individual Values.* New York: Wiley. 2nd edn, 1963.

D'Aspremont, C. and Gevers, L. 1977. Equity and the informational basis of collective choice. *Review of Economic Studies* 44, June, 199–209.

Debreu, G. 1954. Representation of a preference ordering by a numerical function. In *Decision Processes*, ed. R. Thrall, C. Coombs and R. Davis, New York: Wiley, 159–65.

Sen, A.K. 1986. Social choice theory. In *Handbook of Mathematical Economics*, Vol. 3, ed. K. Arrow and M. Intriligator, Amsterdam and New York: North-Holland, 1073–182.

Myopic Decision Rules

MORDECAI KURZ

In a dynamic context a decision maker at any instant t has information about his exogenous economic environment both at time t and at later dates. We represent the environment at t by a vector $x(t)$ of exogenous variables, and their future values by $(x(t+1), x(t+2), \ldots, x(t+T))$. The horizon T is determined by such considerations as length of life, technology, resource limitations etc.; it might be infinite. A decision rule at time t is a map ψ_t associating with a vector of a variables z, the variable d representing the choice of the decision maker. We write $d = \psi_t(z)$. *Myopic decision rules* refer to those maps of the form $d(t) = \psi_t(x(t))$ in which $d(t)$ depends only upon the values of the exogenous variables at time t, disregarding any information about future conditions of the economic environment. A decision rule is said to be *non-myopic* if it is of the form $d(t) = \psi_t(x(t), x(t=1), \ldots, x(t+T))$.

As an example, consider the consumer who wants to maximize the utility function $U_i(c(t), c(t+1), \ldots, c(t+T))$ subject to a budget constraint defined by a vector $(\omega(t), \omega(t+1), \ldots, \omega(t+T))$ of endowments and $(p(t), p(t+1), \ldots, p(t+T))$ of prices. A consumption function like $c(t) = \phi_t(\omega(t), p(t))$ is a myopic choice function whereas a decision function like $c_t = \phi_t(\omega(t), p(t), \omega(t+1), p(t+1), \ldots, \omega(t+T), p(t+T))$ is non-myopic. It is clear from these definitions that myopic decision rules ignore all intertemporal substitution possibilities which may arise from uneven resource distribution, changing needs or prices over time, whereas non-myopic decision rules call upon the decision maker to consider simultaneously all his limitations over the entire relevant period $(t, t+T)$ and make optimal intertemporal substitutions based on his constraints.

HISTORICAL REVIEW. Non-myopic behaviour of firms was the standard means by which capital theory was developed in the 19th and early 20th century. The typical model of the firm identified it with an investment programme and assumed that the firm seeks to maximize the present value of its profits by selecting an optimal stream of actions. In formulating the problem, the optimal decision of the firm at any date depends upon endowments, prices and technology at all dates. A far more complex view was taken of the consumer. With incompletely developed utility theory, economic theorists in the late 19th century developed only implicit non-myopic decision rules. Böhm-Bawerk (1889) clearly analysed the intertemporal choices of a non-myopic consumer and his 'grounds' for time preference and – although confusing technology, preferences and equilibrium conditions – clearly attempted to identify the preferences which would lead to non-myopic decisions of a consumer. Non-myopic consumers may be found in the writings of most early capital theorists; however, the most complete early formulation of non-myopic decisions of consumers and firms was provided by Fisher (1930). It is his model that has remained the foundation of most discrete time models of intertemporal allocations.

Non-myopic decision models of economic agents arise almost always in the context of microeconomic analysis. It is noteworthy that the greatest thrust of myopic decision rules was associated with the development of Keynesian macroeconomics in the 1930s and extended into the growth theory of Harrod (1939), Domar (1946) and Solow (1956). The common formulation of these models held that all economic agents – consumers, producers and investors – select at any date t decision functions which depend only upon economic variables at date t. This gives rise, for example, to an aggregate consumption function such as $c(Y(t), r(t))$, which states that current aggregate consumption depends upon aggregate income $Y(t)$ and the interest rate $r(t)$. Although Keynes's writings demonstrate a deep understanding of the importance of expectations and other intertemporal considerations, the resulting macroeconomics which emerged was founded on entirely myopic decision rules. The two common explanations given to the formulation of myopic decision rules originate in issues of rationality and market imperfection. The first is a simple case of bounded rationality which results in extreme discounting of the future. The second explanation is based on the idea that Keynesian theory is not a theory of perfect competition and perfect price flexibility, rather, it must be interpreted as reflecting economic conditions in which price rigidity, rationing and quantity constraints are operative in various markets so that intertemporal substitutions are not generally feasible. This is particularly true for individuals with liquidity constraints. When such restrictions are operative, a consumer, a producer or an investor can respond only to contemporaneous variables and cannot respond to future changes in prices or endowments.

Even through the period in which Keynesian macroeconomics provided the dominant intellectual tone, non-myopic models of behaviour were being developed. They became very influential through Ramsey (1928) on optimal intertemporal allocations, Modigliani and Brumberg (1954) on the life-cycle hypothesis and Friedman (1957) on the permanent income hypothesis. These contributions laid the foundations for modern thinking about intertemporal substitution and non-myopic decisions. In general, during the postwar period it was the study of consumer and investment behaviour which provided the arena for the debate: non-myopic decision models were derived mostly by micro-theorists whereas both empirical researchers and macroeconomists tended to adopt more myopic decision rules. Apart from the Keynesian justification for myopic decision rules given above, two additional reasons were provided through this research, one empirical and the other conceptual. On the empirical side there is extensive evidence to suggest that individual consumption and investment are more sensitive to contemporaneous variables than would be implied by a non-myopic decision rule. On a more conceptual basis, an individual who wishes to make life-cycle plans must make his decision on the basis of his assessment of future events. Some of these events – like prices – might be observed on futures markets but others like future endowments, transfer payments or technology are uncertain and certainly unobservable by an economic analyst. Hence without some information about the non-observable conjectures of the decision maker about future events, it is not immediately clear how to identify empirically a consumer who follows non-myopic decision rules. In this connection, the 'permanent income hypothesis' may be viewed as a synthetic procedure which integrates the non-myopic nature of the consumer with his relative uncertainty about different components of his wealth (i.e. permanent versus transitory components of income).

In modern times, a further classification was made within the group of myopic decision making consumers by identifying the set of variables over which their utility function is defined. On the one hand there are the 'strict' life-cycle consumers whose utility extends only over consumption vectors consumed by them during their own life. On the other hand, when consumer interdependence is recognized with the extended family, non-myopic behaviour may be extended to allocations over present and future generations. Frequently the strict life-cycle hypothesis is modified by adding the total value of 'bequests' to the set of commodities over which the utility function is defined. Thus the utility function is written as $U(c(t), c(t+1), \ldots, c(t+T), B)$, where B is the value of bequests. Such extensions intend to accommodate an individual's concern for his extended family but is an unsatisfactory device. The fault of this formulation is seen from the fact that the decision rule which it implies is non-myopic over the life of the individual but entirely myopic with respect to dates beyond that. This myopia takes the form of insensitivity of this decision rule to future commodity prices, interest rates, endowments or technology.

MYOPIC DECISION RULES AND INTERTEMPORAL CONSISTENCY. When a non-myopic plan is formulated at time t, the decision maker will take into account all relevant variables $x(t), x(t+1), \ldots, x(t+T))$ and make a plan which will call for actions $(d(t), d(t+1), \ldots, d(t+T))$ to be taken at t and all subsequent dates up to time $t+T$. But now when data $t+\tau$ arrives will he carry out his plan $d(t+\tau)$ for this date? A consumer that would carry out his plans for dates $t+\tau$ for all $1 \leqslant \tau \leqslant T$ is said to be *intertemporally consistent*. In the original paper which raised this question, Strotz (1956) argued that, in general, consumers may not be intertemporally consistent. Alternatively, it was noted by Pollak (1968) that an optimizing individual could take into account future deviations from an initially chosen plan as a further constraint upon the set of feasible plans. For this reason a *sophisticated* planner was viewed by Pollak as an individual who takes into account these restrictions whereas a *naive* planner ignores them. It is clear that even a naive planner always carries out his plans for the first date of the plan. These distinctions lead to the identification of three types of allocations: those planned (and carried out) by a sophisticated planner, those planned by a naive planner and those actually carried out by a naive agent. Both Strotz and Pollak assumed utilities to be additively separable and the discount function to be stationary in the sense that it may be written in the form $\delta(s-t)$, where t is the decision date, s is the date of consumption and $s \geq t$ with $\delta(0) = 1$. Under these conditions, the known theorem is that consistency of plans is equivalent to the condition $\delta(t) = e^{-\delta t}$, where δ is a constant. In this case, all three types of allocations specified above are the same.

Blackorby et al. (1973) extend this concept and analysis to the more general case of nonseparable preferences. Furthermore, Hammond (1976) formally synthesizes this literature on exogenously-changing tastes with a related literature on endogenously changing tastes. Both articles formally demonstrate, for finitely-lived consumers, that inconsistency may arise only if at any time t the individual's ordering of consumption sequences which are identical up to time $t + \tau$ (but diverge thereafter) is different from the ordering of that individual at time $t + \tau$. Such preferences are, quite naturally, termed *inconsistent*. In general, consistent preferences give rise to intertemporally consistent plans for all possible budget constraints whereas inconsistent preferences induce consistent plans only in some special cases. Furthermore, unless preferences are consistent, neither naive nor sophisticated behaviour will, in general, maximize any preference ordering nor even satisfy the weak axiom of revealed preference.

INTERGENERATIONAL EQUILIBRIUM AND THE NEUTRALITY THEORY. The standard intergenerational allocation problem is formulated by specifying a sequence of generations each with its own endowment and preference. The crucial aspect of the problem is the interdependence in utilities where the utility of generation t depends upon the consumption, and, perhaps, the welfare level of generations of later dates. As a result of this interdependence, resources flow from generation t to generation $t + 1$. This structure is analogous to the intertemporal planning problem discussed earlier, since it is natural to think of an individual at different points in time as a different generation of an infinitely lived extended family. However, it is also clear that the concept of *consistent* planning highlights a fundamental flaw in models of the family as an individually rational agent, namely, that future generations will likely reconsider the consumption plan selected by their ancestors. Consequently, for an allocation to be regarded as a possible social outcome, it must satisfy this elementary consistency requirement among the individual decision rules. Since the model of the infinitely lived rational individual may not satisfy this condition, a different conceptual foundation must be introduced. The superior framework which corrects this flaw views the family as a sequence of players in a non-cooperative game. In an intergenerational equilibrium, each generation-player selects an optimal strategy of consumption and capital transfers given the strategies of the others. An equilibrium which is subgame perfect (see Selten, 1975) calls for strategies which satisfy the desired intergenerational consistency property. In this context the non-myopic decision rules are, in fact, non-myopic *strategies*.

The concept of intergenerational equilibrium was first proposed by Phelps and Pollak (1968) who studied it in the context of a simple aggregative model where the allowable strategies are savings functions which are linear in income and where preferences are additively separable. Subsequent contributions considered more general economies with broader strategy spaces. Although the aim of this research has been to provide a general theorem for the existence and characterization of perfect equilibrium (and thus a consistent plan) no such theorem has yet been proved. Significant progress has recently been achieved by Harris (1985).

The most controversial application of the theory of intergenerational equilibrium has been in the area of public policy. The Ricardian Equivalence theory holds that equilibrium utility allocations are invariant to changes in the method used to finance public expenditure. The idea of this theory is that no matter whether the public sector is financed by taxes or debt, the private allocation will be rearranged to neutralize any effect of public finance. This doctrine was recently reexamined by Barro (1974) in a formal model of an intergenerational equilibrium which postulated that preferences have a recursive representation. This means that the utility level of a member of generation t depends upon his own consumption and the utility level of his children, members of generation $t + 1$. Recursive representation is an important special case but such a representation exists only under very specialized conditions which are close to the concept of 'consistent preferences' discussed earlier. For this case, Barro was able to show that the existence of national debt had no real effect on the economy since for every specified method of public finance (debt versus taxes) there exists an intergenerational Nash equilibrium in which the utility allocation is the same as the utility distribution in the equilibrium without any public debt.

The proposed neutrality of public policy under non-myopic equilibrium strategies has dramatic consequences. It contrasts sharply with contemporary views that larger internal debts cause interest rates to increase. It is clear that these views are consistent with the theory which proposes that owing to intertemporal constraints individuals adopt myopic decision rules. Under myopic rules, increased internal debts would, in fact, cause interest rates to increase and private investments to be crowded out.

BIBLIOGRAPHY

Barro, R.J. 1974. Are government bonds net wealth? *Journal of Political Economy* 82(6), 1095–117.

Blackorby, C., Nissen, D., Primont, D. and Russell, R.R. 1973. Consistent intertemporal decision making. *Review of Economic Studies* 40, 239–48.

Böhm-Bawerk, E. von. 1889. *The Positive Theory of Capital*. Trans. William Smart, London: Macmillan, 1891.

Domar, E.D. 1946. Capital expansion, rate of growth, and employment. *Econometrica* 14, April, 137–47.

Fisher, I. 1930. *The Theory of Interest.* New York: Macmillan.

Friedman, M. 1957. *A Theory of the Consumption Function.* Princeton: Princeton University Press.

Hammond, P.J. 1976. Changing tastes and coherent dynamic choice. *Review of Economic Studies* 43, 159–73.

Harris, C. 1985. Existence and characterization of perfect equilibrium in games of perfect information. *Econometrica* 53, May, 613–28.

Harrod, R.F. 1939. An essay in dynamic theory. *Economic Journal* 49, March, 14–33.

Keynes, J. 1936. *The General Theory of Employment, Interest and Money.* London: Macmillan; New York: Harcourt, Brace & World, 1965.

Modigliani, F. and Brumberg, R. 1954. Utility analysis and the consumption function: an interpretation of cross-section data. In *Post-Keynesian Economics*, ed. K. Kurihara, New Brunswick, NJ: Rutgers University Press.

Phelps, E.S. and Pollak, R.A. 1968. On second-best national saving and game-equilibrium growth. *Review of Economic Studies* 35, 185–99.

Pollak, R. 1968. Consistent planning. *Review of Economic Studies* 35, 201–8.

Ramsey, F.P. 1928. A mathematical theory of saving. *Economic Journal* 38, 543–59.

Selten, R. 1975. Reexamination of the perfectness concept of equilibrium points in extensive games. *International Journal of Game Theory* 4, 25–55.

Solow, R.M. 1956. A contribution to the theory of economic growth. *Quarterly Journal of Econometrics* 70, February, 65–94.

Strotz, R. 1956. Myopia and inconsistency in dynamic utility maximization. *Review of Economic Studies* 23, 165–80.

Orderings

C. BLACKORBY

An ordering (also called a complete preordering or a weak ordering) is a binary relation which is reflexive, transitive and complete, that is, it is a preordering that is complete.

A binary relation R defined on a set S is a set of ordered pairs of elements of S, i.e., a subset of the cartesian product of S with itself, $S \times S$. One writes xRy (or $(x, y) \in R$) to mean that $x \in S$ stands in relation R to $y \in S$. An ordering is a binary relation, R, which satisfies three properties: (i) reflexivity: for all $x \in S$, xRx; (ii) transitivity: for x, y, $z \in S$, if xRy and yRx; and (iii) completeness for all x, $y \in S$, xRy or yRx, where 'or' is used in its non-exclusive sense.

A simple example results from letting S be the real line and R the greater than or equal to relation so that xRy if and only if $x \geq y$. The most common use of orderings in economics is in preference theory where S is a commodity space and R stands for 'at least as desirable as'. Every ordering can be separated into its symmetric and asymmetric factors, respectively, as follows:

$$xIy \quad \text{if and only if} \quad xRy \quad \text{and} \quad yRx$$

and

$$XPY \quad \text{if and only if} \quad xRy \quad \text{and not} \quad yRx.$$

In the case of preference theory, these correspond to indifference and strict preference relations.

In consumer theory orderings first appeared in the work of Wold (1943–4). In an attempt to put utility theory on a more solid foundation, Wold posited the existence of an ordering with certain properties and demonstrated that this could be represented by a continuous real-valued function, thus making absolutely clear that this was an ordinal concept. Perhaps the most innovative and useful aspect of Wold's argument was an insightful definition of a continuous ordering. (An ordering is continuous if the sets $\{x | xRy, y \in S\}$ and $\{x | yRx, y \in S\}$ are closed.)

The first modern treatment of the subject appears in Arrow (1951). Agents as well as society as a whole are characterized by their orderings over spaces of alternatives. That the choices of society be consistent with an ordering, and understanding the implications of that requirement, has been particularly important in welfare economics. For example, various compensation criteria have been shown to fail transitivity (see Gorman, 1955) and hence be unsuitable for public decision-making. In addition, by representing agents and society by their orderings, Arrow made the first step toward unravelling a long-standing confusion between the measurability of utility on the one hand and interpersonal comparability on the other. This step was critical if social decision-making was to rest on solid ground; for an accessible discussion of these issues see Blackorby, Donaldson and Weymark (1984).

It is common in economics to represent agents by their preference orderings. This leads to a set of complicated and somewhat unresolved issues: what are the relationships among the notions of preference, choice and happiness or well-being. Either a preference ordering or the choices of an individual may be viewed as a primitive and they may or may not be mutually consistent; the issues at stake can, however, be characterized quite precisely. The relationship between either of these and some notion of happiness or well-being is much less clear; for a good introduction to these problems see Sen and Williams (1982).

BIBLIOGRAPHY

Arrow, K.J. 1951. *Social Choice and Individual Values*. New York: Wiley. 2nd edn, 1963.

Blackorby, C., Donaldson, D. and Weymark, J. 1984. Social choice with interpersonal utility comparisons: a diagrammatic introduction. *International Economic Review* 25(2), 327–56.

Gorman, W. 1955. The intransitivity of certain criteria used in welfare economics. *Oxford Economic Papers* 7, 25–35.

Sen, A. and Williams, B. (eds) 1982. *Utilitarianism and Beyond*. Cambridge: Cambridge University Press.

Wold, H. 1943–4. A synthesis of pure demand analysis, I–III. *Skandinavisk Aktuarietidskrift* 26, 85–118; 220–63; 27, 69–120.

Perfect Foresight

MARGARET BRAY

Perfect foresight is an occasionally convenient theoretical assumption whose total lack of realism is undisputed, and perhaps unrivalled. There are two elements to perfect foresight; firstly that people have definite point expectations, allowing no uncertainty, of future variables, and secondly that these expectations are correct. In practice, as these fortunate perfectly foresightful individuals generally inhabit models with instantaneously clearing perfectly competitive markets, they only need to forecast prices. The pioneering work by Hicks (1939) on intertemporal general equilibrium theory provides a framework in which the issues associated with perfect foresight can be explored. Writing prior to the development of the expected utility theory of choice under uncertainty (von Neumann and Morgenstern, 1944), Hicks had no alternative to a deterministic model in his discussion. He acknowledges the existence and importance of uncertainty in expectation formation, but argues in a somewhat unsatisfactory fashion that point predictions can be interpreted as risk adjusted summaries of underlying probability distributions. Hicks divides time into weeks. Trade takes place weekly. Supply and demand in each week depend upon decisions made in the past, expectations of spot prices in future weeks and current spot prices. In temporary equilibrium these spot prices adjust to clear markets, but expectations may be wrong. In the situation which Hicks terms 'Equilibrium over Time', markets clear at each date, and, crucially, everyone has perfect foresight; price expectations are fulfilled.

Hicks's insight that perfect foresight is an equilibrium concept is important. If people have non-equilibrium expectations, the temporary equilibrium prices in the current spot markets differ from the prices in full equilibrium over time, and the effects of current investment and production decisions based on mistaken expectations reverberate through the future. This can be illustrated in the simplest model of supply and demand in which expectations play a part; the cobweb model, used by Kaldor (1934) in discussing equilibrium adjustments, and by Muth (1961) in the paper which gave us the phrase 'rational expectations'. In the cobweb model, demand at t D_t, depends upon the price at t p_t, $D_t = a - bp_t$. Supply depends upon point expectations p_t^e formed before t about p_t; $S_t = cp_t^e$. In temporary equilibrium supply equals demand, $a - bp_t = cp_t^e$, so $p_t = (a - cp_t^e)/b$. In the perfect foresight equilibrium expectations are correct $p_t^e = p_t = a/(b + c)$. If the price is and has been at the perfect foresight equilibrium level for a long time people will, quite reasonably, expect this price to persist. In an economy in a long-run stationary state with unchanging prices perfect foresight is plausible. Difficulties arise when a shift in an exogenous variable changes the perfect foresight equilibrium price. Suppose that in the cobweb model an increase in costs causes the supply curve to shift to $S_t = c'p^e$. If people are aware of the change, and understand fully the working of their economy, they may at once calculate and expect the new equilibrium price; alternatively they may all believe the forecast generated by the brilliant economist who knows it all. Less well-informed people may be forced to use past prices in forming their expectations. If these expectations are not at the new equilibrium value $a/(b + c')$ actual prices also differ from equilibrium prices; the economy will take some time to adjust to its new equilibrium and may, as Kaldor shows, fail to get there at all. The dynamic adjustment process, as people try to learn from their mistakes, depends very much upon how they learn, and is not understood in any generality (Bray, 1983).

As Hicks argued, equilibrium over time with perfect foresight is most plausible when people expect prices to remain steady, and they do remain steady at the expected level. In the long-run stationary state with no uncertainty there is no need to distinguish between current prices and price expectations. Supply and demand can be thought of as relating to either. In this context the atemporal textbook theory of production and consumption can be reinterpreted to describe a world where production takes time, and is determined by price expectations as well as prices.

In the long-run stationary state tastes and technology must be unchanging; the size of the population and supplies of natural resources static, or possibly in a semi-stationary state growing steadily. These conditions are demanding and implausible. Further, they are not always sufficient for steady prices. As Grandmont (1985) shows, a very simple over-lapping generations model has a constant price equilibrium, but may have other perfect foresight equilibria in which the price follows a very complicated, possibly chaotic, path. Unless people know precisely the underlying non-linear difference equation generating prices they may have great difficulty in inferring prices from past prices.

Postulating perfect foresight allows another reinterpretation of an atemporal general equilibrium model to allow for time (Debreu, 1959). In the atemporal model there is a list of different commodities, and a market and price for each commodity. These markets all operate simultaneously; in general equilibrium they all clear. The same mathematical formalism can be used to describe an intertemporal model, by distinguishing commodities by their date of delivery as well as by their characteristics. Commodities may be produced or consumed at a number of different dates, but all trade takes place at the initial date, in a complete set of spot and contingent futures markets. This of course strains credibility; only a very limited number of futures markets exist. However, as Bliss (1975) shows, the same trades, production and consumption can take place if there is a futures market for one good at each date and spot markets for all other goods, provided everyone foresees the full equilibrium over time prices perfectly. There is little to be gained in realism by exchanging the myth of complete markets for the fantasy of perfect foresight. The value of this approach lies in the handle which the well-understood atemporal general equilibrium theory gives in seeking to understand those aspects of intertemporal economics where mistakes in expectation formation appear unimportant.

The most obvious limitation of perfect foresight models is the absence of uncertainty; but the concept has been extended to allow for uncertainty, in the form of the 'rational expectations hypothesis'. This allows expectations to take the form of a probability distribution rather than a point, and requires the distribution to be correct. This begs the question of what is meant by a correct probability distribution. In a theoretical model this is conceptually straightforward. Writing down a theoretical model quite naturally generates a probability distribution describing people's beliefs about certain variables, and another describing the actual probability distribution of these variables. In a rational expectations equilibrium these are the same. In simple cases it may be easy to show that a rational expectations equilibrium exists, by solving the equations equating the distributions.

Consider, for an example, a slight generalization of the cobweb model discussed earlier, in which demand $D_t = a - bp_t + \varepsilon_t$ where ε_t is a normal random variable with mean 0 and variance 1. The price p_t is now a random variable; suppliers believe that it is normal with mean $\hat{p}_t^e$ and variance $\hat{\sigma}_t^2$, and want to supply $S = c\hat{p}_t^e - \hat{\sigma}_t^2$. In temporary equilibrium supply equals demand, $a - bp_t + \varepsilon_t = c\hat{p}_t^e - \hat{\sigma}_t^2$, so $p_t = (a - c\hat{p}_t^e + \hat{\sigma}_t^2 + \varepsilon_t)/b$. Given the $N(0, 1)$ distribution of ε_t, the price p_t is indeed normally distributed with mean $Ep_t = (a - c\hat{p}_t^e + \hat{\sigma}_t^2)/b$ and variance $1/b^2$. The suppliers have rational expectations if $Ep_t = \hat{p}_t^e$ and $\hat{\sigma}_t^2 = 1/b^2$, in which case $Ep_t = \hat{p}_t^e = (a + 1/b^2)/(b + c)$.

In more complex theoretical models the mathematics is more difficult, but the concept is clear enough. But is it plausible? The very name 'rational expectations equilibrium' is based on the presumption that this is how rational, optimizing economic agents form expectations. This requires, minimally, that they should, at some point, be able to tell whether their beliefs are correct or not. Apart from examples of the card-choosing or coin-tossing type which have little economic relevance, empirical knowledge of the probability distribution of, for example, a price, depends upon repeated observations of that price. If the probability distribution is stationary, given enough observations of the price, the statistical frequency distribution of past prices reveals the underlying probability distribution. But stationary is a very strong condition to require. Even if the exogenous random variable (ε_t in the example) is stationary, the distribution of p_t will change as beliefs change. As noted above, we know very little about dynamic adjustment processes outside perfect foresight or rational expectations equilibria.

Knight (1921) uses the term 'risk' to describe situations where probabilities can be inferred from data giving the results of repeated observations of similar events, or symmetry arguments (e.g. coin-tossing). He reserves 'uncertainty' for situations concerning unique events where there is no such basis for numerical probability assessments. It is a matter of some philosophical debate whether it is in fact possible to interpret probability numerically in situations which Knight calls uncertainty; subjectivists claim that it is possible, but make no claim that different people will make the same probability assessments. Whatever the outcome of this debate the rational expectations hypothesis is in trouble in situations of Knightian 'uncertainty' because there is no single 'correct' probability distribution.

Knight argues that economies with risk, but no uncertainty, are essentially identical to economies with perfect foresight, whereas uncertainty (which he claims is all pervasive in business decisions) has a very great effect on the workings of the economy, accounting for imperfect competition and the existence of profit. Risk is unimportant because its effects are nullified by the ability to hedge, to diversify through stock markets, and most importantly because all risks can be perfectly insured. In the light of more recent theory, Knight is clearly wrong, but his argument anticipates recent developments in a fascinating way.

The formalism of the Arrow–Debreu model can be extended to allow for risk and uncertainty, as well as time, by assuming a complete set of contingent futures markets. Commodities are distinguished by the contingencies in which they are available as well as the date. This provides complete insurance. This model has all the properties of the Arrow–Debreu model without risk (existence of equilibrium and Pareto efficiency); thus far Knight's intuition is correct. Knight is also correct in his observation that in practice complete insurance is not available for many contingencies; we do not live in a world of complete markets. His grand theme is that the presence of uncertainty as opposed to risk renders complete insurances impossible; but in his detailed discussion 'moral hazard' plays a key role. Moral hazard is due to the incentive insurance gives to take less care to avoid accidents, and explains why complete insurance is rarely available. As Knight points out, it is a very widespread phenomenon; any implicit or explicit contract which allows one of the parties a discretion whose exercise cannot be observed by the other, is subject to moral hazard. It is, as Knight argues, all pervasive in business. But it does not require uncertainty in Knight's sense; if there is risk and imperfect information there is moral hazard. The economics of information has been an enormously active area of theoretical research in recent years; considerable progress has been made by formal modelling of situations with imperfect information, giving us a much clearer view of its considerable importance and implication. We know that these make for an economics which is qualitatively quite different from that of the Arrow–Debreu model. We would not have learnt this if theorists had not been willing to make assumptions which cannot be taken literally or completely defended, in order to pursue questions. Quantitative probability, perfect foresight and rational expectations have been crucial tools developing our understanding of economics.

Utility and probability

BIBLIOGRAPHY

Bliss, C.J. 1975. *Capital Theory and the Distribution of Income.* Amsterdam: North-Holland.

Bray, M.M. 1983. Convergence to rational expectations equilibrium. In *Individual Forecasting and Aggregate Outcomes*, ed. R. Frydman and E.S. Phelps, Cambridge: Cambridge University Press.

Debreu, G. 1959. *Theory of Value: an axiomatic analysis of economic equilibrium.* Cowles Foundation Monograph No. 17, New York: Wiley.

Grandmont, J.-M. 1985. On endogenous competitive business cycles. *Econometrica* 53(5), September, 995–1045.

Hicks, J.R. 1939. *Value and Capital.* Oxford: Clarendon Press.

Kaldor, N. 1934. A classificatory note on the determinateness of equilibrium. *Review of Economic Studies* 1, February, 122–36.

Knight, F.H. 1921. *Risk, Uncertainty and Profit.* Boston: Houghton Mifflin.

Muth, J.F. 1961. Rational expectations and the theory of price movements. *Econometrica* 29, July, 315–35.

von Neumann, J. and Morgenstern, O. 1944. *Theory of Games and Economic Behaviour.* Princeton: Princeton University Press.

Preferences

GEORG HENRIK VON WRIGHT

1. The concept of preference holds a pivotal position in value theory. It may even be considered a 'value radical' or common conceptual root of the three main types of evaluative discourse, namely, aesthetic, economic and moral.

In economics and the behavioural sciences generally, the role of this concept has recently been enhanced by the creation of 'exact' theories of 'strategic thinking' such as game theory, Bayesian decision theory, and a general theory of utility.

The concept of (individual) preference is not, on the whole, considered controversial by economists. Philosophical logicians, however, tend to regard the concept as problematic, and there is little agreement among them about the basic principles of a 'logic of preference'. The situation is a little like the one in probability theory. Probability is extensively used and successfully applied in both the physical and the social sciences – and yet philosophers notoriously disagree about its 'true meaning'.

The first systematic inquiry into the foundational problems of preferences seems to have been von Wright (1963). It has at least one noteworthy precursor, Halldén (1957), which explores the related notion of 'betterness'. Significant contributions have been made later by R. Chisholm (1966, 1975), E. Sosa (1966) and N. Rescher (1967, 1969), and by the Swedes S. Danielsson (1968), P. Gädenfors and B. Hansson (1968).

2. A statement of preference of the type which I shall call 'pure' or 'intrinsic' is a *value judgement*. It is *subjective* in the sense that it expresses somebody's preference of something over something else. It is *relative* in the sense that a subject's pure preferences may change in the course of time. Such changes can be spoken of as 'changes of taste'. (Another instance of relativity will be mentioned in section 5 below.)

Sometimes we ask *why* a person prefers, say, *x* to *y*. And sometimes, not always, there is an answer at hand. The person can give a *reason* for his preference. For example: he prefers x to y as a means to the end E because x is, say, cheaper or quicker or safer than y. That x is cheaper (quicker, safer) is a factual statement, true or false, as the case may be. That a person, other things being equal, prefers the cheaper means to the more expensive one is a valuation.

A preference for a reason I shall call 'extrinsic'. As seen from the example, an extrinsic preferences is *linked* to an intrinsic one by means of an objective judgement (the reason). When the intrinsic preference is one which most people share, one often calls the preferred thing *preferable*. For example, the use of a safer means to a given end may be deemed preferable to the use of a less safe one. A judgement of preferability has an 'objective appearance'. It is an open problem in the philosophy of value whether *all* such judgements ultimately depend on subjective valuations expressed in pure preferences.

Sometimes the answer to the above Why? question is that the subject *likes x better* than y. This is not to give a reason for the preference. It is a new verbalization of a pure preference. 'Liking better' is just another term for '(simply) preferring'.

3. The symbol 'xPy' shall mean that x is preferred to y, subject and time left unspecified. For a 'logic' of the preference relation one could lay down the following axiomatic principles:

A1. $$xPy \rightarrow \sim(yPx)$$

A2. $$xPy \rightarrow xPz \lor zPy.$$

The first says that the P-relation is asymmetrical. The second says that if x is preferred to y then any third thing z is such that either x is preferred to it or it is preferred to y. This amounts, in effect, to saying that the P-relation is *connected*, that is, if two things are comparable for preference then any other thing may be compared to them.

From A1 and A2 one easily derives the following two theorems:

T1. $$xPy \,\&\, yPz \rightarrow xPz$$

T2. $$\sim(xPx).$$

They state that the P-relation is transitive and irreflexive.

We can define a relation of indifference as follows:

$$xIy =_{df} \sim(xPy) \,\&\, \sim(yPx).$$

If the P-relation is assumed to obey A1 and A2, it may be proved that the I-relation is reflexive, symmetrical, and transitive. One can then say that xIy means that x and y are of *equal* (intrinsic) *value* to the subject under consideration.

We can now also prove the theorems

T3. $$xPy \,\&\, yIz \rightarrow xPz$$

T4. $$xPy \,\&\, xIz \rightarrow zPy.$$

They state that things of equal value are interchangeable in the preference relation.

150

The assumption that the P-relation is connected is a very strong assumption, the realism of which may be questioned. One might, for example, replace it by the weaker assumption of transitivity.

A P-relation which is (only) asymmetrical and transitive determines a *partial* ordering or ranking of alternatives. A P-relation which is in addition connected determines a *complete* ranking order. In a partial ordering, the I-relation is not provably transitive. Therefore it does not amount to value-equality. In a logic of partial orderings value equality ('strong indifference') is a primitive concept. This concept cannot be defined in terms of preference (and negation), nor preference in terms of it.

4. The terms $x, y,\ldots$ of a P-relation can represent many different types of entity. They can be *goods*, for example when a person prefers apples to pears. Or they can be *means* to an end, for example travelling to a destination by bus rather than by train. Or *states of affairs* when, for example, revolt or war is preferred to continued oppression and slavery.

A person who professes a preference of some good x over another y presumably likes a state of affairs better in which he enjoys or possesses or uses or lives with x than one in which he has y. It may be held true that a relation of (pure) preference is basically a preference between two different states in which a person imagines himself to be.

Economists, it seems, usually treat the terms of the P- and I-relation as goods or other 'thing-like' entities, whereas logicians and philosophers tend to study them as states or otherwise 'proposition-like' entities. Technically, the second approach looks more interesting because it allows us to apply Boolean operations to the terms. As indicated, this may also be the more 'basic' approach.

For P-relations, the terms of which are 'thing-like', the assumption of connectedness seems, in general, too strong. a person prefers, say, (the taste of) apples to (the taste of) pears. He also prefers the music of Bach to that of Beethoven. But if asked whether he prefers apples to Bach or vice versa, his best answer is probably that he finds the alternatives 'incomparable'. By suitably limiting the *range* of things compared, one may, however, be able to secure that the preference order is complete and not only partial. Tastes of fruits, for examples, may be comparable throughout for preference.

5. A theory of P-relations, the terms of which are states of affairs, needs some axiomatic principles in addition to those mentioned in section 3. The new principles concern the 'behaviour' of the Boolean connectives in P-relations. On the details of the matter, however, there is widespread disagreement between researchers.

One could raise the question: What does it *mean* to prefer a state x to another one y? and answer: It means to think it better if the first state obtains but the second does not than the other way round, the second but not the first. One then accepts an equivalence $xPy \leftrightarrow x \mathbin{\&} \sim y \, P \sim x \mathbin{\&} y$. From it one can easily derive a 'law of contraposition' for preferences, $xPy \leftrightarrow \sim yP \sim x$. Objections raised against it on intuitive grounds seem to me to confuse pure preferences between states with some other types of preference.

Another controversial question concerns the case when one or both terms of the relation are *disjunctive* states. An employee says he prefers an increase in salary *or* a shortening of his working day (salary remaining the same) to the status quo of his employment. Does this mean that he both thinks increased salary *and* also thinks reduced working hours preferable to his present position? To interpret the preference thus is to subscribe to an idea that a 'disjunctive preference' is resolvable into a *conjunction* of P-relations, the terms of which are not disjunctive. The reader can easily satisfy himself that, taking 'contraposition' into account, a preference $x \vee yPz \vee u$ then is equivalent to a conjunction of 16 P-relations between 4-termed conjunctions of states and/or their negations.

A P-relation with the above properties his *holistic* in the following sense: A subject's preference of state x over state y obtains in a frame of 'accompanying circumstances'. Of great interest is the case when it obtains *ceteris paribus* or 'other things being equal'. Let these 'other things' be some conjunction of n states and/or their negations. There are, in all, 2^n such conjunctions or 'possible worlds', $C_1, \ldots, C_{2^n}$. That x is preferred to y *ceteris paribus* means that every conjunction $x \& \sim y \& C_i$ is preferred to $\sim x \& y \& C_i$. xPy is then equivalent with the conjunction (totality) of the 2^n relations $x \& \sim y \& C_i P \sim x \& y \& C_i$.

The states x and y and the n states in C_i constitute the *preference horizon* of the person who has the preference. 'Ideally' this horizon should comprise every possible state in the world. In practice, however, it is limited to those states the possible relevance of which to his preference the subject happens to take into account.

Consider three P-relations xPy, yPz and xPz. If we are to be able to infer the third from the first two, the preference must be taken relative to a preference-horizon which includes *at least* the states x, y and z. xPy then means that x is preferred to y regardless of whether z or $\sim z$ obtains; yPz that y is preferred to z regardless of x; xPz that x is preferred to z regardless of y. Thus xPy is explicated as $(x \& zPy \& z) \& (x \& \sim zPy \& \sim z)$. And similarly for yPz and xPz. It is easily seen that transitivity is then secured. If the three preferences had not fallen within one and the same 'horizon', transitivity need not have followed. It has sometimes been questioned whether the P-relation *is* (always) transitive. The answer is that transitivity is there only if due attention is paid to the preference-horizon.

The 'possible worlds' within a given preference-horizon may be ranked in a complete order of preference. But the ranking order of *all* the possible alternatives within such a horizon cannot be complete, but will have to be partial. This is a consequence of the fact that a conception of the P-relation as resolvable into a *conjunction* entails a conception of the I-relation as a *disjunction*. And this I-relation is not an equivalence (a value-equality). Thus a holistic conception of preferences between states entails that one must differentiate between 'mere' indifference and value-equality.

Must preference between states be conceived holistically? The opposite of a holistic conception is to consider the terms of the P-relation 'alone and taken by themselves'. This makes good sense when the terms are 'thing-like'. The taste of apples 'by itself' may be compared with the taste of pears 'by itself'. But whether a similar comparison makes good sense when the terms are 'proposition-like' (states) seems to me debatable. A non-holistic logic of intrinsic preferences between states has been proposed by Chisholm and Sosa (1966).

6. A question of interest to value theory is whether the *absolute* notions of goodness and badness can be defined in terms of the *relative* notion of betterness (preference).

Long ago, A.P. Brogan (1919) suggested that a state of affairs is good if it is better than its contradictory. In terms of preference:

$$\text{Good } x =_{df} xP \sim x.$$

Conversely, a state is bad if its contradictory is preferred to it.

If $xI \sim x$ holds good, x will be called indifferent *in itself*. If xIy holds, x and y will be called indifferent *between themselves*.

A weakness, among others, of the suggested definition of good is that one cannot prove that states which are indifferent in themselves are also indifferent between themselves. Thus it may happen that two states are indifferent in themselves, neither good nor bad, and one of them preferred to (thought better than) the other. This is counter-intuitive. Things which are neither good nor bad have no value and therefore should not be possible to rank as better or worse.

A similar objection can be made against the definition of goodness suggested by R. Chisholm (1975). It says that a state is good if it is preferred to some state which is indifferent in itself. But unless states indifferent in themselves are all equal in value it may happen that one and the same state is both good and bad. This also is counter-intuitive.

The upshot seems to be that the value-absolutes cannot be defined in terms of preference alone. They require in addition an independent concept of *zero*-value or (complete) value-neutrality.

7. One must distinguish between *preference* and (preferential) *choice*. A preference is an attitude, a choice an action.

If a subject has a pure preference for x over y it may be taken as analytic that, if he is offered a choice (option) between the two states, he will choose the former. It is then presupposed that the two states are being presented to him, so to say, 'on a tray' – that he can 'pick out' the one or the other without having to consider further prerequisites for, or consequences of, his choice.

From choices and options of this kind one must distinguish another type. I shall call these other options *conditional*.

A farmer is offered a choice between, on the one hand, getting a horse if it is raining tomorrow and a cow if it is not raining and, on the other hand, a cow if it is raining and a horse if it is not. He prefers getting a horse to getting a cow; this is a 'pure preference'. But which of the offered alternatives does he prefer?

Assume that he professes to be indifferent as between them. How shall we then understand his attitude?

To this question there is an answer, first proposed by F.P. Ramsey, which has later come to play a great role in so-called Bayesian decision theory (Ramsey, 1931; Savage, 1954; Davidson et al., 1955). Ramsey thought that an attitude of indifference here *means* that the person rates the two events, 'rain' and 'not rain', as *equally probable*. Accepting this, one can then proceed as follows:

Assume that our farmer is next presented with this option: On the one hand a horse if it is raining and a sheep if it is not raining and, on the other hand, a cow if it is raining and a hog if it is not raining. Again he says he is indifferent. This, on Ramsey's view, means that the value to him of a cow is *as much less* the value of the horse as the value of a sheep is less than that of a hog. With this the way is open to a *metrization* of value and the introduction of *utility functions*. This done, one can use attitudes of indifference in other, more complex, conditional options for defining arbitrary degrees of (subjective) probability. The product of the value of a good and the probability of its materialization is called *expected utility*. Attitudes of preference in options aim at maximizing this quantity.

Ramsey's method is elegant and ingenious. Nevertheless, it seems to rest on a mistake. It ignores the distinction between the two senses of 'indifference'.

The farmer who, when presented with the first of the above two options, professes an attitude of indifference can do so for one of two reasons. Either he 'simply has no idea' about the chances of rainfall for tomorrow and therefore cannot make up his mind about which alternative is more to his advantage. This does not *mean* that he thinks rain and not-rain equally likely; he simply suspends judgement. *Or*, he considers them equally likely and *therefore* judges the two alternatives to be equally advantageous. He could, for example, support his attitude with the argument that if he repeatedly opted for one of the alternatives, no matter which one, on average half the number of times he would 'probably' get a horse, which is to his advantage, and half the number of times a cow, which is to his disadvantage. So, therefore, he is indifference as between the alternatives. It is, in other words, not his judgement of indifference which gives meaning to the probabilities for him; but it is his prior estimate of the probabilities which determines his attitude of indifference. This estimate, moreover, seems normally to go with a corresponding expectation of frequencies.

The above criticism of Ramsey's procedure is not committed to a frequency theory of the 'meaning' of probability. But it assigns to expected frequencies a much more basic position for understanding probabilities than modern 'Bayesians' have tended to do (cf. von Wright, 1962).

8. By a group-preference one can understand a ranking of alternatives in an order of ('objective') preferability based on the (subjective) rankings for preference of those alternatives by the members of the group. The derivation of the collective preference has to conform to some principles which seem intuitively plausible or 'rational'.

The problem of determining a group-preference is connected with notorious difficulties. Any proposed solution will depend partly upon which rational standards it is thought that the derivation should satisfy, and partly upon which demands are imposed upon the *P*- and *I*-relations involved.

In his influential book *Social Choice and Individual Values* (1951), K.J. Arrow showed that a derivation cannot collectively satisfy certain principles which individually seem plausible. The result is known as Arrow's 'Impossibility Theorem'. It has been the topic of much subsequent discussion both by economists and logicians.

Group-preferences will not be further treated in this article. Let it be mentioned, however, that in the writer's opinion discussion has tended to neglect the complications connected with the concept of *indifference*. It is usually assumed that the *P*-relation is, at least, transitive and that the *I*-relation is an equivalence relation. In a preference ranking which is a partial ordering, this requirement on the *I*-relation is not automatically fulfilled. And even if the *I*-relation for individual preferences were an equivalence, it may not be 'reasonable' to demand or expect the *I*-relation for a group-preference to be this. Observing the distinction between 'mere' indifference and value-equality may therefore be helpful in efforts to cope with the conceptual difficulties in this area.

BIBLIOGRAPHY

Arrow, K.J. 1951. *Social Choice and Individual Values*. New York: Wiley.

Brogan, A.P. 1919. The fundamental value universal. *Journal of Philosophy* 6(4), February, 967–1104.

Chisholm, R.M. 1975. The intrinsic value of disjunctive states of affairs. *Noûs* 9(3), September, 295–308.

Chisholm, R.M. and Sosa, E. 1966. On the logic of 'intrinsically better'. *American Philosophical Quarterly* 3(3), July, 244–9.

Danielsson, S. 1968. *Preference and Obligation*. Uppsala: Scriv Service.

Davidson, D., McKinsey, J.C.C. and Suppes, P. 1955. Outlines of a formal theory of value. *Philosophy of Science* 22(2), April, 140–60.

Halldén, S. 1957. *On the Logic of 'Better'*. Lund: Gleerup.

Hansson, B. 1968a. Fundamental axioms for preference relations. *Synthese* 18(4), 423–42.

Hansson, B. 1968b. Choice structures and preference relations. *Synthese* 18(4), 443–58.

Hansson, B. 1969a. Group preferences. *Econometrica* 37(1), January, 50–54.

Hansson, B. 1969b. Voting and group decision functions. *Synthese* 20(4), 526–37.

Hansson, B. 1970. *Preference Logic, Philosophical Foundations and Applications in the Philosophy of Science*. Lund: Studentlitteratur.

Houthakker, H.S. 1965. On the logic of preference and choice. In *Contributions to Logic and Methodology in Honor of J.M. Bochénski*, ed. A.-T. Tymieniecka, Amsterdam: North-Holland.

Ramsey, F.P. 1931. Truth and probability. In F.P. Ramsey, *Foundations of Mathematics and Other Logical Essays*, London: Kegan Paul; New York: Humanities Press, 1950.

Rescher, N. 1967. Semantic foundations for the logic of preference. In *The Logic of Decision and Action*, ed. N. Rescher, Pittsburgh: Pittsburgh University Press.

Rescher, N. 1969. *Introduction to Value Theory*. Englewood Cliffs, NJ: Prentice-Hall.

Utility and probability

Savage, L. 1954. *The Foundations of Statistics*. New York: Wiley.
Wright, G.H. von. 1962. The epistemology of subjective probability. In *Proceedings of the 1960 International Congress: Logic, Methodology and Philosophy of Science*, ed. E. Nagel, P. Suppes and A. Tarski, Stanford: Stanford University Press.
Wright, G.H. von. 1963. *The Logic of Preference*. Edinburgh: Edinburgh University Press.
Wright, G.H. von. 1972. The logic of preference reconsidered. *Theory and Decision* 3(2). December, 140–69.

Preference Reversals

EDI KARNI

Preference reversal is an experimentally observed phenomenon in which subjects, when asked to choose between suitably matched pairs of lotteries and then to state the lowest amount of money they would be willing to accept in exchange for the right to participate in each of these lotteries, announce the lowest amount for the chosen lottery. Preference reversals were first reported by Lichtenstein and Slovic (1971) and have since been replicated in numerous studies, for example Lindman (1971), Grether and Plott (1979), Pommerehne, Schneider and Zweifel (1982), Reilly (1982). The latter studies introduce variations in the experimental design to increase the motivation and reduce the possibility of confusion and errors on the part of the subjects. This experimental evidence seems inconsistent with transitive preferences and, consequently, with any theory of decision making under risk based on such preferences. Recently, however, Karni and Safra (1986) and Holt (1986) demonstrated that preference reversals may occur even when preferences are transitive, and that the preference reversal phenomenon may be the result of the interaction between the subjects' preferences and the experimental design. According to this interpretation, preference reversals constitute a violation of the independence axiom of expected utility theory.

THE EVIDENCE. Experiments designed to test different hypotheses concerning a given phenomenon must, by their very nature, vary in details. The experiments designed to test the preference reversal phenomenon are no exception. The exposition below focuses upon the essential aspects of these experiments while abstracting from non-essential details.

Let $(x, p; y, 1-p)$ denote the lottery that offers the prizes x and y with probabilities p and $(1-p)$, respectively. A P bet is a lottery that assigns a high probability to winning a modest amount of money, e.g. $A = (-1, \frac{1}{36}; 4, \frac{35}{36})$ and a $\$$ bet is a lottery that assigns a low probability to winning a relatively large amount of money, e.g. $B = (-1.5, \frac{25}{36}p; 16, \frac{11}{36})$. In the first part of a typical preference reversal experimental each subject is presented with a sequence of

157

suitably chosen pairs of lotteries, each pair consisting of a P bet and a $ bet. From each pair the subject is asked to choose the lottery in which he prefers to participate. In the second part of the experiment the same subjects are presented with the same lotteries, one at a time, and are asked to state the lowest amount of money, or the lowest price, which they demand to forego the right to participate in the lottery. To motivate the subject to reveal their minimal prices accurately and to discourage strategic responses that may cause preference reversals, the following relevation scheme was used: The subjects were informed that, after they state their lowest selling price for each lottery, a random number will be drawn from a uniform distribution over a given interval. (The interval is such that its lower bound is smaller than the lowest prize and its upper bound is larger than the largest prize of the lotteries in the experiment.) If the number selected in this way exceeds the price set by the subject for the lottery under consideration, then the subject is paid an amount of money equal to the number that was drawn and foregoes the right to participate in the lottery. If the number drawn randomly falls short of the price set by the subject, the lottery is played out and the participant receives the price according to the outcome.

This method of eliciting the lowest selling price, due originally to Becker, DeGroot and Marschak (1964), is designed to motivate the subjects to reveal the certainty equivalents of the lotteries. (The certainty equivalent of a lottery H for a given decision maker is a sum of money $C(H)$ such that this decision maker is indifferent between H and the lottery $\delta_{C(H)}$ that assigns probability 1 to the prize $C(H)$.) If a subject sets a price of a given lottery exceeding his certainty equivalent and the outcome of the random draw is a value between the stated price and the certainty equivalent, the subject is forced to participate in the lottery even though he would rather take the sum of money that was drawn. Similarly, if he stated a price lower than his certainty equivalent and the outcome of the random drawing were between the certainty equivalent and the price, then he is forced to forego the opportunity to play the lottery when he would rather have participated in it.

The results of the experiments indicate that preference reversals are persistent and systematic. The reversals occur frequently when P bets are chosen over the corresponding $ bets and seldom when $ bets were chosen over P bets. For instance, in an experiment using real money Grether and Plott (1979) found that of a total of 99 choices of P bets over $ bets reversals occurred in 69 cases, or 70 per cent of the time, while only 22 reversals occured in 174 instances where the $ bet was chosen over the corresponding P bet, a reversal rate of 13 per cent. This pattern of reversals is typical and has been replicated with minor changes in other studies.

INTERPRETATION. The claim that the preference reversal phenomenon is inconsistent with transitive preferences is based on the presumption that the selling prices elicited in the experiments are the certainty equivalents of the respective lotteries. To see this, note that if lottery A is chosen (preferred) over lottery B then, by transitivity of the preferences over lotteries, $\delta_{C(A)}$ is preferred over $\delta_{C(B)}$ and $C(A)$ must be larger than $C(B)$. However, the experimental evidence indicates that in many cases, in particular when A is a P bet and B is a $ bet, the elicited selling prices of A and B, $\pi(A)$ and $\pi(B)$, respectively, are such that $\pi(A) < \pi(B)$. Consequently, if $\pi = C$ then this evidence contradicts the transitivity axiom. The significance of this conclusion can hardly be overstated as it undermines the entire body of economic theory that is based on optimizing behaviour.

The alternative interpretation of the preference reversal phenomenon, due to Karni and Safra (1986) and Holt (1986), challenges the validity of the claim that $\pi = C$. In fact, Karni and Safra proved that, under reasonable restrictions on the set of preference relations over lotteries, this claim is valid if and only if these preference relations satisfy the independence axiom of expected utility theory. To grasp the argument, consider the following formal presentation of the experimental design. Let X be a compact interval and let L be the set of cumulative distribution functions on X. Elements of L are lotteries with prizes in X. Let $Q \in L$ be a uniform distribution with a non-trivial, compact support, Supp $Q = [q, r] \subset X$. We shall refer to Q as the base lottery. The experimental design described above may now be formally defined as follows: A Q-experiment is a function $E_Q : \mathbb{R} \times L \to L$, given by:

$$E_Q(\pi, A)(x) = Q(\pi)A(x) + \max{}^E\{0, Q(x) - Q(\pi)\}.$$

$E_Q(\pi, A)$ may be interpreted as a two-stage lottery. Upon announcing the price π the subject participates in a lottery that offers as prizes the lottery A and a uniform lottery on $[\pi, r]$ with probabilities $Q(\pi)$ and $1 - Q(\pi)$, respectively. Thus, given the experimental design, the base lottery Q and the lottery A, a subject will announce the price $\pi^*(A; E_Q)$ so as to obtain the most preferred element in the set $\{E_Q(\pi, A) : \pi \in \mathbb{R}\}$.

Karni and Safra (1986) show that if a preference relation on L is complete, transitive, continuous, monotonic in the sense of satisfying first order stochastic dominance, and smooth in an appropriate sense, then it is representable by a linear real-valued functional on L if and only if $C(A) = \pi^*(A; E_Q)$ for all Q-experiments E_Q and lotteries A such that $C(A) \in$ Supp Q. In other words, given the other restrictions on the preference relations, the condition, that the selling prices of lotteries elicited by Q-experiments are equal to the certainty equivalents of these lotteries, is equivalent to expected utility maximizing behaviour. Consequently, without the independence axiom, any model of decision making under risk implies that $C \neq \pi^*$. Note however that $C(\cdot) \neq \pi^*(\cdot; E_Q)$ is both necessary and sufficient for the preference reversal phenomenon. The necessity is obvious. Sufficiency follows from the observation that by monotonicity of preferences, $\pi^*(\delta_x; E_Q) = x$ for all $x \in$ Supp Q. Hence if $C(A) < \pi^*(A; E_Q)$ there exists x such that $C(A) < x < \pi^*(A; E_Q)$. Clearly δ_x is preferred to A but

$$\pi^*(\delta_x; E_Q) < \pi^*(A; E_Q),$$

is a reversal. A similar argument applies to the case where $C(A) > \pi^*(A; E_Q)$.

Consequently, if the transitivity axiom is maintained, then the preference reversal phenomenon is a violation of the independence axiom. Holt (1986) reached a similar conclusion. However, Holt's analysis is based on a different aspect of the experimental design, namely, that in order to prevent wealth effects from contaminating the data, only one lottery, from the set of lotteries determined by the subject's choices from the original pairs and from the lotteries determined by his announced selling prices, is actually played out at the end of the experiment. This lottery is selected at random. This random selection process determines the compounded lottery essential for generating preference reversals that are consistent with transitivity. Needless to say the abandonment of the independence axiom is much less critical for preference theory than the abandonment of transitivity.

The failure to elicit the certainty equivalents of lotteries under Q-experiments is due to the interaction between the experimental design and the subject's preferences. The design presents the subject with a set of lotteries from which to choose. The subject chooses his response so as to maximize his preferences over the given set. In general this response does not reveal the information sought by the experimenter. This conclusion has been shown by Karni and Safra to apply to a broader class of experiments that may be represented by a function $E: \mathbb{R} \times L \to L$, where the first argument is the index chosen by the subject and represents the elicited observation, the second is the lottery presented to the subject by the experimenter, and the value of E is determined by the experimental design.

BIBLIOGRAPHY
Becker, G.M., DeGroot, M.H, and Marschak, J. 1964. Measuring utility by a single response sequential method. *Behavioural Science* 9, July, 226–32.
Grether, D.M. and Plott, C.R. 1979. Economic theory of choice and the preference reversal phenomenon. *American Economic Review* 69(4), September, 623–38.
Holt, C. 1986. Preference reversals and the independence axiom. *American Economic Review* 76(3), June, 508–15.
Karni, E. and Safra, Z. 1986. Preference reversals and the observability of preferences by experimental methods. *Economics Letters* 20(1), 15–18.
Lichtenstein, S. and Slovic, P. 1971. Reversal of preferences between bids and choices in gambling decisions. *Journal of Experimental Psychology* 89, July, 46–55.
Lindman, H.R. 1971. Inconsistent preferences among gambles. *Journal of Experimental Psychology* 89, May, 390–97.
Pommerehne, W.W., Schneider, F. and Zweifel, P. 1982. Economic theory of choice and the preference reversal phenomenon: a re-examination. *American Economic Review* 73(2), June, 569–74.
Reilly, R.J. 1982. Preference reversal: further evidence and some suggested modifications in experimental design. *American Economic Review* 73(2), June, 576–84.

Preordering

C. BLACKORBY

A preordering (also called a weak ordering or a quasi-ordering) is a reflexive and transitive binary relation which is not necessarily complete.

A binary relation R defined on a set S is a set of ordered parts of elements of S, that is, a subset of the Cartesian product of S with itself, $S \times S$. One writes xRy (or $(x, y) \in R$) to mean that $x \in S$ stands in relation R to $y \in S$. A preordering is a binary relation, R, which satisfies two properties: (i) reflexivity: for all $x \in S$, xRx, and (ii) transitivity: for $x, y, z \in S$, if xRy and yRz, then xRz.

A simple example is given by the binary relation weak vector dominance which we denote V. Suppose S is Euclidean N-space, then xVy if and only if $x_n \geqslant y_n$, $n = 1, \ldots, N$. V is clearly reflexive and transitive; it is just as clearly not complete, that is, not all elements of S are ranked. For example if $N = 2$, $x = (1, 2)$ and $y = (2, 1)$ then it is not the case that xVy or that yVx.

Quasi-orderings have played their largest role in welfare economics where consistency in decision making is a desirable requirement but where one may be dubious about being able to rank all possible outcomes. Two examples follow for which the notion of a subrelation is useful. Suppose R and S are binary relations: S is a subrelation of R if xSy implies xRy. For example, strong vector dominance, $\bar{V}$, is the binary relation which results when the above weak inequality is replaced with a strict inequality. Clearly, $\bar{V}$ is a subrelation of V.

Interpreting the elements of N-space as vectors of utilities, it is possible to define a quasi-ordering which is a subrelation of both the utilitarian and the Rawls criteria: define the binary relation M by xMy if and only if $\Sigma_{i=1}^{N} x_i \geqslant \Sigma_{i=1}^{N} y_i$ and $\min\{x_1, \ldots, x_N\} \geqslant \min\{y_1, \ldots, y_N\}$. M is clearly reflexive, transitive and not complete. The distributional insensitivity of the utilitarian principle is tempered by the Rawls's difference principle.

As an alternative, consider evaluating social states by weighted utility sums where the weights represent utility comparisons but these comparisons are not precisely fixed. Instead, the weights are drawn from a subset of N-dimensional Euclidean space, say B. More formally, define the quasi-ordering F by xFy if and only if $\Sigma_{i=1}^{N} b_i x_i \geqslant \Sigma_{i=1}^{N} b_i y_i$ for all $(b_1, \ldots, b_N) \in B$. Suppose that we try to evaluate the desirability of burning down Rome while Nero fiddles. The quasi-ordering F may show a gain for burning Rome only if the set of interpersonal weights is such that Nero is given extreme consideration. (These examples are taken from the articles listed below.)

BIBLIOGRAPHY

Blackorby, C. and Donaldson, D. 1977. Utility vs. equity: some plausible quasi-orderings. *Journal of Public Economics* 7, 365–82.

Sen, A.K. 1970. Interpersonal aggregation and partial comparability. *Econometrica* 38, 393–409.

Probability

IAN HACKING

Probability denotes a family of ideas that originally centred on the notion of credibility, or reasonable belief falling short of certainty. There have arisen two quite distinct uses of this group of ideas, namely in the modelling of physical or social processes, and in drawing inferences from, or making decisions on the basis of, inconclusive data.

1. MODELLING. We imply the most elementary of probability models when we say that a roulette is fair, meaning that the probability of the ball settling in any one segment of the wheel is equal to that of its settling in any other. Talk of fair coins or biased dice is represented in a model that is typically used to predict the relative frequency with which the possible outcomes will occur. More formal models arise from a natural abstraction and generalization of this ancient idea. In proposing a probability model for some phenomenon, one is making a claim about how some aspect of the natural, social or human world is arranged and how it behaves. Such assertions are contingent propositions that should be susceptible of empirical testing. In economic theory they are typically embedded in models employing other theoretical constructs, such as utility, but the present article is restricted to probability itself.

2. INFERENCE. Probability is also used for drawing inferences from inadequate information. When combined with an assessment of utilities, it is also used for deciding what to do in the face of uncertainty. Probability is here a tool for reasoning from data and for adjusting one's beliefs or actions in the light of new evidence. Such use in reasoning is more akin to logic than to the empirical science of which probability modelling is a part.

Evidently modelling and inference are tools that need not conflict. Often, they are complementary, for methods of inference or decision are often required to choose among competing models. Conversely, a probability model may, in suitable circumstances, be invaluable for drawing probable inferences and making decisions. Despite the compatibility of inference and modelling, there has been a great deal of controversy about the foundations of probability and statistics, partly but only partly arising from confusing these two distinct uses to which probability ideas can be put. The present article will describe these foundational and conceptual issues, but not the applications of probability to special topics.

3. FREQUENCY CONCEPTIONS OF PROBABILITY. It has often been urged, in order to diminish controversy, that there are two distinct and compatible conceptions of probability that perhaps deserve to be called by different names.

One idea derives from our experience of the fairly stable relative frequency of some kinds of events in repeated trials. We appear to be familiar with such phenomena, not only in man-made gambling devices, but also in nature, ranging from radioactivity to the relative frequency of births of the two sexes. A precise definition is, however, elusive.

Some writers propose that we should represent this idea in terms of an infinite sequence of trials. If the relative frequency of event A in a countably infinite series tends in the limit to p, and certain other conditions are met, then the probability of A is p. The chief additional condition is that the relative frequency of A should also tend to p in all sub-sequences that can be picked out in advance. This requirement makes a 'gambling system' impossible (von Mises, 1928); for a precise analysis of such randomness in terms of complexity see work reported in Fine (1973, ch. V).

If it often objected that limiting frequencies are too much of an idealization. Coins are seldom tossed very often, and they wear out unevenly. A chief alternative to limits is that of propensity (Popper, 1959). Here a probability is taken to apply to a physical or social system, and is the tendency or disposition of the system to deliver event A on a single trial. This may manifest itself in a stable relative frequency if sufficiently many trials are made, but the propensity is thought of as a property of the system itself. A comparison would be with the malleability of a piece of copper, taken to be a fact about the structure of the metal. It is often objected that there has never been a lucid analysis of any kind of propensity, tendency or disposition, and that talk of propensities is obscurantism. The American philosopher C.S. Peirce (1839–1914) held each idea in succession, first favouring the limiting frequency view (Peirce, 1878, II, 651) and later the dispositional account (Peirce, 1910, II, 664). In fact it may not be necessary to take a position on these matters. Although talk of limiting frequencies and of tendencies plays an important heuristic role in forming intuitive ideas of probability, it is not of final importance. The substantial connection between probability and frequency is provided by the limiting theorems of §8 below.

4. DEGREES OF BELIEF. Here the paradigm is a statement such as; 'The probability that it will be warm and sunny tomorrow is 80%'. Of itself this cannot express a relative frequency (even if meteorological frequencies are part of the evidence

for the statement), because tomorrow comes but once. The statement expresses the credibility of the thought that it will be a nice day tomorrow. There are two ways to explicate it.

First, the oldest, is the idea of rational confidence: the extent to which it is rational to be confident of hypothesis A (a fine day) in the light of available evidence B. This approach has often been called subjective, because its early proponents spoke of probability being relative in part to our ignorance and in part to our knowledge (Laplace, 1795). However, it is now generally agreed that the term is misleading, for one is concerned with an objective relation between the hypothesis A and the evidence B, a probability relation analogous to the deductive relations of logic (Keynes, 1921). One is concerned with reasonable degrees of belief relative to evidence, and this theory is best called a *rationalist* one.

The label 'subjective theory' should be avoided; when used, it should be applied to another account that starts with the following observation by F.P. Ramsey: a 'fundamental criticism of Mr Keynes' views,... is the obvious one that there really do not seem to be any such things as the probability relations that he describes' (Ramsey, 1926, p. 2). This scepticism led Ramsey, B. de Finetti (1973) and L.J. Savage (1954) to develop what Savage called a theory of personal probability. Here a statement of probability is the speaker's own assessment of the extent to which he or she is confident of a proposition. It is remarkable that a seemingly subjective idea like this is arguably constrained by exactly the same mathematical rules as govern the frequency conception of probability. It is to these rules that we must now turn.

5. MATHEMATICAL PROBABILITY. Probability theory is a branch of the mathematical discipline known as measure theory, with the further condition that all measures are normalized, i.e. lie in the interval $[0, 1]$. The formal theory is open to numerous interpretations, including those mentioned in the two preceding sections.

In what follows, $P(A)$ is read as the probability of A. In the frequency interpretation, A will be an event of some kind, while in a belief interpretation, A is a proposition or hypothesis. This proposition/event nomenclature is of little moment, for we can speak of the proposition that an event occurred, or of the event that a proposition is true. In the event reading, events are represented by sets and we are concerned with an algebra of sets closed under union ($\cup$) and complementation. Intersection is denoted ($\cap$). In a propositional algebra, these correspond to disjunction, negation and conjunction. Ω denotes the sure event or certain proposition, the union of all events (or disjunction of all propositions) in the algebra.

Informally the basic laws of probability for an algebra of finitely many events (such as the six possible outcomes of a die, closed under union and complementation) are as follows:

(1) Normalization. $P(\Omega) = 1$.
(2) Non-negativity. For all events A, $P(A) = 1$.
(3) Additivity. For disjoint A, B, $P(A \cup B) = P(A) + P(B)$.

Two fundamental concepts, conditional probability and independence, may then be defined. Conditional probability is denoted by $P(A/B)$. In a frequency interpretation this is the relative frequency with which A occurs among trials on which B occurs. In a personal belief interpretation, this may be understood as the rate at which a person would make a conditional bet on A – all bets being cancelled unless condition B is satisfied. Note that in the rational belief interpretation, all probability statements are implicitly statements of conditional probability, and an axiomization will be couched in terms of conditional probabilities.

(4) Conditional probability.

$$P(A/B) = \frac{P(A \cap B)}{P(B)} \quad \text{for} \quad P(B) \neq 0.$$

Finally, the notion of an independent event is vital in frequency applications. Intuitively A is independent of b if the occurrence of B makes no difference to whether A occurs or not, so we expect that $P(A/B) = P(A)$. By virtue of (4), this is equivalent to:

(5) Independence. A and B are pairwise independent if and only if

$$P(A \cap B) = P(A)P(B).$$

Mutual independence of a class of n events is defined analogously.

From the very earliest days of probability calculations, speculators and gambles were preoccupied by the fair price for a stake in a game or other transaction, such as the purchase of an annuity. Expectation, or expected value, is the formalization of this idea. Let there be a quantity X with possible values $x_1, x_2, \ldots, x_n$, and let $P(x_i)$ be the probability that X has the value x_i. In the historical origins, the x_i would be payoffs from a game and the $P(x_i)$ would be the changes of getting payoff x_i. The expectation is then defined:

(6) Expectation. $\Sigma(X) = \Sigma x_i P(x_i)$. The expectation is also called the mean value of X. The usual measure of the 'average deviation' from the mean μ is the standard deviation σ, whose square σ^2 is called the variance.

(7) Variance. $\sigma^2 = E(X - \mu)^2 = \Sigma(x_i - \mu)^2 P(x_i)$.

The concepts present in (1)–(6) are clearly set forth in Huygens (1657), which takes expectation rather than probability as the primitive idea. The classic formulation of these ideas as part of measure theory is due to Kolmogorov (1933). Here a probability space is a triple $(\Omega, \mathscr{F}, P)$.

Ω: a space of mutually exclusive and jointly exhaustive events.

$\mathscr{F}$: a countable algebra of suitable subsets of Ω, that is, an algebra closed under countably infinite union and complementation.

Corresponding to (1)–(3) above we have Normalization, Non-negative and:

(3*) Countable additivity. For any countable sequence $A_1, A_2, \ldots$ of pairwise disjoint elements of $\mathscr{F}$,

$$P(UA_i) = \sum P(A_i).$$

Conditional probability, independence, expectation and variance are explained by measure theoretic generalizations of (4)–(7).

6. PERSONAL DEGREES OF BELIEF AND THE AXIOMS. It is evident that both finite and limiting relative frequencies will satisfy the probability axioms. It is obscure why propensities should do so. This question is seldom addressed by those who favour that approach, but see Suppes (1973). This may be because of deeper connections between the frequency idea and the mathematical formalism; see §8 below. Here we indicate the ground for the more surprising result that, arguably, personal degrees of belief should satisfy the probability axioms.

There are two parts of the argument. (*i*) Construe degrees of belief as betting rates. (*ii*) Establish reasonable constraints on a person's set of betting rates. The best introductory exposition of these ideas is the first place they were proposed (Ramsey, 1926).

Ramsey thought of a probability space as a representation of psychological states of belief. $P(A)$ stands for a person's degree of confidence in A. It is to be evaluated behaviourally by determining the least favourable rate at which this individual would take a bet on A. If the least favourable odds are, for example, 3:1, then that person's probability is $P(A) = 3/4$. Conditional probability may be explained in terms of conditional bets. Thus suppose one bets on horse A winning a race, on condition B that the horse completes the course, all bets being off if the condition B fails and the horse drops out. If a person bets 2:1 on A winning, conditional on B, then that person's conditional probability is $2/3$. Ramsey was well aware that one should not expect that real betting rates should be measured to 'too many places of decimals'.

Betting is all very well, but is hardly a general psychological test, for many people go out of their way to seek or to avoid gambling, and this irrelevant factor will distort or render impossible measures of belief by betting behaviour. To get around this, imagine that a man is offered the choice of one of the two following options, at no cost to himself:

(a) He gets $1 if A occurs.

(b) He gets $1 if B occurs.

If he is indifferent between the two, they are equally probable for him, while if he prefers (a) to (b), then for his personal probabilities $P(A) > P(B)$. Now if this man can generate large sets of equally probably events we can measure his probabilities to any realistic degree of precision. Suppose for example that he acts as if he thought a coin is fair, and regards any sequence of 10 outcomes of heads and tails as probably as any other. Then he has 10! equally probably disjoint events. He can be asked about options such as:

(a) $1 if A occurs.

(b) $1 if heads occurs on the next two consecutive tosses.

Preference for (a) indicates that his $P(A) > 3/4$; for (b), $P(A) < 3/4$, while indifference indicates that his $P(A) = 3/4$. Repeated uses of this 'risk free' technique can refine the measurement of his probabilities without any recourse to outright gambling. Suppose, then, that it makes sense to attach betting rates to a person's beliefs. Why should they satisfy the probability axioms? Why call betting rates 'probabilities' at all? The deepest justification jointly develops probability and utility, and hence is outside the scope of this essay. That was the method of Ramsey (1926), which uses a perspicuous zig-zag exposition. That is, first a constraint is placed upon degrees of belief. This is used to place a constraint on utilities. This in turn is fed back into degrees of belief in the form of a further constraint. The upshot of Ramsey's paper is a full axiomatization of probability and utility. A more sophisticated version of such an approach is given in Savage (1954).

There is, however, a less compelling but easy to follow argument suggested in a throwaway phrase in Ramsey (1926), and independently developed in detail in de Finetti (1937).

De Finetti urged that a set of betting rates should be *coherent* in the following sense. It would be unreasonable or 'incoherent' to offer betting rates on a schedule of propositions such that a clever gambler could make a profit by betting with you no matter what transpires. For a trivial example, let $A =$ Australia retains the America's Cup in the next competition. Suppose a person is willing to bet on A at odds 7:3, and on the opposite, $\bar{A}$, at odds of 3:2, then the personal probabilities are $P(A) = 0.7$ and $P(\bar{A}) + 0.6$. That violates the additivity law that requires $P(A) = P(\bar{A}) = 1$.

Suppose that a gambler bets against this person on A with a stake of $75, and against him on $\bar{A}$ with a stake of $100. The gambler stakes $175 and gets back $250, regardless of who wins the next America's Cup. The pair of betting rates 7:3 and 3:2 are *incoherent*. A coherent set of betting rates is such that it is impossible to place a bet against them in such a way as to make a guaranteed profit in the above sense.

De Finetti proved that the necessary and sufficient conditions that a set of betting rates be coherent, is that they satisfy the probability axioms and conditional probability rule, (1)–(4) of §5 above. He does not extend this result to a fully countably additive algebra of events, because he is rigorous in his construal of personal probability. A person cannot realistically be supposed to have a structure of beliefs over such an algebra of events. However, de Finetti does extend his theory so as to allow for example for integration, in ways reminiscent of intuitionist and constructive approaches to the foundations of mathematical analysis.

De Finetti also gave a personal equivalent of independence, defined as (5) in §5 above. This was particularly important for him, because he held that in nature there are no independent trials or stable frequencies; there are only our beliefs about what will happen on individual trials. Since 'independence' is of great heuristic and mathematical power, de Finetti wished a personal surrogate for it. Corresponding to statistical independence he proposed what he called *exchangeability*. The core idea is that events that may occur in a sequence are exchangeable (in a person's belief structure) if the person is indifferent between all sequences in which the proportions of events of given kinds which occur are the same, regardless of the order in which they occur. Thus a person is indifferent between any *ABBBB, BABBB, BBABB, BBBAB* and *BBBBA*; indifferent between any of the 10 sequences containing $2A$ and $3B$, and so forth. Natural generalizations of this idea lead to a powerful theory of exchangeability (Diaconis and Freedman, 1980a).

7. BAYESIANISM. The probability axioms have an immediate consequence much used in the theory of personal probability. Let $A_1, \ldots, A_n$ be a set of mutually exclusive and jointly exhaustive events. By (4) of §5, for each $i \leqslant n$,

$$P(B)P(A_i/B) = P(A_i)P(B/A_i).$$

Since

$$B = \cup(A_j \cap B)$$

$$P(B) = \sum P(A_j \cap B) = \sum P(A_j)P(B/A_i).$$

The first and third lines imply that

$$P(A_i/B) = \frac{P(A_i)P(B/A_i)}{\sum P(A_j)P(B/A_j)}. \tag{8}$$

(8) is often called Bayes' theorem, due to its tenuous connection with Bayes (1763). As it is a trivial deduction it is better called Bayes' rule. It is of course valid in any interpretation, but it is of serious interest only from a belief point of view. For suppose that the partition $A_1, \ldots, A_n$ is an exhaustive set of mutually exclusive hypotheses of interest, and that B is evidence bearing on the hypotheses. Suppose further that a person has, in the light of prior knowledge, a distribution of belief over the A_i, represented by $P(A_i)$ for each i. Call this the *prior* probability distribution. Let the A's be of such a sort that for each A_i, $P(B/A_i)$ is defined. This is called the *likelihood* of getting B, if A_i is true. For example, let A_1 state that the outcomes of a die are equiprobable, and A_2, that there is bias with $P(6) = 0.3$. Then the likelihood of 6 on A_1 is $1/6$, and A_2 is $3/10$.

Now we may ask, in order to be coherent, how should a person incorporate a new piece of evidence B into a prior probability distribution over the hypotheses A_i? A plausible answer following Bayes' rule is that the 'posterior distribution' (in the light of B) should be the same as the (prior) conditional probability distribution $P(A_i/B)$. Schematically,

Posterior probability α prior probability $\times$ likelihood.

The contrast of proportionality is as in (8) above.

It is argued that this provides a model of reasonable learning from experience. A person at some stage has a purely personal prior probability distribution over some range of possibilities. This is subject only to the constraint of coherence. However, it is urged, coherence entails a uniquely reasonable way to adjust one's probabilities in the light of new information. On learning new B, one should move from prior probabilities $P(A_i)$ to posterior probabilities equivalent to $P(A_i/B)$. If we spoke of personal probabilities at a time, indicated by a superscript t, and if between t and t' we learn just B, then

$$P^{t'}(A_i) \quad \text{should be} \quad P^t(A_i/B). \tag{9}$$

This is an additional postulate that does not follow from the probability axioms, and which is peculiar to the personal interpretation of probability. Nothing in the coherence argument entails that probabilities should be adjusted across time in accord with (9). Attempts to justify statements such as (9) have been interesting but inconclusive (Diaconis and Zabell, 1982). Assertion (9) should be regarded as a pragmatic postulate for the use of personal probabilities. No one has proposed a significantly different and seriously better general rule for personal learning from experience.

Every interpretation of probability appears to require a pragmatic postulate, although what is required is different in each case. Consider the theory of rational belief, in which the conditional probability $P(A/B)$ is interpreted as a logical relation between B and A. This is supposed to be a unique constant determined by something analogous to deductive logic. Here there is no need for a time-spanning postulate such as (9), for in a theory of rational belief, all probabilities are conditional and are held to be uniquely defined. How can such purely logical relations serve as 'the very guide of life' (Butler, 1736, Introduction) that one expects from an applied theory of probability? How can a collection of logical relations help with predictions and decisions? One cannot reply that if the total available evidence bearing on A is B, then the rational probability of A is $P(A/B)$, because on the theory of rational probability, 'the probability of A' makes no sense, all probabilities being relative.

One requires a pragmatic postulate similar to what has been called *the requirement of total evidence* (Carnap, 1950, p. 211). Let $A_1, \ldots, A_n$ be a partition of states of affairs, and B a further proposition. Let $P(A_i/B)$ be a rational probability function defined for fixed B. Let U_i be the value of utility if A_i obtains. The the rational expectation on B is, following (6) of §5,

$$\sum U_i P(A_i/B).$$

A pragmatic posultate would state: if B is the total available evidence relevant to members of the partition A_i, then act so as to maximize the rational expectation on B. Since it is doubtful whether there exist rational probability functions, and since the notion of total available evidence is utterly obscure, such a postulate is of purely academic interest, intended to illustrate a feature of some traditional reflections on probability.

The term Bayesian is at present commonly used for a personal theory of probability that makes heavy use of Bayes' rule and (implicitly) a pragmatic postulate. But it should also include rationalist approaches such as those of Jeffreys (1939) which also make extensive use of Bayes' rule.

8. LIGHT THEOREMS. Bayes' rule is a theorem valid under any interpretation of probability but whose interest is largely confined to degree of belief approaches. We now turn to a fundamental body of work whose immediate application is more evident for frequency approaches. Arguably this work, which results in a series of limit theorems, establishes the essential connection between probability

and finite relative frequencies. It begins with a result proved by Jacob Bernoulli around 1695 (Bernoulli, 1713).

Bernoulli intended his investigations to contribute to an understanding of statistical inference, but they are also important for the very conception of probability.

Regardless of the glosses of §3 above, in terms of limiting frequency or propensity, the intuition underlying an abstract frequency conception of probability is this: if A occurs k times in n independent and 'identical' trials, then, if n is large, k/n should be close to the probability p to A. This is the content of Bernoulli's theorem. In its weak form it states that for any small 'error' ε,

$$P\left(\left|\frac{k}{n} - p\right| < \varepsilon\right) \to 1 \quad \text{as } n \to \infty. \tag{10}$$

A stronger form asserts that for any error ε and small probability δ, there is a number N such that for $n > N$,

$$P\left(\left|\frac{k}{n} - p\right| < \varepsilon\right) \leqslant 1 - \delta. \tag{11}$$

This applies only to 'identical' trials on which the probability is $P(A) = p$ for each trial. S.-D. Poisson coined the term 'law of large numbers' for a generalization (Poisson, 1837). Suppose that the probability of A on successive trials is not constant, but only that there is a suitable regular probability distribution for values of $P(A)$. In Poisson's examples, one would have a sequence of urns, each with a different proportion of black as opposed to white balls. $P(A)$ would be the probability of drawing a black ball from a given urn, and there would be a probability distribution over the proportions of balls in successive urns. Poisson established that a result analogous to (11) holds, in which p is replaced by the mean probability of $P(A)$. The term 'law of large numbers' is now widely used to apply to all results of this type, including Bernoulli's original result (10).

A continuation of this result began with work by A. de Moivre in 1732 and was fully developed by P.S. Laplace and C.F. Gauss around 1800 (Stigler, 1986). It is the beginning of the well known Gaussian or Normal probability distribution with its familiar 'bell shaped curve' once known simply as *the* curve of probability.

Bernoulli had been able to place crude upper bounds on the probability that on n trials the proportion of A occurring should be within the ε of p. De Moivre addressed the more general question of the form of the histogram of k/n (for $k = 0, \ldots, k = n$) as n grows without bound. Let $\Phi(x)$ be a cumulative probability distribution for a real-valued variable x: thus $\Phi(x)$ is the probability of the variable taking a value less than or equal to x. The Normal distribution with mean zero and variance 1 is

$$\Phi(x) = \frac{1}{\sqrt{(2\pi)}} \int_{-\infty}^{x} \exp(-\tfrac{1}{2}y^2)\,dy.$$

In repeated independent trials with fixed probability $P(A) = p$, the following holds. For any fixed $a < b$, as $n \to \infty$,

$$P\left\{ a \leqslant \left| \frac{k}{n} - p \right| \left[\frac{n}{p(1-p)} \right]^{1/2} \leqslant b \right\} \to \Phi(b) - \Phi(a). \tag{12}$$

This establishes with greater precision the connection between probability and stable long-run frequency. It also shows how the probability associated with the simplest chance device, namely coin tossing, relates to the Normal distribution which, for mean μ and variance σ^2 is:

$$\frac{1}{\sqrt{(2\pi)}\sigma} \int_{-\infty}^{x} \exp[-(y-\mu)^2/2\sigma_2] \mathrm{d}y.$$

Proofs of (12) and increasingly general theorems of that type were developed by the Petersburg school of mathematicians in the latter part of the nineteenth century: P.L. Chebyshev, A.A. Markov and A.M. Lyapunov (see Maistrov, 1967). Lyapunov gave one form of the *central limit theorem*. Consider a sequence of mutually independent variables $x_1, \ldots, x_r$ with a common distribution. Suppose that the mean and variance of x_i exist, and are μ and σ^2. Let $k = x_1 + \cdots + x_n$. Then for every fixed ε, as $n \to \infty$,

$$P\left\{ \left| \frac{k}{n} - \mu \right| \left(\frac{n}{\sigma} \right)^{1/2} < \varepsilon \right\} \to \Phi(\varepsilon). \tag{13}$$

From a conceptual point of view, central limit theorems should be regarded as a culmination of a series of results that explicate the fundamental frequency conception of probability. They also illustrate the power of the probability axioms.

9. APPLICATION OF SUCH PROBABILITIES. Although the limit theorems lay bare the intuitive connection between probability and frequency, there remains a question of application to a single and unique event, such as the next outcome of a roll of a die. If we think of probability in terms of relative frequencies, how can it bear on a particular toss? We may believe that the probability of 6 with a die is 1/6, and believe, thanks to the limit theorems, that in a long run the relative frequency of sixes will usually be close to 1/6. But if we are to judge only the next outcome, for example for purposes of making a bet, why should the fraction 1/6 be of special interest? Once again it appears that, just as for a personal probability interpretation, we require a pragmatic postulate, this time in order to decide what to do *next*, in other words, once again in order to make probability 'a very guide of life'. This has in effect been proposed by many writers, for example by Reichenbach (1949, §72), who speaks of single case 'posits' in connection with individual cases.

There is, however, an additional problem, often called the problem of the reference class. A particular future event may be a member of several classes, each of which is associated with a stable relative frequency. A man may be both a heavy smoker and a jogger. Probabilities of living to the age of 60 may be known for smokers of his age, and for joggers of his age, but neither in itself tells us what to expect of this individual. It is commonly proposed that an individual case should be referred to the smallest discernible class for which a frequency is known. Then a pragmatic postulate would instruct one to act so as to maximize expectations relative to the smallest discernible reference classes.

This postulate is curiously similar, in certain respects, to the pragmatic postulate needed for Bayesian learning from experience. Even if expectation may seem a good guide in life in situations where one is to make a series of successive decisions or take a series of successive gambles, there is no compelling reason for employing expectations in a particular case. All the same (just as with (9), the temporal use of Bayes' rule) no alternative yet proposed has, in general, any desirable features at all.

10. NON-QUANTITATIVE PROBABILITY. The classical approach to probability from Huygens (1657) to the present has measured probabilities by rational fractions or real numbers. A minority of workers has rejected this as unrealistic. Thus Keynes supposed that comparisons of probability are often feasible when quantitative measures are not (Keynes, 1921). He had the rationality approach, in which all probabilities are conditional, and he held that the fundamental form of probability statements is:

$$P(A/B) \leqslant P(C/D).$$

This gives rise to a lattice of partially ordered probabilities that has proved attractive from various points of view. Some personalists hold that we can usually only compare our personal degrees of confidence, not measure them. A few frequentists have held that stabilities in nature are seldom secure enough to guarantee quantitative long-run frequencies, but that we have many comparisons furnished by nature. For a survey of these approaches, see Fine (1973, ch. II).

11. INFERENCE AND MODELLING. We now return to the chief uses of probability stated in §§1, 2, namely inference and modelling. It might seem as if inference would naturally employ a belief-oriented conception of probability, and that modelling would be via frequency or propensity. This would imply a quite eclectic approach to interpretations of probability, as is common among day-to-day consumers of probability mathematics. However, a majority of workers on foundations have been dogmatic, arguing that we should use one and only one interpretation of probability for all purposes of interest.

Thus a majority of authors who present theories of statistical inference favour a frequency interpretation. They hold that the only legitimate tool for objective public discussion must be a frequency oriented idea. An account of personal probability is too subjective for scientific inference or public decision making.

Conversely, many adherents to a degree of belief approach hold that there just do not exist any objective propensities or frequencies in macroscopic nature. (Some, but not all, admit a place for them in microphysics). Such writers try to re-express everything valuable in a frequency approach in terms of personal belief. De Finetti's exchangeability of §6 above was intended to provide a subjective surrogate for the notion of objective independence (which de Finetti thinks does not exist in nature).

Such dogmatic personalism precludes any use of modelling of natural processes by frequency-like structures, and reduces all reasoning about nature, where we have incomplete information, to operations with coherent personal probabilities. Inference, on the other hand, is no problem for the personalist, who augments the probability axioms with a (usually implicit) pragmatic postulate (9) as in §7 above. All inference is by Bayes' rule or by a more sophisticiated version of that.

Conversely, the dogmatic frequentist has no problem with modelling natural processes by probability structures interpreted in terms of stable frequencies or propensities. But whereas in a sense the personalist has no theory of statistical inference (all inference being by Bayes' rule), the frequentist has not one but several competing theories of considerable conceptual difficulty. These will now be briefly described.

12. INFERRING BY FREQUENCY. There has evolved an enormous battery of techniques for testing statistical hypotheses, estimating statistical parameters, designing experiments and making decisions. There is less agreement on the foundations for these techniques. From 1920 until his death in 1962, R.A. Fisher was a prolific source of such fundamental ideas as significance tests, maximum likelihood estimators, randomized experimental design, sufficient statistics, information and a host of others. In part because he favoured many different and non-equivalent uses of probability, it is not possible to give a brief simple acount of what he took to be the basics. The opposite is the case for a later and influential pair of workers, Jerzy Neyman and E.S. Pearson, whose theory will be sketched first.

Neyman was a dogmatic frequentist who held that it is never possible to make a probability statement about a particular event or hypothesis. Inductive *inference* is, he said, impossible, and is to be replaced by a theory of inductive *behaviour*. We can at best choose a policy that has desirable 'operating characteristics'. In the case of testing one statistical hypothesis H against a family of others, we require a method that seldom rejects H if it is true, (say 1 per cent of the time), and, given that constraint, usually rejects H if it is false. In most practical situations this goal cannot be uniformly achieved, but Neyman and Pearson introduce other operating constraints so as to design unique tests. Likewise in estimating that an unknown parameter lies in a certain interval on the real line, one requires that on repeated experiments the method of estimation would yield an interval that includes the true parameter most of the time. A 99 per cent confidence interval is derived by a method that is correct 99 per cent of the time (and is subject to other constraints to ensure uniqueness). In a particular case one *cannot* assert that there is 0.99 probability that the unknown parameter is within the bounds of the estimate. One can say only that the interval was derived by a method that is usually right.

Fisher regarded statistical inference as primarily a procedure for data analysis, for maximizing information obtained from experiment, and for producing intelligible information-preserving summations of data that would otherwise be too complex to understand. He thought of the various significance levels (analogous to confidence levels) as convenient standards by means of which experimental workers could judge each others' results. Thus in considering a treatment (of a field with fertilizer, of patients with medicine, of an economy with a rise in interest rates) one wants to know if the treatment is efficacious. Thus one tests the 'null hypothesis' by making a probability model of the hypothesis of no effect. The result of an experiment is significant at the 1 per cent level if, on the model of the null hypothesis, an effect at least as large as that observed would occur with probability less than or equal to 0.01. Otherwise the result is judged not to be significant at the 1 per cent level. In the event that the treatment is judged significant, one is not obliged to reject the null hypothesis. The result of a significance test is always of the following logical form: either something very unusual has occurred by change, as will from time to time happen, or else the null hypothesis is false and the treatment is efficacious (Fisher, 1956, ch. III).

Such a piecemeal approach, in which a statistical report summarizes a situation and leaves other experimenters to make up their own minds, is in apparent contrast with the regimented policies derived by the Neyman–Pearson theory. For Fisher's chief papers, see Fisher (1950); for the joint work of Neyman and Pearson, see Neyman and Pearson (1767).

Most ordinary practitioners do not draw firm lies between the two approaches. There remain significant practical differences. For example, in certain Fisherian analyses based on likelihood (see definition (6) in §5 above) it makes no difference whether the length of an experiment has been determined in advance, or whether the experimenter decides in the course of the experiment when to quit. On the Neyman theory, such optional stopping complete changes the analysis of the data. Likewise there are striking contrasts between frequency theories on the one hand – be they those of Fisher or Neyman – and Bayesian belief theories on the other. The former not only regularly incorporate randomization into the design of experiments, but hold it to be an essential procedure for increasing the amount of information derived from an experiment. On a Bayesian account, however, randomization is of no value and may actually lead to a loss of information. It remains the case that almost all experimenters favour randomization, and in the case of human subjects, urge double blind experimentation when practicable.

13. PROBABILITY AND ECONOMICS. Expectation, defined in terms of utility and probability, is an economic concept. The first book on the probability calculus, one which set the pace in the early days, defined probability in terms of expectation (Huygens, 1657), and this practice continued until at least the time of Bayes (1763). Hence one would anticipate a longstanding relationship between probability and economics. This has not been the case. French pre-revolutionary physiocrats thought that probability should play a central role in 'moral science', which would include what we now call economics. However, this had little direct influence, even if through the mediation of the Marquis de Condorcet it aroused the early interests of that greatest of probability mathematicians, Laplace.

Only during the 19th century did probability become a working tool of a sizeable number of sciences, disciplines and practices. The complete assimilation of probability to almost every topic has occurred only very recently. (For cross-disciplinary studies, suggesting the differential adoption of probability tools and techniques, see Daston et al., 1987.) Despite the fact that maximization of utility has long been an economic adage or even tautology, economics has been one of the slower disciplines to be penetrated by probabilistic thinking.

Economists have usually been eclectic in their use of probability. F.Y. Edgeworth, author of the article *Probability* in the original *Palgrave*, noted in his longer essay for the *Encyclopaedia Britannica* that a belief approach to probability might be rejected on the ground that it was 'merely psychological'. He goes on to mention a limiting frequency approach. But, he continues, 'these views are not so diametrically opposed as might at first appear' (Edgeworth, 1911, p. 377). Many economists would echo his words today.

Some, however, have strongly favoured only one approach to probability. The most notable example is Keynes. Although he became less dogmatic about probability later in life, at the time of his major contribution to the field (Keynes, 1921) he provided the classic statement of the rationalist approach to probability, and also was far ahead of his time in urging that comparative probabilities are fundamental. F.P. Ramsey, who in his very short life had commenced important contributions to economic theory, is of course the founder of the modern personalist approach, and he was the first to see how probability and utility can be jointly axiomatized as concepts that are integrally and necessarily connected.

The theory of games and economic behaviour, set forth in its modern form by von Neumann in a work with that title, settles on the 'perfectly well founded interpretation of probability as frequency in long runs' (von Neumann and Morgenstern, 1953, p. 19). In a footnote it is said that one may instead axiomatize probability and preference jointly. This was done explicitly by L.J. Savage (1954), who had been one of von Neumann's wartime assistants, and who has provided us with the standard exposition of personal probability, one which has, as one of its consequences, von Neumann's theory of utility. The present article has emphasized controversies about the interpretation and application of probability ideas; it must conclude by stating that despite differences in foundation, a great many divergences are washed away in the routine of day-to-day application and derivation.

BIBLIOGRAPHY

Bayes, T. 1763. An essay towards solving a problem in the doctrine of changes. In *Studies in the History of Statistics and Probability*, ed. E.S. Pearson and M.G. Kendall, London: Griffin, 1970; Darien, Conn.: Hafner Publishing Company.

Bernoulli, J. 1713. *Ars conjectandi*. Basle.

Butler, J. 1736. *The Analogy of Religion*. London.

Carnap, R. 1950. *Logical Foundations of Probability*. Chicago: University of Chicago Press.

Daston, R., Heidlberger, M. and Krüger, L. (eds) 1987. *The Probabilistic Revolution*. 2 vols, Cambridge, Mass.: Bradford Books.

de Finetti, B. 1937. Foresight: its logical laws, its subjective sources. Trans. from the French in *Studies in Subjective Probability*, ed. H.E. Kyburg Jr. H.E. Smokler, New York: Wiley, 1964.

Diaconis, P. and Freedman, D. 1980a. De Finetti's generalizations of exchangeability. In *Studies in Induction Logic and Probability*, Vol. II, ed. R.C. Jeffrey, Berkeley and Los Angeles: University of California Press.

Diaconis, P. and Freedman, D. 1980b. De Finetti's theorem for Markov chains. *Annals of Probability* 8(1), 115–30.

Diaconis, P. and Zabell, S. 1982. Updating subjective probability. *Journal of the American Statistical Association* 77, 822–30.

Edgeworth, F.Y. 1911. Probability. In *The Encyclopaedia Britannica*, 11th edn, Vol. XXII, New York: Encyclopaedia Britannica.

Fine, T. 1973. *Theories of Probability*. New York: Academic Press.

Fisher, R.A. 1950. *Contributions to Mathematical Statistics*. New York: Wiley.

Fisher, R.A. 1956. *Statistical Methods and Scientific Inference*. Edinburgh: Oliver & Boyd.

Huygens, Chr. 1657. *Ratiociniis in aleae ludo* (Reasoning in a game of change). In C. Huygens, *Oeuvres complètes*, The Hague: M. Nijhoff, 1888–1950, includes the original Latin, Huygens' original Dutch, and French translation in Vol. 14.

Jeffreys, H. 1939. *Theory of Probability*. 3rd edn, Oxford: Clarendon Press, 1961.

Keynes, J.M. 1921. *A Treatise on Probability*. London: Macmillan; New York: Harper & Row, 1962.

Kolmogorov, A.N. 1933. *Foundations of the Theory of Probability*. Trans. from the German, New York: Chelsea, 1950.

Laplace, P.S. de 1795. *A Philosophical Essay on Probabilities*. Trans. from the French, New York: Dover, 1951.

Maistrov, L.E. 1967. *Probability Theory: A Historical Sketch*. Trans. from the Russian, New York: Academic Press, 1974.

Neyman, J. and Pearson, E.S. 1967. *Joint Statistical Papers*. Cambridge: Cambridge University Press; Berkeley: University of California Press, 1967.

Peirce, C.S. 1878, 1910. *Collected Papers of Charlges Sanders Peirce*. Ed. C. Hartshorne and P. Weiss, Cambridge, Mass.: Harvard University Press, 1965.

Poisson, S.-D. 1837. *Recherches sur la probabilité des jugements en matière criminelle et en matière civile*. Paris.

Popper, K.R. 1959. The propensity interpretation of probability. *British Journal for the Philosophy of Science* 10, May, 25–42.

Ramsey, F.P. 1926. Truth and probability. In *Foundations: Essays by F.P. Ramsey*, ed. D.H. Mellor, London: Routledge & Kegan Paul, 1978; New York: Humanities Press.

Reichenbach, H. 1949. *The Theory of Probability*. Berkeley and Los Angeles: University of California Press.

Savage, L.J. 1954. *The Foundations of Statistics*. New York: Wiley.

Stigler, S. 1986. *The History of Statistics: The Measurement of Uncertainty before 1900*. Chicago: University of Chicago Press.

Suppes, P. 1973. New foundations of objective probability: axioms for propensities. In *Logic, Methodology and Philosophy of Science*, Vol. IV, ed. P. Suppes et al., Amsterdam: North-Holland.

Von Mises, R. 1928. *Probability, Statistics and Truth*. Trans. from the German, London: Allen & Unwin, 1957.

Von Neumann, J. and Morgenstern, O. 1944. *Theory of Games and Economic Behavior*. Princeton: Princeton University Press, 3rd edn, 1953.

Psychology and Economics

CHARLES R. PLOTT

Several developments have joined to stimulate economists to think about issues that have been on the forefront of psychological research. Firstly, the information revolution in economics has focused economists on the subtle nature of individual information processing. Secondly, developments in game theory have so successfully identified new solution concepts that for almost any pattern of market behaviour there exists a reasonable theory consistent with that pattern. Introspection, a few principles of decision making, internal consistency and a few stylized facts do not constrain possibilities enough to be sufficient guides to theory. Theorists are being forced to seek more systematic sources of data and additional principles to reduce the number of competing theories. Thirdly, the rapid development of experimental methods applicable to economics has brought the testing of psychologically based economic theories within the realm of reality. Economists can accurately measure behaviour in economically relevant settings. As behavioural patterns become established that are difficult to reconcile with economic models alone, the profession has begun to look to psychology for answers. The data thus force the attention of economists to a broader class of models.

The interest of economists has also been stimulated directly by the work of psychologists whose own curiosity has brought their research closer to subjects that have been in the traditional domain of economics. Psychologists are deeply involved with risk/benefit analysis and normative decision analysis. Consequently, contact with traditional welfare economics and decision theory cannot be avoided. Psychologists have been actively studying common dilemma problems. The literature has led them to an awareness of public goods, externalities, and notions of incentive compatibility. The trend is reversed in the study of non-human choices where economists interested in testing demand theory as applied to non-humans are being exposed to concepts of conditioning, shaping, reinforcement theory, etc., characteristic of the tools traditionally found useful to those who study animal behaviour in the laboratory.

A few exchanges between psychologists and economists have occurred recently.

The focus of this section is on those exchanges. These are recent cases in which economists have become directly involved and have explored hypotheses that are of psychological origin. There is good reason to limit the material in this way. Almost any behaviour can have economic implications, and psychologists have not been particularly shy about making claims for the relevance of their research for economics. The whole field of psychology could be implicated. Consequently the focus will be on the work of economists that has been influenced by psychology as opposed to the work of psychologists that might have some economic import.

THE OPTIMIZATION HYPOTHESIS. Economists tend to focus on choice and have had little to say about the process of choosing. The focus is natural. For the most part economics is about group phenomena and the behaviour of systems such as markets, whole economies, and political or other social units. The actions taken by each individual are the key contributions to the system behaviour and thus the individual actions are the important data. From this traditional perspective the particular cognitions that might have led to an act are of secondary importance to the action itself. The maintained hypothesis of goal seeking and purposeful actions as summarized by the optimization hypothesis provides a coherence and internal consistency to individual actions, but there has been no pressure to inquire deeper into the substance of the choosing process. The existence of attitudes is clearly acknowledged in the theory by the concepts of subjective probabilities and preferences, but the principles governing these attitudes have been maintained only at the most general level.

Choice is connected to the attitudinal parameters by a principle of optimization. The theory of rational choice claims only that observed choices will have that internal consistency necessary to be rationalized by a theory of optimization. Preferences will be revealed by choice.

There are many different types of rational choice. The choice can be influenced by random elements (McFadden, 1974). The subjective probabilities and preferences can be related in ways not anticipated by the excessively strong expected utility hypothesis (Machina, 1982; Chew, 1983; Loomes and Sugden, 1986). The preferences may not be transitive and instead only be devoid of cycles (Richter, 1971). Only very recently has the literature seen generalizations of the concept of an optimum choice that does not require elements of maximization based on binary comparisons (Aizerman, 1985). These principles are all of a most general nature and do not really address the issues of decision process because economic theory has evolved narrowly, as demanded by the study of system behaviour.

By contrast, recent psychological research has been focused on the process of decisions as opposed to the choice or output of the process. The analysis reflects data generated by experimental methodology and is not constrained by systemic considerations. Perception, confusion, and the dynamics of preference and attitude formation are of central importance to psychologists.

Since the focus of psychological research is on decision processes, a natural tendency when confronted by the optimization hypothesis is to ask if people actually think in optimization terms. Do people consciously attempt to maximize something? The mathematics of optimization gives a rather clear outline of what a conscious process might be. Each option of a feasible set is compared in a series of binary comparisons of preference. The best is thereby identified and chosen. Do people do this? Do they *want* to do it?

Psychologists find little support for an optimization process as derived from the mathematical definitions. The lack of support for such a process is especially the case when uncertainty and information processing is involved. The natural response of the economics community when confronted by data that suggest that individuals do not consciously solve mathematical optimization problems has been to ask first, 'so what?'. If the choices made by individuals naturally exhibit the internal consistency property of revealed preference then the cognitive processes are of minor consequence because the individuals would choose 'as if' optimizing and the substance of the theory of markets would be left intact. A second natural response of economists is to ask the psychologists if they have a theory that will 'do better' in explaining system behaviour. In the absence of an alternative theory, criticism of existing theory is not very compelling.

Psychologists have convincingly demonstrated that the 'as if optimizing' principle is not generally reliable. The easiest demonstrations of the lack of generality of the principle involves the preference reversal phenomenon. The subject is given a choice between two lotteries. Lottery A is a 0.99 probability of winning $4 and a 0.01 probability of winning nothing. Lottery B is a 0.33 probability of winning \$16 and a 0.67 probability of winning nothing. When asked to choose between the two, lottery A is the typical choice. When asked which lottery is valued the most, e.g., which of the lotters has the highest reservation price or which has the highest selling price, then B is indicated. In other words the observed preference switches from A to B depending upon the way preference is measured. The phenomenon characterizes the behaviour of many people. It persists with monetary incentives and control for a variety of economic considerations (Grether and Plott, 1979), training (Reilly, 1982), and has been observed by a number of different researchers employing different techniques (Slovic and Lichtenstein, 1983). The existence of the phenomenon is well documented.

The phenomenon is of interest to economists because it can be interpreted as an immediate intransitivity. Let W = existing wealth, ϕ = the empty set, $\succsim$ indicate a preference relation, and $h(x)$ = the reservation price of lottery x. The pair (W, x) describes the possible states of an individual. The chain $(W + h(A), \phi) \sim (W, A) \succ (W, B) \sim (W + h(B), \phi)$ is observed from choice. Which do you prefer, A or B? Typically the subject chooses A as indicated. The minimum selling price when measured yields $h(A)$. Transitivity and the positive utility of money imply $h(A) > h(B)$, which contradicts the typical subject's expression of value; that B is valued more (has a higher reservation price) than A. The phenomenon is not only inconsistent with the expected utility hypothesis, it is inconsistent with all economic theories of preference. It demonstrates that choice is not universally consistent with an 'as if' optimization principle. Furthermore, since a single individual choosing among lotteries is a (degenerate) class of markets, the phenomenon bears directly on market choices.

Is there an alternative theory? The jury is still out on alternative explanations of preference reversals (Goldstein and Einhorn, 1986; Loomes and Sugden, 1982). However, the general approach to theories of decision processes taken by psychologists has been to retain the basic structure of optimization theory. People have transitive preferences but they might not be completely aware of them. Rather than ask what does a person want, the tendency of psychologists is to ask how a person *expects* to feel as a result of taking an act (March, 1978). Perception, limited capacities for calculation, and perhaps the dependence of preferences on previous choices are integral aspects of the modified theory.

Choice is preceded by an editing phase of activities. Alternatives are first examined for attributes, which are coded as a gain or loss relative to some reference point. The reference point could be a status quo or it could be a level of aspiration. This editing phase is sometimes referenced as 'framing' (Tversky and Kahneman, 1981).

The evaluation phase follows editing. Almost all psychological theories of the process of choice postulate that the individual compares options attribute by attribute. This is in contrast to a holistic assessment in which the individual evaluates all attributes of a single option and, having assessed the option, the process moves to another option which is wholly assessed. Studies that involve the tracing of eye movements during the process of choice support the psychologists's presumptions (Russo and Dosher, 1983). Eye movement tends to fix on an attribute and move across options, remaining fixed on that attribute. After surveying objects, a new attribute is chosen. This process should be contrasted to one in which all attributes of an object are examined as if to gain a total assessment of the utility of the object before moving to the next object.

Slovic and Lichtenstein (1983) think of evaluation in terms of anchoring and adjustment. This process begins with the identification and evaluation of a single attribute. The value of that attribute is attached to the option and then the evaluation is adjusted upward or downward to compensate for other attributes. Inconsistencies such as those observed in preference reversals are the result of incomplete adjustments according to this model. Risk averse people tend to choose option A when the choices are offered. Then, when such people are asked to place a value on the options, they focus first on the monetary amount, attach that initial value to the object, and then adjust the amount downward to compensate for the probability. Incomplete adjustment for the probability and other attributes yields a higher value for B than for A, which began with a lower initial value for B than for A, which began with a lower initial valuation because of the lower dollar figure from which base adjustments are made. The result is the observed inconsistency with choice.

Other evaluation models exist. Lexicographic rules involve an ordering of attributes. The chosen alternative has the highest level of the best attribute. Prospect theory (Tversky and Kahneman, 1981) involves valuing attributes but the theory incorporates an asymmetry between losses and gains. When the options

181

are lotteries, prospect theory holds that people are risk avoiders in gains and risk seekers in losses. Of course, since lexicographic rules and prospect theory are optimization theories, neither an account for the preference reversal phenomena.

Another class of models are suggestive of what Simon (1955, 1979) has called satisficing. The choosing agent is viewed as being involved in a costly search problem as objects are examined and attributes are compared. The theoretical problem becomes one of isolating the rules governing search and decision. Two important classes of such rules are conjunctive and disjunctive (Einhorn, 1970). Conjunctive and disjunctive rules require that cutoff levels be set on each attribute. A conjunctive rule requires that any option with an attribute below cutoff is rejected. Disjunction requires that options with attributes above cutoff be accepted.

Economists have pursued some aspects of this theory (Grether and Wilde, 1984). Optimal risk-neutral conjunction decision rules were calculated by the researchers for an experimental economics setting involving sequential (search) decisions. In addition, a set of non-optimal rules were calculated. The non-optimal rules were approximations of the optimal rules in which the cross derivative terms in the first-order conditions of an optimal sequential decision were ignored. Subjects were restricted to the use of conjunctive rules so the test was whether or not consumers used optimal rules or the postulated non-optimal rules, given that a particular type of decision rule had to be used. Subjects tended to use the non-optimal rules in which 'second-order' tradeoffs are ignored.

The Grether and Wilde study has two major dimensions of interest. First, their theoretical methods incorporate a way to identify 'rules of thumb' that have a systematic and theoretical departure from optimal. They have a way of using optimal rules to generate simplifications of the rule that can be interpreted as satisficing. Secondly, the experimental methods provide a way of testing such modified theories and getting good measurements on the nature of their inadequacies.

BAYES' LAW. Economic models tend to treat individuals as if they were intuitive statisticians. Of course Bayes' law is a central tenet. It is used in the theory without modification any time an economic agent is exposed to information.

By contrast, the psychological approach to subjective probability is similar to the psychological approach to decisions in general. People are viewed as using rules of thumb which may or may not reflect an appropriate statistical principle.

One of these rules, called the representativeness heuristic, has caught the attention of economists. According to this rule individuals will view samples as having come from the population that is most representative of the sample. The rule suggests a tendency to ignore prior probabilities or, in a sense, put too much weight on the sample while generating a posterior. The phenomenon has been studied extensively in the psychology literature. The following is an example of what is observed. Suppose urn A contains black balls and white balls with $Pr(black) = 0.75$ and $Pr(white) = 0.25$. Urn B has the opposite probabilities. A sample of four balls with replacement will be drawn from one of these urns. The subject must guess the urn that was used and is rewarded cash for correct choices. The urn to be used in the draw is decided from a draw from a third urn with $Pr(A) = 0.01$ and $Pr(B) = 0.99$.

Now suppose a sample of four balls is drawn. Three of the four are black. Which urn was used?

Bayes' law gives $Pr(A) \approx 0.02$. Nevertheless, the representativeness hypothesis predicts that A will be chosen. The reason is the similarity between the sample and the distribution of balls in A. The prior probabilities will be underweighted according to this theory.

An experiment conducted by Grether (1980) was of the form used in the example. Rewards provide a financial incentive to choose the urn that the subject thinks is the most likely. That is, subjects are paid for guessing the correct urn. For a given sample, x, urn A is chosen when $Pr(A|x)/Pr(B|x) > 1$ and B is chosen otherwise.

The use of Bayes law gives the model

$$\frac{Pr(A|x)}{Pr(B|x)} = \left[\frac{Pr(x|A)}{Pt(x|B)} \right]^{\beta_1} \left[\frac{Pr(A)}{Pr(B)} \right]^{\beta_2}$$

where $\beta_1 = \beta_2 = 1$ and $Pr(A)$ and $Pr(B)$ are prior probabilities. Letting Y_{it}^* be the subjective log odds in favour of A for person i at time t so $e^{Y_{it}^*}$ is the posterior odds in favour of A. By taking the logarithm of

$$e^{Y_{it}^*} = e^{\alpha} \left[\frac{Pr(x|A)}{Pr(x|B)} \right]^{\beta_1} \left[\frac{Pr(A)}{Pr(B)} \right]^{\beta_2} e^{u_{it}},$$

where u_i is a random variable, a model suitable for estimation by logit is obtained. Of course Y_{it}^* is not observed but the observed choice provides a variable $Y_{it} = 1$ when $Y_{it}^* \geq 0$ and $Y_{it} = 0$ otherwise. Bayes' law yields the hypothesis $\alpha = 0$, $\beta_1 = \beta_2 > 0$ and the representativeness hypothesis, $\beta_1 > \beta_2 \geq 0$.

The qualitative predictions of the representativeness hypothesis have been supported by the experimental data. However, the coefficient β_2 tends to be strictly greater than zero so the prior probabilities are not ignored. Generally speaking the Bayes' law model has very good predictive ability. Bayes' law is not 'bad' as a model but its predictive power is increased by allowing for the possibility of a representativeness heuristic.

CONCLUSION. When examining psychologically motivated theories, economists have differed from psychologists in three methodological ways. First, economists have tended to use as the dependent variables an act or an observed choice. By contrast, psychologists have tended to elicit attitudes, such as a degree of preference, belief, or numerical probability. Secondly, economists have been more sensitive to the possibility that motivated choice might differ from unmotivated choice. The third difference is the context. Economists have tended to avoid the rich descriptive hypothetical contexts and scenarios used by psychologists. This no doubt reflects a fear that the verbal descriptions will influence behaviour.

For the most part, when testing directly, economists have observed for themselves what psychologists claimed they would observe. Incentives do matter but so far incentives have not been observed overriding the tendencies that psychologists have observed when incentives were absent. It is too early to speculate about what future research will uncover regarding this issue.

Whether or not the psychologically based theories will account for significant market behaviour remains to be established. The potential for such theories has been recognized (Thaler, 1980) but so far the psychological theories, when applied to experimental markets, have not been sufficiently supported to suggest the need for a substantial overhaul in economic theory (Plott, 1986). Nevertheless, the field has only just begun and, given the persistence and magnitude of effects uncovered at the individual level of analysis, it is reasonable to expect that the effects will soon be detected in experimental markets.

BIBLIOGRAPHY

Aizerman, M.A. 1985. New problems in the general choice theory: review of a research trend. *Social Choice and Welfare* 2, 235–82.

Chew, S.H. 1983. A generalization of the quasilinear mean with applications to the measurement of income inequality and decision theory resolving the Allais paradox. *Econometrica* 51, 1065–92.

Einhorn, H. 1970. The use of nonlinear, noncompensatory models in decision making. *Psychological Bulletin* 73, 221–30.

Goldstein, W.M. and Einhorn, H. 1986. Expression theory and the preference reversal phenomena. *Psychological Review.*

Grether, D.M. 1980. Bayes' rule as a descriptive model: the representativeness heuristic. *Quarterly Journal of Economics* 95, November, 537–57.

Grether, D.M. and Plott, C.R. 1979. Economic theory of choice and the preference reversal phenomenon. *American Economic Review* 69, September, 623–38.

Grether, D.M. and Wilde, L.L. 1984. An analysis of conjunctive choice: theory and experiments. *Journal of Consumer Research* 10, March, 373–85.

Loomes, G. and Sugden, R. 1982. Regret theory: an alternative theory of rational choice under uncertainty. *Economic Journal* 92, December, 805–24.

Loomes, G. and Sugden, R. 1986. Disappointment and dynamic consistency in choice under uncertainty. *Review of Economic Studies* 53, April, 271–82.

Machina, M.J. 1982. Expected utility analysis without the independence axiom. *Econometrica* 50, March, 277–323.

March, J.G. 1978. Bounded rationality, ambiguity and the engineering of choice. *Bell Journal of Economics* 9, Autumn, 587–610.

McFadden, D. 1974. Conditional logit analysis of qualitative choice behavior. In *Frontiers in Econometrics*, ed. P. Zarembka, New York: Academic Press, 105–42.

Plott, C.R. 1986. Rational choice in experimental markets. *Journal of Business* 59(2), Pt. 2, S301–34.

Reilly, R.J. 1982. Preference reversal: further evidence and some suggested modifications in experimental design. *American Economic Review* 72, 576–84.

Richter, M.K. 1971. Rational choice. In *Preference, Utility and Demand*, ed. J.S. Chipman et al., San Francisco: Harcourt, Brace, Jovanovich.

Russo, J.E. and Dosher, B.N. 1983. Strategies for multiattribute binary choice. *Journal of Experimental Psychology: Learning, Memory and Cognition* 9, 676–96.

Simon, H.A. 1955. A behavioural model of rational choice. *Quarterly Journal of Economics* 69, February, 99–118.

Simon, H.A. 1979. Rational decision making in business organizations. *American Economic Review* 69, September, 493–513.

Slovic, P. and Lichtenstein, S. 1983. Preference reversals: a broader perspective. *American Economic Review* 73, 596–605.

Thaler, R. 1980. Toward a positive theory of consumer choice. *Journal of Economic Behavior and Organization* 1, March, 39–60.

Tversky, A. and Kahneman, D. 1981. The framing of decisions and the psychology of choice. *Science* 211, 453–8.

Frank Plumpton Ramsey

PETER NEWMAN

There are interesting parallels in the careers of Frank Ramsey and John von Neumann. Each was born in 1903, one the product of the 'High Intelligentsia of England' (Keynes, 1933, p. vii) and the other the son of a wealthy banker in Budapest (Ulam, 1976, p. 79). Each was a creative mathematician of high order but each also made major contributions to at least two other disciplines. Each wrote just three papers in economic theory, all six of which were of fundamental importance. Moreover, with one exception every one of these seminal papers had to wait many years for its proper recognition; even the exception – the utility theory set out in the Appendix to von Neumann and Morgenstern (1947) – at first encountered serious misunderstanding within the profession. Indeed, considering them purely as economists, one wonders how these two geniuses would fare today, when promotion and tenure so often depend on a good immediate showing in citation indexes and the like.

The three papers of Ramsey are in subjective probability and utility (1926), optimal taxation (1927) and optimal one-sector growth (1928), while those of von Neumann are in game theory (1928, 1944), optimal multi-sector growth ([1937], 1945–6) and objective probability and utility (1947). It is quite striking that their work both on growth theory and on choice under uncertainty should be so complementary, especially since there is no evidence that von Neumann knew of Ramsey's work in either field.

Another and grievous similarity was that both men died early; Ramsey on 19 January 1930 of complications associated with jaundice, and von Neumann (twice Ramsey's age) on 8 February 1957 of cancer. Both losses were tragic, especially that of the 26-year-old Frank Ramsey, whose 'death at the height of his powers deprives Cambridge of one of its intellectual glories and contemporary philosophy of one of its profoundest thinkers' (Braithwaite's Introduction to Ramsey, 1931, p. ix).

186

I. LIFE

Frank Plumpton Ramsey was born in Cambridge on 22 February 1903. His father was a mathematician, Fellow and later President of Magdalene College (Harrod, 1951, pp. 141, 320), and his brother Michael became Archbishop of Canterbury. He was educated at Winchester and at Trinity College Cambridge, and was a Scholar of both those ancient foundations. In the autumn of 1924 he became Fellow of King's College and University Lecturer in Mathematics and soon afterwards married Lettice Baker, who had been a student in the Moral Sciences Tripos. After his death she became a founder of Ramsey and Muspratt, a firm of portrait photographers that has long been an Oxbridge institution. She survived into the 1980s, in vigorous old age.

In physical appearance Ramsey was tall and portly, the latter a feature he shared with von Neumann; 'I take no credit for weighing nearly 17 stone [238 pounds]' (1931, p. 291). All accounts agree as to his simplicity and modesty, qualities which are happily reflected in his engaging literary style. 'Ramsey reminds one of Hume more than of anyone else, particularly in his common sense and a sort of hard-headed practicality towards the whole business' (Keynes, 1933, p. 301). But his unfailing cheerfulness did not disguise 'the amazing, easy efficiency of the intellectual machine which ground away behind his wide temples and broad, smiling face' (ibid., p. 296). 'He comes down to earth, however, with a satisfying bump, and earth is certainly the natural element of my old friend Lettice,' (Partridge, 1981, p. 129).

RAMSEY AND WITTGENSTEIN. For many years it was thought that while still an undergraduate Ramsey assisted in the translation of the German text of Wittgenstein's *Tractatus Logico-Philosophicus* (1922). It now appears that 'the first draft of the translation was produced by F.P. Ramsey alone' (von Wright, 1982, p. 102). Just 19, he dictated it directly to a stenographer in the University Typing Office in Cambridge in the winter of 1921–2 (reminiscent, on a smaller scale, of the 19-year-old 'John S. Mill' beginning in 1825 to edit Bentham's massive *Rationale of Judicial Evidence*). Wittgenstein seems to have been pleased with Ramsey's translation (1973, p. 77), and a fast friendship was thereby established between the two philosophers that lasted for the rest of Ramsey's short life.

In September 1923 the *Tractatus* had been published for almost a year. Not only had Ramsey been its main translator but he had also written a long and penetrating review of it for *Mind* (reprinted in 1931, pp. 270–86). But still there were many passages which remained unclear to him. To remedy this he made a special journey to Austria, where Wittgenstein was teaching in the local school of a small village and living in spartan conditions. The eccentric philosopher and the brilliant undergraduate hit it off immediately. Ramsey stayed two weeks, spending every afternoon from 2 to 7 elucidating the great man's work: 'we get on about a page an hour' (ibid., p. 79).

In the several letters that Ramsey afterwards wrote to Wittgenstein we can glimpse what Keynes meant in referring to 'the simplicity of his feelings and reactions, half-alarming sometimes and occasionally almost cruel in their directness and literalness' (Keynes, 1933, p. 296). Consider for example these passages from his letters of 12 November and 20 December 1923 (Wittgenstein, 1973, pp. 81–3):

> I have not been doing much towards reconstructing mathematics; partly because I have been reading miscellaneous things, a little Relativity and a little Kant, and Frege...But I am awfully idle; and most of my energy has been absorbed since January by an unhappy passion for a married woman, which produced such psychological disorder, that I nearly resorted to psychoanalysis, and should probably have gone at Christmas to live in Vienna for nine months and be analysed, had not I suddenly got better a fortnight ago, since when I have been happy and done a fair amount of work.
>
> I think I have solved all problems about finite integers, except such as are connected with the axiom of infinity, but I may well be wrong.
>
> [December 20th] I was silly to think I had solved those problems. I'm always doing that and finding it a mare's nest... *I have been trying to prove a proposition in the Mengenlehre* either $2^{\aleph_0} = \aleph_1$, or $2^{\aleph_0} \neq \aleph_1$, which it is no one knows but I have had no success (his italics).

In 1924 Ramsey actually did spend six months in Vienna in psychoanalysis (rarer then than now), after which 'I feel that people know far less about themselves than they imagine, and am not nearly so anxious to talk about myself as I used to be, having had enough of it to get bored,' (1931, p. 290). The mathematical problem referred to in his second letter was of course the famous Continuum Hypothesis. His lack of success in this is scarcely surprising, since in the 1960s Paul Cohen showed the Hypothesis to be an undecidable proposition within Zermelo–Fraenkel set theory (see e.g. Cohen, 1966). It was, incidentally, a continual disappointment to von Neumann that it was not him but his hero Kurt Gödel who made the startling discovery, in 1930–31, of the necessary existence of such undecidable propositions (Ulam, 1976, pp. 76, 80).

Wittgenstein returned to Cambridge early in 1929 and began those 'innumerable conversations' with Ramsey that are acknowledged in the Preface/Foreword (dated January 1945) to his *Philosophical Investigations* (1953, p. x). Unfortunately, these were cut short by Ramsey's tragic death, a moving account of which may be found in Frances Partridge's *Memories* (1981, 169–82); the grieving Wittgenstein was at Ramsey's bedside in the hospital until a few hours before he died.

The only other person acknowledged by name in the Preface to the *Investigations*, and for even greater help than Ramsey gave, was Piero Sraffa. The trio of Ramsey, Sraffa and Wittgenstein must have been a formidable discussion group indeed; a treasured piece of Cambridge folklore is a lunch at which the three of them discussed Keynes's theory of probability with its author. The odd pattern of belated recognition of intellectual indebtedness was continued in Sraffa's acknowledgement (1960, pp. vi–vii) of Ramsey's help, a mere thirty years after the fact.

II. WORKS

Ramsey's early work in philosophy was a continuation of the methods of Russell and Whitehead's *Principia*, but it is clear that the influence of Wittgenstein and the evolution of his own thinking were moving him towards the end of his life in a quite different, more pragmatic direction. These later contributions were left fragmentary and incomplete at his death, but a very brief account of them and their relations to modern philosophy may be gleaned from the first two Introductions to the revised edition (1978) of (1931).

In mathematics proper, as distinct from the foundations of mathematics, his main contribution is a fundamental theorem which appeared actually as a byproduct of a paper of 1928 on formal logic (reprinted in 1931, pp. 82–111). It reads (1931, p. 82):

> *Theorem* A. Let Γ be an infinite class, and u and r positive integers; and let all those sub-classes of Γ which have exactly r members, or, as we may say, let all r-combinations of the members of Γ be divided into μ mutually exclusive classes $C_i (i = 1, 2, \ldots, \mu)$, so that every r-combination is a member of one and only one C_i; then, assuming the Axiom of Selections [i.e. the Axiom of Choice], Γ must contain an infinite sub-class Δ such that all the r-combinations of the members of Δ belong to the same C_i.

This beautiful result was ignored until 1935, when it was essentially rediscovered by Paul Erdös and Esther Szekeres. Gradually, it led to the formation of a subdiscipline of Combinatorial Analysis known as *Ramsey Theory*, which already contains many hundreds of papers and is growing at a remarkable rate (see the survey by Graham, Rothschild and Spencer, 1980).

Ramsey's pioneering paper on optimal taxation seems to have been written in response to a request by Pigou to look into the problem (see Pigou, 1928, pp. 126–8) but his work on the theory of growth was apparently his alone, although greatly admired by and discussed with Keynes. These two sterling contributions are the subject of separate essays in *The New Palgrave: a Dictionary of Economics*.

Mathematical expectation, probability and utility. The present discussion of Ramsey's great Chapter VII (1931, pp. 156–98) will consider it quite narrowly, as a contribution only to the theory of choice under uncertainty, and thus neglect the important question of its relation to traditional theories of probability. Ramsey himself adopted throughout a modest and peaceable tone towards probability theory, stressing that 'the meaning of probability in logic' may be quite different from 'its meaning in physics' (p. 157).

The chapter is entitled 'Truth and Probability' and dated 1926; presumably most of it was written then, in spite of a reference which bears the date 1927. It contains almost all of what he has to say on the subject, although further on in

Chapter VIII and pages 256–7 there are a few unsystematic comments and glosses on the earlier work. The first ten pages form a critique of Keynes's theory of probability (1921), which may well have stimulated his own interest in the whole subject, so it is not until Section 3 that Ramsey begins his 'inquiry...[into]...the logic of partial belief'.

Ignoring here all his careful qualifications, the theory outlined in that Section begins as follows (pp. 172–4):

> The old-established way of measuring a person's belief is to propose a bet, and see what are the lowest odds which he will accept. This method I regard as fundamentally sound;...I propose to take as a basis a general psychological theory...that we act in the way we think most likely to realize the objects of our desires...The question then arises how...to take account of varying degrees of certainty in his beliefs. I suggest that we introduce as a law of psychology that his behaviour is governed by what is called the mathematical expectation;...We thus define degree of belief in a way which *presupposes* the use of the mathematical expectation (my italics).

Ramsey was fully aware of the crucial dependence of his approach on mathematical expectation. Later in the *Foundations* he asks: 'The question...why just this law of mathematical expectation. The answer to this is that if we use probability to measure utility, as explained in my paper, then consistency [for which see below] requires just this law' (p. 251).

Putting the matter in its crudest (and so necessarily inaccurate) form, mathematical expectation as a principle of choice involves the use for any risky line of action α of a 'probability' π_i and a 'valuation' v_i attached to each of the possible outcomes α_i that constitute α, in such a way that: (i) the expected valuation $E(\alpha)$ of α is $\Sigma \pi_i v_i$ (or an appropriate integral if α has infinitely many members, an alternative which Ramsey expressly rejects: pp. 183–4); and (ii) α is chosen rather than another risky line of action β if and only if $E(\alpha) > E(\beta)$.

Implicit in this crude form is a conflation between events and outcomes. Outcomes depend upon decisions and events, and it is in events and not outcomes that the randomness present is usually held to reside, so that given the occurrence of an event the relevant outcome on which it depends follows deterministically. Nevertheless, the randomness that inheres in the events may be transferred to the outcomes that are conditional upon those events. In the words of Arrow (1951; 1971, p. 26): 'no matter how complicated the structure of a game of chance is, we can always describe it by a single probability distribution of the final outcomes'.

Notice that because mathematical expectation depends linearly both on the probabilities and on the valuations, choice that follows this principle is made according to a *bilinear* form; there is however no necessity for the valuations of the possible outcome themselves to depend linearly upon those outcomes.

Essentially, given any two of the three concepts: mathematical expectation, probabilities and valuations, the remaining one follows more or less naturally.

For example, in Daniel Bernoulli's account of the theory of risk ([1738], 1954), the π_i are apparently given 'objectively', for example by the tosses of a coin. Wishing to preserve the principle of mathematical expectation, and citing the St Petersburg Paradox as evidence for the inappropriateness of using money itself as valuation, Bernoulli was thus led to a specific *utility function* to compute the correct valuations, this being a nonlinear (actually, concave) function of wealth. This did not in fact resolve the basic difficulty of the Paradox (which resides in the unboundedness of the mathematical expectation) but it was a novel and important idea that was very influential.

A quite different approach was used by Bayes ([1763], 1958),who actually *defined* probability in terms of mathematical expectation: 'The *probability of any event* is the ratio between the value at which an expectation depending on the happening of the event ought to be computed, and the value of the thing expected upon its happening' (1958, p. 298; Jeffreys (1961, pp. 30–34) stresses the similarity here between Bayes and Ramsey). Possibly in ignorance of the earlier contribution, Bayes retained monetary valuations rather than replace them by Bernoullian utilities.

Both authors regarded the maximization of the mathematical expectation of gain as the appropriate principle of choice in an uncertain situation. But whereas Bernoulli accepted probabilities from the outside and altered the meaning of valuations so as to achieve consonance between the maximization of mathematical expectation and rational choice, Bayes started with the outside monetary valuations and thence determined probabilities so as to square rational choice with mathematical expectation.

Ramsey was more subtle. He effectively 'bootstrapped' both the valuations *and* the probabilities from mathematical expectation, at the small cost of: (a) a very general assumption about preferences; (b) an assumed existence of a certain kind of event; and (c) a further principle, original with him, that no agent's subjective probabilities should be *inconsistent*. To be inconsistent means that 'He could have a book made against him by a cunning better and would then stand to lose in any event' (1931; p. 182); this no-win situation is now usually called a *Dutch book*.

Sketch of a proof. Ramsey provided sufficient detail for a formal proof of the existence of valuations and probabilities to be constructed from his system of axioms, but he did not construct one himself. Such proofs, for varying circumstances, have been given by Davidson and Suppes (1956) and Vickers (1962), while more informal discussions may be found in Jeffrey (1965, 1983, ch. 3) and Luce and Suppes (1965, pp. 291–4). Only the merest sketch is attempted here, and its mild technical detail follows Davidson and Suppes (1956) rather than Ramsey's original treatment, which was couched mainly in the concepts of Wittgenstein's *Tractatus* and the language of Russell and Whitehead's *Principia*, both long since unfamiliar.

Ramsey begins by considering the case where the agent has 'certain [i.e. sure] beliefs about everything'. He then adopts assumption (a) above, which expressed in modern language says that the agent has a complete preference preordering over 'all possible courses of the world ... [though] ... we ... have no definite way of representing them by numbers' (1931, p. 176). Vickers points out that if different preferences can themselves be parts of different 'courses of the world' then the argument is ambiguous, and if not then the question is begged (1962, pp. 6–11); however, he shows how to resolve these problems by suitable amendment of Ramsey's definitions.

When 'the subject is capable of doubt' (1931, p. 177), the theory proceeds by offering options. Suppose that the agent has two options: the first is α, in which he receives x if an event e occurs and a preferentially different outcome y if it does not; and the other is β, in which he receives r if e occurs and another outcome s if it does not. Assuming that probabilities $\pi(e)$ and $\pi(e')$ can be attached to the events e and to e' (the complement of e), respectively, and that valuations $v(x)$, $v(y)$, etc. can be placed on the outcomes, x, y, r and s, then the principle of mathematical expectation says that α is better than, indifferent to, or worse than β, according as

$$\pi(e)v(x) + \pi(e')v(y) > ; = ; < \pi(e)v(r) + \pi(e')v(s). \tag{1}$$

Ramsey's next assumption is (b) above, to the effect that there exists some event, say e^*, such that for *every* pair (m, n) of preferentially distinct outcomes the subject is indifferent between the option γ consisting of m if e^* and n if not e^*, and another option δ consisting of n if e^* and m if not e^*. According to the principles of mathematical expectation, this implies

$$\pi(e^*)v(m) + \pi(e^{*'})v(n) = \pi(e^*)v(n) + \pi(e^{*'})v(m). \tag{2}$$

Since m and n are preferentially distinct, their valuations must be such that $v(m) \neq v(n)$. Then from this and (2) it follows that necessarily

$$\pi(e^*) = \pi(e^{*'}). \tag{3}$$

Although quantitative probabilities have not yet been defined, (3) shows that there is a clear qualitative sense in which event e^* has a (subjective) probability of $1/2$, *provided* that the subjective probabilities of an event and its complement sum to unity. Ramsey terms *ethically neutral* any event (in his language, proposition) that has the properties of e^*; the force of the word 'ethically' is not explained (1931, p. 177). The assumption that such events (propositions) exist is perhaps the weakest part of his theory of choice under uncertainty, although before it is rejected out of hand the careful philosophical discussion of it by Vickers (1962) and the equally careful empirical applications of it discussed by Davidson and Suppes (1956) should be consulted.

Now take the case of (1) where e is an ethically neutral event e^*, and the option α is indifferent to the option β. Then from (1) and (3),

$$v(x) - v(r) = v(s) - v(y). \tag{4}$$

This says that differences in valuations can be equated, so that the latter are measurable by an *interval scale*; or what comes to the same thing, that they are measurable up to choice of unit and origin, so that for any other such scale μ, $\mu(\cdot) = \alpha + bv(\cdot)$, where $b > 0$.

A valuation having been obtained in this fashion for each outcome, and assuming again that for any event e, $\pi(e) + \pi(e') = 1$, it follows from the case of equality in (1) that

$$[\pi(e)]^{-1} = 1 + [v(x) - v(r)]/[v(s) - v(y)]. \tag{5}$$

This gives a way of calculating the subjective probabiltiy $\pi(e)$ of any event, ethically neutral or not, in a way compatible simultaneously with the principle of mathematical expectation and with the valuations $v(\cdot)$ of the possible outcomes. Thus both valuations ('utilities') and subjective probabilities have been bootstrapped, in that order, from the simple assumptions (a) and (b), plus the assumption that any event and its negation have subjective probabilities that add up to one. Ramsey dispenses with this last, auxiliary assumption by means of his principle (c) of consistency, which in effect insists upon the impossibility of Dutch books.

Dutch books. Although his paper is crystal clear that consistency means that the subjective probabilities of any set of disjoint and exhaustive events must sum to one, and it is twice stated explicitly (1931, pp. 182–3) that anyone who is not consistent in this sense can have a Dutch book made against him, Ramsey provided no formal proof of equivalence between these two ideas. Hence this result is usually attributed to de Finetti (1937), who gave a very neat proof. Not having read Ramsey's paper, de Finetti like Bayes worked with monetary valuations in his account of personal probability, though he admitted later (1964, p. 102, fn. (a)) that 'Such a formulation could better, like Ramsey's, deal with expected *utilities*; I did not know of Ramsey's work before 1937, but I was aware of the difficulty of money bets.' What follows is a free adaptation of de Finetti's proof to Ramsey's problem.

Let there be n mutually incompatible and together exhaustive events e_i, e.g. the faces of a die. Suppose then that I, knowing your subjective probabilities π_i, offer you the following wager: If e_i occurs I pay you σ_i. In return, you pay me an initial stake of $\Sigma \pi_i \sigma_i$ valuation units, where the sum is taken over the n events. If you behave according to Ramsey's theory of choice under uncertainty, then you should be on the margin of accepting this wager, since for you to attach probability π_i to e_i is to say that you would be indifferent between the following offers: receive σ_i valuation units contingent on the occurrence of e_i, and the amount $\pi_i \sigma_i$ for sure. Since by hypothesis the e_i are exclusive events, the separate amounts $\pi_i \sigma_i$ may be added together.

If event e_h occurs, your gain is

$$\gamma_h = \sigma_h - \Sigma \pi_i \sigma_i \qquad h = 1, 2, \ldots, n. \tag{6}$$

These are n linear equations, which can be put into matrix–vector notation. Writing g and s for the vectors of the γ_i and σ_i, respectively, I for the $n \times n$ identity matrix, and P for the matrix whose (i,j)th element is π_j, the equations (6) become

$$g = (I - P)s. \tag{7}$$

193

Computation shows that $\det(I - P) = 1 - \Sigma\pi_i$. So if $\Sigma\pi_i \neq 1$, then for any desired vector of gains g, stakes $s = (I - P)^{-1}g$ can be computed that will guarantee me the vector $-g$. In particular, I can specify g to be strictly negative, thus ensuring that you will lose whatever event occurs.

Conversely, suppose that your subjective probabilities are what de Finetti called coherent (and Ramsey, consistent), so that by definition $\Sigma\pi_i = 1$. Then, multiplying each equation in (6) by π_h and adding over all events,

$$\Sigma\pi_h\gamma_h = \Sigma\pi_h\sigma_h - \Sigma\pi_h\Sigma\pi_i\sigma_i = 0. \tag{8}$$

Since each $\pi_h \geqslant 0$ and their sum is non-zero, it follows from (8) that not all the γ_h can be negative. Hence the condition that your subjective probabilities π_i sum to one for all complete sets of incompatible events e_i, i.e. that you obey the rules of probability calculus, is necessary and sufficient in order that no Dutch book can be made against you.

The reception of 'Truth and Probability'. Ramsey's theory of choice under uncertainty was deeply original. Emile Borel, in his review (1924) of Keynes's theory of probability, had earlier sketched an interesting theory of subjective probability in terms of bets (note in particular his remark that 'the method of betting permits us in the majority of cases a numerical evaluation of probabilities that has exactly the same characteristics as the evaluation of prices by the methods of exchange' (1964, p. 57), but nobody had come close to the depth and comprehensiveness of Ramsey's theory. He was characteristically modest about its range of application: 'I only claim for what follows approximate truth...like Newtonian mechanics...[it] can, I think, still be profitably used even though it is known to be false' (1931, p. 173).

Perhaps because the theory was too original, such modesty did not help its author, any more than his high reputation as a philosopher. I can find no evidence that anyone, let alone any economist, took any serious notice of Ramsey's work until after von Neumann and Morgenstern's quite separate utility theory had appeared in 1947. The latter theory was very much in the Bernoullian tradition, in which the probabilities are given from outside, 'objectively'. Coupling these with a complete preference preordering for such alternatives, suitable continuity and the principle of mathematical expectation in the form of the Independence Axiom, the authors were able to deduce the existence of a utility function, unique up to positive affine transformations, which gave valuations compatible both with the outside probabilities and that principle.

The first published reference to Ramsey's theory known to me appears in Little (1950, p. 29, fn. 1), who considered it 'essentially the same' as that of von Neumann and Morgenstern. Little's reference was soon followed by one in Arrow (1951), who acknowledged that Ramsey was brought to his attention by Norman Dalkey. Though complaining that 'Ramsey's work was none too clear' (1971, p. 26), Arrow did see that it originated 'a new stage' in decision theory, 'in which a priori probabilities are derived from behavior postulates' (1971, p. 22). Thereafter there was a gradual increase in the appreciation of Ramsey's contribution, although even as late as 1954 an excellent collection of papers on decision theory (Thrall, Coombs and Davis, 1954) contained not one reference to his work.

It is a common mistake to suppose that the line of descent in the theory of personal probability is direct from Ramsey to de Finetti (1937) to Savage (1954). We have seen that de Finetti did not know of Ramsey's work, his own remarkable contribution being very much in the Bayesian tradition which takes the valuations from outside and thence derives the probabilities. Moreover, a careful reading of Savage's fine book shows that Ramsey's influence was at best peripheral, the axiomatization of probabilities and valuations proceeding far more along the lines developed by de Finetti.

There have in fact been relatively few explicit exponents of Ramsey's approach. The most notable are probably Davidson and Suppes (e.g. 1956) and Anscombe and Aumann (1963), who used an interesting bootstrapping argument to go from assumed probabilities for what they called 'roulette' lotteries to valuations, and thence to subjective probabilities for the much wider class of 'horse' lotteries, all very much in the Ramsey manner.

The direct heirs to Ramsey's work have been few but there is no doubt that its influence has been pervasive, to such extent that chairs in decision theory at US business schools have been named after him (though with what warrant is hard to say). Arrow (1965, p. 57) claimed that all arguments involving the expected-utility hypothesis 'are only variations of Ramsey's', while Savage (1962, p. 10) wrote that the 'more thorough-going... formulation of Ramsey (1931)... is in no way obsolete'. Even now, not to experience that 'clear purity of illumination with which the writer's mind is felt by the reader to play about its subject' (Keynes on Ramsey, 1928) is a sad loss for the modern student.

SELECTED WORKS

1926. Truth and probability. Chapter VII, pages 156–98 in (1931). Reprinted in (1978) and in Kyburg and Smokler (1964), 61–92.
1927. A contribution to the theory of taxation. *Economic Journal* 37, 47–61. Reprinted in (1978).
1928. A mathematical theory of saving. *Economic Journal* 38, 543–9. Reprinted in (1978).
1931. *The Foundations of Mathematics*. Edited by R.B. Braithwaite, with a Preface by G.E. Moore, London: Routledge & Kegan Paul; New York: Humanities Press, 1950.
1978. *Foundations*. Edited by D.H. Mellor, with Introductions by the editor, L. Mirsky, T.J. Smiley and J.R.N. Stone, London: Routledge & Kegan Paul; New York: Humanities Press.

BIBLIOGRAPHY

Anscombe, F.J. and Aumann, R.J. 1963. A definition of subjective probability. *Annals of Mathematical Statistics* 34, 199–205.
Arrow, K.J. 1951. Alternative approaches to the theory of choice in risk-taking situations. *Econometrica* 19, 404–37.
Arrow, K.J. 1965. *Aspects of the Theory of Risk-Bearing*. Helsinki: Yrjö Jahnsson Foundation.

Arrow, K.J. 1971. *Essays in the Theory of Risk-Bearing*. Chicago: Markham.

Bayes, T. 1763. An essay towards solving a problem in the doctrine of chances. *Philosophical Transactions of the Royal Society* 53, 370–418. Reprinted in *Biometrika* 45, (1958), 293–315.

Bernoulli, D. 1738. Specimen theoriae novae de mensura sortis. *Commentarii Academiae Scientiarum Imperialis Petropolitanae*, Vol. V, 175–92. Translated as 'Exposition of a new theory on the measurement of risk', *Econometrica* 22, 1954, 23–36.

Borel, E. 1924. A propos d'un traité de probabilité. *Revue Philosophique* 98, 321–36. Translated in Kyburg and Smokler (1964), 45–60.

Cohen, P.J. 1966. *Set Theory and the Continuum Hypothesis*. New York: W.A. Benjamin.

Davidson, D. and Suppes, P. 1956. A finitistic axiomatization of subjective probability and utility. *Econometrica* 24, 264–75.

de Finetti, B. 1937. La prévision, ses lois logiques, ses sources subjectives. *Annales de l'Institut Henri Poincaré* 7, 1–68. Translated in Kyburg and Smokler (1964), 93–158.

Graham, R.L., Rothschild, B.L. and Spencer, J.H. 1980. *Ramsey Theory*. New York: John Wiley & Sons.

Harrod, R.F. 1951. *The Life of John Maynard Keynes*. London: Macmillan; New York: St. Martin's Press, 1963.

Jeffrey, R.L. 1965. *The Logic of Decision*. New York: McGraw-Hill. 2nd edn, Chicago: University of Chicago Press, 1983.

Jeffreys, H. 1961. *Theory of Probability*. 3rd edn, Oxford: Clarendon Press.

Keynes, J.M. 1921. *A Treatise on Probability*. London: Macmillan; New York: Harper & Row, 1962.

Keynes, J.M. 1933. *Essays in Biography*. London: Macmillan. Reprinted as Vol. X of *The Collected Writings of John Maynard Keynes*, New York: St. Martin's Press, 1972.

Kyburg, H.E. and Smokler, H.E. (eds) 1964. *Studies in Subjective Probability*. New York: John Wiley & Sons.

Little, I.M.D. 1950. *A Critique of Welfare Economics*. Oxford: Clarendon Press.

Luce, R.D. and Suppes, P. 1965. Preference, utility, and subjective probability. In *Handbook of Mathematical Psychology*, Vol. III, ed. R.D. Luce, R.R. Bush and E. Galanter, New York: John Wiley & Sons, 249–410.

Partridge, F. 1981. *Memories*. London: Victor Gollancz.

Pigou, A.C. 1928. *A Study in Public Finance*. London: Macmillan.

Savage, L.J. 1954. *The Foundations of Statistics*. New York: John Wiley & Sons.

Savage, L.J. et al. 1962. *The Foundations of Statistical Inference: A discussion*. London: Methuen; New York: J. Wiley, 1962.

Sraffa, P. 1960. *Production of Commodities by Means of Commodities*. Cambridge: Cambridge University Press.

Thrall, R.M., Coombs, C.H. and Davis, R.L. (eds) 1954. *Decision Processes*. New York: John Wiley & Sons.

Ulam, S.M. 1976. *Adventures of a Mathematician*. New York: Charles Scribner's Sons.

Vickers, J.M. 1962. A critical investigation of Frank Ramsey's Theory of Value and Belief. PhD dissertation in the Department of Philosophy, Stanford University.

von Neumann, J. 1928. Zur Theorie der Gesellschaftsspiele. *Mathematische Annalen* 100, 295–320.

von Neumann, J. 1937. Über ein ökonomisches Gleichungssystem und eine Verallgemeinerung des Brouwerschen Fixpunksatzes. *Ergebnisse eines mathematischen Kolloquiums* 8, 78–83. Translated as 'A model of general economic equilibrium', *Review of Economic Studies* 13, 1945–6, 1–9.

von Neumann, J. and Morgenstern, O. 1944. *Theory of Games and Economic Behavior*. Princeton: Princeton University Press.

von Neumann, J. and Morgenstern, O. 1947. 2nd edn of (1944).

Wittgenstein, L. 1922. *Tractatus Logico-Philosophicus*, with an Introduction by Bertrand Russell. London: Kegan Paul, Trench, Trubner & Co; New York: Humanities Press, 1951.

Wittgenstein, L. 1953. *Philosophical Investigations*. Translated by G.E. Anscombe, Oxford: Basil Blackwell; New York: Macmillan.

Wittgenstein, L. 1973. *Letters to C.K. Ogden*. Edited by G.H. von Wright, Oxford: Basil Blackwell.

Wright, G.H. von. 1982. *Wittgenstein*. Minneapolis: University of Minnesota Press.

Rational Behaviour

AMARTYA SEN

The concept of rational behaviour is frequently used in economic theory. The interest in this concept springs from two quite distinct motivations. First, insofar as economic exercises often take a perspective form, it is interesting to know how one could behave rationally in a given situation. This may be called the 'prescriptive motivation'. It should be warned that the prescription need not be necessarily of an ethical kind. Indeed, the prescriptive motivation is sometimes described in clearly non-ethical terms, involving the pursuit of self-interest only. In a classic presentation of this position, Harsanyi (1977) describes 'perfectly rational behaviour' in the context of game theory in the following terms:

> ... our theory is a *normative* (prescriptive) theory rather than a *positive* (descriptive) theory. At least formally and explicitly it deals with the question of how each player *should* act in order to promote his own interests most effectively in the game and not with the question of how he (or persons like him) *will* actually act in a game of this particular type (Harsanyi, 1977, p. 16).

The second motivation concerns the possible use of models of rational behaviour in explaining and predicting *actual* behaviour. This exercise is done, as it were, in two steps. The first step consists in characterizing rational behaviour and the second, following that, bases actual behaviour on rational behaviour. In this way the characterization of rational behaviour may end up specifying the predicted actual behaviour as well. This motivation underlies much of the theory of general equilibrium (see, for example, Edgeworth, 1881; Arrow, 1951; Debreu, 1959; Arrow and Hahn, 1971). The argument is that while actual behaviour can, in principle, take any form, it is reasonable to assume that much of the time it will, in fact, be of the kind that can be described as 'rational'.

In reviewing the theory of rational behaviour, this duality of motivations has to be borne in mind. Even though the primary concern of this essay is with the way rational behaviour has been characterized, the nature of the second motivation makes it imperative that the possible use of rational behaviour models for explaining and predicting actual behaviour must not be overlooked.

RATIONALIZABILITY, BINARINESS AND SELF-INTEREST. In the presence of uncertainty, rational behaviour requires an appreciation of possible variations in the outcome of any chosen action, and such behaviour must, therefore, be based on systematic reading of uncertainties regarding the outcome and ways of dealing with them. Rational behaviour under uncertainty will be presently taken up, but before that the more elementary case when there is no uncertainty has to be dealt with. In fact, behaviour under certainty can be formally seen as an extreme case of behaviour under uncertainty when the uncertainty in question is not only small but simply absent. In this sense, rational behaviour under certainty must be subsumed by any theory that deals with rational behaviour in the presence of uncertainty.

Although there are many different approaches to rational behaviour under certainty, it is fair to say that there are two *main* approaches to this question. The first emphasizes *internal consistency*: rationality of behaviour is identified with a requirement that choices from different subsets should correspond to each other in a cogent and systematic way. Various conditions of internal consistency have been proposed in the literature, but the one which seems to command most attention in formal economic theory is *binariness* which requires that the choices from different subjects can be seen as maximizing solutions from the respective subsets according to some binary relation R (often interpreted as 'preference', e.g. xRy standing for 'x being preferred or indifferent to y'). Or, to put it another way, rational behaviour, in this interpretation, amounts to our ability to find a binary relation R over the universal set of alternatives such that the choice from any particular subset of that universal set consists of exactly the R-maximal elements of that subset. Richter (1971) calls this 'rationalizability'.

In other formulations – still within the general approach of internal consistency – the condition of rationalizability has been relaxed, demanding only a part of the kind of consistency that binary maximization must entail. On the other hand, in some other formulations, the demands have been made stronger than that of maximization according to a binary relation by requiring further that the binary relation in question be an ordering, satisfying both completeness and transitivity.

An enormous variety of conditions of internal consistency have been proposed in the literature, but it can be shown that many of them are equivalent to each other, and indeed altogether they fall into a number of classes, with each class containing different, but essentially equivalent, demands. Such reductionist analyses can be found, for example, in Houthakker (1956), Uzawa (1956), Arrow (1959), Richter (1971), Sen (1971), Herzberger (1973), Suzumura (1983). For critiques (and arguments for the rejection of) the binary approach to rationality, see Kanger (1976), Gauthier (1985), Sen (1985a, 1985b) and Sugden (1985).

The second common approach to rational behaviour under certainty sees it in terms of reasoned pursuit of self-interest. The origins of this approach are often traced to Adam Smith, and it is frequently asserted that the father of modern economics saw human beings as tirelessly fostering their respective self-interests. As a piece of history of economic thought, this is, to say the least, dubious, since Adam Smith's (1776, 1790) belief in the hold of self-interest in some spheres of activity (e.g., exchange) was qualified by his conviction that many other motivations are important in human behaviour in general (on this see Winch, 1978; Brennan and Lomasky, 1985; and Sen, 1987). But it is certainly true that the assumption of the 'economic man' relentlessly pursuing self-interest in a fairly narrowly defined form has played a major part in the characterization of individual behaviour in economics for a very long time.

SELF-INTEREST AND CONSISTENCY. Rational behaviour in the form of maximization in pursuit of self-interest makes the analysis of individual behaviour a good deal more tractable than a less structured assumption would permit. This is certainly one of its appeals. In addition this behavioural assumption is also quite crucial for the derivation of certain central results in traditional and modern economic theory, for example, Pareto optimality of competitive equilibria and *vice versa* (Arrow, 1951; Debreu, 1959; Arrow and Hahn, 1971). This is sometimes called the 'Fundamental Theorem of Welfare Economics'. Roughly stated, it claims, first, that every perfectly competitive equilibrium (with each person maximizing utility, given the prices) under certain assumptions (such as no externalities) achieves Pareto optimality, and second, under a slightly different set of assumptions (including the requirement of no externalities, but also some additional requirements, e.g., the absence of increasing returns to scale), every Pareto optimal state is a perfectly competitive equilibrium with respect to some set of prices and some initial distribution of resources. This correspondence between Pareto optimality and competitive equilibria works neatly given individual self-interested behaviour precisely because Pareto optimality is one characteristic of self-interest maximization of a group, in the sense that in such a situation no one's self-interest can be further enhanced without hurting the self-interest of somebody else. It is the assumption of rational behaviour in the form of the pursuit of self-interest that established the close relationship between competitive equilibria and Pareto optimality (with price-taking behaviour and absence of externalities preventing people from getting in each other's way in their respective pursuit of self-interest). In this result and in many other similar ones, the particular characterization of rational behaviour chosen plays a strategically crucial role.

It can be argued that rational behaviour under the self-interest approach is a special case of that under the consistency approach. If a person does pursue self-interest, it may follow that his or her behaviour will have the consistency needed for maximization of a cogent function. On the other hand, a person can be consistent without necessarily maximizing self-interest, since the maximizing function may have a different interpretation altogether (e.g., the pursuit of some moral values of political goals). Thus internal consistency of choice may be taken to be necessary but not sufficient for self-interested behaviour. There is undoubtedly something in this way of seeing the correspondence between the two common approaches to rational behaviour.

However, that alleged correspondence is also somewhat misleading, since the nature of self-interest need not necessarily take the uncomplicated form of being binary in character. Strictly speaking, neither does the self-interest thesis entail the consistency thesis, nor of course the other way round. While this must, in general, be correct, nevertheless the way self-interest has been actually viewed in standard economic theory has made it clearly binary and more typically an ordering (and often seen as being numerically representable). If self-interest must take this form, then it would indeed be the case that the self-interest approach is just a special case of the consistency approach.

In some treatises on rational behaviour, the distance between the self-interest approach and the consistency approach is bridged by some careful definitions. For example, in the 'revealed preference theory', pioneered by Samuelson (1938), consistency is demanded in the form of the 'Weak Axiom of Revealed Preference', to wit: if x is chosen from a set containing y, then y will not be chosen from any set containing x. This type of consistency is, on its own, without a particular substantive interpretation, except that it corresponds generally to some kind of maximization. However, the term 'revealed preference' might indicate that the chosen alternative is always also the preferred one. Insofar as preference reflects self-interest (as is typically assumed to be the case), this established, through the terminology of 'revealed preference', what looks like a congruence of choice and self-interest.

The consistency entailed by the Weak Axiom of Revealed Preference does not, in general, entail transitivity, which is a property that might be thought to be a natural one to impose on the relation of self-interest. But that hole can be plugged by *either* demanding stronger conditions (such as Houthakker's, 1950, 'Strong Axiom of Revealed Preference'), *or* by demanding that the consistency of the Weak Axiom be satisfied over all finite subsets, which makes the strong axiom equivalent to the weak (on this see Arrow, 1959; Sen, 1971). One way or another, the consistency imposed by revealed preference axioms can lead to a 'preference' relation that has the regularity properties normally associated with the concept of self-interest, and then the gap between the two could be seen as fully bridged.

However, that entire bridging exercise is based on *defining* the relation of choice as a relation of 'preference' which happens to be 'revealed' by the act of choice. But that terminology is arbitrarily imposed, and it is possible that the binary relation of choice, even when fully transitive and complete, may in fact reflect neither the person's preference, nor his or her self-interest. There is, obviously, scope for methodological arguments on this point, and these issues have often been joined.

In the philosophical literature, it is common to distinguish between 'instrumental rationality' and 'substantive rationality' (see Latsis, 1976). It is clear that the self-interest view of rational behaviour is one of substantive rationality requiring that rational behaviour must take the form of pursuing some independently defined self-interest. Obviously, this characteristic of substantiveness is not satisfied by the theory of revealed preference, since there the identification of choice with preference or self-interest takes the form of *defining* the relation of choice as a relation of preference, which is not an independent way of characterizing preference or self-interest. But in other theories, the substantive exercise is carefully done, for example, in the typical general equilibrium theory (see Arrow, 1951; Debreu, 1959; Arrow and Hahn, 1971). The starting point of individual behaviour is, then, not a choice function but a utility function, representing the self-interest of the person in question. Choices follow from constrained maximization of that utility function. In this form, the substantive nature of the characterized rationality is strongly asserted, in the shape of pursuit of self-interest.

A number of criticisms have been recently made about the special nature of the assumption of self-interest maximization. Human beings may well have other motivations, and self-interest is just one of various things that a person might wish to pursue. Different types of criticisms of this substantive assumption have been made by such authors as Nagel (1970), Kornai (1971), Sen (1973, 1977, 1987), Scitovsky (1976), Leibenstein (1976), Schelling (1978), Wong (1978), Elster (1979, 1983), Hirschman (1982, 1983), McPherson (1982), Margolis (1982), Akerlof (1984), Schick (1984) and others.

If the assumption of self-interest maximization is seen as too narrow, it can be argued that merely requiring internal consistency is much too permissive. Indeed, it is tempting to think of the consistency approach as belonging to the 'instrumental' view of rationality. But this is not quite so, since the instrumental view requires that the person pursues some independently defined objective (even though the objective need not be based on self-interest only). In the consistency view there is no such independently defined function at all, and the binary relation that is precipitated by the choice function is a *reflection* of choice rather than a *determinant* of it. It is rather that the consistency approach opens the way to some instrumental view of rationality, involving the maximization of some objective function. Indeed, in this sense, the consistency approach can be seen as permissively admitting the approach of instrumental rationality implicit in the self-interest approach, where the objective function maximized happens to be the self-interest of the person in question.

The consistency approach can be criticized on grounds of inadequacy in characterizing rationality of behaviour. A person's choice function may be internally consistent in the sense that the different things chosen from different subsets correspond to each other in an apparently cogent and coherent way, but this does not in itself indicate that the person's behaviour is consistent with his or her aims or objectives. Indeed, a person who systematically does exactly the *opposite* of what has to be done for the pursuit of his or her objective function may end up producing a consistent choice behaviour, but the binary relation that will be revealed by the choices – the 'opposite' of the person's objective function – will be, clearly, at war with the goals and aims of that person. To describe such a person as behaving rationally would, obviously, lead to some interesting methodological difficulties.

MAXIMIZING, SATISFICING AND BOUNDED RATIONALITY. These problems with the standard views of rationality tend to undermine the very foundations of these approaches. Some other approaches have involved more qualified use of the standard presumptions. For example, Herbert Simon (1957, 1979) has argued powerfully that individuals may not actually *maximize* any function at all, and their behaviour may take the form of what has been called 'satisficing'. There are various ways of characterizing satisficing, but it can be thought of in terms of a person having a certain target level of achievement which he or she will try to reach, but beyond which he or she may not try to improve the achievement any further.

There is a genuine problem of interpretation involved in analysing satisficing, and it can be argued that satisficing behaviour really is maximization according to an effectively incomplete relation, such that the states satisfying the target level of achievement are all put in a non-comparable class as far as choice behaviour is concerned. Maximization can indeed be defined in terms of such incomplete relations (see, for example, Debreu's 1959 analysis of 'maximal' sets based on 'pre-orderings'), and if it is seen in these terms, the gap between satisficing and maximizing may be, at least formally, reduced. However, the content of the claim of satisficing is that the person in question *can* tell between the different levels of achievement which are all beyond the target level required, and despite this discernibility, choice behaviour departs from relentless maximization of the level of achievement. In this version of the story, a substantial difference is indeed made by the notion of satisficing, and the implications of satisficing behaviour may, in this interpretation, be quite different from those of maximization.

Variations of the maximization assumption and the related consistency conditions can be justified by seeing the use of reason in human affairs in terms of what has been called 'bounded rationality'. In this structure human choice is seen not in terms of grand maximizing behaviour, but as a series of particular decisions, not fully integrated with each other, taken in situations of partial information and based on limited reflection. This approach has been developed by Herbert Simon (1957, 1979, 1983) both at a theoretical level and in the context of specific empirical applications. The results differ quite substantially from that of rational behaviour seen in terms of consistency, or in terms of optimization according to self-interest. As Simon (1983) puts it:

> Rationality of the sort described by the behavioural model [of bounded rationality] doesn't optimize, of course. Nor does it even guarantee that our decisions will be consistent. As a matter of fact, it is very easy to show that choices made by an organism having these characteristics will often depend on the order in which alternatives are presented (Simon, 1983, p. 23).

NATURAL SELECTION AND MOTIVES. Supporters of optimizing models have typically used two different types of arguments to defend the practice, against models of the kind characterized by 'bounded rationality' and other behavioural departures. One argument takes the direct form of arguing that human beings do optimize and take care to do so. The second argument suggests that natural selection will lead to this result: those who optimize do better, and those who do not, get eliminated by natural selection. For example, non-profit-maximizing firms may go to the wall, so that only the profit-maximizing ones may survive (see Friedman, 1953). This type of indirect justification of what has been called 'enforced maximization' has many pitfalls, since the analogy with natural selection in biology is at best tenuous (see Helm, 1984; Matthews, 1984), and the biological story itself is far from straightforward (Dawkins, 1982; Maynard Smith, 1982).

It is by no means clear that individual self-interest-maximizers will typically do relatively better in a group of people with diverse motivations. More importantly, when it comes to comparisons of survival of different *groups*, it can easily be the case that groups that emphasize values other than pure self-interest maximization might actually do better (see Sen, 1973, 1974, 1985b; Akerlof, 1984). It has been argued that economic success has often come more plentifully in cultures that emphasize norms of conduct quite different from that of persistent maximization of individual self-interest, focusing on other values (e.g., what Morishima, 1982, calls 'the Japanese ethos'; see also Dore, 1983). The relation between social norms and individual conduct is an enormously complex field, and the simple assumptions of self-interest maximization, or straightforward models of apparent 'consistency', may overlook important aspects of the individual–society relationships (see, for example, Hirschman, 1970, 1982). This is not to argue that 'natural selection' arguments are worthless in economics – they may be far from that – but the results of the selection may lack the simplicity demanded by supporters of simple optimization and may take a more complex form (see Hirshleifer, 1977; Helm, 1984; Matthews, 1984).

In assessing the overall value of standard models of rational behaviour, it is important to pay attention to the distinction made earlier between the value of these structures as representations of *rationality* and their usefulness in terms of predicting *actual* behaviour. Some of the deficiencies of the optimizing structure apply specifically to the latter. For example, models of 'bounded rationality' are often defended by claims of greater plausibility in explaining actual human conduct.

In fact, the entire enterprise of getting to actual behaviour via models of rationality may itself be seen as methodoligically quite dubious. There is scope for argument here on both sides, since the unrealism of rational behaviour may be large, but the unrealism of any *specific kind* of 'irrational' behaviour could be larger still. Whether 'bounded rationality' is the right kind of compromise in getting a grip on actuality via limited use of rationality remains an interesting question.

REASON AND RATIONALITY. As far as the other objective of rational behaviour models is concerned, i.e., the ability of these models to capture the essence of rationality (no matter how people do actually behave), there are a number of complex philosophical issues underlying the question. It is easy enough to argue that mere internal consistency of choice cannot be adequate for rationality, nor can self-interest maximization be seen as uniquely rational in a way that pursuing other kinds of objectives (such as altruism, public spirit, class consciousness, group solidarity) must fail to be. What is much harder to do is to develop an alternative structure for rationality that would be regarded as satisfactory for the purpose of capturing what can be demanded of reason in human choice (whether or not it also serves the second purpose of giving us a good guess regarding actual behaviour). This question remains, to a great extent, an open one, which has been as yet rather inadequately explored.

Two difficulties, in particular, may be worth mentioning in this context. First, while 'instrumental rationality' must have some place in economics, and the role of reasoned choice of means for serving *given* ends cannot be dismissed, it is hard to believe that any kind of objectives – no matter how bizarre – must be seen as okay, i.e., not compromising the rationality of the person pursuing it. The need for rational assessment of objectives and preferences have been analysed by John Broome (1978), Derek Parfit (1984) and others, and both the procedural and substantive features of this type of assessment do deserve serious attention.

Second, even when goals are clearly given, the translation of these into actions depends on the pattern of social interdependence assumed in group behaviour, with members having partly divergent goals. As the discussions on the so called 'Newcomb's problem' and other complex cases have brought out, the correct individual decision may not be entirely unproblematic even when there appears to exist a strictly dominant strategy (see Nozick, 1969; Brams, 1975; Levi, 1975; Gibbard and Harper, 1978; Jeffrey, 1983, among others). The nature of beliefs permits alternative interpretations of the nature of the decision problem, and this philosophical question is of relevance to decision problems in economics as much as it is in other fields of human choice.

The Prisoner's Dilemma has been frequently used in economic arguments to illustrate the nature of inefficiencies of atomistic non-cooperative behaviour when the interdependence incorporates both congruence and conflict of interests in such a way that the combination of each person's dominant strategies produces an outcome that is inferior in terms of the goals of everyone in the group (see Luce and Raiffa, 1957). Attempts to resolve the problem by assuming temporal repetition of the game have not been easy, since it can be demonstrated that with complete knowledge and standard optimizing behaviour, a finitely repeated Prisoner's Dilemma will continue to produce the inferior outcome throughout (Luce and Raiffa, 1957, pp. 97–101).

Such non-cooperative behaviour is, however, violated in many experimental games as well as in the usual readings of many real-life situations. The apparent dissonance between received theory and observed behaviour has been explained in a variety of ways in the large literature that has developed on the Prisoner's Dilemma. The 'ways out' have included relaxing the assumption of mutual knowledge, for example, introducing uncertainty about the number of times for which the game will be played, admitting ignorance of the players about other people's knowledge and motivation, limiting the range of alternative strategies that can be considered, and other relaxations (see Howard, 1971; Basu, 1977; Davis, 1977; Radner, 1980; Smale, 1980; Kreps, Milgrom, Roberts and Wilson, 1982; Axelrod, 1984). Other analyses have emphasized more complex features of 'practical reasoning' involving various types of action ethics, sensitive beliefs, behavioural commitments, and instrumental use of reciprocity; see Sen (1974, 1985b), Watkins (1974, 1985), Levi (1975, 1987), Gauthier (1985), McClennen (1985). If it has done nothing else, the literature has at least brought out sharply the complexity of the nature of rationality in situations of interdependence as well as various conceptual and logistic difficulties in using models of rationality to understand the nature of actual behaviour.

It seems easy to accept that rationality involves many features that cannot be summarized in terms of some straightforward formula, such as binary consistency. But this recognition does not immediately lead to alternative characterizations that might be regarded as satisfactory, even though the inadequacies of the traditional assumptions of rational behaviour standlardly used in economic theory have become hard to deny. It will not be an easy task to find replacements for the standard assumptions of rational behaviour – and related to it of actual behaviour – that can be found in the traditional economic literature, both because the identified deficiencies have been seen as calling for rather divergent remedies, and also because there is little hope of finding an alternative assumption structure that will be as simple and usable as the traditional assumptions of self-interest maximization, or of consistency of choice.

UNCERTAINTY AND EXPECTED UTILITY. The extension of the modelling of rational behaviour from certainty to uncertainty involves both (1) the characterization of uncertainty, and (2) taking note of uncertainty thus characterized in making actual decisions over alternative courses of actions. The model that has been most extensively used in this context is that of 'expected utility'. This takes the form of weighing the value of each of the outcomes by the respective probabilities of the different outcomes. The probability-weighted overall 'expected value', thus derived, is then maximized in this approach to rational choice under uncertainty.

The use of probability calculus involves interpretational problems as to what the probabilities stand for. While the view of probability as a measure of relative frequency is a natural one to consider, there is clearly much cogency in interpreting probability as a measure of the degree of belief (as argued by Fisher, 1921, and Keynes, 1921).

Actual decision-taking operations involve a reading of the likelihood of different outcomes and an assessment of the different outcomes in the light of the respective likelihoods. In a pioneering contribution in axiomatizing conjointly characterized probabilities and utilities, Frank Ramsey (1931) provided the structure (and a possible derivation) of the expected utility calculus. Another major contribution in this area came from Von Neumann and Morgenstern (1947). Given the probabilities of different outcomes, consistent and complete rankings of the possible lotteries over the outcomes (including lotteries of lotteries and so forth) permit the construction of cardinal utility functions for the respective rankings associated with the outcomes, provided the rankings in question satisfy certain regularity properties which were specified by Von Neumann and Morgenstern (see also Marschak, 1946). The assigned cardinal utility numbers of the respective outcomes, weighted by the respective probabilities, when summed together, yield the expected values of the lotteries, and provide numerical representations of the overall goodness of the respective lotteries. Rational behaviour under expected utility maximization takes the form of choosing that lottery which has the highest overall value, thus calculated. The expected utility approach can be and has been used extensively both in economic theory and in applied economics (see, for example, Friedman and Savage, 1948; Arrow, 1971).

INDEPENDENCE AND CONSISTENCY. The axioms underlying the derivation of expected utility maximization have been subjected to a good deal of examination and scrutiny. There is scope for disputation both about the exact content and the plausibility of the expected utility axioms (for a very helpful introduction see Luce and Raiffa, 1957; see also Fishburn, 1970, 1981).

The axiom that has perhaps attracted the most criticism is the so-called 'strong independence'. This independence condition can be stated in several different ways, but a rather immediate one is the following. If in a combined lottery over, say, lotteries L^1 and L^2, the latter L^2 is replaced by another lottery L^3 which is preferred to L^2 (leaving the probabilities and L^1 unchanged), then the modified combined lottery (over L^1 and L^3) would be preferred to the original one (over L^1 and L^2). And *vice versa*.

Another axiom, related to this one, is sometimes called 'the sure thing principle', which, in one version, requires that anything that raises the probability of the preferred component in a two-alternative lottery would improve the lottery. These axioms are implicit in expected utility maximization, even though the 'independence' condition can be dispensed with in a more limited ('locally' valid) version of expected utility behaviour (as has been shown by Mark Machina, 1982).

Various 'counter-examples' to expected utility maximization have been proposed in the literature, often on the basis of considering interesting 'hypothetical' cases, but sometimes on the basis of experimental observations as well. In assessing these objections, we must distinguish, once again, between the claims *to* rationality of this model, and the claims of the model to explain actual behaviour *via* rationality.

It is certainly clear that very often people do act in a way that cannot be made consistent with expected utility maximization. (An early critique, with an alternative framework for choice behaviour, came from Shackle, 1938, 1952.) Observations of behaviour and articulated judgements under uncertainty have indicated different types of violations of expected utility behaviour (see, for example, Kahneman, Slovik and Tversky, 1982). There seem to be problems both in risk perception as well as in the utilization of probability information in making actual decisions. These departures from rational behaviour in the form of expected utility maximization have considerable implications on the way economic models may have to be constructed involving uncertainty (on this see Arrow, 1982, 1983). As a framework for understanding actual behaviour, the merits and demerits of the expected utility model are certainly becoming clearer on the basis of recent work. But the 'bottom line' of overall judgement continues to vary. While some have been extremely sceptical, others (such as Harsanyi, 1977) continue to emphasize, with some justice, the usefulness of this model in 'explaining or predicting real-life human behaviour' (p. 16).

The need for departures – small or great – from the expected utility model in explaining *actual* behaviour does not, of course, settle the question of the rationality or irrationality of maximization of expected utility. However, a number of telling and powerful arguments have also been presented in the literature giving reasons for departing from 'consistency' of the kind demanded by the expected utility model (for arguments on both sides, see the collection of papers in Daboni, Montesano and Lines, 1986). Allais (1953) has followed up his empirical critique of expected utility model as representation of actual behaviour by arguments in favour of the reasonableness of the departures, and more arguments on this have been outlined in recent years (see Allais and Hagen, 1979; Stigum and Wenstop, 1983; and Daboni, Montesano and Lines, 1986). Also, the possibility of 'state-dependent utilities' has raised questions of a different sort, requiring reformulation of the original model (see Drèze, 1974).

One of the important considerations that the expected utility model may leave out consists of 'counterfactual' information. One's 'disappointment', 'regret', etc., may well depend on what one anticipated and what did not occur. Earlier discussions of such criteria as 'minimax regret' (see Savage, 1954) have been followed in recent years by various models of disappointment and regret (see, for example, Bell, 1982; Loomes and Sugden, 1982).

It is arguable that something which has not happened, but could have, should not really affect one's decision, and in particular, it is irrational to regret and sigh about what could have happened. But while it is indeed possible to argue that it is irrational to regret a past decision on the ground of what could have happened in the light of later information, nevertheless *if* it is the case that one would willy-nilly regret the past decision if it turns out to be unfortunate, then it is *not* in any sense obviously irrational to *recognize* that fact and take that inescapable feeling into account. Clarity of analysis requires that we distinguish between (1) and the rationality of what psychology we ought to have, and (2) the rationality of decisions, taking note of what psychology we might not be able to escape. Many counter-examples to expected utility behaviour presented in the literature relate – directly or indirectly – to mental-state considerations, for example, Allais (1953), MacCrimmon (1968), Bernard (1974), Drèze (1974), Tversky (1975), Machina (1981), McClennen (1983) and others.

One reason why the inclusion of mental states among the influences on choice is resisted is the idea that mental state is a particular interpretation of *utility* of which another – alternative – interpretation is given by the numerical representation of choice, with which the expected utility model is concerned. In the context of utilitarianism, the mental-state utility and the numerical representation of choice can indeed be seen as *alternatives*, as they have been viewed in the ethical literature. However, in terms of the description of the world, both mental states and choices are distinct parts of the reality, and the acknowledgement of the existence of one does not deny the existence of the other. Indeed, it is not unreasonable to ask how each might relate to the other. The states of affairs over which choices may be considered (including choices over lotteries of those states) may, quite importantly, include the mental states of the parties involved.

On the other hand, including such mental states in the description of states of affairs makes the scope of such conditions as 'strong independence' rather limited. Varying an *alternative* lottery (e.g., L^3 vis-à-vis L^2) might affect the description of the 'prize' of a given lottery (L^1) through variations of mental states (now included in the outcome of L^1) related to considering and reflecting on the nature of the alternative (L^3 vis-à-vis L^2) and the corresponding disappointment, regret, etc. If L^1 is no longer 'the same' in the two cases, then 'strong independence' would make no demand. Thus 'strong independence' may be saved only at the cost of making it often trivially fulfilled (see Sen, 1985a). The same difficulty applies if strong independence is 'rescued' by including counterfacial information in describing states of affairs.

The basis of rationality implicit in expected utility calculation does, however, require descriptions of states of affairs in sufficient detail such that choices can be made taking all the relevant considerations into account. It can be argued, as indeed Peter Hammond (1986) has, that 'consequential' reasoning taking into account all the relevant considerations, will push us in the direction of expected utility maximization. The important question is whether the relevant considerations would include either counterfactuals or mental states, and if they do so, whether enough scope for the use of such conditions as 'strong independence' can be found to build up utility numbering in a way that would make the expected utility model work in practice. This is not a matter, obviously, of pure theory only, and much depends on the nature of people's psychology and what considerations might be regarded as rational, in taking note of the complexities of our psychology.

CONCLUDING REMARKS. Attempts at constructing models of rational behaviour have certainly played a creative part in reducing the intractability of unstructured assessment of (1) the demands of rationality, and (2) facts of actual behaviour. On the other hand, models of rational behaviour actually presented have tended to ignore some of the complexities that have to be faced. This problem arises even when no uncertainty is introduced into the picture.

Neither of the two standard views of rational behaviour – as 'consistent choice' or as 'self-interest maximization – has emerged as being really adequate as representations of rationality or of actuality. Various suggestions as to the directions in which we might go were reviewed earlier. Although none of the suggestions are unproblematic, many fruitful avenues of investigation have certainly been identified in the critical literature.

These difficulties carry over to rational behaviour models accommodating uncertainty. The limitations of characterizing rational behaviour in terms of just internal consistency, as discussed in the context of choice under certainty, obviously would apply to the modelling of choice under uncertainty as well. Similarly, pursuit of self-interest cannot be seen as being *uniquely* rational in models of uncertainty, any more than they can be so seen when everything is certain. However, it is not really necessary that expected utility models be seen in terms of self interest maximization, and indeed some writers, for example, Ramsey (1931), have explicitly repudiated that interpretation. In fact, what the expected utility models do concentrate on is 'consistency' in a very demanding sense, and in this context objections similar to the ones raised in models of choice *without* uncertainty can be raised a *fortiori* with uncertainty.

Rationality may be seen as demanding something other than just consistency of choices from different subsets. It must, at least, demand cogent relations between aims and objectives actually entertained by the person and the choices that the person makes. This problem is not eliminated by the terminological procedure of describing the cardinal representation of choices as the 'utility' of the person, since this does not give any independent evidence on what the person is aiming to do or trying to achieve.

A more difficult issue, as discussed in the context of certainty, concerns the *assessment* of aims and objectives pursued by a person, even if they are fully reflected in the choices actually made. As Patrick Suppes (1984) has put it, the standard normative model of expected utility 'can be satisfied by cognitive and moral idiots'. 'Put another way, the consistency of computations required by the expected-utility model does not guarantee the exercise of judgement and wisdom in the traditional sense' (pp. 207–8). Suppes argues in favour of moving to the Aristotelian view that the rational person acts 'in accordance with good reasons', and is not embarrassed by the fact that this leaves a certain amount of 'pluralism' in the possible approach to rationality.

In addition to those problems of rationality that are shared by models of certainty as well as uncertainty, there are some special problems that apply particularly to considerations of uncertain outcomes. The status of counterfactuals, and their influences on mental states, raise interesting and important questions as to what may or may not be relevant to take into account in rationally assessing alternative courses of action.

While these problems were addressed earlier on in this paper, one issue that has not yet received much attention here concerns the nature of uncertainty itself. Reference was made earlier to the distinction between interpreting probabilities as degrees of belief, and interpreting them as frequencies. There are also other issues (see, for example, Levi, 1982, 1987). Even the very idea of having beliefs about possible outcomes in the form of probabilities in a situation of partial ignorance raises some interesting philosophical questions. At the very least, it is possible to make a distinction that was made by Frank Knight (1921) between 'risk' and 'uncertainty', with probability distributions being specified in the case of the former but not in the latter case. Whether arguments such as 'insufficient reason' can permit one to *construct* probability distributions even when we do not start with them remains a hard question to settle.

The area of expectation formation is also one in which the demands of rationality are not easy to specify. In some models of rational behaviour, no requirements of rationality are imposed on expectations at all, and the problem of rationality arises only in taking note of the actual expectations in arriving at decisions regarding action. In models of 'adaptive expectations' a step is taken in the direction of making expectations responsive – in an intelligent way – to experience. What goes very much further than this is the assumption of 'rational expectation' by which each person anticipates what can, in some sense, be described as objective probabilities; see Muth (1961), Lucas and Sargent (1981).

This approach not only raises the question as to what the philosophical status of objective probabilities might be, but also whether it is really a matter of *rationality* as such whether one is successful in guessing what the objective probabilities are. It is fair to say that the assessment of models of 'rational expectation' cannot be based on the idea of rationality alone, since the demands of such a theory go well beyond the requirements of the use of reason, especially in a situation of ignorance. It is sensible enough to think that there are problems in models of behaviour in which such that people's expectations are systematically wrong, but to try to move from that recognition to one in which everyone manages to take note of objective probabilities fully is quite a dramatic step. Whether that step is worth taking in predicting actual behaviour might well be discussed and assessed in the light of the ability of such a theory to explain actual behaviour, but that, as we have already discussed, is a rather different problem from assessing the *rationality* as such of that behaviour.

In addition to the issue of the role of rationality involved in 'rational expectation' models, even the basic rational behaviour models (without such expectational assumptions), widely used in economics, raises, as we have seen, difficult – sometimes perplexing – questions. It is not hard to see the merit of trying to reduce a complex reality by characterizing rationality in rather narrow terms, but nor is it hard to fathom that such a narrowing might do grave injustice to the notion of rationality, which is, after all, one of the central concerns of human life.

We have to make a clear distinction between (1) what type of behaviour might be described as *rational*, and (2) what rational behaviour models might be useful in making predictions about *actual* behaviour. These different questions are not, of course, independent of each other. But the first step in pursuing their interrelations is to recognize the distinction between the two questions. What issues respectively arise in facing these distinct questions, and how they might possibly be related, were discussed earlier on in this paper in the light of the existing literature. There was, however, no escape from noting the fact that the existing literature is indeed deeply incomplete in that real difficulties have been identified without providing an adequate structure for solutions. The need to go beyond the existing literature is apparent enough, but where to go is less clear.

BIBLIOGRAPHY

Akerlof, G.A. 1984. *An Economic Theorist's Book of Tales.* Cambridge: Cambridge University Press.
Allais, M. 1953. Le comportement de l'homme rationnel devant le risque: critique de postulates et axiomes de l'école Américaine. *Econometrica* 21, October, 503–46.

Allais, M. and Hagen, O. (eds) 1979. *Expected Utility Hypotheses and the Allais Paradox: Contemporary Discussions of Decisions under Uncertainty with Allais' Rejoinder.* Dordrecht: Reidel.

Arrow, K.J. 1951. An extension of the basic theorems of classical welfare economics. In *Proceedings of the Second Berkeley Symposium of Mathematical Statistics*, ed. J. Neyman, Berkeley: University of California Press.

Arrow, K.J. 1959. Rational choice functions and orderings. *Economica* 26, May, 121–7.

Arrow, K.J. 1971. *Essays in the Theory of Risk-Bearing.* Amsterdam: North-Holland.

Arrow, K.J. 1982. Risk perception in psychology and economics. *Economic Inquiry* 20(1), 1–9.

Arrow, K.J. 1983. Behaviour under uncertainty and its implications for policy. In Stigum and Wenstop (1983).

Arrow, K.J. and Hahn, F.H. 1971. *General Competitive Analysis.* San Francisco: Holden-Day. Republished, Amsterdam: North-Holland, 1979.

Axelrod, R. 1984. *The Evolution of Cooperation.* New York: Academic Press.

Basu, K. 1977. Information and strategy in iterated Prisoners' Dilemma. *Theory and Decision* 8(3), 293–8.

Bell, D.E. 1982. Regret in decision making under uncertainty. *Operations Research* 30(5), 961–81.

Bernard, G. 1974. On utility functions. *Theory and Decision* 5(2), 205–42.

Brams, S.J. 1975. *Game Theory and Politics.* New York: Free Press.

Brennan, G. and Lomasky, L. 1985. The impartial spectator goes to Washington: toward a Smithian theory of economic behavior. *Economics and Philosophy* 1(2), October, 189–211.

Broome, J. 1978. Choice and value in economics. *Oxford Economic Papers* 30(3), November, 313–33.

Broome, J. 1984. Uncertainty and fairness. *Economic Journal* 94, 624–32.

Campbell, R. and Sowden, L. (eds) 1985. *Paradoxes of Rationality and Cooperation.* Vancouver: University of British Columbia Press.

Chipman, J.S., Hurwicz, L., Richter, M.K. and Sonnenschein, H.F. 1971. *Preferences, Utility, and Demand.* New York: Harcourt, Brace.

Daboni, L., Montesano, A. and Lines, M. (eds) 1986. *Recent Developments in the Foundations of Utility Theory and Risk.* Dordrecht: Reidel.

Davis, L.M. 1977. Prisoners, paradox and rationality. *American Philosophical Quarterly* 14. Also in Campbell and Sowden (1985).

Dawkins, R. 1982. *The Extended Phenotype.* Oxford: Clarendon Press.

Davidson, D., Suppes, P. and Siegel, S. 1957. *Decision Making: An Experimental Approach.* Stanford: Stanford University Press.

Debreu, G. 1959. *A Theory of Value.* New York: Wiley.

Dore, R. 1983. Goodwill and the spirit of market capitalism. *British Journal of Sociology* 34, December, 459–82.

Drèze, J.H. 1974. Axiomatic theories of choice, cardinal utility and subjective probability: a review. In *Allocation under Uncertainty: Equilibrium and Optimality*, ed. J.H. Drèze, London: Macmillan; New York: Halsted Press.

Edgeworth, F. 1881. *Mathematical Physics.* London: Kegan Paul; New York: A.M. Kelley, 1967.

Elster, J. 1979. *Ulysses and the Sirens.* Cambridge and New York: Cambridge University Press.

Elster, J. 1983. *Sour Grapes.* Cambridge: Cambridge University Press.

Fishburn, P.C. 1970. *Utility Theory and Decision Making.* New York: Wiley.

Fishburn, P.C. 1981. Subjective expected utility: a review of normative theories. *Theory and Decision* 31(2), 139–99.

Fisher, R.A. 1921. On the mathematical foundations of theoretical statistics. *Philosophical Transactions of the Royal Society of London,* Series A 222, April, 309–68.

Friedman, M. 1953. *Essays in Positive Economics.* Chicago: Chicago University Press.

Friedman, M. and Savage, L.J. 1948. The utility analysis of choices involving risk. *Journal of Political Economy* 56, August, 279–304.

Gauthier, D. 1985. Maximization constrained: the rationality of cooperation. In Campbell and Sowden (1985).

Gibbard, A. and Harper, W.L. 1978. Counterfactual and two kinds of expected utility. In Hooker, Leach and McClennen (1978).

Hammond, P.J. 1976. Changing tastes and coherent dynamic choice. *Review of Economic Studies* 43(1), February, 159–73.

Hammond, P.J. 1986. Consequentialism and rationality in dynamic choice under uncertainty. In *Social Choice and Public Decision Making: Essays in Honor of K.J. Arrow,* ed. W. Heller, D. Starrett and R. Starr, Vol. I, Cambridge: Cambridge University Press.

Harsanyi, J.C. 1977. *Rational Behaviour and Bargaining Equilibrium in Games and Social Situations.* Cambridge and New York: Cambridge University Press.

Helm, D. 1984. Predictions and causes: a comparison of Friedman and Hicks on method. *Oxford Economic Papers* 36, Supplement, November, 118–34.

Herzberger, H. 1973. Ordinal preference and rational choice. *Econometrica* 41(2), March, 187–237.

Hirschman, A.O. 1970. *Exit, Voice, and Loyalty.* Cambridge, Mass.: Harvard University Press.

Hirschman, A.O. 1982. *Shifting Involvements.* Princeton: Princeton University Press.

Hirschman, A.O. 1983. Against parsimony: three easy ways of complicating some categories of economic discourse. *American Economic Review, Papers and Proceedings* 74(2), May, 89–96.

Hirschleifer, J. 1977. Economics from a biological viewpoint. *Journal of Law and Economics* 20(1), April, 1–52.

Hooker, C.A., Leach, J.J. and McClennen, E.F. (eds) 1978. *Foundations and Applications of Decision Theory.* Dordrecht: Reidel.

Houthakker, H.S. 1950. Revealed preference and the utility function. *Economica* 15, May, 159–72.

Houthakker, H.S. 1956. On the logic of preference and choice. In *Contributions to Logic and Methodology in Honor of J.J. Bochenski,* ed. A. Tymieniecka, Amsterdam: North-Holland.

Howard, N. 1971. *Paradoxes of Rationality.* Cambridge, Mass.: MIT Press.

Jeffrey, R.C. 1965. *The Logic of Decision.* New York: McGraw-Hill, 2nd edn, Chicago: University of Chicago Press, 1983.

Kahneman, D. and Tversky, A. 1979. Prospect theory: an analysis of decisions under risk. *Econometrica* 47(2), March, 263–91.

Kahneman, D., Slovik, P. and Tversky, A. 1982. *Judgement under Uncertainty: Heuristics and Biases.* Cambridge: Cambridge University Press.

Kanger, S. 1976. Preference based on choice. Mimeographed, Uppsala University.

Keynes, J.M. 1921. *A Treatise on Probability.* London: Macmillan; New York: Harper & Row, 1962.

Knight, F. 1921. *Risk, Uncertainty and Profit.* New York: Houghton Mifflin.

Kornai, J. 1971. *Anti-Equilibrium*. Amsterdam: North-Holland.

Kreps, D.M., Milgrom, P., Roberts, J. and Wilson, R. 1982. Rational cooperation in the finitely repeated Prisoners' Dilemma. *Journal of Economic Theory* 27(2), August, 245–52.

Latsis, S.J. (ed.) 1976. *Method and Appraisal in Economics*. Cambridge and New York: Cambridge University Press.

Leibenstein, H. 1976. *Beyond Economic Man: A New Foundation for Microeconomics*. Cambridge, Mass.: Harvard University Press.

Levi, I. 1975. Newcomb's many problems. *Theory and Decision* 6(2), 161–75.

Levi, I. 1982. Ignorance, probability and rational choice. *Synthése* 53(2), December, 287–417.

Levi, I. 1987. *Hard Choices*. Cambridge: Cambridge University Press.

Loomes, G. and Sugden, R. 1982. Regret theory: an alternative theory of rational choice. *Economic Journal* 92(368), December, 805–24.

Lucas, R.E. and Sargent, T.J. 1981. *Rational Expectation and Econometric Practice*. Minneapolis: University of Minneapolis Press; London: Allen & Unwin, 1982.

Luce, R.D. and Raiffa, H. 1957. *Games and Decisions*. New York: Wiley.

MacCrimmon, K.R. 1968. Descriptive and normative implications of decision theory postulates. In *Risk and Uncertainty*, ed. K. Borch and J. Mossin, London: Macmillan.

Machina, M. 1981. 'Rational' decision making vs. 'rational' decision modelling? *Journal of Mathematical Psychology* 24.

Machina, M. 1982. 'Expected utility' analysis without the independence axiom. *Econometrica* 50(2), March, 277–323.

McClennen, E.F. 1983. Sure-thing doubts. In Stigum and Wenstop (1983).

McClennen, E.F. 1985. Prisoners' dilemma and resolute choice. In Campbell and Sowden (1985).

McPherson, M.S. 1982. Mill's moral theory and the problem of preference change. *Ethics* 92(2), 252–73.

Margolis, H. 1982. *Selfishness, Altruism and Rationality*. Cambridge: Cambridge University Press.

Marschak, J. 1946. Von Neumann's and Morgenstern's new approach to static economics. *Journal of Political Economy* 54, April, 91–115.

Matthews, R.C.O. 1984. Darwinism and economic change. *Oxford Economic Papers* 36, Supplement, November, 91–117.

Maynard Smith, J. 1982. *Evolution and the Theory of Games*. Cambridge: Cambridge University Press.

Morishima, M. 1982. *Why Has Japan 'Succeeded'? Western Technology and Japanese Ethos*. Cambridge: Cambridge University Press.

Muth, J.F. 1961. Rational expectations and the theory of price movements. *Econometrica* 29, July, 315–35.

Nagel, T. 1970. *The Possibility of Altruism*. Oxford: Clarendon Press.

Nozick, R. 1969. New comb's problem and two principles of choice. In *Essays in Honor of Carl G. Hempel*, ed. N. Rescher, Dordrecht: Reidel.

Parfit, D. 1984. *Reasons and Persons*. Oxford: Clarendon Press.

Radner, R. 1980. Collusive behaviour in non-cooperative epsilon-equilibria of oligopolies with long but finite lives. *Journal of Economic Theory* 22(2), April, 136–54.

Ramsey, F.P. 1931. Truth and probability. In F.P. Ramsey, *The Foundations of Mathematics and other Logical Essays*, London: Kegan Paul; New York: Humanities Press, 1950.

Richter, M.K. 1971. Rational choice. In Chipman, Hurwicz, Richter and Sonnenschein (1971).

Samuelson, P.A. 1938. A note on the pure theory of consumers' behaviour. *Economica* 5, February, 61–71.

Savage, L.J. 1954. *The Foundations of Statistics.* New York: Wiley.

Schelling, T.C. 1978. *Micromotives and Macrobehaviour.* New York: Norton.

Schelling, T.C. 1984. Self-command in practice, in policy, and in a theory of rational choice. *American Economic Review, Papers and Proceedings* 74(2), May, 1–11.

Schick, F. 1984. *Having Reasons: An Essay on Rationality and Sociality.* Princeton: Princeton University Press.

Scitovsky, T. 1976. *The Joyless Economy.* London: Oxford University Press.

Sen, A.K. 1971. Choice functions and revealed preference. *Review of Economic Studies* 38, July, 307–17.

Sen, A.K. 1973. Behaviour and the concept of preference. *Economica* 40, August, 241–59. Reprinted in Sen (1982).

Sen, A.K. 1974. Choice, orderings and morality. In *Practical Reason,* ed. S. Körner, Oxford: Blackwell; New Haven: Hale University Press. Reprinted in Sen (1982).

Sen, A.K. 1977. Rational fools: a critique of the behavioural foundations of economic theory. *Philosophy and Public Affairs* 6, Summer, 317–44. Reprinted in Sen (1982).

Sen, A.K. 1982. *Choice, Welfare and Measurement.* Oxford: Blackwell; Cambridge, Mass.: MIT Press.

Sen, A.K. 1985a. Rationality and uncertainty. *Theory and Decision* 18. Also in Daboni, Montesano and Lines (1985).

Sen, A.K. 1985b. Goals, commitment and identity. *Journal of Law, Economics and Organization* 1.

Sen, A.K. 1987. *On Ethics and Economics.* Oxford: Blackwell.

Shackle, G.L.S. 1938. *Expectations, Investment and Income.* Cambridge: Cambridge University Press.

Shackle, G.L.S. 1952. *Expectations in Economics.* 2nd edn, Cambridge: Cambridge University Press.

Simon, H.A. 1957. *Models of Man.* New York: Wiley.

Simon, H.A. 1979. *Models of Thought.* New Haven: Yale University Press.

Simon, H.A. 1983. *Reason in Human Affairs.* Oxford: Blackwell; Stanford: Stanford University Press.

Smale, S. 1980. The Prisoner's Dilemma and dynamic systems associated to non-cooperative games. *Econometrica* 48(7), November, 1617–34.

Smith, A. 1776. *An Inquiry into the Nature and Causes of the Wealth of Nations.* Ed. by R.H. Campbell and A.S. Skinner, Oxford: Clarendon Press, 1976.

Smith, A. 1790. *The Theory of Moral Sentiments.* Ed. by D.D. Raphael and A.L. Macfie, Oxford: Clarendon Press, 1974.

Stigum, B.P. and Wenstop, F. (eds) 1983. *Foundations of Utility and Risk Theory with Applications.* Dordrecht: Reidel.

Sugden, R. 1985. Why be consistent? A critical analysis of consistency requirements in choice theory. *Economica* 52, May, 167–83.

Suppes, P. 1984. *Probabilistic Metaphysics.* Oxford: Blackwell.

Suzumura, K. 1983. *Rational Choice, Collective Decisions and Social Welfare.* Cambridge: Cambridge University Press.

Tversky, A. 1975. A critique of expected utility theory: descriptive and normative considerations. *Erkenntnis* 9, 163–73.

Uzawa, H. 1956. A note on preference and axioms of choice. *Annals of the Institute of Statistical Mathematics* 8(1), 35–40.

Von Neumann, J. and Morgenstern, O. 1947. *Theory of Games and Economic Behavior.* Princeton: Princeton University Press, 1st edn, 1944.

Watkins, J. 1974. Comment: self-interest and morality. In *Practical Reason,* ed. S. Körner, Oxford: Blackwell; New Haven, Yale University Press.

Watkins, J. 1985. Second thoughts on self-interest and mortality. In Campbell and Sowden (1985).

Winch, D. 1978. *Adam Smith's Politics.* Cambridge: Cambridge University Press.

Wong, S. 1978. *Foundations of Paul Samuelson's Revealed Preference Theory.* London and Boston: Routledge.

Representation of Preferences

PETER C. FISHBURN

Three facets of subjective preferences have played central roles in economics. They are the qualitative structure of an agent's preferences, numerical representations of preferences, and the use of numerical representations or utility functions in economic analysis. We consider various representations and their ties to qualitative preference structures.

Preferences themselves are described by a binary relation $\succ$, *is preferred to*, on a non-empty set X. Axioms or assumptions about the behaviour of $\succ$ on X identify a qualitative preference structure. A representation provides a correspondence between this structure and properties of real valued functions based on X.

Elements in X are often viewed as decision alternatives or outcomes of choice. They may be arbitrary or have a prescribed structure, as when each x in X is a commodity bundle in some Euclidean space or a probability distribution (lottery) on wealth or on increments to current wealth.

Representations of preferences between lotteries date to Bernoulli (1738), who sought to explain why agents often prefer a sure level of wealth to a lottery with larger expected value than the sure level. Representations of preferences between commodity bundles were used by Jevons, Menger, Walras and Edgeworth in the late 19th century to examine the economic consequences of consumer behaviour within the theory of marginal analysis (Samuelson, 1947; Stigler, 1950). The commodity space and lottery contexts remain the preeminent structures for research in the representation of preferences.

Despite the early beginnings, detailed attention to qualitative preference structures for various representations is comparatively recent. Three examples are Frisch's axiomatization of comparable preference differences and Ramsey's theory of utility and subjective probability for decisions under uncertainty from the 1920s, and the axioms for expected utility of von Neumann and Morgenstern (1944).

217

CLASSIFICATION. The structure of X and the degree of transitivity are two useful factors for classifying representations. The five most prominent structures are

S1 X is arbitrary except perhaps for cardinality or topological properties,
S2 $X = X_1 \times X_2 \times \cdots \times X_n$ or $X = X_1 \times X_2 \times \ldots$,
S3 X is a set of probability distributions,
S4   same as S3 except the outcomes are multidimensional as in S2,
S5 X is a set of mappings from a set S of states into an outcome set.

S2 includes commodity spaces and time streams, S3 is the setting for expected utility, and S5 is Savage's (1954) formulation for decisions under uncertainty. When S is countable, S2 can be used instead of S5 with X_i the possible outcomes for state i.

Our discussion is organized around S1 to S5 with transitivity as a subsidiary factor. It is assumed in all cases that $\succ$ is asymmetric, so $x \succ y$ precludes $y \succ x$. The agent's indifference relation $\sim$ and preference-or-indifference relation are defined by

$$x \sim y, \qquad \text{if neither } x \succ y \text{ nor } y \succ x,$$
$$x \succsim y, \qquad \text{if } x \succ y \text{ or } x \sim y,$$

Comparable preferences differences are discussed in the final section.

The preference relation $\succ$ is *transitive* if, for all x, y and z in X, $x \succ z$ whenever $x \succ y$ and $y \succ z$. Similar definitions pertain to $\sim$ and $\succsim$. Three levels of transitivity are

T1   both $\succ$ and $\sim$ are transitive,
T2   only $\succ$ is assumed to be transitive,
T3   neither $\succ$ nor $\sim$ is assumed to be transitive.

T1 is the usual assumption employed in economic analysis. T2 has little relevance before 1960 and T3 has little relevance before 1970.

T1 implies that $\succsim$ also is transitive. Under T1, $\succ$ is a 'weak order', and $\succsim$ is a 'weak order' or 'complete preorder'. T2 says that preferences are partially ordered; indifference need not be transitive. I include acyclic preferences – it is never true that $x_1 \succ x_2 \succ \cdots \succ x_k \succ x_1$ – under T2. Unordered or non-transitive preferences fall under T3, which allows preference cycles such as $x \succ y$, $y \succ z$ and $z \succ x$, or $x \succ y \succ z \succ x$ for short.

Arbitrary sets: S1. The basic representation for weak orders is

$$x \succ y \Leftrightarrow u(x) > u(y), \tag{1}$$

where u is a real function on X. This and later expressions apply to all $x, y, \ldots$ in X. The function u in (1) is unique up to transformations that preserve order and is called an *ordinal* utility function.

T1 is necessary and sufficient for (1) when X is countable, but not otherwise.

The general case also requires X to have a countable *order-dense* subset Y (Cantor, 1985) such that, whenever $x \succ z$ then $x \succsim y \succsim z$ for some y in Y. When (1) fails under T1 because no countable subset is order-dense in X, $\succ$ can be represented by vectors of utilities ordered lexicographically (Chipman, 1960; Fishburn, 1974). The finite-dimensional lexicographic representation is

$$x \succ y \Leftrightarrow [u_1(x), \ldots, u_n(x)] >_L [u_1(y), \ldots, u_n(y)], \tag{2}$$

where each u_i is real valued and $(a_1, \ldots, a_n) >_L (b_1, \ldots, b_n)$ if $a_i \neq b_i$ for some i and $a_i > b_i$ for the smallest such i.

Other conditions than order denseness can be used for (1) when X is a topological space. If X is connected and separable and T1 holds, there is a continuous u that satisfies (1) if, for each y in X, $\{x : x \succ y\}$ and $\{x : y \succ x\}$ are open sets in X's topology. This and related contributions on continuity appear in Debreu (1964) and Fishburn (1970a).

Under T2, (1) is replaced by the one-way representation

$$x \succ y \Rightarrow u(x) > u(y). \tag{3}$$

T2 is sufficient for (3) when X is countable, but not otherwise (Fishburn, 1970a, 1970b). For comments on continuity, see Sondermann (1980). Specialized partial orders use two functions for two-way representations. For example, if X is countable and $\{x \succ a, y \succ b\}$ implies $x \succ b$ or $y \succ a$, then there are real functions f and $\rho > 0$ on X such that

$$x \succ y \Leftrightarrow f(x) > f(y) + \rho(y).$$

Such an $(X, \succ)$ is called an *interval order*. The more specialized case in which ρ is a positive constant is known as a *semiorder*; see Fishburn (1985) for details.

Under T3, $(X, \succ)$ can be represented by a skew-symmetric $[\phi(y, x) = -\phi(x, y)]$ real function ϕ on $X \times X$ as

$$x \succ y \Leftrightarrow \phi(x, y) > 0. \tag{4}$$

This requires only asymmetry, and $\phi(x, y)$ can be set equal to 1, 0 or -1 when $x \succ y$, $x \sim y$ or $y \succ x$ respectively. We can view (1) as the specialization of (4) in which $\phi(x, y) = u(x) - u(y)$.

Product sets: S2. When $X = X_1 \times X_2 \times \cdots \times X_n$ with $x = (x_1, x_2, \ldots, x_n)$, (1) is

$$x \succ y \Leftrightarrow u(x_1, x_2, \ldots, x_n) > u(y_1, y_2, \ldots, y_n). \tag{1*}$$

It is often assumed that each X_i is a real interval or a convex subset of a connected and separable topological space, and that u increases and is continuous in each component (Debreu, 1964; Fishburn, 1970a). When X is the positive orthant of n-dimensional Euclidean space, the indifference classes form a layered array of isoutility contours away from the origin. Isoutility contours that are convex to the origin are often presumed in the marginal analysis of consumption theory.

Houthakker (1961) provides a survey of consumption theory, including the fundamentals of demand as a function of prices and income, revealed preference, direct utility as a function of commodity bundles and indirect utility. An example of the indirect approach, which expresses utility as a function of prices $p_1, \ldots, p_n$ and total expenditure $m > 0$, is the indirect addilog function

$$v(p_1/m, \ldots, p_n/m) = \sum_{i=1}^{n} a_i(p_i/m)^{b_i}.$$

A related direct addilog function for quantities $q_i, \ldots, q_n$ is

$$u(q_1, \ldots, q_n) = \sum_{i=1}^{n} \alpha_i q_i^{\beta_i}.$$

These functions are special cases of the additive-utility specialization of (1), i.e.

$$x \succ y \Leftrightarrow u_1(x_1) + \cdots + u_n(x_n) > u_1(y_1) + \cdots + u_n(y_n), \qquad (5)$$

where u_i is a real function on X_i. This presumes the *independence condition* which says that, whenever the n factors are partitioned into two parts, the preference order over one part conditioned on fixed values of the X_i in the other part is independent of the particular fixed values used. Other axioms are also needed for (5).

Necessary and sufficient conditions for (5) and its one-way counterpart under T2 when X is finite appear in Fishburn (1970a) and Krantz et al. (1971). Conditions sufficient for (5) with infinite X_i appear in Fishburn (1970a) and Krantz et al. (1971). The latter conditions imply that the u_i in (5) are unique up to similar positive linear transformations, so that $v_1, \ldots, v_n$ satisfy (5) in place of $u_1, \ldots, u_n$ if and only if there are numbers $\beta_1, \ldots, \beta_n$ and $\alpha > 0$ such that

$$v_i(x_i) = \alpha u_i(x_i) + \beta_i, \qquad \text{for all } i \text{ and all } x_i \text{ in } X_i.$$

Debreu and Koopmans (1982) study the conjunction of additive utilities and quasiconcavity of u when $u(x) = u_1(x_1) + \cdots + u_n(x_n)$.

The basic lexicographic representation for $X = X_1 \times X_2 \times \cdots$ (Chipman, 1960) with hierarchical importance ordering $1, 2, \ldots$ is

$$x \succ y \Leftrightarrow [u_1(x_1), u_2(x_2), \ldots] >_L [u_1(y_1), u_2(y_2), \ldots].$$

Luce (1978) combines the lexicographic and additive ideas in a two-factor model whose lexicographic part applies under significant differences in the dominant factor, and whose additive part applies otherwise.

One T3 representation is the additive-difference model in Tversky (1969) where

$$x \succ y \Leftrightarrow \sum_{i=1}^{n} f_i[u_i(x_i) - u_i(y_i)] > 0.$$

This is a special case of (4). Here f_i is an odd $[f_i(-a) = -f_i(a)]$, continuous and increasing real function. Fishburn (1980) combines the additive-difference and lexicographic notions.

Other T3 representations are implicit in Mas-Colell (1974) and elsewhere in a topological setting. A key axiom in this work is that $\{y: y \succ x\}$ is a convex subset of X for each x in X.

The homogeneous case $X = A^n$ or $X = A \times A \times \cdots$ provides a setting for time preference. Notions of persistence, impatience and stationarity for denumerable-period contexts are analysed by Koopmans (1960), Koopmans et al. (1964), and Fishburn and Rubinstein (1982). Fishburn (1970a) considers finite periods. One representation here is

$$x \succ y \Leftrightarrow \pi_1 u(x_1) + \pi_2 u(x_2) + \cdots > \pi_1 u(y_1) + \pi_2 u(y_2) + \ldots, \qquad (6)$$

where $\pi_i \geq 0$ is an importance weight for period i. A particular case is $\pi_i = \sigma^{i-1}$, which obtains for the additive model (5) if preferences are 'stationary'.

Probability distributions: S3. This section and the next assume that X is a convex set of probability measures (distributions) on an outcome algebra $\mathscr{A}$. $x(A)$ is the probability that x yields an outcome in set A. When $0 \leq \lambda \leq 1$ and x and y are in X, $\lambda x + (1 - \lambda)y$ denotes the linear convex combination of x and y that has $[\lambda x + (1 - \lambda)y](A) = \lambda x(A) + (1 - \lambda)y(A)$ for each A in $\mathscr{A}$. We say that $(X, \succ)$ is *linear* if $\lambda x + (1 - \lambda)z \succ \lambda y + (1 - \lambda)z$ whenever $x \succ y$, z is in X, and $0 < \lambda < 1$.

The von Neumann–Morgenstern theory (Fishburn, 1970a, 1982a) uses T1, linearity and a continuity condition to obtain a u on X that satisfies (1) and

$$u[\lambda x + (1 - \lambda)y] = \lambda u(x) + (1 - \lambda)u(y). \qquad (7)$$

Such a u is unique up to an arbitrary positive linear transformation $[v(x) = \alpha u(x) + \beta, \alpha > 0]$ and is sometimes called a *cardinal utility function*. If the outcome set C is finite and $\mathscr{A}$ includes each singleton $\{c\}$ for c in C, then (7) yields the expected-utility form

$$u(x) = \sum_C x(c)u(c).$$

The extension of this to $u(x) = \int u(c)\mathrm{d}x(c)$ for infinite outcome sets is discussed in Fishburn (1970a, 1982a).

Generalizations of the von Neumann–Morgenstern theory that retain T1 but weaken the linearity axiom are discussed by Allais (1953), Kahneman and Tversky (1979), Machina (1982), Chew (1983) and Fishburn (1983). For example, Machina assumes a smooth preference field over X that is approximately linear locally, and Chew and Fishburn axiomatize the representation

$$x \succ y \Leftrightarrow u(x)w(y) > u(y)w(x), \qquad (8)$$

in which each of u and w is linear, as in (7), and w is non-negative. When w is constant, (8) reduces to the von Neumann–Morgenstern case.

Generalizations that retain linearity but weaken T1 to T2 appear in Fishburn (1970a, 1982a). Other generalizations retain T1 and linearity but drop continuity to obtain lexicographic expected-utility representations (Chipman, 1960; Fishburn, 1982a).

Axioms for unordered and nonlinear preferences over X are presented in Fishburn (1982b). Assumptions of continuity, convexity, such as $x \succ y$ and $z \succ y$

imply $\lambda x + (1 - \lambda)z \succ y$, and symmetry are shown to be necessary and sufficient for the unordered representation (4) in which ϕ on $X \times X$ is skew-symmetric and *bilinear*, that is linear separately in each argument. Such a ϕ is unique up to an arbitrary similarity transformation of the form $\phi'(x, y) = \alpha\phi(x, y)$ with $\alpha > 0$. The von Neumann–Morgenstern model results when ϕ can be decomposed as $\phi(x, y) = u(x) - u(y)$, and (8) corresponds to $\phi(x, y) = u(x)w(y) - u(y)w(x)$.

Multiple attributes under risk: S4. Continuing with X as a set of probability distributions, we now assume that the outcome set C is a product set with $C = C_1 \times C_2 \times \cdots \times C_n$. We assume also that the basic expected-utility axioms hold for $(X, \succ)$, so that, for all distributions x and y in X with finite supports,

$$x \succ y \Leftrightarrow \sum_C x(c_1, \ldots, c_n)u(c_1, \ldots, c_n) > \sum_C y(c_1, \ldots, c_n)u(c_1, \ldots, c_n). \qquad (9)$$

A generalization of (9) is noted at the end of the section.

Representation (9) has several specializations involving decompositions of $u(c_1, \ldots, c_n)$. Many of these are reviewed in Keeney and Raiffa (1976), Fishburn (1977) and Farquhar (1978).

The additive decomposition is

$$u(c_1, \ldots, c_n) = u_1(c_1) + \cdots + u_n(c_n), \qquad (10)$$

in which u_i is a real function on C_i and the u_i are unique up to similar positive linear transformations. When (10) holds, the sum in (9) simplifies to

$$\sum_C x(c_1, \ldots, c_n)u(c_1, \ldots, c_n) = \sum_{i=1}^n \sum_{C_i} x_i(c_i)u_i(c_i),$$

where x_i denotes the marginal distribution of x on C_i. Given (9), a necessary and sufficient condition for (10) is $x \sim y$ whenever $x_i = y_i$ for $i = 1, \ldots, n$. The same result holds (Fishburn, 1982a) when C is only assumed to be a subset of $C_1 \times \cdots \times C_n$, but in this case the preceding uniqueness property may fail.

Multiplicative decompositions of $u(c_1, \ldots, c_n)$ arise from independence conditions that are similar to the condition following (5). For any non-trivial two-part partition $\{I, J\}$ of $\{1, 2, \ldots, n\}$ we say that I is *utility independent* of J if the preference order over distributions on the product of the C_i for i in I, conditioned on fixed values of the C_j for all j in J, is independent of those fixed values. Moreover, I is *generalized utility independent* of J if any two such conditional preference orders are identical, duals, or one is empty. The importance of these notions is that if I is generalized utility independent of J then $u(c_I, c_J)$, where c_I is in the product of the C_i for $i \in I$ and similarly for c_J, decomposes as

$$u(c_I, c_J) = f(c_J) + g(c_J)h(c_I).$$

If I is utility independent of J, then g is a strictly positive function.

We mention one consequence of this two-part decomposition. If $\{1, \ldots, i-1, i+1, \ldots, n\}$ is generalized utility independent of $\{i\}$ for each i in $\{1, \ldots, n\}$, then there is a real function u_i on C_i for each i such that either (10) holds or there is a non-zero constant k such that, under a suitable rescaling of u,

$$ku(c_1,\ldots,c_n)+1 = [ku_1(c_1)+1]\cdots[ku_n(c_n)+1].$$

Other types of independence among factors in the context of (9) are analysed by Farquhar (1975), Keeney and Raiffa (1976), and Fishburn and Farquhar (1982).

States of the world: S5. In our final setting, X is a set of functions from a set S of states of the world into a set C of outcomes or consequences. The set C may be unstructured or have one of the forms considered previously. For example, C could be a set of probability distributions defined on another set.

Following Savage (1954), we refer to each x in X as an *act* and to each subset of S as an *event*. It is presumed that exactly one state in S is the true state and that the agent is uncertain as to which state this is. Moreover, the true state, or state that 'obtains', is determined by circumstances beyond the agent's control. If the agent chooses act x and state s obtains, then $x(s)$ in C is the consequence that occurs as the result of the choice.

The best-known representation for $(X, \succ)$ is Savage's (1954) subjective expected-utility model, which was inspired by Ramsey's earlier outline of a theory of preferences and beliefs under uncertainty, de Finetti's (1937) work in subjective probability, and the von Neumann–Morgenstern (1944) theory of expected utility. Savage's representation is

$$x \succ y \Leftrightarrow \int_S u[x(s)]\,\mathrm{d}P(s) > \int_S u[y(s)]\,\mathrm{d}P(s), \tag{11}$$

where u is a real function on C and P is a finitely-additive probability measure on the set of all events that is 'continuously divisible' in the sense that, for every event A and every $0 < \lambda < 1$ there is another event $B \subseteq A$ for which $P(B) = \lambda P(A)$. In addition, u is bounded (Fishburn, 1970a) and unique up to a positive linear transformation, and P is unique.

Savage's assumptions include strong structural conditions on X, T1, a few independence axioms, and a continuity condition that generates the form of P noted above. Criticisms of his conditions and alternative ways of conceptualizing decisions under uncertainty have stimulated a number of people to develop alternatives to Savage's theory with representations that are more or less similar to (11). The alternatives are reviewed in detail in Fishburn (1981).

Several authors (see Fishburn, 1981) derive Savage's representation for finite as well as infinite S by taking C as a set of probability distributions or lotteries. The same device is used extensively in Fishburn (1982a), which includes a one-way representation under T2. Schmeidler (1984) keeps T1 in the lottery approach but weakens independence to obtain a representation with monotonic but non-additive 'probabilities' that accommodates preference patternns that are inconsistent with Savage's theory (Ellsberg, 1961).

Loomes and Sugden (1982) propose a finite-state model for decision under uncertainty that allows non-transitive preferences and therefore falls in transitivity

223

class T3. Their representation for n states is

$$x \succ y \Leftrightarrow \sum_{i=1}^{n} P(s_i)\phi[x(s_i), y(s_i)] > 0,$$

where $P(s_i)$ is the agent's subjective probability for states s_i and ϕ is skew-symmetric. Lottery-based axioms for this and other T3 models appear in Fishburn (1984).

Comparable preference differences. In contrast to preceding representations, we now consider representations based on a binary relation $\succ^*$ on $X \times X$. A common intuitive interpretation of $\succ^*$ is that $(x, y) \succ^* (z, w)$ signifies that the difference in preference between x and y exceeds the difference in preference between z and w, or that the intensity of preference for x over y exceeds the intensity of preference for z over w. When $\succ^*$ is used, $\succ$ is usually defined by $x \succ y$ if and only if $(x, y) \succ^* (y, y)$.

A basic representation in this setting is

$$(x, y) \succ^* (z, w) \Leftrightarrow u(x) - u(y) > u(z) - u(w). \tag{12}$$

This requires $\succ^*$ to be a weak order on $X \times X$ and entails other conditions like $(x, y) \succ^* (z, w) \Leftrightarrow (x, z) \succ^* (y, w)$ and $(x, y) \succ^* (z, y) \Leftrightarrow (x, w) \succ^* (z, w)$.

Early axiomatizations of (12) from the 1920s and 1930s are due to Frisch, Lange and Alt. Comments on these and more recent axiomatizations appear in Fishburn (1970a, chapter 6). The axioms for infinite X essentially use a bisection procedure to determine utility midpoints, as when $u(x) - u(z) = u(z) - u(y)$, or $u(z) = [u(x) + u(y)]/2$, and the resultant u is unique up to a positive linear transformation.

Specialized representations in the context of (12) arise when $X = X_1 \times \cdots \times X_n$. Dyer and Sarin (1979) and Kirkwood and Sarin (1980) consider decompositions of $u(x_1, \ldots, x_n)$ that are similar to ones mentioned under S4, and Fishburn (1970a) discusses the weighted additive form used in (6) when $X = A^n$.

BIBLIOGRAPHY

Allais, M. 1953. Le comportement de l'homme rationnel devant le risque: critique des postulats et axiomes de l'école Americaine. *Econometrica* 21, 503–46.

Bernoulli, D. 1738. Specimen theoriae novae de mensura sortis. *Commentarii Academiae Scientarium Imperialis Petropolitanae* 5, 175–92. Trans. L. Sommer, *Econometrica* 22, (1954), 23–36.

Cantor, G. 1895. Beiträge zur Begrüdung der Transfinite Mengenlehre. *Mathematische Annalen* 46, 481–512 and 49 (1897), 207–46. English translation: *Contributions to the Founding of the Theory of Transfinite Numbers*. New York: Dover, n.d.

Chew, S.H. 1983. A generalization of the quasilinear mean with applications to the measurement of income inequality and decision theory resolving the Allais paradox. *Econometrica* 51, 1065–92.

Chipman, J.S. 1960. The foundations of utility. *Econometrica* 28, 193–224.

Debreu, G. 1964. Continuity properties of Paretian utility. *International Economic Review* 5, 285–93.

Debreu, G. and Koopmans, T.C. 1982. Additively decomposed quasiconvex functions. *Mathematical Programming* 24, 1–38.

de Finetti, B. 1937. La prévision: ses logiques, ses sources subjectives. *Annales de l'Institut Henri Poincaré* 7, 1–68. Trans. by H.E. Kyburg in *Studies in Subjective Probability*, ed. H.E. Kyburg and H.E. Smokler, New York: Wiley, 1964, 93–158.

Dyer, J.S. and Sarin, R.K. 1979. Measurable multiattribute value functions. *Operations Research* 27, 810–22.

Ellsberg, D. 1961. Risk, ambiguity, and the Savage axioms. *Quarterly Journal of Economics* 75, 643–69.

Farquhar, P.H. 1975. A fractional hypercube decomposition theorem for multiattribute utility functions. *Operations Research* 23, 941–67.

Farquhar, P.H. 1978. Interdependent criteria in utility analysis. In *Multiple Criteria Problem Solving*, ed. S. Zionts, Berlin: Springer-Verlag, 131–80.

Fishburn, P.C. 1970a. *Utility Theory for Decision Making*. New York: Wiley.

Fishburn, P.C. 1970b. Intransitive indifference in preference theory: a survey. *Operations Research* 18, 207–28.

Fishburn, P.C. 1974. Lexicographic orders, utilities, and decision rules: a survey. *Management Science* 20, 1442–71.

Fishburn, P.C. 1977. Multiattribute utilities in expected utility theory. In *Conflicting Objectives in Decisions*, ed. D.E. Bell, R.L. Keeney and H. Raiffa, New York: Wiley, 172–94.

Fishburn, P.C. 1980. Lexicographic additive differences. *Journal of Mathematical Psychology* 21, 191–218.

Fishburn, P.C. 1981. Subjective expected utility: a review of normative theories. *Theory and Decision* 13, 139–99.

Fishburn, P.C. 1982a. *The Foundations of Expected Utility*. Dordrecht, Holland: Reidel.

Fishburn, P.C. 1982b. Nontransitive measurable utility. *Journal of Mathematical Psychology* 26, 31–67.

Fishburn, P.C. 1983. Transitive measurable utility. *Journal of Economic Theory* 31, 293–317.

Fishburn, P.C. 1984. SSB utility theory and decision-making under uncertainty. *Mathematical Social Sciences* 8, 253–85.

Fishburn, P.C. 1985. *Interval Orders and Interval Graphs*. New York: Wiley.

Fishburn, P.C. and Farquhar, P.H. 1982. Finite-degree utility independence. *Mathematics of Operations Research* 7, 348–53.

Fishburn, P.C. and Rubinstein, A. 1982. Time preference. *International Economic Review* 23, 677–94.

Houthakker, H.S. 1961. The present state of consumption theory. *Econometrica* 29, 704–40.

Kahneman, D. and Tversky, A. 1979. Prospect theory: an analysis of decision under risk. *Econometrica* 47, 263–91.

Keeney, R.L. and Raiffa, H. 1976. *Decisions with Multiple Objectives: Preferences and Value Tradeoffs*. New York: Wiley.

Kirkwood, C.W. and Sarin, R.K. 1980. Preference conditions for multiattribute value functions. *Operations Research* 28, 225–32.

Koopmans, T.C. 1960. Stationary ordinal utility and impatience. *Econometrica* 28, 287–309.

Koopmans, T.C., Diamond, P.A. and Williamson, R.E. 1964. Stationary utility and time perspective. *Econometrica* 32, 82–100.

Krantz, D.H., Luce, R.D., Suppes, P. and Tversky, A. 1971. *Foundations of Measurement. Volume I: Additive and Polynomial Representations*. New York: Academic Press.

Loomes, G. and Sugden, R. 1982. Regret theory: an alternative theory of rational choice under uncertainty. *Economic Journal* 92, 805–24.

Luce, R.D. 1978. Lexicographic tradeoff structures. *Theory and Decision* 9, 187–93.

Machina, M.J. 1982. 'Expected utility' analysis without the independence axiom, *Econometrica* 50, 277–323.

Mas-Colell, A. 1974. An equilibrium existence theorem without complete or transitive preferences. *Journal of Mathematical Economics* 1, 237–46.

Samuelson, P.A. 1947. *Foundations of Economic Analysis*. Cambridge, Mass.: Harvard University Press.

Savage, L.J. 1954. *The Foundations of Statistics*. New York: Wiley. 2nd rev. edn, Dover Publications, 1972.

Schmeidler, D. 1984. Subjective probability and expected utility without additivity. Preprint no. 84, Institute for Mathematics and its Applications, University of Minnesota.

Sondermann, D. 1980. Utility representations for partial orders. *Journal of Economic Theory* 23, 183–8.

Stigler, G.J. 1950. The development of utility theory I, II. *Journal of Political Economy* 58, 307–27; 373–96.

Tversky, A. 1969. Intransitivity of preferences. *Psychological Review* 76, 31–48.

von Neumann, J. and Morgenstern, O. 1944. *Theory of Games and Economic Behavior*. Princeton: Princeton University Press; 2nd edn, 1947; 3rd edn, 1953.

Risk

MARK J. MACHINA AND MICHAEL ROTHSCHILD

The phenomenon of *risk* (or alternatively, *uncertainty* or *incomplete information*) plays a pervasive role in economic life. Without it, financial and capital markets would consist of the exchange of a single instrument each period, the communications industry would cease to exist, and the profession of investment banking would reduce to that of accounting. One need only consult the contents of any recent economics journal to see how the recognition of risk has influenced current research in economics. In this essay we present an overview of the modern economic theory of the characterization of risk and the modelling of economic agents' responses to it.

RISK VERSUS UNCERTAINTY. The most fundamental distinction in this branch of economic theory, due to Knight (1921), is that of risk versus uncertainty. A situation is said to involve *risk* if the randomness facing an economic agent can be expressed in terms of specific numerical probabilities (these probabilities may either be objectively specified, as with lottery tickets, or else reflect the individual's own subjective beliefs). On the other hand, situations where the agent cannot (or does not) assign actual probabilities to the alternative possible occurrences are said to involve *uncertainty*.

The standard approach to the modelling of preferences under uncertainty (as opposed to risk) has been the *state preference approach* (e.g. Arrow, 1964; Debreu, 1959, ch. 7; Hirshleifer, 1965, 1966; Karni, 1985; Yaari, 1969). Rather than using numerical probabilities, this approach represents the randomness facing the individual by a set of mutually exclusive and exhaustive *states of nature* or *states of the world* $S = \{s_1, \ldots, s_n\}$. Depending upon the particular application, this partition of all possible futures may either be very coarse, as with the pair of states {it snows here tomorrow, it does not snow here tomorrow} or else very fine, so that the description of a single state might read 'it snows more than three inches here tomorrow *and* the temperature in Paris at noon is 73° *and* the price of platinum in London is over $700.00 per ounce'. The objects of choice in this

227

framework consist of *state-payoff bundles* of the form $(c_1, \ldots, c_n)$, which specify the payoff that the individual will receive in each of the respective states. As with regular commodity bundles, individuals are assumed to have preferences over state-payoff bundles which can be represented by indifference curves in the *state-payoff space* $\{(c_1, \ldots, c_n)\}$.

Although this approach has led to important advances in the analysis of choice under uncertainty (see for example the above references), the advantages of being able to draw on the modern theory of probability has led economists to concentrate on the analysis of risk, where the consequences of agents' actions are alternative well-defined probability distributions over the random variables they face. An important justification for the modelling of randomness via formal probability distributions are those joint axiomatizations of preferences and beliefs which provide consistency conditions on preferences over state-payoff bundles sufficient to imply that they can be generated by a well-defined probability distribution over states of nature and by a von Neumann–Morgenstern utility function over payoffs of the type described in the following section (e.g. Savage, 1954; Anscombe and Aumann, 1963; Pratt, Raiffa and Schlaifer, 1964; and Raiffa, 1968, ch. 5).

CHOICE UNDER RISK – THE EXPECTED UTILITY MODEL. For reasons of expositional ease, we consider a world with a single commodity (e.g. wealth). An agent making a decision under risk can therefore be thought of as facing a choice set of alternative univariate probability distributions. In order to consider both discrete (e.g. finite outcome) distributions as well as distributions with density functions, we shall represent each such probability distribution by means of its cumulative distribution functions $F(\cdot)$, where $F(x) \equiv \text{prob}(\tilde{x} \leqslant x)$ for the random variable $\tilde{x}$.

In such a case we can model the agent's preferences over alternative probability distributions in a manner completely analogous to the approach of standard (i.e. non-stochastic) consumer theory: he or she is assumed to possess a ranking $\succcurlyeq$ over distributions which is complete, transitive and continuous (in an appropriate sense), and hence representable by a real-valued *preference function* $V(\cdot)$ over the set of cumulative distribution functions, in the sense that $F^*(\cdot) \succcurlyeq F(\cdot)$ (i.e. the distribution $F^*(\cdot)$ is weakly preferred to $F(\cdot)$) if and only if $V(F^*) \geqslant V(F)$).

Of course, as in the non-stochastic case, the above set of assumptions implies nothing about the functional form of the preference functional $V(\cdot)$. For reasons of both normative appeal and analytic convenience, economists typically assume that $V(\cdot)$ is a *linear functional* of the distribution $F(\cdot)$, and hence takes the form

$$V(F) \equiv \int U(x)\mathrm{d}F(x) \tag{1}$$

for some function $U(\cdot)$ over wealth levels x, where $U(\cdot)$ is referred to as the individual's *von Neumann–Morgenstern utility function*. (For readers unfamiliar with the *Riemann–Stieltjes integral* $\int U(x)\mathrm{d}F(x)$ it represents nothing more than the expected value of $U(\tilde{x})$, when $\tilde{x}$ possesses the cumulative distribution function $F(\cdot)$. Thus if $\tilde{x}$ took the values $x_1, \ldots, x_n$ with probabilities $p_1, \ldots, p_n$, $\int U(x)\mathrm{d}F(x)$

would equal $\Sigma U(x_i)p_i$, and if $\tilde{x}$ possessed the density function $f(\cdot) = F'(\cdot)$, $\int U(x)\mathrm{d}F(x)$ would equal $\int U(x)f(x)\mathrm{d}x$.)

Since the right side of (1) may accordingly be thought of as the mathematical expectation of $U(\tilde{x})$, this specification is known as the *expected utility model* of preferences over random prospects. Within this framework, an individual's attitudes toward risk are reflected in the shape of his or her utility function $U(\cdot)$. Thus, for example, an individual would always prefer shifting probability mass from lower to higher outcome levels if and only if $U(x)$ were an increasing function of x, a condition which we shall henceforth always assume. Such a shift of probability mass is known as a *first order stochastically dominating shift*.

RISK AVERSION. The representation of individuals' preferences over distributions by the shape of their von Neumann–Morgenstern utility functions provides the first step in the modern economic characterization of risk. After all, whatever the notion of 'riskier' means, it is clear that bearing a random wealth $\tilde{x}$ is riskier than receiving a certain payment of $\tilde{x} = E[\tilde{x}]$, i.e. the expected value of the random variable $\tilde{x}$. We therefore have from Jensen's inequality that an individual would be *risk averse*, i.e. always prefer a payment of $E[\tilde{x}]$ (and obtaining utility $U(E[\tilde{x}])$) to bearing the risk $\tilde{x}$ (and obtaining expected utility $E[U(\tilde{x})]$) if and only if his or her utility function were concave. This condition is illustrated in Figure 1, where the random variable $\tilde{x}$ is assumed to take on the values x' and x'' with respective probabilities 2/3 and 1/3.

Of course, not all individuals need be risk averse in the sense of the previous

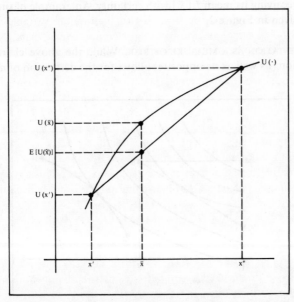

Figure 1 Von Neumann–Morgenstern utility function of a risk averse individual

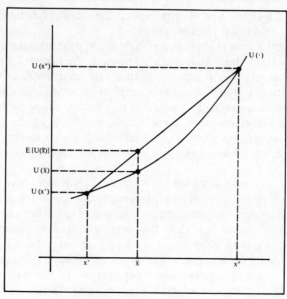

Figure 2   Von Neumann–Morgenstern utility function of a risk loving individual

paragraph. Another type of individual is a *risk lover*. Such an individual would have a *convex* utility function, and would accordingly prefer receiving a random wealth $\tilde{x}$ to receiving its mean $E[\tilde{x}]$ with certainty. An example of such an utility function is given in Figure 2.

STANDARD DEVIATION AS A MEASURE OF RISK. While the above characterization of risk aversion (as well as its opposite) allows for the derivation of many results

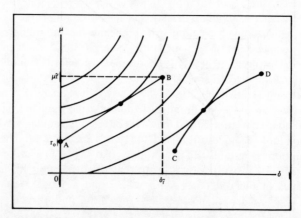

Figure 3   Portfolio analysis in the mean-standard deviation diagram

in the theory of behaviour under risk, it says nothing regarding which of a *pair* of non-degenerate random variables $\tilde{x}$ and $\tilde{y}$ is the most risky. Since real-world choices are almost never between risky and riskless situations but rather over alternative risky situations, such a means of comparison is necessary.

The earliest and best known univariate measure of the riskiness of a random variable $\tilde{x}$ is its *variance* $\sigma^2 = E[(\tilde{x} - \tilde{x})^2]$ or alternatively its *standard deviation* $\sigma = \{E[(\tilde{x} - \tilde{x})]^2\}^{1/2}$. The tractability of these measures as well as their well-known statistical properties led to the widespread use of *mean-standard deviation analysis* in the 1950s and 1960s, and in particular to the development of modern portfolio theory by Markowitz (1952, 1959), Tobin (1958) and others. As an example of this, consider Figure 3. Points A and B correspond to the distributions of a riskless asset with (per dollar) gross return r_0 and a risky asset with random return $\tilde{r}$ with mean $\mu\tilde{r}$ and standard deviation $\sigma\tilde{r}$. An investor dividing a dollar between the two assets in proportions $\alpha:(1 - \alpha)$ will possess a portfolio whose return has a mean of $\alpha \cdot r_0 + (1 - \alpha) \cdot \mu\tilde{r}$ and standard deviation $(1 - \alpha) \cdot \sigma_{\tilde{r}}$, so that the set of attainable (μ, σ) combinations consists of the line segment connecting the points A and B in the figure. It is straightforward to show that if the individual were also allowed to *borrow* at rate r_0 in order to finance purchase of the risky asset (i.e. could sell the riskless asset short), then the set of attainable (μ, σ) combinations would be the ray emanating from A and passing through B.

If we then represent the individual's risk preferences by means of indifference curves in this diagram, we obtain their optimal portfolio (the example in the figure implies an equal division of funds between the two assets). In the more general case of choice between a pair of risky assets, the set of (μ, σ) combinations generated by alternative divisions of wealth between them will trace out a locus such as the one between points C and D in the diagram, with the curvature of this locus determined by the degree of statistical dependence (i.e. covariance) between the two random returns.

As mentioned, the representation and analysis of risk and risk-taking by means of the variance or standard deviation of a distribution proved tremendously useful in the theory of finance, culminating in the mean-standard deviation based *capital asset pricing model* of Treynor (1961), Sharpe (1964), Lintner (1965) and Mossin (1966). However, by the late 1960s the mean-standard deviation approach was under attack for two reasons.

The first reason (known since the 1950s) was that the fact that an expected utility maximizer would evaluate all distributions solely on the basis of their means and standard deviations if and only if his or her von Neumann–Morgenstern utility function took the quadratic form $U(x) \equiv ax + bx^2$ for $b \lessgtr 0$. The sufficiency of this condition is established by noting that $E[U(\tilde{x})] = E[a\tilde{x} + b\tilde{x}^2] = a\tilde{x} + b(\tilde{x}^2 + \sigma^2)$. To prove necessity, note that the distributions which yield a $2/3:1/3$ chance of the outcomes $x - \delta:x + 2\delta$ and a $1/3:2/3$ chance of the outcomes $x - 2\delta:x + \delta$ both possess the same mean and variance for each x and δ, so that $(2/3) \cdot U(x - \delta) + (1/3) \cdot U(x + 2\delta) \equiv (1/3)U(x - 2\delta) + (2/3)U(x + \delta)$ for all x and δ. Differentiating with respect to δ and simplifying yields

$U'(x + 2\delta) + U'(x - 2\delta) \equiv U'(x + \delta) + U'(x - \delta)$ for all x and δ. This implies that $U'(\cdot)$ must be linear and hence that $U(\cdot)$ must be quadratic.

The assumption of quadratic utility is objectionable. If an individual with such a utility function is risk averse (i.e. if $b < 0$), then (i) utility will decrease as wealth increases beyond $1/2b$, and (ii) the individual will be more averse to constant additive risks about high wealth levels than about low wealth levels – in contrast to the observation that those with greater wealth take greater risks (see for example Hicks (1962) or Pratt (1964)).

Borch (1969) struck the second and strongest blow to the mean-standard deviation approach. He showed that for any two points (μ_1, σ_1) and (μ_2, σ_2) in the (μ, σ) plane which a mean-standard deviation preference ordering would rank as indifferent, it is possible to find random variables $\tilde{x}_1$ and $\tilde{x}_2$ which possess these respective (μ, σ) values and where $\tilde{x}_2$ first order stochastically dominates $\tilde{x}_1$. However, *any* person with an increasing von Neumann–Morgenstern utility function would strictly prefer $\tilde{x}_2$ to $\tilde{x}_1$. In response to these arguments and the additional criticisms of Feldstein (1969), Samuelson (1967) and others, the use of mean-standard deviation analysis in economic theory waned. See, however, the recent work of Meyer (1987) for a partial rehabilitation of such two-moment models of preferences.

Besides the variance or standard deviation of a distribution, several other univariate measures of risk have been proposed. Examples include the *mean absolute deviation* $E[|\tilde{x} - \tilde{x}|]$, the *interquartile range* $F^{-1}(0.75) - F^{-1}(0.25)$, and the classical statistical measures of *entropy* $\Sigma p_i \cdot \ln(p_i)$ or $\int f(x) \cdot \ln(f(x)) dx$. Although they provide the analytical convenience of a single numerical index of riskiness, each of these measures are subject to problems of the sort encountered with the variance or standard deviation. In particular, the entropy measure can be particularly unresponsive to the values taken on by the random variable: the 50:50 gambles over the values \$50:\$51 and \$1:\$100 both possess the same entropy level.

INCREASING RISK. By the late 1960s the failure to find a satisfactory univariate measure of risk led to another approach to this problem. Working independently, several researchers (Hadar and Russell, 1969; Hanoch and Levy, 1969; and Rothschild and Stiglitz, 1970, 1971) developed an alternative characterization of increasing risk. The appeal of this approach is twofold. First, it formalizes three different intuitive notions of increasing risk. Second, it allows for the straightforward derivation of comparative statics results in a wide variety of economic situations. Unlike the univariate measures described above, however, this approach provides only a partial ordering of random variables. In other words, not all pairs of random variables can be compared with respect to their riskiness.

We now state three alternative formalizations of the notion that a cumulative distribution function $F^*(\cdot)$ is riskier than another distribution $F(\cdot)$ with the same mean (in the following, all distributions are assumed to be over the interval $[0, M]$).

The first definition of increasing risk captures the notion that 'risk is what all risk averters hate'. Thus an increase in risk lowers the expected utility of all risk averters. Formally we may state this condition as:

(A) $F^*(\cdot)$ and $F(\cdot)$ have the same mean and $\int U(x)\mathrm{d}F^*(x) \leqslant \int U(x)\mathrm{d}F(x)$ for all concave utility functions $U(\cdot)$.

This criterion cannot be used to compare every pair of distributions with the same mean. However, if a pair of distributions $F(\cdot)$ and $F^*(\cdot)$ do *not* satisfy condition (A) (in either direction), there must exist a risk averse (i.e. concave) utility function $U_a(\cdot)$ which prefers $F(\cdot)$ to $F^*(\cdot)$ and another risk averse function $U_b(\cdot)$ which prefers $F^*(\cdot)$ to $F(\cdot)$.

The second characterization of the notion that a random variable $\tilde{y}$ with distribution $F^*(\cdot)$ is riskier than a variable $\tilde{x}$ with distribution $F(\cdot)$ is that $\tilde{y}$ consists of the variable $\tilde{x}$ plus an additional noise term $\tilde{\varepsilon}$. One possible specification of this is that $\tilde{\varepsilon}$ be statistically independent of $\tilde{x}$. However, this condition is too strong in the sense that it does not allow the variance of $\tilde{\varepsilon}$ to depend upon the magnitude of $\tilde{x}$, as in the case of heteroskedastic noise. Instead, Rothschild and Stiglitz (1970) modelled the addition of noise by the condition:

(B) $F(\cdot)$ and $F^*(\cdot)$ are the cumulative distribution functions of the random variables $\tilde{x}$ and $\tilde{x} + \tilde{\varepsilon}$, where $E[\tilde{\varepsilon}|x] \equiv 0$ for all x.

The third notion of increasing risk involves the concept (due to Rothschild and Stiglitz, 1970) of a *mean preserving spread*. Intuitively, such a spread consists of moving probability mass from the centre of a probability distribution to its tails in a manner which preserves the expected value of the distribution, as seen in the top panels of Figures 4 and 5. Formally we say that $F^*(\cdot)$ differs from $F(\cdot)$ by a mean preserving spread if they have the same mean and there exists a single crossing point x_0 such that $F^*(x) \geqslant F(x)$ for all $x \leqslant x_0$ and $F^*(x) \leqslant F(x)$ for all $x \geqslant x_0$ (see the middle panels of these figures). Since it is clear that *sequences* of such spreads will also lead to riskier distributions, our third characterization of increasing risk is:

(C) $F^*(\cdot)$ may be obtained from $F(\cdot)$ by a finite sequence, or as the limit of an infinite sequence, of mean preserving spreads.

Although the single crossing property of the previous paragraph serves to characterize cumulative distribution functions which differ by a *single* mean preserving spread, distributions which differ by a sequence of such spreads will typically not satisfy the single crossing condition. If we consider the *integral* of the cumulative distribution function, however, we see from the bottom panels of Figures 4 and 5 that a mean preserving spread will always serve to raise or preserve the value of this integral for each x and (since $F^*(\cdot)$ and $F(\cdot)$ have the same mean) to preserve it for $x = M$. It is clear that this condition *will* continue to be satisfied by distributions which differ by a sequence of mean preserving

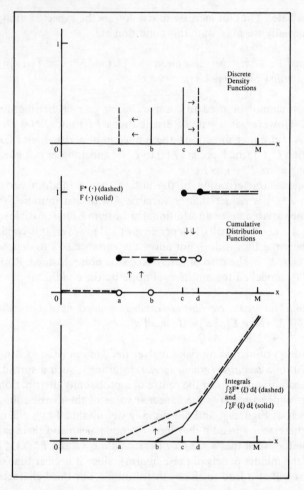

Figure 4   A mean preserving spread of a discrete distribution

spreads. Accordingly, we may rewrite condition (C) above by the analytically more convenient:

(C′) *The integral $\int_0^x [F^*(\xi) - F(\xi)] \cdot d\xi$ is non-negative for all $x > 0$, and is equal to 0 for $x = M$.*

Rothschild and Stiglitz (1970) showed that *these three concepts of increasing risk are the same* by proving that conditions (A), (B) and (C/C′) are equivalent. Thus, a single partial ordering of distribution functions corresponds simultaneously to the notion that risk is what risk averters hate, to the notion that adding noise to a random variable increases its risk, and to the notion that moving probability mass from the centre of a probability distribution to its tails increases the risk of that distribution.

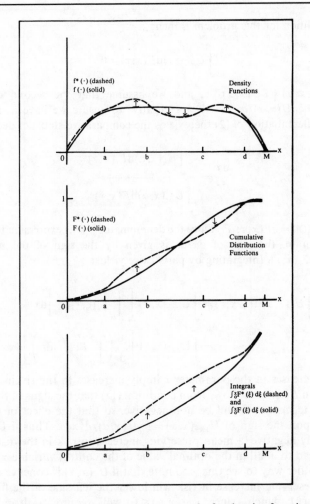

Figure 5 A mean preserving spread of a density function

This characterization of increasing risk permits the derivation of general and powerful comparative statics theorems concerning economic agents' response to increases in risk. The general framework for these results is that of an individual with a von Neumann–Morgenstern utility function $U(x, \alpha)$ which depends upon both the outcome of some random variable $\tilde{x}$ as well as a *control variable* α which the individual chooses so as to maximize expected utility $\int U(x, \alpha)dF(x; r)$, where the distribution function $F(\cdot; r)$ depends upon some exogenous parameter $r(x$ for example might be the return on a risky asset, and α the amount invested in it). For convenience, we assume that $F(0; r) = \text{prob}(\tilde{x} \leqslant 0) = 0$ for all r. The first order condition for this problem is then:

$$\int U_\alpha(x, \alpha) dF(x; r) = 0 \tag{2}$$

where $U_\alpha(x, \alpha) = \partial U(x, \alpha)/\partial \alpha$, and we assume that the second derivative $U_{\alpha\alpha}(x, \alpha) = \partial^2 U(x, \alpha)/\partial \alpha^2$ is always negative to ensure we have a maximum. Implicit differentiation of (2) then yields the comparative statistics derivative:

$$\frac{d\alpha}{dr} = \frac{- \int U_\alpha(x, \alpha) dF_r(x; r)}{\int U_{\alpha\alpha}(x, \alpha) dF(x; r)} \tag{3}$$

where $F_r(x; r) = \partial F(x; r)/\partial r$. Since the denominator of this expression is negative by assumption, the sign of $d\alpha/dr$ is given by the sign of the numerator $\int U_\alpha(x, \alpha) dF_r(x; r)$. Integrating by parts twice yields:

$$\int U_\alpha(x, \alpha) dF_r(x; r) = \int U_{xx\alpha}(x, \alpha) \cdot \left[\int_0^x F_r(\xi, r) d\xi \right] dx$$
$$= \int U_{xx\alpha}(x, \alpha) \cdot \left[\frac{d}{dr} \left(\int_0^x F(\xi, r) d\xi \right) \right] dx. \tag{4}$$

Thus, if increases in the parameter r imply increases in the riskiness of the distribution $F(\cdot; r)$, it follows from condition (D) that the signs of the square bracketed terms in (4) will be non-negative, so that the effect of r upon α depends upon the sign of $U_{xx\alpha}(x, \alpha) = \partial^3 U(x, \alpha)/\partial^2 x \partial \alpha$. Thus if $U_{xx\alpha}(x, \alpha)$ is uniformly negative, a mean preserving increase in risk in the distribution of x will lead to a fall in the optimal value of the control variable α and vice versa. Another way to see this is to note that if $U_\alpha(x, \alpha)$ is concave in x then a mean preserving increase in risk will lower the left side of the first order condition (2), which (since $U_{\alpha\alpha}(x, \alpha) \leqslant 0$) will require a drop in α to re-establish the equality. Economists routinely use this technique when analysing models involving risk; see for example Rothschild and Stiglitz (1971).

RELATED TOPICS. The characterization of risk outlined in the previous section has been extended along several lines. Diamond and Stiglitz (1974), for example, have replaced the notion of a mean preserving spread with that of a mean *utility* preserving spread to obtain a general characterization of a *compensated increase in risk*. They related this notion to the well-known Arrow–Pratt characterization of comparative risk aversion.

In addition, researchers such as Ekern (1980), Fishburn (1982), Fishburn and Vickson (1978), Hansen, Holt, and Peled (1978), Tesfatsion (1976) and Whitmore

(1970) have extended the above work to the development of a general theory of *stochastic dominance*, which provides a whole sequence of similarly characterized partial orders on distributions, each presenting a corresponding set of equivalent conditions involving algebraic conditions on the distributions, types of spreads, and classes of utility functions which prefer (or are averse) to such spreads, etc. The comparative statistics analysis presented above may be similarly extended to such characterizations (e.g. Machina, 1987). An extensive bibliography of the stochastic dominance literature is given in Bawa (1982). Finally, various extensions of the notions of increasing risk and stochastic dominance to the case of multivariate distributions may be found in Epstein and Tanny (1980), Fishburn and Vickson (1978), Huang, Kira and Vertinsky (1978), Lehmann (1955), Levhari, Parousch and Peleg (1975), Levy and Parousch (1974), Russell and Seo (1978), Sherman (1951) and Strassen (1965) (see also the mathematical results in Marshall and Olkin, 1979).

BIBLIOGRAPHY

Anscombe, F. and Aumann, R. 1963. A definition of subjective probability. *Annals of Mathematical Statistics* 34, 199–205.

Arrow, K. 1964. The role of securities in the optimal allocation of risk-bearing. *Review of Economic Studies* 31, 91–6.

Bawa, V. 1982. Stochastic dominance: a research bibliography. *Management Science* 28, 698–712.

Borch, K. 1969. A note on uncertainty and indifference curves. *Review of Economic Studies* 36, 1–4.

Debreu, G. 1959. *Theory of Value: An Axiomatic Analysis of General Equilibrium.* New Haven: Yale University Press.

Diamond, P. and Rothschild, M. (eds) 1978. *Uncertainty in Economics: Readings and Exercises.* New York: Academic Press.

Diamond, P. and Stiglitz, J. 1974. Increases in risk and in risk aversion. *Journal of Economic Theory* 8, 337–60.

Ekern, S. 1980. Increasing n'th degree risk. *Economic Letters* 6, 329–33.

Epstein, L. and Tanny, S. 1980. Increasing generalized correlation: a definition and some economic consequences. *Canadian Journal of Economics* 13, 16–34.

Feldstein, M. 1969. Mean-variance analysis in the theory of liquidity preference and portfolio selection. *Review of Economic Studies* 36, 5–12.

Fishburn, P. 1982. Simplest cases of n'th degree stochastic dominance. *Operations Research Letters* 1, 89–90.

Fishburn, P. and Vickson, R.G. 1978. Theoretical foundations of stochastic dominance. In Whitmore and Findlay (1978).

Hadar, J. and Russell, W. 1969. Rules for ordering uncertain prospects. *American Economic Review* 59, 25–34.

Hanoch, G. and Levy, H. 1969. The efficiency analysis of choices involving risk. *Review of Economic Studies* 36, 335–46.

Hansen, L., Holt, C. and Peled, D. 1978. A note on first degree stochastic dominance. *Economics Letters* 1, 315–19.

Hicks, J. 1962. Liquidity. *Economic Journal* 72, 787–802.

Hirshleifer, J. 1965. Investment decision under uncertainty: choice-theoretic approaches. *Quarterly Journal of Economics* 79, 509–36.

Hirshleifer, J. 1966. Investment decision under uncertainty: applications of the state-preference approach. *Quarterly Journal of Economics* 80, 252–77.

Huang, C., Kira, D. and Vertinsky, I. 1978. Stochastic dominance for multi-attribute utility functions. *Review of Economic Studies* 45, 611–16.

Karni, E. 1985. *Decision Making Under Uncertainty: The Case of State Dependent Preferences.* Cambridge, Mass.: Harvard University Press.

Knight, F. 1921. *Risk, Uncertainty and Profit.* Boston: Houghton Mifflin Co.

Lehmann, E. 1955. Ordered families of distributions. *Annals of Mathematical Statistics* 26, 399–419.

Levhari, D., Parousch, J. and Peleg, B. 1975. Efficiency analysis for multivariate distributions. *Review of Economic Studies* 42, 87–91.

Levy, H. and Parousch, J. 1974. Toward multivariate efficiency criteria. *Journal of Economic Theory* 7, 129–42.

Lintner, J. 1965. The valuation of risk assets and the selection of risky investments in stock portfolios and capital budgets. *Review of Economics and Statistics* 44, 243–69.

Machina, M. 1987. *The Economic Theory of Individual Behavior Toward Risk: Theory, Evidence and New Directions.* Cambridge: Cambridge University Press.

Markowitz, H. 1952. Portfolio selection. *Journal of Finance* 7, 77–91.

Markowitz, H. 1959. *Portfolio Selection: Efficient Diversification of Investment.* New Haven: Yale University Press.

Marshall, A. and Olkin, I. 1979. *Inequalities: Theory of Majorization and Its Applications.* New York: Academic Press.

Meyer, J. 1987. Two moment decision models and expected utility maximization. *American Economic Review*, 421–30.

Mossin, J. 1966. Equilibrium in a capital asset market. *Econometrica* 34, 768–83.

Pratt, J. 1964. Risk aversion in the small and in the large. *Econometrica* 32, 122–36.

Pratt, J., Raiffa, H. and Schlaifer, R. 1964. The foundations of decision under uncertainty: an elementary exposition. *Journal of the American Statistical Association* 59, 353–75.

Raiffa, H. 1968. *Decision Analysis: Introductory Lectures on Choice Under Uncertainty.* Reading, Mass.: Addison-Wesley.

Rothschild, M. and Stiglitz, J. 1970. Increasing risk: I. A definition. *Journal of Economic Theory* 2, 225–43. Reprinted in Diamond and Rothschild (1978).

Rothschild, M. and Stiglitz, J. 1971. Increasing risk: II. Its economic consequences. *Journal of Economic Theory* 3, 66–84.

Rothschild, M. and Stiglitz, J. 1972. Addendum to 'Increasing risk: I. A definition'. *Journal of Economic Theory* 5, 306.

Russell, W. and Seo, T. 1978. Ordering uncertain prospects: the multivariate utility functions case. *Review of Economic Studies* 45, 605–11.

Samuelson, P. 1967. General proof that diversification pays. *Journal of Financial and Quantitative Analysis* 2, 1–13.

Savage, L. 1954. *The Foundations of Statistics.* New York: John Wiley and Sons. Revised and enlarged edition, New York: Dover Publications, 1972.

Sharpe, W. 1964. Capital asset prices: a theory of market equilibrium under conditions of risk. *Journal of Finance* 19, 425–42.

Sherman, S. 1951. On a theorem of Hardy, Littlewood, Polya, and Blackwell. *Proceedings of the National Academy of Sciences* 37, 826–31. (See also 'Errata', *Proceedings of the National Academy of Sciences* 38, 382.)

Strassen, V. 1965. The existence of probability measures with given marginals. *Annals of Mathematical Statistics* 36, 423–39.

Tesfatsion, L. 1976. Stochastic dominance and the maximization of expected utility. *Review of Economic Studies* 43, 301–15.

Tobin, J. 1958. Liquidity preference as behavior toward risk. *Review of Economic Studies* 25, 65–86.

Whitmore, G. 1970. Third-degree stochastic dominance. *American Economic Review* 60, 457–9.

Whitmore, G. and Findlay, M. 1978. *Stochastic Dominance: An Approach to Decision Making Under Risk.* Lexington, Mass.: Heath.

Yaari, M. 1969. Some remarks on measures of risk aversion and on their uses. *Journal of Economic Theory* 1, 315–29.

Leonard J. Savage

I. RICHARD SAVAGE

L.J. (Jimmie) Savage, né Leonard Ogashevitz, was born in Detroit on 20 November 1917 and died in New Haven on 1 November 1971. His interests were encyclopaedic: as a youth he immersed himself in the *Book of Knowledge*, and at the time of his death he was preparing for the Peabody Museum a demonstration-exhibit on animal odorants. The dominant theme of Savage's professional work was the mathematical analysis of normative behaviour.

He received a BS (1938) and PhD (1941) from the University of Michigan. In the early 1940s he obtained a broad post-doctoral exposure to pure and applied mathematics at the Institute for Advanced Study in Princeton, at Cornell, Brown, the Statistical Research Group of Columbia, the Courant Institute at New York University and at Woods Hole Marine Biological Laboratory. From 1946 to 1960 he was at the University of Chicago, where he was central to the development of the statistics programme. Subsequently, he held professorships at Michigan and at Yale. Always, he was intellectually generous with students, colleagues, visitors and correspondents.

Savage's basic views and results on normative behaviour appear in his *Foundations* (1954). His essential theme, still being elaborated, is the relation between a person's probability for an event and his utility for the event. In particular, his probabilities and utilities must be consistent with the principle of maximizing his expected utility. These results flow from compelling axioms of coherent behaviour and they recommend specific strategies for applied statistics, such as the use of Bayesian statistics and the likelihood principle.

Savage's axioms imply that all probabilities reflect individual experience so that there is no reason for two people to have the same probability for a particular event. His theory conflicts with traditional views that hold probabilities to be basic constants of nature. At first Savage thought this conflict would not be significant in applying statistical theory, but he remarked in the preface to the second edition of the *Foundations* (1972) that he was not successful in bringing the theories of statistics together at the applied level. He recognized the long process from elegant theory to serious applications. His paper on elicitation of probabilities (1971) develops methods to implement his theory of personal probability. And Savage (1977) warns against holding theoretical foundations as adequate for all aspects of applied statistics.

Savage's work on the foundations of statistics had major antecedents in Frank Ramsey and B. de Finetti, whose work was developed, polished and taught to a generation of scholars by Savage himself. Hewitt and Savage (1955) is both elegant mathematics and an extension of a basic result of de Finetti in the foundations of statistics. Dubins and Savage (1965) stems from a normative problem and bears mathematical fruit. Exposition of the basic ideas of applied Bayesian statistics combined with the new theory of stable estimation appears in Edwards, Lindman and Savage (1963). Additional biographical and critical analysis as well as most of Savage's published papers appear in Ericson et al (1981).

SELECTED WORKS

1948. (With M. Friedman.) The utility analysis of choices involving risk. *Journal of Political Economy* 56, 279–304.

1954. *The Foundations of Statistics.* New York: John Wiley & Sons. 2nd revised edn, New York: Dover Publications, 1972.

1955. (With E. Hewitt.) Symmetric measures on Cartesian products. *Transactions of the American Mathematical Society* 80, 470–501.

1963. (With W. Edwards and H. Lindman.) Bayesian statistical inference for psychological research. *Psychological Review* 70, 192–242.

1965. (With L.E. Dubins.) *How to Gamble If You Must: Inequalities for Stochastic Processes.* New York: McGraw-Hill. Reprinted with a new Bibliographic Supplement and Preface by L.E. Dubins as *Inequalities for Stochastic Processes (How to Gamble If You Must)*, New York: Dover Publications, 1976.

1971. Elicitation of personal probabilities and expectations. *Journal of the American Statistical Association* 66, 783–801.

1977. The shifting foundations of statistics. In *Logic, Laws and Life: Some Philosophical Complications*, ed. R.G. Colodny, Pittsburgh: University of Pittsburgh Press.

1981. *The Writings of Leonard Jimmie Savage – A Memorial Selection.* Prepared by a Committee (W.H. DuMouchel, W.A. Ericson (chair), B. Margolin, R.A. Olshen, H.V. Roberts, I.R. Savage and A. Zellner) for the American Statistical Association and the Institute of Mathematical Statistics, Washington, DC.

State-dependent Preferences

EDI KARNI

It is commonplace to formulate theories of individual decision-making under uncertainty using three sets: the set of *states of nature*, S, the set of *consequences*, C, and the set of *acts*, L. Following Savage (1954) we define nature as the object of concern to the decision-maker and a state of nature as a portrayal of nature leaving no relevant aspect undescribed. A consequence is anything that may happen to a person. An act is a course of action. Each combination of an act $f \in L$ and a state of nature $s \in S$ determines a unique consequence denoted $c(f, s)$ in C. In addition, the theory postulates the existence of a preference relation, $\succcurlyeq$, on acts. For our purposes preference relations are taken to be complete and transitive binary relations on L, with the symbol $\succcurlyeq$ being interpreted as 'preferred or indifferent'.

Loosely speaking a preference relation is state-dependent when the prevailing state of nature is of direct concern to the decision maker. To define this notion formally we let f, f', g, g' be acts in L. Then given $\succcurlyeq$ and $s \in S$, we define *preferences over acts conditional on* s, $\succcurlyeq_s$, by $f \succcurlyeq_s f'$ if $g \succcurlyeq g'$ whenever $c(f, s) = c(g, s)$, $c(f', s) = c(g', s)$ and $c(g, s') = c(g', s')$ for all $s' \in S \setminus \{s\}$. Since $c: L \times S \to C$ is defined uniquely, $\succcurlyeq_s$, defines a preference relation on C conditional on $s \in S$. We denote this preference relation by $\succcurlyeq_s$.

A state $s \in S$ is said to be *null* if $f \succcurlyeq_s f'$ for all f, f' in L. Finally, we say that $\succcurlyeq_s$ and $\succcurlyeq_{s'}$ *agree* if for all $c, c' \in C$, $c \succcurlyeq_s c'$ if and only if $c \succcurlyeq_{s'} c'$ that is, $\succcurlyeq_s$ and $\succcurlyeq_{s'}$ are the same preference ordering on C.

Definition: A preference relation $\succcurlyeq$ on L is said to be *evidently state-dependent* if $\succcurlyeq_s$ and $\succcurlyeq_{s'}$ do not agree for some non-null s, s' in S.

Notice that if s is null and s' is non-null then, by definition, $\succcurlyeq_s$ and $\succcurlyeq_{s'}$ do not agree. This, however, does not imply that the preference relation is state-dependent since s may be null as a result of the decision-maker's belief that s being the true state is virtually impossible. Notice also that even if $\succcurlyeq_s$ and $\succcurlyeq_t$ agree for all non-null

242

s and t in S, the preference relation is not necessarily state-independent since $s' \in S$ may be null as a result of all the consequences being equally preferred if s' is the true state. Thus, a preference relation may be state-dependent but not evidently state-dependent.

Circumstances in which the dependence of the decision-maker's preferences on the state of nature constitute an indispensable feature of the decision-problem include the choice of health insurance coverage (see Arrow, 1974; Karni, 1985); the choice of air travel insurance coverage (see Eisner and Strotz, 1961); the choice of optimal consumption and life-insurance plans in the face of uncertain life-time (see Yaari, 1965; Karni and Zilcha, 1985); and the provision of collective protection (see Cook and Graham, 1977).

REPRESENTATION. Preferences among acts are a matter of personal judgement, presumably combining the decision-maker's evaluation of the consequences with his beliefs regarding the likely realization of alternative states of nature. Expected utility theory postulates preference structures that permit the numerical representation of preference relations over acts separating in a unique way, tastes, which are represented by a utility function, from beliefs, which are represented by a subjective probability distribution over states of nature. Under the usual assumptions of expected utility theory when the preference relation is state-dependent, a unique separation along these lines is impossible and additional structure is called for.

To convey the issues involved in obtaining an expected utility representation of state-dependent preferences we present in some detail the theory developed by Karni, Schmeidler and Vind (1983), followed by brief comments on the alternative theories.

Following Anscombe and Aumann (1963) let the space of consequences be lotteries with objectively known probabilities over finite, non-empty sets of prizes. Let $X(s)$ be the set of prizes available in state s, and let $Y(s)$ be the set of lotteries in s that have elements of $X(s)$ as prices, that is, the set of probability distributions on $X(s)$. Denote by $|X(s)|$ the cardinality of $X(s)$ and by l the cardinality of the space of prizes, $\Sigma_{s \in S}|X(s)|$. The set of acts is $L = \{f \in R^l | f(s) \in Y(s) \text{ for } s \in S\}$. Decision-makers are assumed to have preference relations $\geqslant$ on L that satisfy the von Neumann–Morgenstern axioms of weak order (completeness and transitivity), continuity and independence. Under these conditions a version of the classic von Neumann–Morgenstern theorem holds, namely, that for each $s \in S$ there exists a real valued function $w(s, \cdot): X(s) \to R$ such that for all $f, g \in L$:

$$f \geqslant g \Leftrightarrow \sum_{s \in S} w(s) f(s) \geqslant \sum_{s \in S} w(s) g(s),$$

where $w(s)$ is a von Neumann–Morgenstern utility function associated with s, and $w(s)f(s)$ is the inner product $\Sigma_{x \in X(s)} w(s, x) f(s, x)$ in $R^{|X(s)|}$. Furthermore, if some other utility $w' \in R^l$ represents $\geqslant$ on L then there exist $b > 0$ and real numbers $a(s)$ one for each state such that $w'(s) = bw(s) + a(s)$ for all $s \in S$. We say that $w = (w(s)) \in R^l$ is unique up to a cardinal unit comparable transformation.

243

The representation of $\succcurlyeq$ by w in this manner does not imply a unique subjective probability distribution on S. Indeed, *any* list of positive numbers $p(s)$, $s \in S$ that sum to 1 is consistent with $\succcurlyeq$, provided that $p(s)u(s) = w(s)$. To obtain a unique subjective probability distribution on S we need to restrict $\succcurlyeq$ further. One way of doing so is to postulate the existence of a preference relation on acts compatible with a hypothetical, strictly positive, probability distribution p' on S that satisfies the von Neumann–Morgenstern axioms, and to assume that the hypothetical preference relation is consistent with $\succcurlyeq$. To grasp the significance of consistency let $L_{p'} = \{f' \in R^l_+ \,|\, \text{for all } s \in S: \Sigma_{x \in X(s)} f'(s, x) = p'(s)\}$, and denote by $\succcurlyeq'$ a hypothetical preference relation on $L_{p'}$. The restriction on $\succcurlyeq$ is then the condition that $\succcurlyeq$ and $\succcurlyeq'$ are consistent in the sense that they are induced by the same utilities and the difference between them is fully explained by the difference in the underlying probabilities. The preference relation $\succcurlyeq'$ captures the decision-maker's evaluation of acts if he has reason to believe that the probability distribution p' reflects the likely realization of alternative states. The consistency condition attributes the difference between the hypothetical preference relation $\succcurlyeq'$ and the actual preference relation $\succcurlyeq$ to the difference between the hypothetical and actual probability beliefs, respectively.

To present these ideas formally, define a bijective mapping $H: L_{p'} \to L$ as follows: For all $f' \in L_{p'}$, $H(f'(s)) = f'(s)/p'(s)$. Using this notation we define a state $s \in S$ to be *evidently null* with respect to $\succcurlyeq'$ if $f \succcurlyeq_s g$ for all $f, g \in L$ and not $f' \succcurlyeq_s g'$ for all f', g' in $L_{p'}$. A state $s \in S$ is *evidently non-null* if not $f \succcurlyeq_s g$ for all $f, g \in L$.

Weak Consistency Axiom: For all $s \in S$ and $f', g' \in L_{p'}$, if f' agrees with g' outside s and $H(f') \succ H(g')$ then $f' \succ' g'$. Moreover, if s is evidently non-null then if f' agrees with g' outside s, $f' \succ' g'$ implies $H(f') \succ H(g')$.

Finally, a preference relation $\succcurlyeq$ is non-trivial if not $f \succcurlyeq g$ for all $f, g \in L$.

Theorem: (Karni, Schmeidler and Vind, 1983). Suppose that two binary relations are given: a nontrivial relation $\succcurlyeq$ on L and $\succcurlyeq'$ on $L_{p'}$ for some strictly positive p'. Assume that each of the two relations satisfies the von Neumann–Morgenstern axioms of Weak Order, Continuity and Independence and that jointly they satisfy the Weak Consistency axiom. Then:

(a) There exists a real valued function on $\{(s, x) \,|\, s \in S, x \in X(s)\}$ and a probability distribution p on S such that for all $f, g \in L$

$$f \succcurlyeq g \Leftrightarrow \sum_{s \in S} p(s)u(s)[f(s) - g(s)] \geqq 0,$$

where

$$u(s) \in R^{|X(s)|} \quad \text{for all} \quad s \in S, \quad \text{and for all} \quad f', g' \in L_{p'}$$

$$f' \succcurlyeq g' \Leftrightarrow \sum_{s \in S} u(s)[f'(s) - g'(s)] \geqq 0.$$

(b) The u of part (a) is unique up to a cardinal unit comparable transformation.

(c) For s evidently null $p(s) = 0$ and for s evidently non-null $p(s) > 0$. Furthermore, the probability p restricted to the event of all evidently non-null states is unique.

Wakker (1985) has adapted the theory presented above to the case where the set of consequences is a connected topological space. This permits the derivation of unique subjective probabilities without the use of objective lotteries. However, foregoing the linearity of the utility functions, which is implied by the Anscombe and Aumann framework, requires the replacement of the weak consistency axiom by a stronger 'cardinal consistency' condition. Loosely speaking this condition requires that the intensity of preferences of the hypothetical and actual preference relations are never contradictory.

ALTERNATIVE THEORIES. The first axiomatic treatment of expected utility theory with subjective probabilities appears in Ramsey (1931). Ramsey's method of defining subjective probabilities does not rule out state-dependent preferences. It does require, however, that there be at least two states ('propositions' in Ramsey's terminology) that are 'ethically neutral', that is two states in which preferences over consequences are identical. Ramsey did not elaborate on this point.

Drèze (1961, 1985) presents a theory of individual decision-making under uncertainty with moral hazard and state-dependent preferences. Departing from the theory of Savage (1954), which requires that the occurrence of events lies beyond the control of the decision-maker, Drèze exploits the fact that in many circumstances the decision-maker does exercise some control over events by adapting his behaviour. He then shows that if there are as many behavioural modes yielding linearly independent probability distributions as there are states of nature then, under additional assumptions, it is possible to obtain a unique separation of state-dependent utilities from behaviourally dependent probability distributions over the set of states of nature.

According to Drèze's theory, the elicitation of subjective probabilities can be accomplished in principle with exclusive reliance upon observed choices among acts. In this respect Drèze's theory enjoys a methodological advantage over theories that must, to obtain the same objective, rely on comparisons of hypothetical acts using direct questions. Its shortcoming is the restriction that it imposes on the decision problems. One restriction is the need for a large degree of freedom in the manipulation of probabilities, which is not always available. The second is the requirement that there exist at least two acts that yield constant utility. The latter requirement may be irreconcilable with some applications of the theory (e.g. the choice of life insurance coverage).

Fishburn (1973) presents a theory based on preference relations over the set of acts conditional on events (non-empty subsets of S). These preference relations are assumed to satisfy axioms analogous to those of von Neumann and Morgenstern and several additional structural restrictions. In particular, Fishburn requires that for every two disjoint events not all the consequences conditioned upon one event are preferred to all the consequences conditioned upon the other.

This restriction renders the theory inapplicable to important decision problems involving state-dependent preferences, such as the choice of life, and some health, insurance coverage.

THE MEASUREMENT OF RISK AVERSION AND OF RISK. As with state-independent preferences, the economic analysis of many decision problems involving state-dependent preferences requires measures of risk aversion and of risk. Such measures are developed in Karni (1985). The key notion required for comparability of attitudes towards risk and for the definition of increasing risk is the reference set, defined as the optimal allocation of wealth across states that would obtain under fair insurance. For classes of preferences that are comparable in the sense of inducing identical reference sets the Arrow (1965) and Pratt (1964) measures of risk aversion and the Rothschild and Stiglitz (1970) definition of increasing risk apply, with some modifications. Unlike the case of state-independent preferences, however, in the case of state-dependent preferences not all preference relations are comparable in this sense. Despite its limited applicability expected utility theory with state-dependent preferences is a generalization of the same theory with state-independent preferences.

BIBLIOGRAPHY

Anscombe, F.J. and Aumann, R.J. 1963. A definition of subjective probability. *Annals of Mathematical Statistics* 34(1), March, 199–205.

Arrow, K.J. 1965. The theory of risk aversion. In *Aspects of the Theory of Risk-Bearing*. Helsinki: Yrjö Jahnsson Foundation.

Arrow, K.J. 1974. Optimal insurance and generalized deductibles. *Scandinavian Actuarial Journal*.

Cook, P.J. and Graham, D.A. 1977. The demand for insurance and protection: the case of irreplaceable commodities. *Quarterly Journal of Economics* 91(1), February, 143–56.

Drèze, J.H. 1961. Les foundements logique de l'utilité cardinale et de la probabilité subjective. *La Dècision*. Colloques Internationaux du CNRS.

Drèze, J.H. 1985. Decision theory with moral hazard and state-dependent preferences. In *Essays on Economic Decision under Uncertainty*, Cambridge: Cambridge University Press.

Eisner, R. and Strotz, R.H. 1961. Flight insurance and the theory of choice. *Journal of Political Economy* 69(4), August, 355–68.

Fishburn, P.C. 1973. A mixture-set axiomatization of conditional subjective expected utility. *Econometrica* 41(1), January, 1–25.

Karni, E. 1985. *Decision Making under Uncertainty: The Case of State-Dependent Preferences*. Boston: Harvard University Press.

Karni, E., Schmeidler, D. and Vind, K. 1983. On state-dependent preferences and subjective probabilities. *Econometrica* 51(4), July, 1021–31.

Karni, E. and Zilcha, I. 1985. Uncertain lifetime, risk aversion and life insurance. *Scandinavian Actuarial Journal*.

Pratt, J.W. 1964. Risk aversion in the small and in the large. *Econometrica* 32(1–2), January–April, 122–36.

Ramsey, F.P. 1931. Truth and Probability. In *The Foundation of Mathematics and Other Logical Essays*, ed. R.B. Braithwaite, London: Kegan Paul, Trench, Trubner and Co; New York: Humanities Press, 1950.

Rothschild, M. and Stiglitz, J.E. 1970. Increasing risk I: a definition. *Journal of Economic Theory* 2(3), September, 225–43.

Savage, L.J. 1954. *The Foundations of Statistics*. New York: John Wiley.

Wakker, P. 1985. Subjective probabilities for state-dependent continuous utility. Report 8506, Department of Mathematics, Catholic University, Nijmegen, The Netherlands.

Yaari, M.E. 1965. Uncertain lifetime, life insurance and the theory of the consumer. *Review of Economic Studies* 32, 137–50.

State Preference Approach

H.M. POLEMARCHAKIS

Under certainty, with commodities $i \in I$, individual preferences are defined over commodity bundles $c = (c_i : i \in I)$, which are the objects of choice of individuals. Under uncertainty, production possibilities and individual and aggregate endowments, for instance, may vary with the realization of random states of nature $s \in S$. It is then necessary to define individual preferences over plans $\vec{c} = (c(s); s \in S)$ which assign to each state of nature a commodity bundle.

Rationality, under certainty, is identified with the assumption that an individual's preference relation over commodity bundles is complete and transitive. Under regularity conditions it is then possible to show that a continuous utility function $u(c)$ represents this preference relation. Furthermore, it is a common additional assumption that the preference relation is convex; equivalently, that a utility function which represents it is quasi-concave: if the individual is indifferent between two commodity bundles c_1 and c_2: $u(c_1) = u(c_2)$, he finds any convex combination $c_\lambda = \lambda c_1 + (1 - \lambda)c_2, 0 \leqslant \lambda \leqslant 1$, at least as good: $u(c_\lambda) \geqslant u(c_1) = u(c_2)$. Note that quasi-concavity of the utility function is not an aspect of rationality but rather a qualitative assumption. The stronger assumption of concavity, according to which $u(c_\lambda) \geqslant \lambda u(c_1) + (1 - \lambda)u(c_2)$ for any two commodity bundles c_1 and c_2, is not well taken: unlike quasi-concavity, concavity is not preserved by monotonically increasing transformations and thus does not derive from the underlying preference relation. The utility function $u(c)$ is ordinal.

It is possible to maintain that, beyond completeness and transitivity, rationality imposes no further restrictions on an individual's preference over plans. The *state preference approach* to choice under uncertainty then obtains. With the set of commodities extended from I under certainty to $I \times S$ under uncertainty, individual and aggregate behaviour remain unaffected.

The state preference approach, as exposited, for example, in Debreu (1959, ch. 7) analytically reduces uncertainty to certainty. It poses, however, a dilemma. It is often of interest to associate with a utility function $u(\vec{c})$ over plans a utility function $v(c; s)$ over consumption bundles conditional on the realization of the

248

state of nature. This is necessary, for instance, in order to answer the question whether the individuals find it desirable to revise their choices after the uncertainty has been resolved, and the related question of ex-ante versus ex-post optimality. The state preference approach either is agnostic on this issue or it adopts the following solution: Given a plan

$$\vec{c}^*, v(c; s) = u(\vec{c}), \qquad \text{where } c(s) = c$$

and

$$c(s') = c^*(s'), \qquad \text{for } s' \neq s.$$

That is, individuals behave as if the states of nature which failed to occur did occur and their plan conditional on those states was carried out. This is analytically consistent, but it is contrived.

Alternatively, rationality under uncertainty can be argued to extend beyond completeness and transitivity. A series of postulates, most definitively developed by Savage (1954), implies that the utility function $u(\vec{c})$ over plans has an expected utility representation $u(\vec{c}) = E_p v(c)$ for some probabilty measure p over the set of states of nature S. Note that well defined probability beliefs are derived from the postulates which characterize rationality and are not taken for granted. The function $v(c)$ over consumption bundles is the individual's cardinal utility index; it is unique up to monotonically increasing, linear transformations.

Two of the postulates which yield the expected utility representation have been most consistently criticized. The 'sure thing principle', which corresponds to the 'strong independence axiom' when the state probabilities are given, asserts that the preference between two plans $\vec{c}_1$ and $\vec{c}_2$ does not depend on the commodity bundles they assign to states of nature on which they coincide. This postulate yields the additive separability of the utility function over state contingent commodity bundles; Machina (1982) has argued that it can be understood as an approximation. Note that, with the sure thing principle conditional, preferences are well defined: conditional on an event B, a subset of the set of states of nature, a plan $\vec{c}_1 | B = (c_1(s): s \in B)$ is at least as good as another $\vec{c}_2 | B = (c_2(s): s \in B)$ if and only if there exist extensions $\vec{c}_1$ and $\vec{c}_2$ to S of $\vec{c}_1 | B$ and $\vec{c}_2 | B$ respectively, which coincide on $\sim B = S | B$ and $\vec{c}_1$ is at least as good as $\vec{c}_2$. (An event B is said to be null if, conditional on B, any plan, $\vec{c}_1$, is at least as good as any other, $\vec{c}_2$.)

Consider two plans $\vec{c}_1$ and $\vec{c}_2$, both of which are constant; that is, $c_1(s) = c_1(s')$ and $c_2(s) = c_2(s')$ for any states of nature s, s'. It is then postulated that if c_1 is unconditionally preferred to c_2 it is also preferred conditional on any non-null event B. Thus state-dependent preferences are excluded and the cardinal utility index takes the form $v(c)$, as opposed to the state dependent form $v(c; s)$. For this postulate to be tenable it is necessary to keep clear the distinction between states of nature (or plans) and commodities. State dependence can be introduced in a formal sense, by introducing the state of nature as an additional argument in the commodity bundle: $c^* = (c_i: i \in I, s)$; of course this obliges the individual to contemplate plans which assign to, say, state s the bundle $c^* = (c, s')$, while s

249

and s' are mutually exclusive! This notwithstanding, state dependent cardinal utility indices are indeed employeed, and the term *state preference approach* often refers to state dependence. Note that this is a different use of the term from the one outlined earlier. Both are, however, generalizations of the (state-independent), expected utility approach to choice under uncertainty.

When individual preferences have an expected utility representation, the cardinal utility index is often assumed to be concave. This is a qualitative property. Note that in this context concavity does reflect a property of the underlying preference relation since the latter determines the cardinal utility index up to monotonically increasing, linear transformations which do preserve concavity. It is a straightforward argument to show that concavity of the cardinal utility index implies that the individual is risk-averse (Arrow, 1965; Pratt, 1964). The characterization of risk averse behaviour for the state preference approach was developed, among others, by Yaari (1969); roughly, risk aversion follows from the quasi-concavity of the individual's utility function over plans.

We have considered only static choice under uncertainty. If choice occurs at more than one time period and uncertainty is resolved sequentially, the state preference approach is more problematic. We already mentioned the difficulties it presents in obtaining from a given utility function prior to the resolution of uncertainty an objective function after the uncertainty has been (partly) resolved.

BIBLIOGRAPHY

Arrow, K.J. 1965. *Aspects of the Theory of Risk-Bearing.* Helsinki: Yrjö Hahnsson Foundation.

Debreu, G. 1959. *Theory of Value.* New Haven: Yale University Press.

Machina, M. 1982. 'Expected utility' analysis without the independence axiom. *Econometrica* 55(2), 277–323.

Pratt, J. 1964. Risk aversion in the small and in the large. *Econometrica* 32(1), 122–36.

Savage, L.J. 1954. *The Foundations of Statistics.* New York: John Wiley & Sons.

Yarri, M. 1969. Some measures of risk aversion and their uses. *Journal of Economic Theory* 1(2), 315–29.

Stochastic Dominance

HAIM LEVY

The notion of stochastic dominance is quite old (see, for example, Blackwell, 1953). Although it was (in various forms) used in statistical or economic theory, it was for some reason not developed until 1969–70, when four papers were published by Hadar and Russell (1969), Hanoch and Levy (1969), Rothschild and Stiglitz (1970) and Whitmore (1970). Since then almost 400 papers have been written on this topic; for a good survey article see Kroll and Levy (1980) and for a good bibliography see Bawa (1982).

The stochastic dominance criteria have been developed in three main directions: (a) Further theoretical development, for example, the ordering of uncertain options for specific distributions or for more restricted classes of utility functions, the effect on the stochastic dominance rules of including a riskless asset, and partial ordering in the multi-period case. (b) Application of stochastic dominance rules to empirical data: various algorithms have been developed to this end. (c) Application of stochastic dominance rules to other economic and financial issues, for example, optimum financial leverage with bankruptcy, the analysis and definition of risk, and optimality of diversification.

THE CRITERIA. Given two risky options with cumulative distribution functions F and G, we seek to determine if an order of preference can be establishes between F and G. Obviously, if one has full information on the investor's utility, for example, $u(X) = \log X$, then one has simply to calculate the expected utility $E_F(\log X)$ and $E_G(\log X)$, and the option with the highest expected value is preferable. The importance of stochastic dominance rules is that they enable us to compare options even when there is only partial information on the investor's preference, for example $u' > 0$, $u'' < 0$, etc.

Stochastic dominance rules deal mainly with three classes of utility functions $U_i (i = 1, 2, 3)$, where $u \in U_1$ if $u' \geqslant 0$; $u \in U_2$ if $u' \geqslant 0$ and $u'' \leqslant 0$; and $u \in U_3$ if $u' \geqslant 0$, $u'' \leqslant 0$ and $u''' \geqslant 0$.

251

The decision rules appropriate for the classes $U_i(i = 1, 2, 3)$ are called First, Second and Third degree stochastic dominance (FSD, SSD and TSD respectively).

Theorem 1. Let F and G be the cumulative distribution of two distinct uncertain options. Then F dominates G(FDG) by FSD, SSD and TSD, if and only if:

(1) $\quad F(x) \leqq G(x)$, $\hspace{3cm}$ for all x $\hspace{3cm}$ FSD

(2) $\quad \displaystyle\int_{-\infty}^{x} [G(t) - F(t)]\mathrm{d}t \geqq 0$, $\hspace{1.5cm}$ for all x $\hspace{2.5cm}$ SSD

(3) $\quad \displaystyle\int_{-\infty}^{x} \int_{-\infty}^{v} [G(t) - F(t)\mathrm{d}t \, \mathrm{d}v \geqq 0$, $\quad$ for all x and $E_F(x) \geqq E_G(x)$. $\quad$ TSD

(Obviously we need also a strict inequality for at least one value x.)

STOCHASTIC DOMINANCE WITH A RISKLESS ASSET. Levy and Kroll (1979) applied the *quantile approach* to develop stochastic dominance criteria with a riskless asset (SDR criteria). According to this approach, the FSD, SSD and TSD criteria can be reformulated in terms of the inverse function of the cumulative probability function; that is, they can be restated in terms of $Q_F(P)$, where P is the probability of obtaining values lower than or equal to $Q_F(P)$ under distribution F. According to this formulation F dominates G by FSD if and only if $Q_F(P) \geqslant Q_G(P)$ for all P, with a strict inequality for at least one P; F dominates by G by SSD if and only if

$$\int_0^P Q_P(t)\mathrm{d}t \geqslant \int_0^P Q_G(t)\mathrm{d}t$$

for all P, with a strict inequality for at least one P; and F dominates G by TSD if and only if

$$\int_0^P \int_0^t Q_F(t)\mathrm{d}z \, \mathrm{d}t \geqslant \int_0^P \int_0^t Q_G(t)\mathrm{d}z \, \mathrm{d}t$$

with a strict inequality for at least one P and in addition

$$\int_0^1 Q_F(t)\mathrm{d}t \geqslant \int_0^1 Q_G(t)\mathrm{d}t.$$

Employing the quantile approach, and allowing riskless lending and borrowing, Levy and Kroll (1979) established stochastic dominance rules which allows us to establish preference in a case where the criteria given in Theorem 1 fail.

The SDR criteria have some interesting properties. First, recall that F dominates G by stochastic dominance only if $E_F \geqslant E_G$. Such a requirement is not necessary for dominannce by FSDR, SSDR, or TSDR (when R is added to indicate the existence of a riskless asset) since we can always change the mean of the risky portfolio by changing the proportion of the riskless asset in the mixed portfolio. Second, the stochastic dominance and SDR criteria are related as follows:

$$FSD \rightarrow SSD \rightarrow TSD$$
$$\downarrow \qquad \downarrow \qquad \downarrow$$
$$FSDR \rightarrow SSDR \rightarrow TSDR$$

Since these are all transitive relations, it is obvious that FSD implies TSDR as well as SSDR, and SSD implies TSDR. Thus, the TSDR-efficient set must be a subset of all other efficient sets derived by either stochastic dominance or SDR criteria.

EMPIRICAL STUDIES. Most of the empirical work attempts to give answers to questions such as the relative effectiveness of the criteria, or differences in the contents of the efficient sets produced by the alternative criteria.

The main results are as follows: (1) FSD is, in most cases, a totally ineffective criterion. (2) The SSD criterion is about as effective as the Mean–Variance (M–V) criterion. This means that by using SSD instead of M–V one can avoid the restrictive assumptions on the probability distribution or on the utility function without cost since the size of the efficient set does not change significantly. (3) The assumption of borrowing and lending at a risk-free interest rate (SDR rules) leads to an impressive reduction of the size of the efficient sets for risk averters. However, FSDR remains relatively ineffective. (4) The SSDR and TSDR efficient sets contain only 1–3 risky assets; namely, an almost 'empirical separation' exists. That is, SSDR and TSDR are very effective in yielding small efficient sets. For example, Levy and Kroll (1979) in a study of mutual fund found about 3 per cent of the feasible set remained in the efficient set using SSDR and TSDR.

BIBLIOGRAPHY

Bawa, V.S. 1982. Stochastic dominance: a research bibliography. *Management Science* 28(6), June, 698–712.

Bawa, V.S. 1975. Optimal rules for ordering uncertain prospects. *Journal of Financial Economics* 2(1), March, 95–121.

Blackwell, D. 1953. Equivalent comparisons of experiments. *Annals of Mathematical Statistics* 24, 265–72.

Hadar, J. and Russell, W.R. 1969. Rules for ordering uncertain prospects. *American Economic Review* 59(1), March, 25–34.

Hanoch, G. and Levy, H. 1969. Efficiency analysis of choices involving risk. *Review of Economic Studies* 36(3), July, 335–46.

Kroll, Y. and Levy, H. 1980. Stochastic dominance: a review and some new evidence. *Research in Finance* 2, 163–227.

Levy, H. and Hanoch, G. 1970. Relative effectiveness of efficiency criteria for portfolio selection. *Journal of Financial and Quantitative Analysis* 5(1), March, 63–76.

Levy, H. and Kroll, Y. 1979. Efficiency analysis with borrowing and lending: criteria and their effectiveness. *Review of Economics and Statistics* 61(1), February, 125–40.

Quirk, J.P. and Saposnik, R. 1962. Admissibility and measurable utility functions. *Review of Economic Studies* 29, February, 140–46.

Rothschild, M. and Stiglitz, J.E. 1970. Increasing risk I: a definition. *Journal of Economic Theory* 2(3), September, 225–43.

Rothschild, M. and Stiglitz, J.E. 1971. Increasing risk II: its economic consequences. *Journal of Economic Theory* 3(1), March, 66–84.

Whitmore, G.A. 1970. Third-degree stochastic dominance. *American Economic Review* 60(3), June, 457–9.

Subjective Probability

I.J. GOOD

1. KINDS OF PROBABILITY. The usual meaning of 'probable' in ordinary conversation is closely related to its derivation from a Latin word meaning provable or capable of being made convincing. The concept is even clearer in the derivation of the German word *Wahrscheinlichkeit*, 'having the appearance of truth'. In fact, when we say an event is probably we usually mean that we would not be surprised (or we ought not to be) if it occurred, or that we *would* be somewhat surprised (or ought to be) if it did not occur. Since 'surprise' refers to a personal or subjective experience it seems clear that the ordinary concept of probability is subjectivistic (or else in some sense logical). Also a probability, in this subjective or logical sense, can be more or less large so it can be interpreted as a degree of belief or intensity of conviction. A subjective probability is usually regarded as somewhat more than just a degree of belief – it is a degree of belief that belongs to a body of beliefs from which the worst inconsistencies have been removed by means of detached judgements. In short, the degree of belief should be more or less rational.

To appreciate better the meaning of a subjective probability it is necessary to consider other kinds or interpretations of probability. We begin by contrasting subjective probability with what is often called *physical probability* by considering an example.

Suppose you are given a solid cube that appears superficially symmetrical and you are asked to paint the numbers 1 to 6 on its six faces so that the cube becomes a die (the singular of 'dice'). What is the probability that you will obtain the 6 uppermost on the first throw of the die? Because of the symmetry of the information available to you it seems that your probability, at least for betting purposes, *ought* to be equal to or close to 1/6. (Irrational gamblers, when they say 'When you're hot you're hot' seem to believe that dice have memories.) But, for all you know, the die might not be symmetrical inside, it might be a loaded die, and the intrinsic or material or physical probability or propensity to come up 6 might be far from 1/6. Thus your betting or subjective or personal probability need not be equal to the physical probability. I shall use the term 'subjective' to avoid being too personal.

That there are two kinds of probability was perhaps first emphasized by Poisson (1837, p. 31). He used the French (or English) word for 'chance' for physical probability, and 'probabilité' for something close to subjective probability. I say 'close' because Poisson did not make it clear whether his use of 'probabilité' was intended to denote subjective probability, or, on the other hand, the only rational probability, or objective degree of belief, on the evidence available. This latter kind of probability, the existence of which is controversial, has been called a *credibility* (for example to F.Y. Edgeworth and Bertrand Russell) or a *logical probability*. A probability that is either subjective or logical, or something intermediate, is conveniently called an *epistemic probability* although some writers use the term 'subjective' to mean 'epistemic' in order to avoid sounding too philosophical. A probability agreed upon by a group of people is sometimes called *multisubjective* or multipersonal. The subject whose subjective probability is under discussion is often called 'You'. This has the merit of being ambiguously singular or plural.

For a dendroidal classification of kinds of probability see Figure 1 (based on Good, 1966). This classification mentions 'tautological probability' which is a probability occurring in a mathematical theory without an interpretation outside the mathematics.

Your probability that a die will come up 6 depends on the information available to you; for example, if you have thrown it 6000 times and it has come up 6 exactly 500 times then your subjective probability on the next throw would presumably be close to 500/6000 or 1/12. Furthermore, I think you will agree that if you throw the die an exceedingly large number of times, but not so many that the die or you get worn out, then the credibility is close to 1 that your subjective probability *should* become close to the physical probability (if you are

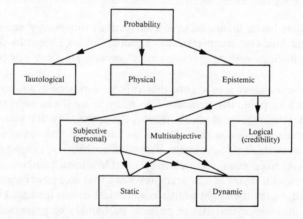

Figure 1   A dendroidal classification of kinds of probability or usages of the term.

rational and if the die is thrown properly). This assumes of course that the die is of durable material and not made of soft clay. If it is made of soft clay the physical probability presumably exists but is more difficult or impossible to measure by long-run relative frequency.

This example makes it entirely clear that a subjective probability should depend on the available information just as a physical probability depends on the 'set-up'. To capture this fact symbolically it is customary in modern books on statistics or mathematical probabilty to write $P(E|F)$ or $\Pr(E|F)$ or $\mathrm{Prob}(E|F)$ or $p(E|F)$, etc., for the probability of E given F. Here E and F might denote events, hypotheses, or propositions and the notation is often used whatever kind of probability is meant. The expressions are read 'the probabiltiy of E given F'. Sometimes the vertical stroke is replaced by other notations, especially by those philosophers of statistics who do not have a vertical stroke in their typewriter fonts.

In some contexts it is convenient to use distinct symbols for physical and epistemic probability. For example, one could use C for chance, or, to reverse the notation, one could use P for physical probability and C for credibility.

It has been argued by de Finetti (1937, 1968/70) that it is sufficient to assume the existence of only one kind of probability, namely subjective probability. His argument depends on his remarkable theorem concerning 'permutable' or 'exchangeable' sequences of events but we shall have to be satisfied with a reference (Good, 1965, pp. 13, 21–3) where further references are cited.

De Finetti's definition of $P(E|F)$ is the fraction of a rouble that you would pay for the privilege of receiving one rouble if the event E obtains, the whole set being cancelled if F does not obtain.

2. A THEORY OF SUBJECTIVE PROBABILITY. Except when it is folly to be wise most of us would like our probabilities to be in some sense rational or approximately so. For example, if $P(E_1|F_1)$, though not necessarily numerical, in some sense 'exceeds' $P(E_2|F_2)$ and the latter exceeds $P(E_3|F_3)$ then we would want $P(E_1|F_1)$ to exceed $P(E_3|F_3)$, for the sake of rationality. This property is known as 'transitivity'. (Condorcet's paradox of voting is *not* a serious objection to the assumption of transitivity but only shows that a familiar voting procedure is faulty.) For example, probabilities might be only 'partially ordered', that is, we might not always be able to state whether $P(E_1|F_1)$ exceeds, 'subceeds', or equals $P(E_2|F_2)$. The concept that logical probabilities are only partially ordered was emphasized by Keynes (1921) and Koopman (1940a, 1940b), while the partial ordering of *subjective* probabilities has been emphasized by the present author in countless publications beginning in Good (1950).

The purpose of a theory of subjective probability is *to make your subjective probabilities more objective*. We all have subjective probabilities but those libertines without a theory are free to be as subjective and irrational as they like. They call themselves objectivists! In nearly all theories of subjective probability there is a set of axioms resembling the following set (Good, 1950, p. 19). These

257

axioms contain equality signs, but a theory of partially ordered probabilities can nevertheless be based on them as will be explained below.

(A1) *Numerical probability.* $P(E|H)$ is a non-negative real number.

(A2) *The addition law.* If $P(E \& F|H) = 0$, then $P(E \vee F|H) = P(E|H) + P(F|H)$, where the symbol $\vee$ denotes the (inclusive) 'or'

(A3) *The product law.* $P(E \& F|H) = P(E|H) \cdot P(F|E \& H)$.

(A4) *Equivalence.* If E and F logically imply one another, given H, then $P(E|H) = P(F|H)$ and $P(H|E = P(H|F)$.

(A5) $P(H^*|H^*) \neq 0$, where H^* is logically true. (One can deduce that $P(H^*|H^*) = 1$.)

(A6) $P(E^*|H^*) = 0$ for some proposition E^*.

For attempts to justify some such set of axioms, based on one's intuitive understanding of language, without introducing bets, see, for example, Jeffreys (1939, ch. 1), Cox (1946, 1961), Schroedinger (1947), and Good (1950, pp. 1–20, 33, and 105–106). For attempts based on your behaviour (choice of actions), which many people find more convincing because actions speak louder than words, see Ramsey (1926/31), de Finetti (1937), and Savage (1954). (Indeed the mathematical theory of probability arose out of gambling problems.) The implication of these writers is that if your behaviour, including your linguistic behaviour, satisfies certain seemingly compelling desiderata for rationality then you will behave *as if* you had subjective probabilities and 'utilities' (values), satisfying a familiar set of axioms, and that you appear to be trying to maximize your mathematical expectation of utility. Of course 'utility' is not necessarily monetary value, in fact anyone who equated utility with money in all circumstances would be extremely irrational. Your calculations need not be done at a conclusion level: nice people are not 'calculating'. It is not even obvious whether animals are less rational than humans according to this interpretation of rationality, for language can lead to irrationality as well as to rationality.

In Savage's book a main desideratum is the 'sure-thing' principle, that if action A is to be preferred if E occurs and also if E does not occur, then A is to be preferred, period. Some people have questioned the sure-thing principle by reference to the *amalgamation paradox* or Pearson–Yule paradox (Pearson, 1899; Yule, 1903), sometimes incorrectly attributed to Simpson. The amalgamation paradox is exemplified by the fact that a drug can be beneficial for men and also for women, but, when the samples (2-by-2 contingency tables) are amalgamated, can appear to be harmful to the mixed population. The appearance is of course deceptive so the amalgamation paradox is not a genuine objection to the sure-thing principle.

From the axioms we can deduce non-trivial probabilities only from other probabilities, so we have to begin with some judgemental ones.

Axioms expressed explicitly in terms of partially-ordered probabilities have been derived in various ways by Koopman (1940a, b), Good (1960–62) and Smith (1961).

As mentioned above, a theory of partially-ordered probability can be based on numerical axioms. This can be done by introducing the notion of a 'black box' or 'abstract theory'. A collection of non-numerical inequality *judgements* of the kind '$P'(E_1|H_1)$ exceeds $P'(E_2|H_2)$' are plugged into the black box where P' refers to a degree of belief, not necessarily numerical. Such a judgement is interpreted by the black box as $P(E_1|H_1) > P(E_2|H_2)$, where the probabilities are now treated as numbers. The abstract or mathematical theory, based on the numerical axioms, is then used to produce new inequalities such as $P(E_3|H_3) > P(E_4|H_4)$, which are reinterpreted as *discernments*, such as $P'(E_3|H_3)$ *exceeds* $P'(E_4|H_4)$, at the output of the black box, and are fed back into the 'body of beliefs'. The input and output specifications are not axioms, but are *rules of application* of the abstract theory. (See Figure 2.)

Because 'landmark probabilities' can be introduced by imagining perfectly shuffled packs of cards, or rotating pointers, a partially-ordered theory is equivalent to a theory of interval-valued probabilities, or upper and lower probabilities, denoted by P^* and P_*. (In practice, however, even P^* and P_* are fuzzy.) From the black-box theory one can deduce axioms satisfied by the upper and lower probabilities, such as

$$P^*(E \& F|H)/P_*(F|E \& H) \geqslant P^*(E|H).$$

This approach was used by Good (1960–62), whereas the independent approach by Smith (1961) was based on betting behaviour and resembled the behavioural method used by Savage (1954) for sharp numerical probabilities.

Even if you support the theory of partially-ordered, or upper and lower probabilities, you might often work with a theory of sharp probabilities for the sake of simplicity, and especially for simplicity of exposition. You will then find that axiom (A4) is only an ideal, not always attainable. For example, you might be asked to bet whether the billionth digit of π, after the decimal point, is a 7. (Good, 1950, p. 49, considered the millionth digit, but that digit is now known.) Your betting probability is presumably $1/10$, but it you could complete the calculations the probability would become 1 or 0. Thus a subjective probability can be changed by calculation or by pure thought, as in the analysis of a chess position, without any change of empirical evidence. Such probabilities have been

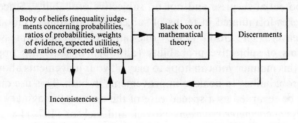

Figure 2 The black-box theory of subjective probabilities. The discernments are fed back into the body of beliefs. This enables you to enlarge the body of beliefs and to check it for consistency. Observed inconsistencies encourage more mature judgement

called 'evolving' or, better, *dynamic* and the topic is reviewed by Good (1977). To allow for dynamic probabilities one can replace (A4) by (A4'). If you have *seen* or proved that E and F are logically equivalent given H then

$$P(E|H) = P(F|H) \quad \text{and} \quad P(H|E) = P(H|F)$$

(Good, 1950, p. 49).

Dynamic probabilities have an important application in the philosophy of science (Good, 1968, p. 129; 1983a, p. 223; 1985b): it is there pointed out that the philosophy of explanation definitely requires the concept of dynamic probability when an explanation, like the inverse square law of gravitation, does not involve any new empirical observations.

3. 'SUGGESTIONS'. In practice a theory that deals with judgements needs more than axioms and rules of application; it also needs suggestions or hints for forming and adjusting judgements. There are apt to be an almost unlimited supply of possible suggestions because they relate largely to your psychology. Experiments on the psychology of probability judgements have been reviewed by Hogarth (1975). You can use the results to help you to avoid pitfalls when making your own judgements.

Let us now consider a few suggestions.

(i) *The device of imaginary results* (Good, 1983, indexes). A theory of subjective probability is basically a theory of consistency of judgements, a point made by Ramsey (1926/31). (When dynamic probability, or axiom (A4'), is incorporated, the consistency can be intended only at a given time or *in a given report*.) Hence, when formulating our judgements we can usefully imagine possible outcomes of experiments and use these to help us to form judgements. This suggestion will be made clearer after we discuss Bayes' theorem in Section 4. An example of the device of imaginary results is sensitivity analysis where we vary our initial model and see whether the conclusions are affected too much (in our judgement).

(ii) *Surprise indexes.* Shackle (1949) suggested that entrepreneurs rely on the concept of potential surprise and not on subjective probability. Since there are surprise indexes formulated in terms of subjective probability (Good, 1953/57 who cites Weaver, 1948; Good, 1986b), one can in my opinion express Shackle's views in terms of subjective probability (although Shackle has opposed this opinion). In this manner you can hope to play off your judgements about surprise and about probabilities to achieve improvements in both. This use on potential surprise can be regarded as a special case of the device of imaginary results.

(iii) *The use of computer programs.* Novick and Jackson (1974) have described computer programs that can help you to deduce consequences interactively and rapidly from your probability judgements, thus carrying out the purpose of a black-box theory as described above, almost as if the computer were the black box. To make rapid deductions is clearly an advantage because, if you have the facilities, it enables you to make deductions from your judgements that you otherwise might not have had the time or energy to make.

4. BAYES' THEOREM AND WEIGHTS OF EVIDENCE. Suppose that we are interested in discriminating between two or more hypothesis $H_1, H_2, \ldots, H_n$ $(n \geqslant 2)$, and we have evidence E in addition to background information B. The probabilities $P(H_i|B)$ $(i = 1, 2, \ldots, n)$ are known as prior or initial probabilities (prior to the taking of E into account, but not necessarily chronologically prior to the occurrence of E), and the $P(H_i|B \& E)$ are known as posterior or final probabilities. Then, leaving aside the possibility of zero probabilities, it follows very quickly from the axioms that

$$P(H_i|E) = \frac{P(E|H_i)P(H_i)}{\sum_j P(E|H_j)P(H_j)} \tag{1}$$

and this is known as Bayes' theorem, though he did not use the modern notation. It is interesting that so simple a theorem can have far-reaching consequences. Bayes' work was published posthumously, having been found among his papers by Price who made contributions to the publication (Bayes, 1763/65). The fact that Bayes did not publish the theorem during his lifetime has several possible explanations, one being that he was perhaps not satisfied with the part of the work dealing with the values of the prior probabilities.

$P(E|H_i)$, or $\lambda P(E|H_i)$, where λ does not depend on i, is called the likelihood of H_i given E, so Bayes' theorem can be expressed in the form 'the posterior probability of H_i is proportional to its prior probability times its likelihood' (Jeffreys, 1939, p. 29).

When subjective probabilities are used in statistics, in conjunction with Bayes' theorem, the approach is called *Bayesian* or *neo-Bayesian*. (There are, however, at least 6^6 possible shades of meaning: see Good, 1983a, ch. 3, or twice this number if allowance is made for dynamic versus static probabilities. One of the 2×6^6 is known as Doogian: see Berger, 1984.) Non-Bayesian methods of statistical inference are exemplified by the use of tail-area probabilities ('Fisherian') and confidence intervals ('Neyman–Pearsonian'). Non-Bayesian methods are also called *frequentist* or *sampling-theory* methods. The Bayesian would claim that these methods, when they can be justified at all, can be justified only by means of informal or formal Bayesian arguments. One example will be given in Section 5.

The case $n = 2$ of Bayes' theorem is especially interesting. It leads very easily to the further simple identity (almost as important as Bayes' theorem itself),

$$\frac{O(H|E \& B)}{O(H|B)} = \frac{P(E|B \& H)}{P(E|B \& H)} \tag{2}$$

where $-H$ denotes the negation of H and O denotes *odds*. (The odds corresponding to a probability p are defined as $p/(1-p)$.) The ratio of the posterior to the prior odds of H is now known as the *Bayes factor* in favour of H provided by E (given B all along), although Bayes never mentioned it. Its logarithm is sometimes called the *weight of evidence in favour of H provided by E given B*, and can be denoted by $W(H:E|B)$. The base of the logarithms merely defines the unit in terms of which the weight of evidence is measured. The expression 'weight of evidence' was seemingly first proposed in this sense by Peirce (1878) for the special case in which the initial probability of H was $1/2$ (Good, 1983c) but the expression in this technical sense dropped out of use until the publication of Good (1950). (Peirce proposed but did not *use* the expression for he was a non-Bayesian.) The expression was temporarily called 'support' by Jeffreys (1936) and the concept, though not the name, was introduced into the cryptanalysis of the Enigma by A.M. Turing during World War II. (He never mentioned Jeffreys, 1936, and probably had not seen that publication.) When the base was 10, Turing called the unit a ban, one-tenth of which he called a deciban. The deciban is about the smallest unit of weight of evidence that the human mind can apprehend and is analogous to the decibel in acoustics. For the Enigma publication a weight of evidence was called a 'score' or a 'decibannage'.

To justify the expression 'weight of evidence' in this technical sense, imagine that H represents the guilt of an accused man and its negation his innocence, and let E denote the evidence presented in court. Let $W_1(H:E)$ denote the weight of evidence if favour of guilt *provided by the evidence E alone* (though *given* the background information), where here 'weight of evidence' is to be interpreted in its intuitive and ordinary sense of the *balance* of the evidence (*not* as the sum of the favourable and unfavourable pieces of evidence). The background information B can be included in the notation by writing $W_1(H:E|B)$ but we omit B to simplify the exposition. The following desiderata seem natural:

(i) $W_1(H:E)$ should depend only on $P(E|H)$ and $P(E|-H)$;

(ii) $P(H|E)$ should depend only on $W_1(H:E)$ and on the initial probability $P(H)$.

It can be proved that $W_1(H:E)$ must be a function of $W(H:E)$ (Good, 1984). We may as well take $W_1 = W$ because we have the desirable additive property

$$W[H:(E\,\&\,F)] = W(H:E) + W(H:F|E). \qquad (3)$$

Bayes factors have a corresponding multiplicative property, but, when talking about 'weights' additivity is more appropriate. A survey of properties of weights of evidence is given by Good (1985a).

It is necessary that magistrates, jurymen and doctors doing differential diagnoses, should have at least implicit judgements of final probabilities of the form $P(H|E)$, the probability of a hypothesis H when evidence E is provided. A 'suggestion', that can be appended to those listed in Section 3, is that such judgements would be aided by introducing semi-quantitative judgements of weights of evidence or of inequalities between them. (They can be used as inputs to the Black Box.) This would be especially valuable when there are approximately independent pieces of evidence such as evidence from reliable witnesses, fingerprints, motivation, behaviour of the accused in court, previous convictions (!) and previous convictions of the unreliable witnesses!

Bayes' theorem, and especially the concept of a Bayes factor or of a weight of evidence, can be combined with the device of imaginary results to work backwards from a final probability (based on an imagined outcome) to an initial probability. The words 'prior' (or 'initial') and 'posterior' (or 'final') have repeatedly misled people into overlooking this possibility although it has been recognized since at least 1950. Note too that what is called 'prior' might often be better called 'intermediate'.

The use of Bayes' theorem in reverse exemplifies that neo-Bayesianism is basically a theory of (approximate) consistency of judgements.

An important part of statistics is not primarily inferential, namely descriptive statistics and exploratory data analysis, both of which consist of techniques for presenting salient features or interesting patterns or 'clues' in data to the eye–brain system. Exploratory data analysis leans a little further towards scientific discovery than does descriptive statistics. A case is made by Good (1983b) that there is an implicit Bayesian component even in these seemingly non-inferential activities. The reason is that you need to judge whether a pattern is a mere 'kinkus', that is, probably has no physical cause. Cranks take kinkera seriously. A *scientifically interesting* pattern is one that probably has a cause even if the cause is unknown. When you conjecture *specific* causes you have begun doing science rather than statistics.

5. BAYES/NON-BAYES OR BAYES-FREQUENTIST COMPROMISES. If a statistic X takes a value x for which the tail-area probability or P-value, $P = P(X \geqslant x | H)$, is 'small', the Fisherian will regard this as evidence against the null hypothesis H, whereas the Bayesian will measure the evidence by $W = W(-H-X = x)$, the weight of evidence against H provided by the knowledge that X took the value x. In other words the Bayesian requires that the Bayes factor $P(X = x | H)/P(X = x | -H)$ should be 'large'; but the non-Bayesian will usually regard the expression $P(X = x | -H)$ as meaningless when $-H$ is not a 'simple statistical hypothesis'. In many cases there is some very rough mathematical anticorrelation between the P-value and W. When this is so one has a rough informal justification of the use of P-values, but when it is not so the Bayesian will regard the use of the P-value as misleading. I have often found that a 'single-tailed' P-value of precisely 0.05 corresponds to a Bayes factor of only about 3 or 4, and as such it is only weak evidence against the null hypothesis. Indeed, if the null hypothesis had prior odds of more than 4 to 1 on, then it might very well be 'odds on' after suffering from a P-value of 0.05. Note, however, that an intelligent and honest Fisherian who, because, being human (and not merely a statistician) is also a convert or informal Bayesian in his heart, happens to regard the prior odds of H as more than 4 to 1 on, then he will perhaps choose the rejection threshold for P as say 0.01 or lower. (He might of course report a P-value without either accepting or rejecting the null hypothesis.)

Note too that when a Fisherian makes the choice between single-tail and double-tail probabilities he is allowing for the class of non-null hypotheses that are of interest to him. This too is consistent with a Bayesian outlook.

When a sample size N is large enough, a P-value of 0.05 can be strong *support* for the null hypothesis (see, for example, Good, 1983d, where this is made abundantly clear). Good (1982b) suggests that any P-value should be 'standardized' to a fixed sample size, say 100, like adjusting to 'constant dollars' to allow for inflation. The proposed formula is $\min[\frac{1}{2}, P(N/100)^{1/2}]$. For other examples of Bayes/non-Bayes (or Bayes-frequentist) compromises see Good (1983a, Indexes; 1986a).

6. INDUCTION. The concept of epistemic probability is necessary for any constructive theory of scientific induction. Induction is usually defined as arguing from the particular to the general. For example, if all of many swans you have seen in the past have been white then it would be natural to conjecture that all swans are white, at least under similar circumstances. When circumstances are different in some way judged to be important, for example, if the observation is carried out in Australia, the inference seems less probable (and in fact is false).

We can regard an inference about the next case as another form of induction because it is so similar to induction yet does not argue from the particular directly to the general. It may be called *induction to the next case*. The earliest formula proposed for induction to the next case is known as *Laplace's Law of Succession*. It relates to Bernoulli trials or binomial sampling. For example, we might throw a drawing-pin (thumb-tack) on the table and define a 'success' as each occasion that it comes to rest pointing downwards. Let the physical probability of a success be denoted by p. Initially, if your are a 'sharp' Bayesian (one with sharp probability estimates), you have a prior subjective probability density concerning the value of p. Laplace assumed that this 'prior' was uniform, that is, that the subjective or logical probability density of the physical probability p is the same (and therefore equal to 1) at each value of n. This assumption is called a *Bayes postulate*. Then, if we have had n successes in n throws, the probability of a success in the next trial is found to be

$$(n + 1)/(n + 2). \tag{4}$$

This is Laplace's Law of Succession. It is by no means a perfect estimate, and has even been called 'notorious', but it is much better than the maximum-liklihood estimate which is unity and absurd in this application.

Laplace's Law of Succession can be applied to the case of the US Space Shuttle disaster of February 1986. There had been 24 successful launchings of the Shuttle, so Laplace's Law of Succession would lead to an estimated probability of 1/26 for a failure on the 25th attempt. But conditions were different in an important manner, for the temperature on the 25th occasion was far below that on any previous occasion, so, having no inside information, your subjective probability of a disaster could well have been much larger than 1/26. (Apart from the temperature there had been other engineering concerns.)

We now return to general discussion of Laplace's Law of Succession. It follows from this 'law' that the probability of successes on each of the next m trials (after the original n) is equal to

$$\frac{n+1}{n+2} \cdot \frac{n+2}{n+3} \cdots \frac{n+m}{n+m+1},$$ (5)

because, for example, after the $(n+1)$th success the probability of a success on the $(n+2)$th trial is $(n+2)/(n+3)$ (by a second application of Laplace's Law of Succession) and so on. The product (5) reduces at once to

$$(n+1)/(n+m+1),$$ (6)

a formula with interesting implications. It suggests, for example, by taking $m = n + 1$, that, putting it roughly, what has gone on for a certain length of time will, with subjective probability $\frac{1}{2}$, continue for about the same length of time again – which has been somewhat facetiously called the first law of meterology. In the meterological application the length of time must not exceed about one month because we all have background knowledge about seasons. But in other contexts we might let $m \to \infty$ and infer that the probability of a general law is zero. Jeffreys (1957, p. 51) attributed this conclusion to Karl Pearson and inferred that the Bayes postulate needed amendment. Haldane (1931) and Jeffreys (1939, p. 114) proposed that non-zero epistemic positive probabilities q_0 and q_1 should be assumed at $p = 0$ and $p = 1$ in the prior, the remaining probability being (perhaps) uniformly spread. This observation is also fairly explicit in Pearson ([1892], 1937, p. 125). It comes to the same thing as assuming two null hypotheses, each with positive prior probability, the Bayes postulate being assumed conditional on the falsity of both null hypotheses. (Other 'null hypotheses', with positive prior probabilities, might be natural such as the hypotheses that $p = \frac{1}{2}$.) Such modifications of Bayes' postulate permit induction to a general law. Under these assumptions, the 'likelihoods' of the three hypotheses $p = 0$, $p = 1$ and $p \neq 0$ or 1, after n successes in n trials, are 0, 1 and $1/(n+1)$ so, by Bayes' theorem, the final odds of the 'general law' $p = 1$ are

$$(n+1)q_1/(1 - q_0 - q_1)$$ (7)

which tends to infinity with n. In particular, if $q_0 = 0$ and $q_1 = \frac{1}{2}$, the final probability that $p = 1$ is $(n+1)/(n+2)$ (Jeffreys, 1957, p. 53). This just happens to equal formula (4), but its meaning is different.

When we have substantial background knowledge these results break down for a variety of reasons. For example, when tossing a coin for the first time the prior probability density of p is (if you are sensible) sharply peaked at $p = \frac{1}{2}$. The Bayes postulate is often generalized to a 'beta' prior for p whose density is proportional to $p^{a-1}(1-p)^{b-1}$ ($a > 0, b > 0$) (Hardy, 1889). This is flexible enough on most occasions to binomial sampling and has the merit of being a 'conjugate prior'; that is, after r successes and s failures, the posterior density of p belongs to the same (beta) family and is obtained by adding r to a and s to b. One way to judge the values of a and b is to judge the lower and upper quartiles of the prior.

Closely related is a paper by W.E. Johnson (1932) in which he introduced some assumptions related to multiple or multinomial sampling. His argument was incorrect for the special case of binomial sampling: see Good (1965, p. 26), but for the sake of simplicity I consider the binomial case here. Johnson's work anticipated the basic idea of the 'continuum of inductive methods' (Carnap, 1952) in which Laplace's formula is replaced by $(n+k)/(n+2k)$ $(k>0)$. (For each value of k there is a distinct 'inductive method'.) Good (1965) proposed putting a 'hyperprior' on k, the method being a special case of what is now called the *hierarchical Bayesian* method. For a review of this method as applied especially to multinomials and contingency tables see Good (1979/81), 1981/83). The latter paper again indicates that induction to the next case (or to the next several cases) is much more convincingly attainable than induction to a general law. Fortunately, in many practical situations, induction to the next several cases is more important than induction to a general law. For example, we would like to be able to say with confidence that our next 100 aircraft flights will probably be successful, but we are not concerned with eternally safe flights.

Similarly, in general applications of Bayesian methods in statistics, prediction to the next several cases is usually more important than the estimation of parameters as such. In recent years the Bayesian predictivist point of view has been especially emphasized by de Finetti and, for numerous applications, by Geisser: see, for example, de Finetti (1968/70) and Geisser (1983/85). The over-preoccupation with parameters, which are usually denoted by Greek letters, has been called the worship of Greek gods. Nevertheless the religion of parameters and even of hyperparameters (parameters in priors) is at least psychologically useful.

7. DECISION THEORY. We have already mentioned the close relationship of the theory of subjective probability to decision theory. The black box theory extends in a straightforward manner to this theory (Good, 1952). We have to append to the axioms the principle of rationality, *maximize the mathematical expectation of the utility*, and input judgements need to be extended to include preferences. It is often necessary to allow for the costs of calculation and thought and when you do so you can be regarded as applying a principle of rationality of 'type 2'. It is unlikely that this principle can be fully formalized but it cannot be avoided in practice.

The large influence of Bayesianism (the explicit use of epistemic probability) on statistics is typified by the opinion that is sometimes held that the whole of inferential statistics should be regarded as an application of Bayesian decision theory. Historically, Bayesianism received a set-back in the second quarter of the 20th century under R.A. Fisher's influence. He was a great practitioner but a mediocre philosopher. But statistics needed an adequate philosophical background and the pendulum swung back a long way in the third quarter of the century. In the writer's opinion, the swings will soon be damped and a Bayes/non-Bayes compromise will emerge as the majority position among statisticians for the next hundred years (Good, 1983a, p. 95).

BIBLIOGRAPHY

For an article covering somewhat similar ground to the present one see Good (1982a). On some points it says more and on some less.

For books giving applications of subjective or logical probability in statistics see, for example, Jeffreys (1939–61), Lindley (1965), Zellner (1971, 1980), De Groot (1970), Box and Tiao (1973), Rosenkratz (1977), Good (1965, 1983a) and Berger (1985).

Bayes, T. 1763. An essay toward solving a problem in the doctrine of chances (with discussion and a foreword by Richard Price). *Philosophical Transactions of the Royal Society* 53, 370–418; 54, 295–35. Reprinted by the Graduate School, US Department of Agriculture, Washington, DC (1940; and in *Biometrika* 45 (1958), 293–315.

Berger, J.O. 1984. The robust Bayesian viewpoint. In *Robustness of Bayesian Analysis*, ed. J.B. Kadane, Amsterdam: North-Holland, 64–144.

Berger, J.O. 1985. *Statistical Decision Theory and Bayesian Analysis*. 2nd edn, New York: Springer-Verlag.

Bernardo, J.M., De Groot, M.H., Lindley, D.V. and Smith, A.F.M. (eds) 1983–5. *Bayesian Statistics 2*: *Proceedings of the Second Valencia International Meeting* September 6–10, 1983. Amsterdam: North-Holland.

Box, G.E.P. and Tiao, G.C. 1973. *Bayesian Inference in Statistical Analysis*. Reading, Mass.: Addison-Wesley.

Carnap, R. 1952. *The Continuum of Inductive Methods*. Chicago: University of Chicago Press.

Cox, R.T. 1946. Probability, frequency and reasonable expectation. *American Journal of Physics* 14, 1–13.

Cox, R.T. 1961. *The Algebra of Probable Inference*. Baltimore: Johns Hopkins University Press.

de Finetti, B. 1937. La prévision: ses lois logiques, ses sources subjectives. *Annales de l'Institut Henri Poincaré* 7, 1–68. Translated in Kyburg and Smokler (1980).

de Finetti, B. 1968–70. Initial probabilities: a prerequisite for any valid induction. *Synthese* 20, 1969, 2–24 (with discussion). Also in *Induction, Physics and Ethics: Proceedings and Discussions of the 1968 Salzburg Colloquium in the Philosophy of Science*, ed. P. Weingartner and G. Zechs, Dordrecht, Holland: D. Reidel, 1970.

De Groot, M.H. 1970. *Optimal Statistical Decisions*. New York: McGraw-Hill.

Geisser, S. 1983–5. On the prediction of observables: a selective update. In Bernardo et al. (1983–5), 203–29 (with discussion).

Good, I.J. 1950. *Probability and the Weighing of Evidence*. London: Charles Griffin; New York: Hafners.

Good, I.J. 1952. Rational decisions. *Journal of the Royal Statistical Society B*, 14, 107–114. Reprinted in Good (1983a).

Good, I.J. 1953–7. The appropriate mathematical tools for describing and measuring uncertainty. In *Uncertainty and Business Decisions*, ed. C.F. Carter, G.P. Meredith and G.L.S. Shackle, Liverpool: Liverpool University Press, 20–36. Partly reprinted in Good (1983a).

Good, I.J. 1960–62. Subjective probability as the measure of a non-measurable set. In *Logic, Methodology, and Philosophy of Science*, ed. E. Nagel, P. Suppes and A. Tarski, Stanford: Stanford University Press, pp. 319–29. Reprinted in Kyburg and Smokler (1980) and in Good (1983a).

Good, I.J. 1965. *The Estimation of Probabilities: An Essay on Modern Bayesian Methods*. Cambridge, Mass.: MIT Press.

Good, I.J. 1966. How to estimate probabilities. *Journal of the Institute of Mathematics and its Applications* 2, 364–83.

Good, I.J. 1968. Corroboration, explanation, evolving probability, simplicity, and a sharpened razor. *British Journal for the Philosophy of Science* 19, 123–43.

Good, I.J. 1977. Dynamic probability, computer chess, and the measurement of knowledge. In *Machine Intelligence* 8, ed. E.W. Elcock and D. Michie, Chichester: Ellis Horwood, 139–150. Reprinted in Good (1983a).

Good, I.J. 1979–81. Some history of the hierarchical Bayesian methodology. *Bayesian Statistics: Proceedings of the First International Meeting held in Valencia (Spain), May 28 to June 2, 1979*, ed. J.M. Bernardo, M.H. De Groot, D.V. Lindley and A.F.M. Smith, University of Valencia, 1981, 489–510 and 512–19 (with discussion).

Good, I.J. 1981–3. The robustness of a hierarchical model for multinomials and contingency tables. In *Scientific Inference, Data Analysis, and Robustness*, ed. G.E.P. Box, Tom and Leonard and Chien-Fu Wu, New York: Academic Press.

Good, I.J. 1982a. Degrees of belief. In *Encyclopaedia of Statistical Sciences*, Vol. 2, ed. S. Kotz and N.L. Johnson, New York: Wiley, 287–93.

Good, I.J. 1982b. Standardized tail-area probabilities. C140 in *Journal of Statistical Computation and Simulation* 16, 65–6.

Good, I.J. 1983a. *Good Thinking: The Foundations of Probability and its Applications*. Minneapolis: University of Minnesota Press.

Good, I.J. 1983b. The philosophy of exploratory data analysis. *Philosophy of Science* 50, 283–95.

Good, I.J. 1983c. A correction concerning my interpretation of Neyman–Pearson 'hypothesis determination'. C165 in *Journal of Statistical Computation and Simulation* 18, 71–4.

Good, I.J. 1983d. The diminishing significance of a fixed P-value as the sample size increases: a discrete model. C144 in *Journal of Statistical Computation and Simulation* 16, 312–14.

Good, I.J. 1984. The best explicatum for weight of evidence. C197 in *Journal of Statistical Computation and Simulation* 19, 294–9.

Good, I.J. 1985a. Weight of evidence: a brief survey. In Bernardo et al. 1983–5, 249–69 (with discussion).

Good, I.J. 1985b. A historical comment concerning novel confirmation. *British Journal for the Philosophy of Science* 36, 184–5.

Good, I.J. 1986a. Statistical evidence. In *Encyclopaedia of Statistical Sciences*, Vol. 8, ed. S. Kotz, N.L. Johnson and C. Read, New York: Wiley.

Good, I.J. 1986b. Surprise index. In *Encyclopaedia of Statistical Sciences*, Vol. 9, ed. S. Kotz, N.L. Johnson and C. Read, New York: Wiley.

Haldane, J.B.S. 1931. A note on inverse probability. *Proceedings of the Cambridge Philosophical Society* 28, 55–61.

Hardy, G.F. 1889. In correspondence in *Insurance Record*, reprinted in *Transactions of the Faculty of Actuaries* 8, (1920), 174–82, esp. 181.

Hogarth, R.M. 1975. Cognitive processes and the assessment of subjective probability distributions. *Journal of the American Statistical Association* 70, 271–94.

Jeffreys, H. 1936. Further significance tests. *Proceedings of the Cambridge Philosophical Society* 32, 416–45.

Jeffreys, H. 1939. *Theory of Probability*. Oxford: Clarendon Press; 2nd edn, 1961.

Jeffreys, H. 1957. *Scientific Inference*. 2nd edn, Cambridge: Cambridge University Press.

Johnson, W.E. 1932. Appendix (ed. R.B. Braithwaite) to 'Probability: deductive and inductive problems'. *Mind* 41, 421–3.

Keynes, J.M. 1921. *A Treatise on Probability*. London: Macmillan; New York: Harper & Row, 1962.

Koopman, B.O. 1940a. The basis of probability. *Bulletin of the American Mathematical Society* 46, 763–74.

Koopman, B.O. 1940b. The axioms and algebra of intuitive probability. *Annals of Mathematics* 41, 269–92.

Kyburg, H.E. and Smokler, H.E. (eds) 1980. *Studies in Subjective Probability*. 2nd edn, Huntington: New York, Robert E. Krieger. (1st edn New York: John Wiley, 1964.)

Lindley, D.V. 1965. *Introduction to Probability and Statistics*, Vol. 2. Cambridge: Cambridge University Press.

Novick, M.R. and Jackson, P.H. 1974. *Statistical Methods for Educational and Psychological Research*. New York: McGraw-Hill.

Pearson, K. 1982. *The Grammar of Science*. Reprinted, London: J.M. Dent & Sons, 1937.

Pearson, K. 1899. Theory of genetic (reproductive) selection. *Philosophical Transactions of the Royal Society of London (A)* 192, 260–78, esp. 277–8, 'On the spurious correlation produced by forming a mixture of heterogeneous but uncorrelated materials'.

Peirce, C.S. 1878. The probability of induction. *Popular Science Monthly*; reprinted in *The World of Mathematics* 2, ed. James R. Newman, New York: Simon & Schuster, 1956, 1341–54.

Poisson, S.-D. 1937. *Recherches sur la probabilité des jugements en matière criminelle et en matière civile*. Paris: Bachelier.

Ramsey, F.P. 1926. Truth and probability. In *The Foundations of Mathematics and Other Logical Essays*, London: Kegan Paul; New York: Harcourt, Brace & Co. Reprinted in Kyburg and Smokler (1980).

Rosenkrantz, R.D. 1977. *Inference, Method and Decision*. Dordrecht, Holland: Reidel.

Savage, L.J. 1954. *The Foundations of Statistics*. New York: John Wiley.

Schroedinger, E. 1947. The foundation of probability. *Proceedings of the Royal Irish Academy* 51A, 51–66 and 141–6.

Shackle, G.L.S. 1949. *Expectation in Economics*. Cambridge: Cambridge University Press.

Smith, C.A.B. 1961. Consistency in statistical inference and decision. *Journal of the Royal Statistical Society*, Series B, 23, 1–37 (with discussion).

Weaver, W. 1948. Probability, rarity, interest and surprise. *Scientific Monthly* 67, 390–92.

Yule, G.U. 1903. Notes on the theory of association of attributes in statistics. *Biometrika* 2, 121–34. Reprinted in *Statistical Papers of George Udny Yule*, ed. A. Stuart and M.G. Kendall, London: Griffin, 1971, 71–84.

Zellner, A. 1971. *An Introduction to Bayesian Inference in Econometrics*. New York: John Wiley.

Zellner, A. (ed.) 1980. *Bayesian Analysis in Econometrics and Statistics: Essays in Honor of Harold Jeffreys*. Amsterdam: North-Holland.

Time Preference

MURRAY N. ROTHBARD

Time preference is the insight that people prefer 'present goods' (goods available for use at present) to 'future goods' (present expectations of goods becoming available at some date in the future), and that the social rate of time preference, the result of the interactions of individual time preference schedules, will determine and be equal to the pure rate of interest in a society. The economy is pervaded by a time market for present as against future goods, not only in the market for loans (in which creditors trade present money for the right to receive money in the future), but also as a 'natural rate' in all processes of production. For capitalists pay out present money to buy or rent land, capital goods, and raw materials, and to hire labour (as well as buying labour outright in a system of slavery), thereby purchasing expectations of future revenue from the eventual sales of product. Long-run profit rates and rates of return on capital are therefore forms of interest rate. As businessmen seek to gain profits and avoid losses, the economy will tend toward a general equilibrium, in which all interest rates and rates of return will be equal, and hence there will be no pure entrepreneurial profits or losses.

In centuries of wrestling with the vexed question of the justification of interest, the Catholic scholastic philosophers arrived at highly sophisticated explanations and justifications of return on capital, including risk and the opportunity cost of profit foregone. But they had extreme difficulty with the interest on a riskless loan, and hence denounced all such interest as sinful and usurious.

Some of the later scholastics, however, in their more favourable view of usury, began to approach a time preference explanation of interest. During a comprehensive demolition of the standard arguments for the prohibition of usury in his *Treatise on Contracts* (1499), Conrad Summenhart (1465–1511), theologian at the University of Tübingen, used time preference to justify the purchase of a discounted debt, even if the debt be newly created. When someone pays $100 for the right to obtain $110 at a future date, the buyer (lender) doesn't profit usuriously from the loan because both he and the seller (borrower) value the future $110 as being worth $100 at the present time (Noonan, 1957).

A half-century later, the distinguished Dominican canon lawyer and monetary theorist at the University of Salamanca, Martin de Azpilcueta Navarrus (1493–1586) clearly set forth the concept of time preference, but failed to apply it to a defence of usury. In his *Commentary on Usury* (1556), Azpilcueta pointed out that a present good, such as money, will naturally be worth more on the market than future goods, that is, claims to money in the future. As Azpilcueta put it:

> a claim on something is worth less than the thing itself, and ... it is plain that that which is not usable for a year is less valuable than something of the same quality which is usable at once (Gordon, 1975, p. 215).

At about the same time, the Italian humanist and politician Gian Francesco Lottini da Volterra, in his handbook of advice to princes, *Avvedimenti civili* (1574), discovered time preference. Unfortunately, Lottini also inaugurated the tradition of moralistically deploring time preference as an over-estimation of a present that can be grasped immediately by the sense (Kauder, 1965, pp. 19–22).

Two centuries later, the Neapolitan abbé, Ferdinando Galiani (1728–87) revived the rudiments of time-preference in his *Della Moneta* (1751) (Monroe, 1924). Galiani pointed out that just as the exchange rate of two currencies equates the value of a present and a spatially distant money, so the rate of interest equates present with future, or temporally distant, money. What is being equated is not physical properties, but subjective values in the minds of individuals.

These scattered hints scarcely prepare one for the remarkable development of a full-scale time preference theory of interest by the French statesman. Anne Robert Jacques Turgot (1727–81), who, in a relatively few hastily written contributions, anticipated almost completely the later Austrian theory of capital and interest (Turgot, 1977). In the course of a paper defending usury, Turgot asked: why are borrowers willing to pay an interest premium for the use of money? The focus should not be on the amount of metal repaid but on the usefulness of the money to the lender and borrower. In particular, Turgot compares the 'difference in usefulness which exists at the date of borrowing between a sum currently owned and an equal sum which is to be received at a distant date', and notes the well-known motto, 'a bird in the hand is better than two in the bush'. Since the sum of money owned now 'is preferable to the assurance of receiving a similar sum in one or several years' time', returning the same principal means that the lender 'gives the money and receives only an assurance'. Therefore, interest compensates for this difference in value by a sum proportionate to the length of the delay. Turgot added that what must be compared in a loan transaction is not the value of money lent with the value repaid, but rather the 'value of the *promise* of a sum of money compared to the value of money available now' (Turgot, 1977, pp. 158–9).

In addition, Turgot was apparently the first to arrive at the concept of *capitalization*, a corollary to time preference, which holds that the present capital value of any durable good will tend to equal the sum of its expected annual rents, or returns, discounted by the market rate of time preference, or rate of interest.

Turgot also pioneered in analysing the relation between the quantity of money and interest rates. If an increased supply of money goes to low time preference people, then the increased proportion of savings to consumption lowers time preference and hence interest rates fall while prices rise. But if an increased quantity goes into the hands of high time preference people, the opposite would happen and interest rates would rise along with prices. Generally, over recent centuries, he noted, the spirit of thrift has been growing in Europe and hence time preference rates and interest rates have tended to fall.

One of the notable injustices in the historiography of economic thought was Böhm-Bawerk's brusque dismissal in 1884 of Turgot's anticipation of his own time-preference theory of interest as merely a 'land fructification theory' (Böhm-Bawerk, I, 1959). Partly this dismissal stemmed from Böhm's methodology of clearing the ground for his own positive theory of interest by demolishing, and hence sometimes doing injustice to, his own forerunners (Wicksell, 1911, p. 177). The unfairness is particularly glaring in the case of Turgot, because we now know that in 1876, only eight years before the publication of his history of theories of interest, Böhm-Bawerk wrote a glowing tribute to Turgot's theory of interest in an as yet unpublished paper in Karl Knies's seminar at the University of Heidelberg (Turgot, 1977, pp. xxix–xxx).

In the course of his demolition of the Ricardo–James Mill labour theory of value on behalf of a subjective utility theory, Samuel Bailey (1825) clearly set forth the concept of time preference. Rebutting Mill's statement that time, as a 'mere abstract word', could not add to value, Bailey declared that 'we generally prefer a present pleasure or enjoyment to a distant one', and therefore prefer present goods to waiting for goods to arrive in the future. Bailey, however, did not go on to apply his insight to interest.

In the mid-1830s, the Irish economist Samuel Mountifort Longfield worked out the later Austrian theory of capital as performing the service for workers of supplying money at present instead of waiting for the future when the product will be sold. In turn the capitalist receives from the workers a time discount from their productivity. As Longfield put it, the capitalist

> pays the wages immediately, and in return receives the value of [the worker's] labour, ... [which] is greater than the wages of that labour. The difference is the profit made by the capitalist for his advances ... as it were, the discount which the labourer pays for prompt payment (Longfield, 1834).

The 'pre-Austrian' time analysis of capital and interest was most fully worked out, in the same year 1834, by the Scottish and Canadian eccentric John Rae (1786–1872). In the course of attempting an anti-Smithian defence of the protective tariff, Rae, in his *Some New Principles on the Subject of Political Economy* (1834), developed the Böhm-Bawerkian time analysis of capital, pointing out that investment lengthens the time involved in the processes of production. Rae noted that the capitalist must weigh the greater productivity of longer production processes against waiting for them to come to fruition. Capitalists will sacrifice present money for a greater return in the future, the difference – the interest return – reflecting the social rate of time preference. Rae saw that people's time preference rates reflect their cultural and psychological willingness to take a shorter or longer view of the future. His moral preferences were clearly with the low time preference thrifty as against the high time preference people who suffer from a 'defect of the imagination'. Rae's analysis had little impact on economics until resurrected at the turn of the 20th century, whereupon it was generously hailed in the later editions of Böhm-Bawerk's history of interest theories (Böhm-Bawerk, I, 1959).

Time preference, as a concept and as a foundation for the explanation of interest, has been an outstanding feature of the Austrian School of economics. Its founder, Carl Menger (1840–1921), enunciated the concept of time preference in 1871, pointing out that satisfying the immediate needs of life and health are necessarily prerequisites for satisfying more remote future needs. In addition, Menger declared, 'all experience teaches that we humans consider a present pleasure, or one expected in the near future, more important than one of the same intensity which is not expected to occur until some more distant time' (Wicksell, 1924, p. 195; Menger, 1871, pp. 153–54). But Menger never extended time preference from his value theory to a theory of interest; and when his follower Böhm-Bawerk did so, he peevishly deleted this discussion from the second edition of his *Principles of Economics* (Wicksell, 1924, pp. 195–6).

Böhm-Bawerk's *Capital and Interest* (1884) is the *locus classicus* of the time preference theory of interest. In his first, historical volume, he demolished all other theories, in particular the productivity theory of interest, but five years later, in his *Positive Theory of Capital* (1889), Böhm brought back the productivity theory in an attempt to combine it with a time preference explanation of interest (Böhm-Bawerk, I, II, 1959). In his 'three grounds' for the explanation of interest, time preference constituted two, and the greater productivity of longer processes of production the third, Böhm ironically placing greatest importance upon the third ground. Influenced strongly by Böhm-Bawerk, Irving Fisher increasingly took the same path of stressing the marginal productivity of capital as the main determinant of interest (Fisher, 1907, 1930).

With the work of Böhm-Bawerk and Fisher, the modern theory of interest was set squarely on the path of placing time preference in a subordinate role in the explanation of interest: determining only the rate of consumer loans, and the supply of consumer savings, while the alleged productivity of capital determines the more important demand for loans and for savings. Hence, modern interest theory fails to integrate interest on consumer loans and producer's returns into a coherent explanation.

In contrast, Frank A. Fetter, building on Böhm-Bawerk, completely discarded productivity as an explanation of interest and constructed an integrated theory of value and distribution in which interest is determined solely by time preference, while marginal productivity determines the 'rental prices' of the factors of production (Fetter, 1915, 1977). In his outstanding critique of Böhm-Bawerk, Fetter pointed out a fundamental error of the third ground in trying to explain the return on capital as 'present goods' earning a return for their productivity in the future; instead, capital goods are *future* goods, since they are only valuable in the expectation of being used to produce goods that will be sold to the consumer at a future date (Fetter, 1902). One way of seeing the fallacy of a productivity explanation of interest is to look at the typical practice of any current microeconomics text: after explaining marginal productivity as determining the demand curve for factors with wage rates on the *y*-axis, the textbook airily shifts to interest rates on the *y*-axis to illustrate the marginal productivity determination of interest. But the analog on the *y*-axis should not be interest, which is a ratio and not a price, but rather the *rental price* (price per unit time) of a capital good. Thus, interest remains totally unexplained. In short, as Fetter pointed out, marginal productivity determines rental prices, and time preference determines the rate of interest, while the capital value of a factor of production is the expected sum of future rents from a durable factor discounted by the rate of time preference or interest.

The leading economist adopting Fetter's pure time preference view of interest was Ludwig von Mises, in his *Human Action* (Mises, 1949). Mises amended the theory in two important ways. First, he rid the concept of its moralistic tone which had been continued by Böhm-Bawerk, implicitly criticizing people for 'under'-estimating the future. Mises made clear that a positive time preference rate is an essential attribute of human nature. Secondly, and as a corollary, whereas Fetter believed that people could have either positive or negative rates of time preference, Mises demonstrated that a positive rate is deducible from the fact of human action, since by the very nature of a goal or an end people wish to achieve that goal as soon as possible.

BIBLIOGRAPHY

Bailey, S. 1825. *A Critical Dissertation on the Nature, Measure, and Causes of Value.* New York: Augustus M. Kelly, 1967.

Böhm-Bawerk, E. von 1884–9. *Kapital und Kapitalzins. Zweite Abteilung: Positive Theorie des Kapitales.* 4th edn. Trans by I.D. Huncke as *Capital and Interest*, Vols I and II. South Holland, Ill.: Libertarian Press, 1959.

Fetter, F.A. 1902. The 'Roundabout process' in the interest theory. *Quarterly Journal of Economics* 17, November, 163–80. Reprinted in F.A. Fetter, *Capital, Interest and Rent: Essays in the Theory of Distribution*, ed. M. Rothbard, Kansas City: Sheed Andrews and McMeel, 1977.

Fetter, F.A. 1915. *Economic Principles*, Vol I. New York: The Century Co.

Fetter, F.A. 1977. *Capital, Interest, and Rent: Essays in the Theory of Distribution.* Ed. M. Rothbard, Kansas City: Sheed Andrews and McMeel.

Fisher, I. 1907. *The Rate of Interest.* New York: Macmillan.

Fisher, I. 1930. *The Theory of Interest.* New York: Kelley & Millman, 1954.

Gordon, B. 1975. *Economic Analysis Before Adam Smith; Hesiod to Lessius.* New York: Barnes & Noble.

Kauder, E. 1965. *A History of Marginal Utility Theory*. Princeton: Princeton University Press.

Longfield, S.M. 1971. *The Economic Writings of Mountifort Longfield*. Ed. R.D.C. Black, Clifton, NJ: Augustus M. Kelley.

Menger, C. 1871. *Principles of Economics*. Ed. J. Dingwall and B. Hoselitz, Glencoe, Ill.: Free Press, 1950.

Mises, L. von. 1949. *Human Action: a treatise on economics*. 3rd revised edn, Chicago: Regnery, 1966.

Monroe, A. (ed.) 1924. *Early Economic Thought*. Cambridge, Mass.: Harvard University Press.

Noonan, J.T., Jr. 1957. *The Scholastic Analysis of Usury*. Cambridge, Mass.: Harvard University Press.

Rae, J. 1834. *Some New Principles on the Subject of Political Economy*. In *John Rae: Political Economist*, ed. R.W. James, Toronto: University of Toronto Press, 1965.

Turgot, A.R.J. 1977. *The Economics of A.R.J. Turgot*. Ed. P.D. Groenewegen, The Hague: Martinus Nijhoff.

Wicksell, K. 1911. Böhm-Bawerk's theory of interest. In K. Wicksell, *Selected Papers on Economic Theory*, ed. E. Lindahl, Cambridge, Mass.: Harvard University Press, 1958.

Wicksell, K. 1924. The new edition of Menger's *Grundsatze*. In K. Wicksell, *Selected Papers on Economic Theory*, ed. E. Lindahl, Cambridge, Mass.: Harvard University Press, 1958.

Transitivity

WAYNE SHAFER

Transitivity is formally just a property that a binary relation might possess, and thus one could discuss the concept in any context in economics in which an ordering relation is used. Here, however, the discussion of transitivity will be limited to its role in describing an individual agent's choice behaviour. In this context transitivity means roughly that if an agent choses A over B, and B over C, that agent ought to choose A over C, or at least be indifferent. On the surface this seems reasonable, even 'rational', but this ignores how complicated an agent's decision making process can be. For an excellent discussion of this issue see May (1954). Given a model of agent behaviour, transitivity can be imposed as a direct assumption, or can be an implication of the model for choice behaviour. The standard model of agent behaviour in economics is that the agent orders prospects by means of a utility function, which in effect assumes transitivity. With appropriate continuity and convexity restrictions on utility functions, the model allows one to demonstrate that: (1) Individual demand functions are well defined, continuous, and satisfy the comparative static restriction, the Strong Axiom of Revealed Preference (SARP). (In the smooth case, this corresponds to the negative semidefiniteness and symmetry of the Slutsky matrix.) (2) Given a finite collection of such agents with initial endowments of goods, a competitive equilibrium exists. What will be discussed in the remaining part of this essay is to what extent one can obtain results analogous to (1) and (2) above while using a model of agent behaviour which does not assume or imply transitive behaviour. To keep the discussion as simple as possible, we will only consider the situation in which the agent's set of feasible commodity vectors is the non-negative orthant of n-dimensional Euclidean space, and the agent's problem is to choose a commodity vector x when faced with positive prices and income. A vector p in the positive orthant of Euclidean n-space will denote the vector of price–income ratios, or a 'price' system.

Two models of agent behaviour which have a long history in economics will now be described. The first, which will be called the 'local' theory, takes as its primitive the assumption that if an agent is currently consuming at a vector x, he is able to determine if an infinitesimal change in x, say x to $x + dx$, is a change for better or worse. This idea is represented by a function $x \rightarrow g(x)$, mapping each vector x into a n-vector $g(x)$ such that a small movement from x in the direction of y is an improvement if $g(x)(y - x) > 0$, and not an improvement otherwise. Given a price system p, an affordable x is an equilibrium point for the agent if $g(x)(y - x) \leqslant 0$ for all affordable y. That is, no small movement from x in the direction of an affordable y is an improvement. A basic question is whether for every p, an equilibrium x exists. This approach goes back at least to Pareto, and most economists, including Pareto, concerned themselves with the 'integrability' problem; when is there a quasi-concave utility function such that $g(x)$ is a positive scalar multiple of the vector of marginal utilities, for each x? Note that if an agent has a differentiable quasi-concave utility function u, and one defines g by $g(x) = \lambda(x)Du(x)$ for any $\lambda(x) > 0$, then $g(x)(y - x) > 0$ is equivalent to $Du(x)(y - x) > 0$, and this implies $u(x + t(y - x)) > u(x)$ for t positive and sufficiently small. Thus if g is 'integrable', the agent acts as if he maximizes a utility function, and thus results (1) or (2) above will be satisfied. Some economists, however, believed that the local theory could be used to describe agent behaviour without assuming the integrability conditions. Most notable is the work of Allen (1932), Georgescu-Roegen (1936; 1954) and Katzner (1971). Without the integrability conditions and the implied utility function (and thus implied transitivity) the existence of an equilibrium x given any p is nontrivial. This problem was solved by Georgescu-Roegen (1954), who showed that if g is continuous and g satisfied the 'Principal of Persistent Nonpreference' (PPN), that is, $g(x)(y - x) < 0$ implies $g(y)(x - y) > 0$, then an equilibrium point will exist in any budget set. It should be noted that the integrability problem mentioned above requires PPN (for quasi-concave utility), as well as the Frobenius conditions for mathematical integrability. It is easy to show that Georgescu-Roegen's assumptions imply that the resulting demand correspondence will be upper-hemicontinuous.

The second basic approach to modelling agent behaviour will be called the 'global' theory. In this approach, the primitive of the theory is a binary relation R on the commodity space with xRy having the interpretation 'x is at least as good as y'. Define the strict preference relation P by xPy is equivalent to not yRx. (P could also be taken as the primitive.) Given a price system p, an affordable x is an equilibrium point if yPx implies $py > 1$, i.e., any vector y preferred to x is not affordable. A basic question is whether such an equilibrium point will exist. This approach dates back to Frisch (1926), and the usual approach was to specify conditions on R which imply R has a representation by a continuous utility function, i.e., $u(x) \geqslant u(y)$ equivalent to xRy. This problem was solved by Debreu (1954), who showed that R must be reflexive, complete, transitive and continuous. With the addition of appropriate convexity conditions, this approach yields the results (1) and (2) above. However, in a remarkable paper, Sonnenschein (1971) showed that one could remove transitivity from the list of standard assumptions and still have a well defined demand correspondence which is upper-hemicontinuous.

Specifically, he demonstrated that if R is continuous, reflexive, and $P(x) = \{y: yPx\}$ is convex for all x, then an equilibrium point will exist in any budget set, and the resulting demand correspondence is upper-hemicontinuous. (He also assumed R is complete, but that assumption was used only to show that an equilibrium point is comparable to every affordable y.) Note that if g represents local theory, and g is continuous, then the R defined by xRy is equivalent to $g(x)(y - x) < 0$, satisfies Sonnenschein's conditions, and an equilibrium x for R is an equilibrium point for g, in any budget. Thus Sonnenschein demonstrated that Georgescu–Roegen's condition PPN is not necessary for the existence of equilibrium points in a budget set.

In order to resolve question (1) above, a theory must predict a unique equilibrium point in each budget set, in order to get a well defined demand function. In the local theory, if one assumes $g(x) \neq 0$ for all x and strengthens PPN to SPPN: $g(x)(y - x) \leqslant 0$, $x \neq y$ implies $g(y)(x - y) > 0$, then the equilibrium point x will be unique in any budget, and the resulting demand function will be continuous and satisfy the Weak Axiom of Revealed Preference (WARP). Thus the local theory, without assuming mathematical integrability (implies transitivity), yields a theory of individual demand functions satisfying WARP. On the other hand, given a continuous demand function h satisfying WARP, if h has a continuous inverse, then $g = h^{-1}$ yields a local theory with g satisfying SPNN and generating h. Now consider the global theory. If R is represented by a continuous, strictly quasi-concave nonsatiated utility function, then R will be reflexive, complete, transitive, strongly convex and nonsatiated. If one simply removes the assumption of transitivity from this list, then Sonnenschein's result implies that an equilibrium point will exist, and the remaining assumptions imply that this point will be unique, and that the resulting demand function will be continuous and satisfy WARP (see Shafer, 1974). Furthermore, Kim and Richter (1986) showed, that with a slight variation in the assumptions on R, any continuous demand function h satisfying a modified version of WARP can be generated by such an R. Thus, from the point of view of having single value demand functions, the absence of transitivity, either assumed as in the global theory or implied as in the local theory, is essentially equivalent to Samuelson's theory of observed demand satisfying WARP. Since WARP includes the 'law of demand', i.e., normal goods have downward sloping demand, in my view little is lost by not assuming transitivity.

Now question (2) above: the problem of existence of competitive equilibrium will be discussed. Again, Sonnenschein observed that if one took the standard assumptions on R normally used in proofs of existence of a competitive equilibrium, and removed the transitivity assumption, then demand correspondences would be well defined and convex valued, and the standard proof techniques would still work, so equilibrium would exist. Thus transitivity is irrelevant to demonstrating the internal consistency of the competitive model. Note, however, that the assumptions needed by Sonnenschein to demonstrate that individual demand correspondences are well defined and upper-hemicontinuous, namely continuity and convex preferred sets, are too weak to ensure convex valued demand correspondences. Nevertheless, Mas-Colell (1974) demonstrated that with only these assumptions on preferences, competitive equilibria will exist. Thus the only properties of individual preferences which are important to the existence of competitive equilibrium are continuity and convexity.

BIBLIOGRAPHY

Allen, R.G.D. 1932. The foundations of a mathematical theory of exchange. *Economica* 12, 197–226.

Debreu, G. 1954. Representation of a preference ordering by a numerical function. In *Decision Processes*, ed. R.M. Thrall, C.H. Combs and R.L. Davis, New York: Wiley, 159–65.

Frisch, R. 1926. Sur un problème d'èconomie pure. *Norsk mathematisk forenings skrifter* 16, 1–40.

Gorgescu-Roegen, N. 1936. The pure theory of consumer's behavior. *Quarterly Journal of Economics* 50, August, 545–93.

Georgescu-Roegen, N. 1954. Choice and revealed preference. *Southern Economic Journal* 21, October, 119–30.

Katzner, D. 1971. Demand and exchange analysis in the absence of integrability conditions. In *Preferences, Utility, and Demand*, ed. J. Chipman et al., New York: Harcourt, Brace, Jovanovich, 254–70.

Kim, T. and Richter, M. 1986. Nontransitive-nontotal consumer theory. *Journal of Economic Theory* 38, April, 324–63.

Mas-Colell, A. 1974. An equilibrium existence theorem without complete or transitive preferences. *Journal of Mathematical Economics* 1, 237–46.

May, K. 1954. Intransitivity, utility, and aggregation in preference patterns. *Econometrica* 22, January, 1–13.

Shafer, W. 1974. The nontransitive consumer. *Econometrica* 42, 913–19.

Sonnenschein, H. 1971. Demand theory without transitive preferences, with applications to the theory of competitive equilibrium. In *Preferences, Utility, and Demand*, ed. J. Chipman et al., New York: Harcourt, Brace, Jovanovich, 215–23.

Uncertainty

PETER J. HAMMOND

Nothing is more certain than the prevalence of uncertainty about the consequences of any economic decision. It is therefore entirely appropriate that uncertainty has been the subject of a large literature that grew out of important work in the early 1950s, and is still flourishing, as testified by the number of recent surveys and books such as Balch, McFadden and Wu (1974), Diamond and Rothschild (1978), Hirshleifer and Riley (1979), Lippman and McCall (1981), Fishburn (1982), Schoemaker (1982), Sinn (1983). No attempt will be made here to provide a comprehensive new survey. Rather, the devices of state contingent consequence functions and state preferences will be explained, and various types of uncertainty categorized. Following the pioneering work of Ramsey (1926), Savage (1954), and Anscombe and Aumann (1963) in particular, I shall discuss decision theory and when uncertainty can be described by subjective probabilities, based on an analysis of decision trees in the spirit of Raiffa (1968). While uncertainty *per se* can be largely treated through devices such as Debreu (1959) state contingent commodity contracts, the problems posed by asymmetric information and the lack of common knowledge are much more fundamental and intractable.

STATES OF THE WORLD AND CONTINGENT CONSEQUENCES. Economics is the scientific study of decisions affecting the allocation of scarce resources between competing ends. *Uncertainty* arises whenever a decision can lead to more than one possible consequence. Following Savage (1954, ch. 2) the term *state of the world* is commonly used to describe whatever determines the uncertain consequence of a decision. Formally, states of the world s in the set S, decisions d in the set D, and consequences c in the set C must be defined in a way which ensures that the consequences $c(d, s)$ of any decision d in any state of the world s is uniquely determined. Thus, states of the world must be defined so finely that no decision can possibly have more than one consequence in a given state of the world. Given the set S of possible states of the world, any decision d gives rise to a *contingent consequence function* (CCF) γ_d mapping S into the set of consequences C, given by:

$$\gamma_d(s) = c(d, s) \qquad (\text{all } s \in S). \tag{1}$$

Savage (1954) even defines an 'act' (or decision) as such a contingent consequence function, but this may be confusing because decisions which seem very different a priori may lead to identical CCFs. Jeffrey (1974) especially questions seriously whether decisions can ever have their consequences described so precisely in practice, and Jeffrey (1965) and Bolker (1967) have constructed a decision theory without using CCFs. But one might argue that their objections can be met by employing a much richer space of consequences.

CATEGORIES OF ECONOMIC UNCERTAINTY. In economics several different kinds of uncertainty arise, according to what aspect of the 'state of the world' is being considered. The first kind is *exogenous uncertainty*, concerning variables like consumers' tastes and firms' technologies which the economist usually treats as exogenous. An obvious example is the weather which affects both consumers' tastes and farmers' production possibilities in predictable ways. Other examples are medical uncertainties affecting a person's contracting a disease and recovery from it, as well as various kinds of accident. Often insurance against adverse exogenous uncertainty is available.

No economic system can reduce exogenous uncertainty although insurance may help to mitigate its impact upon individuals. Other kinds of uncertainty, however, concern the operation of the economic system itself. In market economies, a buyer may be uncertain whether he will meet a suitable seller, and vice versa. Both may be uncertain about the terms at which trade will take place, as in the extensive literatures on search theory and bargaining. Such uncertainty can be reduced, to some extent, by individuals who take the trouble to search extensively. It can also be created by sellers who change their prices frequently and unpredictably, as currently exemplified by de-regulated airlines in the USA. Such uncertainty is *endogenous*; it results from the decisions of economic agents, which it is the task of the economist to explain and/or predict. Notice too that endogenous and exogenous uncertainty can interact, as when a dam bursts because of a combination of cost-cutting carelessness by the constructor – which is endogenous – and an exceptionally severe rainstorm – which is exogenous. The unhealthy effects of cigarette smoking also result from a combination of endogenous decisions affecting smoking and exogenous factors determining a smoker's susceptibility to disease.

An important kind of uncertainty in modern economies concerns economic policy and its impact on the tax system, interest rates, the provision of public goods, etc. This is *policy uncertainty* which, to the economist at least, is really a form of exogenous uncertainty, since it is the task of political science to explain policy.

Finally, a recent development is work on *extrinsic uncertainty*, due to Cass and Shell (1983). By 'extrinsic' uncertainty, they mean that there is no uncertainty about the usual exogenous variables such as tastes and technology, which would

281

constitute 'intrinsic' uncertainty of a kind one naturally expects to affect the allocation of resources in an economy. They give 'sunspots' as an example of extrinsic uncertainty. They show that, in market economies where there are some agents who cannot insure themselves against extrinsic uncertainty before they are born, there may exist 'sunspot' equilibria in which the allocation depends upon the outcome of extrinsic uncertainty. This may be so even though there is a unique equilibrium in which extrinsic uncertainty does not matter. Thus the 'sunspot' equilibrium is not just some randomization of 'non-sunspot' equilibria, and the competitive market system is quite capable of producing uncertainty which is completely unrelated to any intrinsic uncertainty. It should be added that recent work on equilibrium with incomplete financial markets shows that there is likely to be a continuum of multiple equilibria, which suggests an even more prevalent form of extrinsic uncertainty regarding equilibrium prices and the resulting allocation of resources.

FROM STATE PREFERENCES TO RANDOM CONSEQUENCES. Earlier, contingent consequence functions (CCFs) were defined to describe uncertainty about the consequences of a decision. Particular examples of CCFs are the contingent commodity contracts of Debreu (1959, ch. 7). Arrow's (1953) ingenious device of contingent securities is closely related, provided that agents always foresee correctly at what prices they will be able to trade later on. For the 'Arrow–Debreu' theory of complete markets, it suffices to postulate that consumers have 'regular' preferences – obeying the standard properties – over the space of contingent commodity bundles, with goods distinguished by the state of the world in which they are available, as well as by physical properties including location and date. Indeed, a great deal of standard economic analysis applies in this case, as was realized by Hirshleifer (1966). His 'state-preference' approach to economic decisions under uncertainty relies precisely upon preferences over contingent commodity bundles.

The state preference approach makes no explicit reference to probabilities of states of the world, although implicitly a consumer's marginal willingness to pay for consumption in a specific state s will be higher, the more likely the occurrence of state s is believed to be. This observation suggests that it may be useful to consider how state preferences depend upon probabilities in those cases where probabilities are known. Of course, this is the subject of expected utility theory, discussed below, whose origins can be traced back at least to D. Bernoulli's (1738) attempt to resolve the 'St Petersburg paradox'. If probabilities are indeed known, then two CCFs which yield the same probability distribution of consequences may be regarded as equivalent. For example, suppose there are three states s_1, s_2, s_3 each with probability $1/3$. Let c_1, c_2 be any pair of consequences. Then the three CCF's γ_1, γ_2 and γ_3 given by:

$$\gamma_1(s_1) = c_1, \quad \gamma_1(s_2) = c_1, \quad \gamma_1(s_3) = c_2$$
$$\gamma_2(s_1) = c_2, \quad \gamma_2(s_2) = c_1, \quad \gamma_2(s_3) = c_1$$
$$\gamma_3(s_1) = c_1, \quad \gamma_3(s_2) = c_2, \quad \gamma_3(s_3) = c_1 \tag{2}$$

all yield the same probability distribution of consequences, in which c_1 occurs with probability $2/3$ and c_2 occurs with probability $1/3$.

So, if every state of the world s happens to have an associated probability π_s, then uncertain consequences are equivalent to random consequences. For, given any CCF $\gamma: S \to C$, there is an associated probability distribution $\mu(\gamma, \pi)$ on C defined by:

$$\mu(\gamma, \pi)(B) = \sum_{s \in S(\gamma, B)} \pi_s \tag{3}$$

for every set of consequences B, a subset of C, where:

$$S(\gamma, B) = \{s \in S \mid \gamma(s) \in B\}. \tag{4}$$

(There are some technical problems of measurability here, which I shall avoid by assuming that the set S of possible states of the world is finite.)

Thus, corresponding to a preference ordering $\succsim$ on the space $M(C)$ of probability distributions over C, and to the probability distribution π on S the set of states of the world, there exists a unique corresponding preference ordering $\succsim(\pi)$ on the set S^C of CCF's $\gamma: S \to C$, with:

$$\gamma_1 \succsim(\pi)\gamma_2 \Leftrightarrow \mu(\gamma_1, \pi) \succsim \mu(\gamma_2, \pi) \tag{5}$$

for all pairs $\gamma_1, \gamma_2: S \to C$. Preferences over probability distributions in $M(C)$ then induce preferences over CCF's because each CCF γ gives rise to a unique probability distribution μ_γ in $M(C)$.

In principle, one could go on to ask whether, even if probabilities π_s are not known, there may be a (unique) probability distribution $\bar{\pi}$ on S such that $\succsim(\bar{\pi})$ is the preference ordering for CCF's.

If this is true for a unique probability distribution $\bar{\pi}$ on S, then one can say that $\bar{\pi}$ is the *subjective probability distribution*. The existence of subjective probabilities for general preferences $\succsim$ over $M(C)$ may appear to be a problem of some theoretical interest, in the spirit of Machina's (1982) recent work. Yet, understandably, the literature has concentrated upon a particularly appealing special case, in which the preference ordering $\succsim$ has an expected utility representation, relying upon the independence axiom which I shall discuss next. This leads to the theory of the simultaneous determination of subjective probabilities and utility which Savage (1954) and Anscombe and Aumann (1963) based on the fundamental ideas of Ramsey (1926) who was in turn apparently stimulated by Keynes (1921).

THE INDEPENDENCE AXIOM AND EXPECTED UTILITY. The independence axiom can be motivated as follows, using an idea due to Raiffa (1968, pp. 82–3). Suppose there is a decision tree with a chance node n_0, which is succeeded either by node n_1 with probability λ (where $0 < \lambda \leqslant 1$) or by node n_2 with probability $1 - \lambda$. Suppose too that at n_1 the decision maker chooses between two acts a_1 and a_2, and that act a_j results in the random consequence $\mu_j \in M(C)$ $(j = 1, 2)$. At n_2, on the other hand, there is no decision to make and the random consequence is μ_0. Then the decision maker chooses a_1 over a_2 at node n_1 if and only if he prefers μ_1 to μ_2. On the other hand, at node n_0, the decision maker will plan to choose a_1 over a_2 if and only if the random consequence $\lambda\mu_1 + (1 - \lambda)\mu_0$ is preferred to the alternative random consequence $\lambda\mu_2 + (1 - \lambda)\mu_0$. For, when μ_0 is still a possible random consequence because the decision maker does not know whether n_1 or n_2 will occur, the random consequence of planning to choose a_j if n_1 does occur is indeed $\lambda\mu_j + (1 - \lambda)\mu_0$ $(j = 1, 2)$. Thus, requiring plans to be consistent with actual later choices implies that:

$$\lambda\mu_1 + (1 - \lambda)\mu_0 \gtrsim \lambda\mu_2 + (1 - \lambda)\mu_0 \Leftrightarrow \mu_1 \gtrsim \mu_2 \tag{6}$$

for all random consequences μ_0, μ_1 and μ_2 and for all λ satisfying $0 < \lambda \leqslant 1$. This is the *independence axiom*, originally formulated by Samuelson (1952).

The *expected utility hypothesis* requires the existence of a 'von Neumann–Morgenstern utility function' (NMUF) v, defined on C the space of consequences, with the property that for all pairs μ', μ'' of random consequences in $M(C)$:

$$\mu' \gtrsim \mu'' \Leftrightarrow E_{\mu'}v \geqslant E_{\mu''}v \tag{7}$$

where $E_\mu v$ is defined, for every μ in $M(C)$, as the expected utility expression:

$$E_\mu v = \sum_{c \in C} \mu(\{c\})v(c). \tag{8}$$

The NMUF v can be replaced by any other NMUF $\tilde{v}$ which is cardinally equivalent, in the sense that:

$$\tilde{v}(c) \equiv \alpha v(c) + \beta \tag{9}$$

for some positive multiplicative constant α and an arbitrary additive constant β.

It is easy to check that the expected utility hypothesis implies the independence axiom. The converse is not true; without an extra assumption such as preferences being continuous in probabilities, the independence axiom does not imply the expected utility hypothesis – one can still have multidimensional or lexicographic utilities (see Hausner (1954), Thrall (1954) and Skala (1975)). But such a continuity condition or 'Archimedean axiom' is sufficient (see Herstein and Milnor, 1953) and is anyway mostly just a technical requirement.

THE SURE-THING PRINCIPLE. Now we can return to the question posed earlier concerning the existence of subjective probabilities, but making use of the expected utility framework. Given that the preference ordering $\gtrsim$ is represented by the expected utility expression $E_\mu v$, do there exist unique subjective probabilities $\pi_s (s \in S)$ for which the preference ordering $\gtrsim(\pi)$ on C^S, the space of CCF's, is represented by the subjectively expected utility expression:

$$\sum_{s \in S} \pi_s v(\lambda(s))? \tag{10}$$

Just as the independence axiom is necessary for (7) to hold, a corresponding 'sure-thing principle' is required if (10) is indeed to represent the ordering $\succsim(\pi)$. This sure-thing principle has a similar motivation, moreover. Indeed, suppose that there is a decision tree in which 'nature' determines at node n_0 which of two disjoint events, either E or F, occurs. If E occurs at n_0, then the next node of the tree is n_1 at which the decision maker chooses between the two acts a_1 and a_2; if a_j is chosen, the consequences are described by $\gamma_j(s)$ ($s \in E; j = 1, 2$). On the other hand, if F occurs at n_0, there is no decision to make, and the consequences are described by $\gamma(s)$ ($s \in F$). Now the decision maker chooses a_1 over a_2 at n_1 if and only if the CCF $\gamma_1 : E \to C$ is preferred to the alternative CCF $\gamma_2 : E \to C$. On the other hand, suppose that the two CCF's $\bar{\gamma}_j : S \to C$ ($j = 1, 2$) are defined by:

$$\bar{\gamma}_j(s) = \begin{cases} \gamma_j(s) & (s \in E) \\ \gamma(s) & (s \in F). \end{cases} \tag{11}$$

Then the decision maker at node n_0 will plan to choose a_1 over a_2 if and only if he prefers the CCF $\bar{\gamma}_1$ to $\bar{\gamma}_2$, because the CCF $\bar{\gamma}_j$ is what results from a combination of the uncertainty at node n_0 about the event E or F with the consequences of choosing act a_j at node n_1. For consistency of plans with actual choices later on, it must be true that:

$$\bar{\gamma}_1 \succsim^*_S \bar{\gamma}_2 \Leftrightarrow \gamma_1^E \succsim^*_E \gamma_2^E \tag{12}$$

where $\succsim^*_S$ denotes the preference ordering over C^S, the space of CCF's $\gamma : S \to C$, and $\succsim^*_E$ is the preference ordering over C^E, the space of restricted CCF's $\gamma^E : E \to C$ conditional upon event E having occurred. The equivalence (12) is the *sure-thing principle*, so called because the same CCF $\gamma(s)(s \in F)$ is a 'sure-thing', regardless of whether a_1 or a_2 is chosen at n_1. Really, both the sure-thing principle and the independence axiom are like weak dominance relations which feature prominently in both decision theory and game theory (cf. Arrow, 1971, p. 50).

Another appealing restriction on preferences arises when a restricted CCF $\gamma^E : E \to C$ yields the same consequence c in every state s of E. Then γ^E is effectively identical to the sure-consequence c. So the *sure-consequence principle* (which is closely related to the sure-thing principle is defined above; indeed, that corresponds to Savage's (1954) P2, while the new principle corresponds to P3, and both seem regarded by Savage as part of his 'sure-thing principle') requires the existence of a *sure-consequence preference ordering* $\succsim_C$ on the set of consequences C such that:

$$\text{If} \quad \gamma_1(s) = c_1, \quad \gamma_2(s) = c_2 \quad (\text{all } s \in E),$$

then

$$\gamma_1^E \succsim^*_E \gamma_2^E \Leftrightarrow c_1 \succsim_C c_2 \tag{13}$$

for every event E and pair of consequences c_1, c_2.

Utility and probability

HORSE LOTTERIES AND SUBJECTIVE PROBABILITIES. Savage (1954) and Arrow (1965, 1971) proceed to derive subjective probabilities from a number of additional postulates, in particular one called 'ordering of events' whose motivation is not nearly so appealing to this author as the independence axiom of the sure-thing principle. In addition, Savage and Arrow both assume that events can be partitioned arbitrarily finely so that, in the end, to every possible number p between zero and one, there exist events with subjective probabilities arbitrarily close to p. An alternative and simpler derivation of subjective probabilities was first suggested by Anscombe and Aumann (1963) through the device of 'horse lotteries', which combine uncertain states of the world determined by nature with 'extraneous uncertainty' determined through artificial lotteries with known probabilities.

Formally, a *horse lottery* is a probability distribution μ on C^S, the space of CCF's. The uncertain consequence of a horse lottery therefore depends both on the realization of a random process with known probabilities μ and on the state of the world s. The probability distribution μ is therefore really the joint multivariate distribution of the random consequences $\gamma(s)(s\in S)$.

The independence axiom is equally appealing for horse lotteries. Together with continuity in probabilities, it implies the existence of an NMUF U^E for every $E \subset S$, defined on C^E the space of CCF's, whose expected value represents preferences on $M(C^E)$. The sure-thing principle is justified for *independent* random CCF's in the sense that for any $\mu_1^E, \mu_2^E \in M(C^E)$ and $\mu^F \in M(C^F)$, where E and F are disjoint:

$$\mu_1^E \times \mu^F \succsim_S^* \mu_2^E \times \mu^F \Leftrightarrow \mu_1^E \succsim_E^* \mu_2^E \tag{14}$$

where for $j = 1, 2$, $\mu_j^E \times \mu^F$ is the random CCF $v_j \in M(C^S)$ for which:

$$v_j(\{\gamma^E, \gamma^F\}) = \mu_j^E(\{\gamma^E\}) \times \mu^F(\{\gamma^F\}) \tag{15}$$

for all $\gamma^E \in C^E$, $\gamma^F \in C^F$.

Horse lotteries also suggest a *random* sure-consequence principle, as follows. Suppose that $\mu_1, \mu_2 \in M(C^E)$ each have the property that consequences in different states of the world are perfectly correlated, so that for $j = 1, 2$ one has $\mu_j(\{\gamma^E\}) = 0$ unless there is a constant consequence c for which $\gamma^E(s) = c$ (all $s \in E$). Then μ_j is equivalent to a random 'sure-consequence' distribution λ_j on C with the property that:

$$\lambda_j(\{c\}) = \mu_j(\{\gamma^E | \gamma^E(s) = c \text{ (all } s \in E)\}). \tag{16}$$

The natural counterpart of (13) then requires the existence of an NMUF v on C, independent of E, whose expected value represents the preference ordering for all pairs of random sure-consequences – this is the *random sure-consequence principle*.

Invoking the axioms so far – the independence axiom, the sure-thing principle for independent random CCF's, the random sure-consequence principle, and continuity in probabilities – does not quite suffice to guarantee the existence of subjective probabilities. If there are only two possible consequences in the set C, preferences which amount to preferring known probabilities, as against 'unreliable probabilities', are still possible, as in 'Ellsberg's paradox' (1961) – see also Drèze (1974) and Gärdenfors and Sahlin (1982). When, however, C contains at least three consequences, of which no two are indifferent according to the ordering $\succsim_C$, then there do exist an NMUF v on C and positive constants $\alpha_s (s \in S)$ such that, for every $E \subset S$ and all CCF's $\gamma_1^E, \gamma_2^E : E \to C$:

$$\gamma_1^E \succsim_E^* \gamma_2^E \Leftrightarrow \sum_{s \in E} \alpha_s v[\gamma_1(s)] \geqslant \sum_{s \in E} \alpha_s v[\gamma_2(s)]. \qquad (17)$$

Thus the utility function

$$U^E(\gamma^E) = \sum_{s \in E} \alpha_s v(\gamma(s))$$

represents $\succsim_E^*$ over C^E, the space of CCF's $\gamma^E : E \to C$, and its expected value represents preferences over $M(C^E)$, the set of random CCF's. Normalizing by taking:

$$\pi(s|E) := \alpha_s \Big/ \sum_{s' \in S} \alpha_{s'}, \qquad (s \in E) \qquad (18)$$

implies that the NMUF U^E on C^E takes the subjectively expected utility form:

$$U^E(\gamma^E) = \sum_{s \in E} \pi(s|E) v[\gamma(s)] \qquad (19)$$

(ignoring an irrelevant positive multiplicative constant). Notice that one of the assumptions of Anscombe and Aumann (1963), Harsanyi (1978) and Myerson (1979) is logically entailed by the assumptions given here; specifically, the assumption that preferences on $M(C^E)$ depend only on the marginal probabilities $\mu(s) \in M(C)$ for every state $s \in E$. This is immediate from the fact that the expected value of (19) can be written in the form:

$$E_\mu U^E(\gamma^E) = \sum_{s \in E} \pi(s|E) E_{\mu(s)} v[\gamma(s)] \qquad (20)$$

where $\mu(s)$ is the marginal distribution of consequences in state s induced by the joint distribution μ of CCF's.

It is noteworthy that each α_s must be *positive*, so there can be no zero probabilities in this formulation. Zero probabilities give rise to inconsistencies in some decision trees if an event with zero probability does occur, because acts which were originally indifferent will cease to be indifferent, in general. Events which cannot occur must be omitted from the decision tree. Of course, the finiteness of the set S is crucial here.

Also noteworthy is the fact that consistency implies Bayes' rule (Weller, 1978) because for any pair of events E' and E'':

$$\pi(E'|E'') = \sum_{s \in E'} \pi(s|E'') = \sum_{s \in E' \cap E''} \alpha_s \Bigg/ \sum_{s' \in E''} \alpha_{s'}$$

from which it follows that:

$$\pi(F|E \cap G) = \pi(E|F \cap G)\pi(F|G)/\pi(E|G). \tag{21}$$

This is indeed Bayes' rule for the posterior probability of F given E and G, in terms of the prior probability of F given G and the likelihood of E given F and G. In particular, (21) is equivalent to:

$$\frac{\pi(F_1|E \cap G)}{\pi(F_2|E \cap G)} = \frac{\pi(E|F_1 \cap G)\pi(F_1|G)}{\pi(E|F_2 \cap G)\pi(F_2|G)} \tag{22}$$

which has posterior probabilities proportional to the product of prior probabilities with likelihoods.

CONTINGENT FEASIBILITY OF CONSEQUENCES. The above discussion treated the space of consequences C as the same in every state of the world. Yet as Jones-Lee (1979) and others have rightly emphasized, when uncertainty concerns events such as death or injury, not all consequences are feasible in every state. So let C_s denote the set of consequences which are possible in state s, for every $s \in S$, and let C denote $\cup_{s \in S} C_s$. For every $E \subset S$, let C^E denote the product space $\Pi_{s \in S} C_s$.

In this more general framework, the sure-thing principle (12) retains its appeal, as does the sure-consequence principle (13) provided that CCF's $\gamma^E : E \to C$ are restricted to satisfy the obvious requirement:

$$\gamma^E(s) \in C_s \quad \text{(all } s \in E\text{).} \tag{23}$$

Equation (17) no longer follows from the independence axiom, the sure-thing principle, the sure-consequence principle and continuity of probability, even if C does contain at least three members. To rule out Ellsberg-like paradoxes, it suffices to assume that there are two states s', s'' and three consequences c_1, c_2, c_3 – no two of which are indifferent according to the sure-consequence ordering $\succsim_C$ – such that c_1, c_2, c_3 all belong to $C_{s'} \cap C_{s''}$. Even then, however, all that can be shown is the existence of state-dependent NMUF's $w(s, \cdot)$, defined on C_s for every $s \in S$, such that the NMUF whose expected value represents preferences on $M(C^E)$ takes the additive form:

$$U^E(\gamma^E) = \sum_{s \in E} w[s, \gamma(s)]. \tag{24}$$

Following Wilson (1968) and Myerson (1979), the function w is called an *evaluation function*.

One problem which remains in showing that (24) can be expressed in the form (19) for well defined subjective probabilities $\pi(s|E)$ is that the probabilities may not be uniquely defined; obviously this happens whenever S can be partitioned into two events S' and S'' such that $\cup_{s \in S'} C_s$ and $\cup_{s \in S''} C_s$ are disjoint. To overcome this difficulty, Karni, Schmeidler and Vind (1983) assume that there is some set of all positive probabilities $\bar{\pi}_s (s \in S)$ such that the decision-maker could conceivably be convinced that these were the true probabilities, and would then maximize the expected value accordingly. Here, the expected value is the following sum (where the first sum is as c^E varies over the whole of C^E):

$$\sum \mu(c^E) \sum_{s \in E} \bar{\pi}_s v(c_s) \tag{25}$$

for every $\mu \in M(C^E)$ and $E \subset S$, where v is a well defined NMUF on C, the whole set of possible consequences. Now, when state s is known to have occurred, (24) implies maximizing the expected value of $w(s, c)$ while (25) implies maximizing the expected value of $v(c)$. So these must be cardinally equivalent NMUF's, which implies that there exist positive multiplicative constants α_s and arbitrary additive constants β_s such that:

$$w(s, c) = \alpha_s v(c) + \beta_s \qquad \text{(all } s \in S, \ c \in C_s\text{).} \tag{26}$$

Ignoring the irrelevant additive constants and normalizing using (18), gives the subjectively expected form (19) of (24). The positive conditional probabilities $\pi(s|E)$ emerge as before as marginal rates of substitution, in effect, between measures of von Neumann–Morgenstern utility in state s and in even E, whenever $s \in E \subset S$.

The crucial new assumption here, of course, was the possibility of having objective probabilities $\bar{\pi}_s (s \in S)$. Yet this is obviously a necessary condition for the existence of subjective probabilities, because having subjective probabilities become objectively known should not affect behaviour. It is interesting that the same condition is also sufficient; indeed, only *one* set of possible objective probabilities are needed, whereas when probabilities are unknown one could well argue that whole ranges of objective probabilities should be viewed as possibilities.

Maximization of subjectively expected utility has been called *Bayesian rationality* by Harsanyi (1975, 1978) and others. The last few sections have presented the following six sufficient conditions for Bayesian rationality – (i) existence of a preference ordering, (ii) the independence axiom, (iii) continuity with respect to objective probabilities, (iv) the sure-thing principle, (v) the sure-consequence principle, and (vi) rationality (in the sense of the previous five conditions) for some possible set of probabilities attached to states of the world.

BAYESIAN RATIONAL SOCIAL CHOICE WITH COMMON PROBABILITIES. So far I have considered rationality just for individual choice under uncertainty. But the same standards of rationality apply to policy objectives as well, which are the subject of Arrow's (1951, 1953) social choice theory. When there is uncertainty, however, Harsanyi's (1955) approach seems more suitable. There must exist subjective probabilities $\pi_s(s \in S)$ for society and a 'von Neumann–Bergson social welfare function' (NMBSWF) W such that the social objective is to maximize the expected value of:

$$W^E(c^E) = \sum_{s \in E} \pi(s \mid E) w(c_s). \tag{27}$$

Suppose that society consists of individuals in the finite membership set M. To ensure the existence of subjective probabilities, suppose that it is possible for all individuals to know that $\bar{\pi}_s(s \in E)$ are the true probabilities. In this case, society's NMBSWF is:

$$\bar{W}^E(c^E) = \sum_{s \in E} \bar{\pi}_s w(c_s) \tag{28}$$

while each individual i has an NMUF of the form:

$$\bar{U}_i^E(c^E) = \sum_{s \in E} \bar{\pi}_s v_i(c_s). \tag{29}$$

As shown by Harsanyi (1955) and (under less restrictive conditions) by Border (1985), the usual Pareto condition of social choice theory then implies the existence of positive welfare weights $\omega_i (i \in M)$ for which:

$$w(c_s) = \sum_{i \in M} \omega_i v_i(c_s). \tag{30}$$

Returning to (27), this now becomes:

$$W^E(c^E) = \sum_{s \in E} \pi(s \mid E) \sum_{i \in M} \omega_i v_i(c_s). \tag{31}$$

When each individual i has his own subjective probabilities $\pi_i(s \mid E)$, i's objective is

$$U_i^E(c^E) = \sum_{s \in E} \pi_i(s \mid E) v_i(c_s) \tag{32}$$

and the usual Pareto condition is then generally violated unless

$$\pi_j(s \mid E) = \pi(s \mid E) \qquad (\text{all } i \in M) \tag{33}$$

whenever $s \in E \subset S$. Thus Paretian social choice experiences difficulties except when individuals have identical subjective probabilities, as was first realized by Diamond (1967). In particular, there is a contradiction between the ex-ante and ex-post approaches to welfare economics under uncertainty. For the ex-ante approach suggests combining individuals' ex-ante expected utilities into an ex-ante social welfare function, such as the expected value of:

$$\sum_{i \in M} \omega_i \sum_{s \in E} \pi_i(s \mid E) v_i(c_s). \tag{34}$$

Whereas the ex-post approach suggests taking the socially expected value of ex-post social welfare:

$$\sum_{s \in E} \pi(s|E) \sum_{i \in M} \omega_i v_i(c_s) \tag{35}$$

which generally differs from (34) unless (33) is satisfied. Apart from Diamond (1967), the contrast between ex-ante and ex-post has been discussed by Starr (1973) and many others, including Hammond (1983).

These difficulties for Paretian social choice and welfare economics have proved intractable. One feels that the ex-ante approach embodied in (34) pays too much heed to probabilities $\pi_i(s|E)$ that may be based on poor information. Yet the ex-post approach smacks of paternalism if the probabilities $\pi(s|E)$ are imposed, as it seems that they must be. A possible resolution may be to construct individual types $t_i(i \in M)$ broadly enough, as in Mertens and Zamir's (1985) recent elaboration of Harsanyi's (1967, 1968) games of incomplete information, so that there is a common joint conditional prior probability distribution $\pi^*(s, t^M|E)$ on combinations of social states s and profiles $t^M = (t_i)_{i \in M}$ of individuals' types, for every $E \subset S$. Then, provided that $\bar{t}^M$ is known, the natural NMBSWF to use is:

$$\sum_{s \in E} \pi^*(s|\bar{t}^M, E) \sum_{i \in M} \omega_i v_i(c_s) \tag{36}$$

with probabilities conditional upon $\bar{t}^M$ and E. This is so even though each individual i, knowing only t_i, desires to maximize the expected value of the sum over all possible t^M of:

$$\sum_{s \in E} \pi^*(s, t^M|t_i, E) v_i(c_s) \tag{37}$$

with probabilities conditional upon t_i and E, and even though the Pareto condition is then violated in general unless it happens that:

$$\pi^*(s|\bar{t}^M, E) = \pi^*(s, t^M|t_i, E) \qquad \text{(all } s \in E, i \in M) \tag{38}$$

which generally implies that $\pi^*(s|t^M, E)$ is independent of t^M – i.e., individuals have common subjective probabilities. If t^M is not known, the natural NMBSWF is the sum over all possible t^M of:

$$\sum_{s \in E} \pi^*(s, t^M|E) \sum_{i \in M} \omega_i v_i(c_s). \tag{39}$$

This is only a *possible* resolution, however, whose full implications remain unexplored as this is written. Reconciling conflicting subjective probabilities raised conceptual issues far beyond anything else yet discussed in this essay.

DIFFERENCES IN INDIVIDUALS' INFORMATION. In the discussion of single person decision theory, uncertainty was handled in principle by the device of contingent consequence functions. Thereafter conditions were given for a person's decisions to be Bayesian rational – i.e., correspond to maximizing the expected value of an NMUF, attaching subjective probabilities to each state of the world. Provided that all individuals also share the same information and the same subjective probabilities throughout, it is also straightforward in principle to use contingent consequence functions (or Debreu's contingent commodity contracts in economies) in order to adapt any piece of standard static economic analysis to allow for uncertainty. It is true that expected utility maximization introduces a special additive structure to preferences which permit special results to be derived, as in the theory of risk-aversion. But really this is incidental rather than fundamental.

As the discussion of the previous section begins to illustrate, fundamental new issues arise once one recognizes that individuals do not all share the same information and probability beliefs. There, the contrast between ex-ante and ex-post and the dilemma posed for Paretian social choice and welfare economics were noted. Far more important, however, is the realization that the environment in which an individual makes decisions is not just determined by an uncertain 'state of the world' which is chosen passively by 'nature' who, one presumes, has no objectives of her own. In addition, in a game of imperfect or incomplete information, there is uncertainty about the strategic choices by other 'players' who may well have very definite objectives (even if there is uncertainty about these objectives, as indeed there is in games of incomplete information). Such uncertainty is much better able to justify Knight's (1921) claim that 'risk' offers no profit opportunities whereas 'uncertainty' does – after all, complete Arrow–Debreu markets for contingent commodities may well remove profit opportunities that arise from uncertain states of the world, but not those that result because some traders are better informed than others about profit opportunities.

So, uncertainty *per se* really introduces little that is fundamentally new into economics. It is when individuals have different information as well that the position changes dramatically.

BIBLIOGRAPHY

Anscombe, F.J. and Aumann, R.J. 1963. A definition of subjective probability. *Annals of Mathematical Statistics* 34, 199–205.

Arrow, K.J. 1951. *Social Choice and Individual Values.* New York: John Wiley; 2nd edn, New Haven: Yale University Press, 1963.

Arrow, K.J. 1953, 1963. The rôle of securities in the optimal allocation of risk-bearing. *Review of Economic Studies* 31, 91–6; first published as 'Le rôle des valeurs boursières pour la répartition la meilleure des risques', *Économetrie* (Colloques Internationaux du Centre National de la Recherche Scientifique) 11, 41–7; reprinted as ch. 4 of Arrow (1971) and as ch. 3 of Arrow (1983).

Arrow, K.J. 1965. *Aspects of the Theory of Risk-Bearing.* Helsinki: Yrjö Jahnsson Foundation.

Arrow, K.J. 1971. *Essays in the Theory of Risk-Bearing.* Amsterdam: North-Holland; Chicago: Markham.

Arrow, K.J. 1983. *Collected Papers of Kenneth J. Arrow, 2: General Equilibrium.* Cambridge, Mass.: The Belknap Press of Harvard University Press.

Balch, M., McFadden, D. and Wu, S. (eds) 1974. *Essays on Economic Behavior under Uncertainty.* Amsterdam: North-Holland.

Bernoulli, D. 1738. Specimen theoriae novae de mensura sortis. *Commentarii academiae scientiarum imperialis Petropolitanae* 5, 175–92. Translated by L. Sommer (1954) as 'Exposition of a new theory on the measurement of risk', *Econometrica* 22, 23–36.

Bolker, E.D. 1967. A simultaneous axiomatization of utility and subjective probability. *Philosophy of Science* 34, 333–40.

Border, K.C. 1985. More on Harsanyi's utilitarian cardinal welfare theorem. *Social Choice and Welfare* 1, 279–81.

Cass, D. and Shell, K. 1983. Do sunspots matter? *Journal of Political Economy* 91, 193–227.

Debreu, G. 1959. *Theory of Value: An Axiomatic Analysis of General Equilibrium.* New York: John Wiley.

Diamond, P.A. 1967. The role of a stock market in a general equilibrium model with technological uncertainty. *American Economic Review* 57, 759–76.

Diamond, P.A. and Rothschild, M. (eds) 1978. *Uncertainty in Economics: Reading and Exercises.* New York: Academic Press.

Drèze, J.H. 1974. Axiomatic theories of choice, cardinal utility and subjective probability: A review. In *Allocation under Uncertainty* ed. J.H. Drèze, London: Macmillan, 3–23.

Ellsberg, D. 1961. Risk, ambiguity and the Savage axioms. *Quarterly Journal of Economics* 75, 643–69.

Fishburn, P.C. 1982. *The Foundations of Expected Utility.* Dordrecht: Reidel.

Gärdenfors, P. and Sahlin, N.-E. 1982. Unreliable probabilities, risk taking, and decision making. *Synthèse* 53, 361–86.

Hammond, P.J. 1983. Ex-post optimality as a dynamically consistent objective for collective choice under uncertainty. In *Social Choice and Welfare*, ed. P.K. Pattanaik and M. Salles, Amsterdam: North-Holland, 175–205.

Harsanyi, J.C. 1955. Cardinal welfare, individualistic ethics, and interpersonal comparisons of utility. *Journal of Political Economy* 63, 309–21.

Harsanyi, J.C. 1967, 1968. Games with incomplete information played by 'Bayesian' players, I–III. *Management Science; Theory* 14, 159–82, 320–34 and 486–502.

Harsanyi, J.C. 1975. Nonlinear social welfare functions: do welfare economists have a special exemption from Bayesian rationality? *Theory and Decision* 6, 311–32.

Harsanyi, J.C. 1978. Bayesian decision theory and utilitarian ethics. *American Economic Review, Papers and Proceedings* 68, 223–8.

Hausner, M. 1954. Multidimensional utilities. In R.M. Thrall et al. (eds) (1954), 167–90.

Herstein, I.N. and Milnor, J. 1953. An axiomatic approach to measurable utility. *Econometrica* 21, 291–7.

Hirshleifer, 1966. Investment decision under uncertainty: applications of the state-preference approach. *Quarterly Journal of Economics* 80, 252–77.

Hirshleifer, J. and Riley, J.G. 1979. The analysis of uncertainty and information: an expository survey. *Journal of Economic Literature* 17, 1375–421.

Jeffrey, R.C. 1965. *The Logic of Decision.* New York: McGraw-Hill.

Jeffrey, R.C. 1974. Frameworks for preference. In Balch, McFadden and Wu (1974), 74–9.

Jones-Lee, M.W. 1979. The expected conditional utility theorem for the case of personal probabilities and state conditional utility functions: a proof and some notes. *Economic Journal* 89, 834–49.

Karni, E., Schmeidler, D. and Vind, K. 1983. On state dependent preferences and subjective probabilities. *Econometrica* 51, 1021–31.

293

Keynes, J.M. 1921. *A Treatise on Probability*. London: Macmillan; New York: Harper & Row, 1962.

Knight, F.H. 1921, 1971. *Risk, Uncertainty and Profit*. Chicago: University of Chicago Press.

Kyburg, H.E., Jr and Smokler, H.E. (eds) 1964. *Studies in Subjective Probability*. New York: John Wiley.

Lippman, S.A. and McCall, J.J. 1981. The economics of uncertainty: selected topics and probabilistic methods. In *Handbook of Mathematical Economics*, Vol. 1, ed. K.J. Arrow and M.D. Intriligator, Amsterdam: North-Holland, 211–84.

Machina, M. 1982. 'Expected utility' analysis without the independence axiom. *Econometrica* 50, 277–323.

Mertens, J.-F. and Zamir, S. 1985. Formalization of Harsanyi's notions of 'type' and 'consistency' in games with incomplete information. *International Journal of Game Theory* 14, 1–29.

Myerson, R.B. 1979. An axiomatic derivation of subjective probability, utility and evaluation functions. *Theory and Decision* 11, 339–52.

Raiffa, H. 1968. *Decision Analysis: Introductory Lectures on Choices under Uncertainty*. Reading, Mass.: Addison-Wesley.

Ramsey, F.P. 1926. Truth and probability. In F.P. Ramsey, *The Foundations of Mathematics and Other Logical Essays*, ed. R.B. Braithwaite, New York: Humanities Press, 1950, and in Kyburg and Smokler (1964).

Samuelson, P.A. 1952. Probability, utility and the independence axiom. *Econometrica* 20, 670–78.

Savage, L.J. 1954. *The Foundations of Statistics*. New York: John Wiley, and Dover. 2nd revised edn, 1972.

Schoemaker, P.J.H. 1982. The expected utility model: its variants, purposes, evidence and limitations. *Journal of Economic Literature* 20, 529–63.

Sinn, H.-W. 1983. *Economic Decisions Under Uncertainty*. Amsterdam: North-Holland.

Skala, H.J. 1975. *Non-Archimedean Utility Theory*. Dordrecht: D. Reidel.

Starr, R. 1973. Optimal production and allocation under uncertainty. *Quarterly Journal of Economics* 87, 668–90.

Thrall, R.M. 1954. Applications of multidimensional utility theory. In R.M. Thrall et al. (eds), 181–6.

Thrall, R.M., Coombs, C.H. and Davis, R.L. (eds) 1954. *Decision Processes*. New York: John Wiley.

Weller, P.A. 1978. Consistent intertemporal decision making under uncertainty. *Review of Economic Studies* 45, 263–6.

Wilson, R.B. 1968. The theory of syndicates. *Econometrica* 36, 119–32.

Utility

R.D. COLLISON BLACK

Utility is a term which has a long history in connection with the attempts of philosophers and political economists to explain the phenomenon of value. It has most frequently been given the connotation of 'desiredness', or the capacity of a good or service to satisfy a want, of whatever kind. Its use with that meaning can be traced back at least to Gershom Carmichael's 1724 edition of Pufendorf's *De Officio Hominis et Civis Iuxta Legem Naturalem*, and arguably came down to him through the medieval schoolmen from Aristotle's *Politics*.

Utility in the sense of desiredness is a purely subjective concept, clearly distinct from usefulness or fitness for a purpose – the more normal everyday sense of the word and the first meaning given for it by the *Oxford English Dictionary*.

While most political economists of the 19th and 19th centuries used the term in this subjective sense, the distinction was not always kept clear, most notably in the writings of Adam Smith. In a famous passage in the *Wealth of Nations* Smith wrote:

> The word VALUE, it is to be observed, has two different meanings, and sometimes expresses the utility of some particular object, and sometimes the power of purchasing other goods which the possession of that object conveys. The one may be called 'value in use'; the other, 'value in exchange'. The things which have the greatest value in use have frequently little or no value in exchange; and, on the contrary, those which have the greatest value in exchange have frequently little or no value in use. Nothing is more useful than water; but it will purchase scarce any thing; scarce any thing can be had in exchange for it. A diamond, on the contrary, has scarce any value in use; but a very great quantity of other goods may frequently be had in exchange for it (1776, Book I, ch. IV).

Smith has sometimes been accused, because of the wording of this passage, of falling into the error of claiming that things which have *no* value in use can have value in exchange, which is tantamount to saying that utility is not a necessary

295

condition for a good to have value. It would appear, however, that Smith was not here using the theme 'value in use', or utility, in the subjective sense of desiredness but in the normal objective sense of usefulness (cf. Bowley, 1973, p. 137; O'Brien, 1975, pp. 80 and 97). Most other classical economists and even Smith himself in his *Lectures on Jurisprudence*, used the term in its subjective sense, but the passage in the *Wealth of Nations* gave rise to considerable confusion and misinterpretation. Nor was this the only source of confusion in the early writing on the subject: even those who used the term utility in its subjective sense were not always clear as to whether it should be considered a feeling in the mind of the user or a property of the good or service used. Thomas De Quincey, for example, referred to the 'intrinsic utility' of commodities (*Logic of Political Economy*, 1844, p. 14).

Most classical economists, however, were not greatly concerned with the subtleties of meaning which the term utility might contain. Generally they used it in the broad sense of desiredness, and Ricardo employed it in a typically classical way when he wrote:

> Utility then is not the measure of exchangeable value, although it is absolutely essential to it. If a commodity were in no way useful – in other words, if it could in no way contribute to our gratification – it would be destitute of exchangeable value, however scarce it might be, or whatever quantity of labour might be necessary to procure it (*Principles of Political Economy and Taxation*, 1817, ch. I, sect. I).

'Useful' here is interpreted as 'contributing to gratification' but the very word carries an echo of Smith's confusion.

For Ricardo and others in the mainstream classical tradition down to J.S. Mill and Cairnes utility became a necessary but not a sufficient condition for a good to possess value. In this context, the utility referred to was generally the total utility of the good to the purchaser, or the utility of a specific quantity which is all that is available in the circumstances of the example – for example, the utility of a single item of food to a starving person.

As a result of this approach it followed, in the words of J.S. Mill, that 'the utility of a thing in the estimation of the purchaser is the extreme limit of its exchange value: higher the value cannot ascend; peculiar circumstances are required to raise it so high' (*Principles of Political Economy*, 1848, Book III, ch. II, §1). Classical economists like Mill accepted the view put forward by J.B. Say that 'labour is not creative of objects, but of utilities' but could see the weakness in Say's contention that price measured utility. Clearly in the case of competitively produced commodities it did not and it was cost of production and not utility (in the total sense) which determined value.

Since the classical economists were mainly interested in 'natural' rather than 'market' price, that is, in long-run normal values which were mainly determined by supply and cost, the fact that they had no theory to explain fully the relationships between utility, demand and market price was not a matter of concern to most of them. Nevertheless in the period from about 1830 to 1870 a number of attempts were made to work out these relationships more fully or to clarify aspects of them. Some of these attempts took place in Britain, within the framework of the classical system, but not surprisingly some of the best work was done at this time in France, where the tradition of demand analysis was stronger.

The full explanation of the relation between utility and demand requires the distinction between total utility and increments of utility, and the recognition of the principle that consumption of successive increments of a commodity yields not equal but diminishing increments of satisfaction or utility to the consumer. A number of writers in the mid-19th century showed an understanding of this point, but only a few stated it explicitly and correctly. Among those in Britain who did so were William Foster Lloyd (*A Lecture on the Notion of Value, delivered before the University of Oxford in Michaelmas Term*, 1833) and Nassau Senior (*An Outline of the Science of Political Economy*, 1836), but neither proceeded to develop their insights into a complete theory of the relationship between utility, demand and market values.

The French engineer A.J. Dupuit was the first to present an analysis which clearly explained the concept of marginal utility and related it to a demand curve, in his paper 'On the Measurement of the Utility of Public Works' (*Annales des Ponts et Chaussées*, 1844; English translation, 1952). Dupuit also extended his analysis to show that the total area under the demand curve represents the total utility derived from the commodity; deducting from this the total receipts of the producer he arrived at the 'utility remaining to consumers' or what was later to be termed 'consumers' surplus'.

The significance of Dupuit's contribution is now well recognized, but at the time of its appearance it had little impact. The same is even more true of the work of Hermann Heinrich Gossen, one of the few German contributors to utility theory in this period. His book *Entwicklung der Gesetze des menschlichen Verkehrs*, published in 1854, contained not only a statement of the 'law of satiable wants', or diminishing marginal utility, but also of the proposition that to maximize satisfaction from any good capable of satisfying various wants it must be allocated between those uses so as to equalize its marginal utilities in all of them.

Gossen's analysis of the principles of utility maximization was thus more complete than any which had preceded it. Yet his one book, which foreshadowed many features of general equilibrium as well as utility theory, received virtually no attention until 1878, twenty years after the author's death, when Robert Adamson, W.J. Jevons's successor as Professor of Philosophy and Political Economy at Manchester, obtained a copy of it and drew it to the attention of Jevons himself.

By that time the whole character of utility analysis and its place in economic theory had begun to change significantly. This change is usually dated from the very nearly simultaneous publication of Jevons's *Theory of Political Economy* in England and Menger's *Grundsätze der Volkswirtschaftslehre* in Austria, both in 1871, and Walras's *Eléments d'économie politique pure* in Switzerland in 1874. All these works contained a treatment of the theory of value in which the analysis of diminishing marginal utility (under a variety of other names) played a considerable part, but each of the three authors seems to have arrived independently at the main ideas of his theory without indebtedness to the others or to the predecessors already mentioned above.

This remarkable example of multiple discovery in the history of ideas has come to be known as 'the Marginal Revolution'. Discussion of its causes and character lies outside the scope of this article, but it is generally accepted that, as Sir John Hicks has said, 'the essential novelty in the work of these economists was that instead of basing their economics on production and distribution, they based it on exchange' (Hicks, 1976, p. 212).

A major element in this 'shift in attention' undoubtedly was a change from the classical concept of value in use, or total utility, as a necessary but not sufficient condition to explain the normal values of freely reproducible commodities, to the concept of what Jevons called 'the degree of utility' and of adjustments in it, through exchange of quantities of goods held or consumed, in order to maximize satisfaction. Marginal analysis can, however, be applied to questions of production and distribution as well as consumption, and hence the 'Marginal Revolution' involved more than a new stage in the development of utility theory.

Although all three pioneers of the Marginal Revolution did contribute to that development they also contributed in other ways to the theory of pricing and exchange. Perhaps only for Jevons was the theory of utility genuinely central to the structure of his economic work. On the opening page of his *Theory of Political Economy* he emphatically asserted that '*value depends entirely upon utility*' and he went on to say that 'Political Economy must be founded upon a full and accurate investigation of the conditions of utility' (1871, p. 46). Jevons indeed appears to have shared with his classical predecessors the view that a theory of value must go beyond the phenomena of demand and supply to some more fundamental explanation which for him was to be found in utility rather than in labour. 'Labour is found often to determine value, but only in an indirect manner, by varying the degree of utility of the commodity through an increase or limitation of supply' (Jevons, 1871, p. 2).

Apart from differences of terminology, Walras's treatment of utility in relation to the problem of exchange had substantial similarities with that of Jevons; but Walras saw the problem in a different context:

> His whole attention was focused on market phenomena and not on consumption... while the driving force in the theory of exchange is, as Walras saw it, the endeavour of all traders to maximize their several satisfactions, it is marketplace satisfactions rather than dining-room satisfactions which Walras had in mind (Jaffé, 1973, pp. 118–19).

For Menger, as for Walras, the concepts of utility theory formed only a part of a much larger analytical structure (concerned in his case not so much with equilibrium as with development), but unlike both Walras and Jevons he refused to state his theories in mathematical terms.

Menger developed a theory of economizing behaviour showing how the individual would seek to satisfy his subjectively felt needs in the most efficient manner. In the process he elaborated the essential propositions of a theory of maximizing behaviour for the consumer, but he expressed them in terms of the satisfaction of needs by the consumption of successive units of goods. In his discussion of this process Menger used the same phrases – use-value and exchange-value – which Smith had used almost a century earlier, and with similar connotations. Use-value he defined as 'the importance that goods acquire for us because they *directly* assure us the satisfaction of needs that would not be provided for if we did not have the goods at our command. Exchange value is the importance that goods acquire for us because their possession assures the same result *indirectly*' (Menger, [1871], 1951, p. 228). Menger did use the term 'utility', but not as a synonym for use-value; he viewed it as an abstract relation between a species of goods and a human need, akin to the general term 'usefulness'. As such it constituted a prerequisite for a good to have economic character, but had no quantitative relationship to value.

The three pioneers of the Marginal Revolution thus saw the problem of the relationship of utility to exchange value in different contexts and expressed their solutions to it in different ways. Inevitably also their first solutions were incomplete in various respects. For example, the precise relationships between the individual's utility function and demand function, the market demand function and the market price were not clearly specified in some of the earlier formulations; it remained for later contributors such as Marshall, Wicksteed and Edgeworth to deal with these points.

Nevertheless, despite their differences of terminology and approach, the writings of the pioneers did contain a common core which gradually gained wider acceptance, and by 1890, with the appearance of Marshall's *Principles of Economics* it seemed that the new analysis of market values had been effectively integrated with an analysis of supply and cost which served to explain long-run 'normal' values. It did provide some things which the classical system had not contained, among them a consistent theory of consumer behaviour, expressed in terms of utility.

So in 1899 it was possible for Edgeworth to write that:

> the relation of utility to value, which exercised the older economists, is thus simply explained by the mathematical school. The value in use of a certain quantity of commodity corresponds to its total utility; the value in exchange to its marginal utility (multiplied by the quantity). The former is greater than the latter, since the utility of the final increment of commodity is less than that of every other increment (Edgeworth, 1899, p. 602).

At this stage utility analysis appeared to have evolved to something approaching finality, and in 1925 Jacob Viner could still say:

> In its developed form it is to be found sympathetically treated and playing a prominent role in the exposition of value theory in most of the current authoritative treatises on economic theory by American, English, Austrian, and Italian writers.

Yet Viner immediately went on to add:

In the scientific periodicals, however, in contrast with the standard treatises, sympathetic expositions of the utility theory of value have become somewhat rare. In their stead are found an unintermittent series of slashing criticisms of the utility economics (Viner [1925], 1958, p. 179).

The principal criticisms which Viner noted were the apparent involvement of utility theory with hedonistic psychology and the problems of measuring welfare in terms of utility. In later years questions of the measurement and summation of utility came to trouble economists more and more.

The two basic problems involved here are whether utility can be measured cardinally or simply ordinally, and whether interpersonal comparisons of utility are possible. The pioneers of the Marginal Revolution were not unaware of these problems; Jevons nowhere attempted to define a unit of utility, and indeed said that 'a unit of pleasure or pain is difficult even to conceive', but he went on to say that 'it is from the quantitative effects of the feelings that we must estimate their comparative amounts' (Jevons, 1871, p. 14). However they may be estimated, Jevons did not hesitate to refer to 'quantity of utility', and his whole analysis proceeds by treating utility as it could be measured. The question was not examined in detail by Walras or Menger, but both their analyses treat utilty as cardinally measurable.

On the question of interpersonal comparisons of utility, Menger and Walras seemed to find no difficulty, and Walras was prepared to speak of a 'maximum of utility' for society (Walras [1874], 1954, p. 256). Jevons on the other hand declared that 'every mind is... inscrutable to every other mind, and no common denominator of feeling seems possible' (Jevons, 1871, p. 211) – but this did not always prevent him from comparing and aggregating utilities.

In the early editions of his *Principles of Economics* Marshall fully accepted the idea of utility as cardinally measurable and allowed the possibility if not of interpersonal certainly of inter-group comparisons of utility (1890, pp. 151–2). In later years he became more reticent and defensive on these points, and he was always more concerned than Jevons with the effects of feelings rather than the feelings of themselves; yet cardinal utility always remained the basis of Marshall's demand theory.

Now, as Sir John Hicks said:

if one starts from a theory of demand like that of Marshall and his contemporaries, it is exceedingly natural to look for a welfare application. If the general aim of the economic system is the satisfaction of consumer wants, and if the satisfaction of individual wants is to be conceived of as a maximising of utility, cannot the aim of the system be itself conceived of as a maximizing of utility – universal utility, as Edgeworth called it? If this could not be done and some measure of universal utility could be found, the economist's function could be widened out, from the understanding of cause and effect to the judgement of the effects – whether, from the point of view of want-satisfaction, they are to be judged as successful or unsuccessful, good or bad (Hicks, 1956, p. 6).

This was, in effect, the task which was undertaken by Marshall's successor, A.C. Pigou, in his *Economics of Welfare* (1920; earlier version published under the title *Wealth and Welfare*, 1912). Pigou made no attempt to establish a measure of universal utility; instead he took what Marshall had called 'the national dividend', aggregate real income, as the 'objective counterpart' of economic welfare. Pigou argued that economic welfare would be greater when aggregate real income increased, when fluctuations in its amount were reduced, and when it was more equally distributed among persons. It was in the context of this last point that interpersonal utility comparisons were most evident; Pigou argued that

the old 'law of diminishing utility' thus leads securely to the proposition: Any cause which increases the absolute share of real income in the hands of the poor, provided that it does not lead to a contraction in the size of the national dividend... will in general, increase economic welfare' (1920, p. 89).

In the 1930s most economists became increasingly uncomfortable with the idea of measurement and interpersonal or inter-group comparisons of utility. In 1934, in a famous article entitled 'A Reconsideration of the Theory of Value', Hicks and Allen used the technique of indifference curves originated by Edgeworth and developed by Walras's successor at Lausanne, Vilfredo Pareto, in presenting a theory of consumer behaviour involving only ordinal comparisons of satisfaction. A few years later a further step towards eliminating what were now considered dubious psychological assumptions from that theory was taken by treating consumer behaviour solely on the basis of revealed preference.

Accompanying these changes there was a movement away from the type of welfare economics developed on the basis of utility theory by Marshall and Pigou towards that based on Pareto's concept of an economic optimum as a position from which it is impossible to improve anyone's welfare without damaging that of another.

Indifference analysis and revealed preference theory are now standard features of microeconomic theory; but the utility concept has not disappeared; the most widely used introductory economics texts still tend to begin their treatments of household behaviour with an account of utility theory.

BIBLIOGRAPHY

Bowley, M. 1973. Utility, the pardox of value and 'all that' and classical economics. In M. Bowley, *Studies in the History of Economic Theory Before 1870,* London: Macmillan.

Dupuit, A.J. 1844. On the measurement of the utility of public works. *Annales des Ponts et Chaussées*, 2nd Series, Vol. VIII. Translated in *International Economic Papers* No. 2, 1952, London: Macmillan, 83–110.

Edgeworth, F.Y. 1899. Utility. In *Dictionary of Political Economy*, Vol. III, ed, R.H.I. Palgrave, London: Macmillan, 602.

Gossen, H.H. 1854. *Entwicklung der Gesetze des menschlichen Verkehrs und der daraus fliessenden Regeln für menschliches Handeln.* Brunswick: Viewig. Translated as *The Laws of Human Relations and the Rules of Human Action Derived Therefrom,* Cambridge, Mass.: MIT Press, 1983.

Hicks, J.R. 1956. *A Revision of Demand Theory.* Oxford: Clarendon Press.

Hicks, J.R. 1976. 'Revolutions' in economics. In *Method and Appraisal in Economics,* ed. S.J. Latsis, Cambridge and New York: Cambridge University Press.

Hicks, J.R. and Allen, R.G.D. 1934. A reconsideration of the theory of value. *Economica,* NS 1, 52–76; 196–219.

Howey, R.S. 1960. *The Rise of the Marginal Utility School, 1870–1889.* Lawrence, Kansas: University of Kansas Press.

Jaffé, W. 1973. Léon Walras's role in the 'marginal revolution' of the 1870s. In *The Marginal Revolution in Economics,* ed. R.D. Collison Black, A.W. Coats and C.D. Goodwin, Durham, North Carolina: Duke University Press.

Jevons, W.S. 1871. *The Theory of Political Economy.* London: Macmillan; 5th edn, New York: A.M. Kelley, 1965.

Kauder, E. 1965. *A History of Marginal Utility Theory.* Princeton: Princeton University Press.

Lloyd, W.F. 1833. A lecture on the notion of value, delivered before the University of Oxford in Michaelmas Term 1833. Reprinted in *Economic History,* supplement to the *Economic Journal,* No. 2, (1927), 168–83.

Marshall, A. 1890. *Principles of Economics.* 9th (Variorum) edn, ed. C.W. Guillebaud, London and New York: Macmillan, 1961.

Menger, C. 1871. *Grundsätze der Volkswirtschaftslehre.* Trans. by J. Dingwall and B.F. Hoselitz as *Principles of Economics,* Glencoe, Ill.: Free Press, 1951.

Mill, J.S. 1848. *Principles of Political Economy.* Ed. W.J. Ashley, London: Longmans, 1909; New York: A.M. Kelley, 1961.

O'Brien, D.P. 1975. *The Classical Economists.* Oxford: Clarendon Press.

Pigou, A.C. 1912. *Wealth and Welfare.* Expanded and republished as *The Economics of Welfare,* London: Macmillan, 1920; New York: St. Martin's Press, 1952.

Ricardo, D. 1817. *The Principles of Political Economy and Taxation.* Vol. I of *The Works and Correspondence of David Ricardo,* ed. P. Sraffa, Cambridge: Cambridge University Press, 1951; New York: Cambridge University Press, 1973.

Senior, N.W. 1836. *An Outline of the Science of Political Economy.* London: W. Clowes. Reprinted, London: Allen & Unwin, 1938.

Smith, A. 1776. *An Inquiry into the Nature and Causes of the Wealth of Nations.* Ed. R.H.Campbell and A.S. Skinner, Oxford: Clarendon Press, 1976.

Stigler, G.J. 1950. The development of utility theory. Pts I and II. *Journal of Political Economy* 58, 307–27; 373–96. Reprinted in G.J. Stigler, *Essays in the History of Economics,* Chicago: University of Chicago Press, 1965.

Viner, J. 1925. The utility concept in value theory and its critics. *Journal of Political Economy* 33, 369–87. Reprinted in J. Viner, *The Long View and the Short,* Glencoe, Ill.: Free Press, 1958.

Walras, L. 1874. *Eléments d'économie politique pure.* Lausanne: Corbaz et Cie. Trans. by W. Jaffé as *Elements of Pure Economics,* London: Allen & Unwin, 1954; Homewood, Ill.: R.D. Irwin.

Utility Theory and Decision Theory

PETER C. FISHBURN

The conjunction of utility theory and decision theory involves formulations of decision making in which the criteria for choice among competing alternatives are based on numerical representations of the decision agent's preferences and values. Utility theory as such refers to those representations and to assumptions about preferences that correspond to various numerical representations. Although it is a child of decision theory, utility theory has emerged as a subject in its own right as seen, for example, in the contemporary review by Fishburn (*see* REPRESENTATION OF PREFERENCES). Readers interested in more detail on representations of preferences should consult that essay.

Our discussion of utility theory and decision theory will follow the useful three-part classification popularized by Luce and Raiffa (1957), namely decision making under certainty, risk and uncertainty. I give slightly different descriptions than theirs.

Certainty refers to formulations that exclude explicit consideration of chance or uncertainty, including situations in which the outcome of each decision is known beforehand. Most of consumer demand theory falls within this category.

Risk refers to formulations that involve chance in the form of known probabilities or odds, but excludes unquantified uncertainty. Games of chance and insurance decisions with known probabilities for possible outcomes fall within the risk category. Note that 'risk' as used here is only tangentially associated with the common notion that equates risk with the possibility of something bad happening.

Uncertainty refers to formulations in which decision outcomes depend explicitly on events that are not controlled by the decision agent and whose resolutions are known to the agent only after the decision is made. Probabilities of the events are regarded either as meaningless, unknowable, or assessable only with reference

303

to personal judgement. Situations addressed by the theory of noncooperative games and statistical decision theory typically fall under this heading.

A brief history of the subject will provide perspective for our ensuing discussion of the three categories.

HISTORICAL REMARKS. The first important paper on the subject was written by Daniel Bernoulli (1738) who, in conjunction with Gabriel Cramer, sought to explain why prudent agents often choose among risky options in a manner contrary to expected profit maximization. One example is the choice of a sure $10,000 profit over a risky venture that loses $5000 or gains $30,000, each with probability $1/2$. Bernoulli argued that many such choices could be explained by maximization of the expected utility ('moral worth') of risky options, wherein the utility of wealth increases at a decreasing rate. He thus introduced the idea of decreasing marginal utility of wealth as well as the maximization of expected utility.

Although Bernoulli's ideas were endorsed by Laplace and others, they had little effect on the economics of decision making under risk until quite recently. On the other hand, his notion of decreasing marginal utility became central in consumer economics during the latter part of the 19th century (Stigler, 1950), especially in the works of Gossen, Jevons, Menger, Walras and Marshall.

During this early period, utility was often viewed as a measurable psychological magnitude. This notion of intensive measurable utility, which was sometimes represented by the additive form $u_1(x_1) + u_2(x_2 + \cdots + u_n(x_n)$ for commodity bundles $(x_1, x_2, \ldots, x_n)$, was subsequently replaced in the ordinalist revolution of Edgeworth, Fisher, Pareto and Slutsky by the view that utility represents nothing more than the agent's preference ordering over consumption bundles. A revival of intensive measurable utility occurred after 1920 when Frisch, Lange and Alt axiomatized the notion of comparable preference differences, but it did not regain the prominence it once held.

Bernoulli's long-dormant principle of the maximization of expected utility reappeared with force in the expected utility theory of von Neumann and Morgenstern (1944, 1947). Unlike Bernoulli and Cramer, who favoured an intensive measurable view of utility, von Neumann and Morgenstern showed how the expected utility form can arise solely from simple preference comparisons between risky options. They thus accomplished for decision making under risk what the ordinalists accomplished for demand theory a generation earlier.

Although little noted at the time, Ramsey (1931), in an essay written in 1926 and published posthumously, attempted something more ambitious than the utility theory for risky decisions of von Neumann and Morgenstern. Ramsey's aim was to show how assumptions about preferences between uncertain decisions imply not only a utility function for outcomes but also a subjective or personal probability distribution over uncertain events such that one uncertain decision is preferred to another precisely when the former has greater subjective (probability) expected utility. Ramsey's outline of a theory of decision making under uncertainty greatly influenced the first complete theory of subjective expected utility, due to Savage (1954). Savage also drew heavily on Bruno de Finetti's seminal ideas on subjective probability, which are similar in ways to views espoused much earlier by Bayes and Laplace.

During the historical period, several unsuccessful proposals were made to replace 'utility' by a term better suited to the concepts it represents. Despite these failures, the terms *ordinal utility* and *cardinal utility*, introduced by Hicks and Allen (1934) to distinguish between the ordinalist viewpoint and the older measurability view of utility as a 'cardinal magnitude', caught on. Present usage adheres to the following measurement theoretic definitions.

Let $\succ$ denote the relation *is preferred to* on a set X of decision alternatives, outcomes, commodity bundles, or whatever. Suppose preferences are ordered and can be represented by a real valued function u on X as

$$x \succ y \Leftrightarrow u(x) > u(y), \tag{1}$$

for all x and y in X. We then say that u is an *ordinal utility function* if it satisfies (1) but is subject to no further restrictions. Then any other real function v that preserves the order of $\succ$, or satisfies (1) in place of u, is also an ordinal utility function, and all such functions for the given $\succ$ are equivalent in the ordinal context. A different preference ordering on X will have a different equivalence class of order-preserving functions. If u is also required to be continuous, we may speak of continuous ordinal utility.

If u satisfies (1) and is restricted by subsidiary conditions in such a way that v also satisfies (1) *and* the subsidiary conditions if and only if there are numbers $a > 0$ and b such that

$$v(x) = au(x) + b, \qquad \text{for all } x \text{ in } X, \tag{2}$$

then u is a *cardinal utility function* and is said to be unique up to a positive $(a > 0)$ linear transformation. Subsidiary conditions that force (2) under the appropriate structure for X include additivity $u(x_1,\ldots,x_n) = u_1(x_1) + \cdots + u_n(x_n)$ with $n \geqslant 2$, the linearity property $u[\lambda p + (1 - \lambda)q] = \lambda u(p) + (1 - \lambda)u(q)$ of expected utility, and the ordered preference-difference representation $(x, y) \succ^*(z, w) \Leftrightarrow u(x) - u(y) > u(z) - u(w)$. Only the last of these, where $(x, y) \succ^*(z, w)$ says that the intensity of preference for x over y exceeds the intensity of preference for z over w, involves a view of preference that goes beyond the basic relation $\succ$.

DECISIONS UNDER CERTAINTY. Representation (1) is the preeminent utility representation for decision making under certainty. It presumes that the preference relation $\succ$ is

asymmetric: if $x \succ y$ then not $(y \succ x)$,

negatively transitive: if $x \succ z$ then $x \succ y$ or $y \succ z$,

and, when X is uncountably infinite, that there is a countable subset C_0 in X such that, whenever $x \succ y$, there is a z in C_0 such that $x \succsim z \succsim y$, where $x \succsim z$

means not $(z \succ x)$. An asymmetric and negatively transitive relation is often referred to as a *weak order*, and in this case both $\succ$ and its induced indifference relation $\sim$, defined by

$$x \sim y \text{ if neither } x \succ y \text{ nor } y \succ x,$$

are *transitive*, that is $(x \succ y, \ y \succ z) \Rightarrow x \succ z$ and $(x \sim y, \ y \sim z) \Rightarrow x \sim z$. If X is a connected and separable topological space, the countable C_0 condition can be replaced by the assumption that the preferred-to-x set $\{y: y \succ z\}$ and the less-preferred-than-x set $\{y: x \succ y\}$ are open sets in X's topology for every x in X. When this holds, u can be taken to be continuous. If the countable C_0 condition fails when $\succ$ is a weak order, (1) cannot hold and instead we could represent $\succ$ by vector-valued utilities ordered lexicographically. For details and further references, see Fishburn (1970, 1974).

Economics is often concerned with situations in which any one of a number of subsets of X might arise as the feasible set from which a choice is required. For example, if X is a commodity space $\{(x_1, \ldots, x_n): x_i \geqslant 0 \text{ for } i = 1, \ldots, n\}$, then the feasible set at price vector $p = (p_1, \ldots, p_n) > (0, \ldots, 0)$ and disposable income $m \geqslant 0$ is the *opportunity set* $\{(x_1, \ldots, x_n): p_1 x_1 + \cdots + p_n x_n \leqslant m\}$ of commodity bundles that can be purchased at p and m. The allure of (1) in such situations is that the same u can be used for choice by maximization of utility for each non-empty feasible set Y so long as the set

$$\max_u Y = \{x \text{ in } Y: u(x) \geqslant u(y) \text{ for all } y \text{ in } Y\}$$

is not empty. The existence of non-empty $\max_u Y$ is assured if Y is finite or if it is a compact subset of a connected and separable topological space on which u is upper semi-continuous.

When (1) holds, the set

$$\max \succ Y = \{x \text{ in } Y: y \succ x \text{ for no } y \text{ in } Y\}$$

of maximally-preferred elements in Y is identical to $\max_u Y$. On the other hand, $\max \succ Y$ can be non-empty when no utility function satisfies (1). For example, if X is finite, then $\max \succ Y$ is non-empty for every non-empty subset Y of X if, and only if, X contains no preference cycle, that is no $x_1, \ldots, x_m$ such that $x_1 \succ x_2 \succ \cdots \succ x_m \succ x_1$. In this case it is always possible to define u on X so that, for all x and y in X,

$$x \succ y \Rightarrow u(x) > u(y). \tag{3}$$

Then choices can still be made by maximization of utility since $\max_u Y$ will be a non-empty subset of $\max \succ Y$. However if $\succ$ has cycles, then the principle of choice by maximization breaks down.

The situation for infinite X and suitably constrained feasible sets is somewhat different. Sonnenschein (1971) shows for the commodity space setting that $\succ$

can have cycles while every opportunity set Y has a non-empty $\max \succ Y$. His key assumptions are a semicontinuity condition on $\succsim$ and the assumption that every preferred-to-x set is convex. Thus, choice by maximal preference may obtain when $\succ$ can be characterized by neither (1) nor (3).

$\text{Max} \succ Y$ for opportunity sets Y in commodity space is the agent's *demand correspondence* (which depends on p and m) or, if each $\max \succ Y$ is a singleton, his *demand function*. The revealed preference approach of Samuelson and others represents an attempt to base the theory of consumer demand directly on demand functions without invoking preference as an undefined primitive. If $f(p, m)$ denotes the consumer's unique choice at (p, m) from the opportunity set there, we say that commodity bundle x is *revealed to be preferred to* commodity bundle y if $y \neq x$ and there is a (p, m) at which $x = f(p, m)$ and $p_1 y_1 + \cdots + p_n y_n \leqslant m$. Conditions can then be stated (Uzawa, 1960; Houthakker, 1961; Hurwicz and Richter, 1971) for the revealed preference relation such that there exists a utility function u on X for which $\max_u Y = \{f(p, m)\}$ when Y is the opportunity set at (p, m), for every such Y.

The revealed preference approach in demand theory has stimulated a more general theory of choice functions. A *choice function* C is a mapping from a family of non-empty feasible subsets of X into subsets of X such that, for each feasible Y, $C(Y)$ is a non-empty subset of Y. The *choice set* $C(Y)$ describes the 'best' things in Y. Research in this area has identified conditions on C that allow it to be represented in interesting ways. Examples appear in Fishburn (1973, chapter 15) and Sen (1977). One is the condition

$$\text{if } Y \subseteq Z \text{ and } Y \cap C(Z) \text{ is non-empty,}$$

$$\text{then } C(Y) = Y \cap C(Z).$$

When every two-element and three-element subset of X is feasible, this implies that the revealed preference relation $\succ_r$, defined by $x \succ_r y$ if $x \neq y$ and $C(\{x, y\}) = \{x\}$, is a weak order. The weaker condition

$$\text{if } Y \subseteq z \text{ then } Y \cap C(Z) \subseteq C(Y).$$

implies that $\succ_r$ has no cycles when every non-empty finite subset of X is feasible.

DECISIONS UNDER RISK. Let P be a convex set of probability measures on an algebra $\mathscr{A}$ of subsets of an outcome set X. Thus, for every p in $\mathscr{P}$, $p(A) \geqslant 0$ for all A in $\mathscr{A}$, $p(X) = 1$, and $p(A \cup B) = p(A) + p(B)$ whenever A and B are disjoint sets in $\mathscr{A}$. *Convexity* means that $\lambda p + (1 - \lambda)q$ is in $\mathscr{P}$ whenever p and q are in $\mathscr{P}$ and $0 \leqslant \lambda \leqslant 1$. We assume that each $\{x\}$ is in $\mathscr{A}$ and each measure that has $p(\{x\}) = 1$ for some x in X is in $\mathscr{P}$.

The basic expected utility representation is, for all p and q in $\mathscr{P}$,

$$p \succ q \Leftrightarrow \int_X u(x) dp(x) > \int_X u(x) dq(x), \tag{4}$$

where u is a real valued function on X. When u satisfies (4), it is unique up to a positive linear transformation. The expected utility representation follows from the preference axioms of von Neumann and Morgenstern (1947) when each p in $\mathscr{P}$ has $p(A) = 1$ for a finite A in $\mathscr{A}$. Other cases are axiomatized in Fishburn (1970, 1982a). The most important axiom besides weak order is the *independence condition* which says that, for all p, q and r in P and all $0 < \lambda < 1$,

$$p \succ q \Rightarrow \lambda p + (1 - \lambda)r \succ \lambda q + (1 - \lambda)r. \tag{5}$$

If $5000 with certainty is preferred to a 50-50 gamble for $12,000 or $0, then (5) says that a 50-50 gamble for $5000 or $-$20,000 will be preferred to a gamble that returns $12,000 or $0 or $-$20,000 with probabilities $1/4$, $1/4$ and $1/2$ respectively: $r(-$20,000) = 1$ and $\lambda = 1/2$.

The principle of choice for expected utility says to choose an expected-utility maximizing decision or measure in the feasible subset $\mathscr{Q}$ of $\mathscr{P}$ when such a measure exists. Since convex combinations of measures in $\mathscr{Q}$ can be formed at little or no cost with the use of random devices, feasible sets are often assumed to be convex. Although this will not create a maximizing combination when none existed prior to convexification under the usual expected utility model, it can create maximally-preferred measures in more general theories that allow cyclic preferences. Convex feasible sets are also important in the minimax theory of noncooperative games (Nash, 1951) and economic equilibrium without ordered preferences (Mas-Colell, 1974; Shafer and Sonnenschein, 1975).

Expected utility for the special case of monetary outcomes has sired extensive literatures on risk attitudes (Pratt, 1964; Arrow, 1974) and stochastic dominance (Whitmore and Findlay, 1978; Bawa, 1982). Risk attitudes involve curvature properties of an increasing utility function ($u'' < 0$ for risk aversion) and their economic consequences for expected-utility maximizing agents. Stochastic dominance relates shape features of u to distribution function comparisons. For example, $\int u \, dp \geqslant \int u \, dq$ for all increasing u if and only if $p(\{x: x \geqslant c\}) \geqslant q(\{x: x \geqslant c\})$ for every real c.

Alternatives to expected utility maximization with monetary outcomes base criteria for choice on distribution function parameters such as the mean, variance, below-target semivariance and loss probability (Markowitz, 1959; Libby and Fishburn, 1977). The best known of these are mean (more is better)/variance (more is worse) models developed by Markowitz (1959), Tobin (1965) and others. Whether congruent with expected utility or not (Chipman, 1973), such models assume that preferences between distributions depend only on the parameters used.

Recent research in utility/decision theory of risky decisions has been motivated by empirical results (Allais and Hagen, 1979; Kahneman and Tversky, 1979; Slovic and Lichtenstein, 1983) which reveal systematic and persistent violations of the expected utility axioms, including (5) and transitivity. Alternative utility models that weaken (5) but retain weak order have been proposed by Kahneman and Tversky (1979), Machina (1982), and others. A representation which presumes neither (5) nor transitivity is axiomatized by Fishburn (1982b).

DECISIONS UNDER UNCERTAINTY. We adopt Savage's (1954) formulation in which each potential decision is characterized by a function f, called an *act*, from a set S of *states* into a set X of *consequences*. The consequence that occurs if f is taken and state s obtains is $f(s)$. Exactly one state will obtain, the agent does not know which it is, and the act chosen will not affect its realization. Examples of states are possible temperatures in central London at 12 noon next 14 July and possible closing prices of a company's stock next Thursday.

Suppose S and the set F of available acts are finite, and that there is a utility function u on X that satisfies (1) and perhaps other conditions. Choice criteria that avoid the question of subjective probabilities on $\mathscr{S}$ (Luce and Raiffa, 1957, chapter 13) include

maximum utility: choose f to maximize $\min\limits_{s} u[f(s)]$;

minimax loss: choose f to minimize

$$\max_{S}\left\{\max_{F} u[f(s)] - u[f(s)]\right\};$$

Hurwicz α: given $0 \le \alpha \le 1$, choose f to maximize

$$\alpha \max_{s} u[f(s)] + (1 - \alpha)\max_{s} u[f(s)].$$

Maximin, which maximizes the worst that can happen, is very conservative. Minimax loss (or regret), which is less conservative that maximin, minimizes the maximum difference between the best that could happen and what actually happens. Hurwicz α ranges from maximin ($\alpha = 0$) to 'maximax' ($\alpha = 1$).

Another criterion maximizes the average value of $u[f(s)]$ over s. This is tantamount to the subjective expected utility model with equal probability for each state.

Subjective probability as developed by Ramsey, de Finetti and Savage quantifies partial beliefs by the extent to which we are prepared to act on them. If you would rather bet £100 on horse A than on horse B then, *for you*, A has the higher probability of winning. If your beliefs adhere to appropriate axioms for a comparative probability relation $\succ^{*}$ on the algebra $\mathscr{S}$ of subsets of S (Fishburn, 1986) then there is a probability measure ρ on $\mathscr{S}$ such that, for all A and B in $\mathscr{S}$, $A \succ^{*} B \Leftrightarrow \rho(A) > \rho(B)$.

Savage's axioms for $\succ$ on F (Savage, 1954; Fishburn, 1970, chapter 14) imply the existence of a bounded utility function u on X and a probability measure ρ on $\mathscr{S}$ such that, for all f and g in F,

$$f \succ g \Leftrightarrow \int_{S} u[f(s)]\mathrm{d}\rho(s) > \int_{S} u[g(s)]\mathrm{d}\rho(s), \tag{6}$$

with u unique up to a positive linear transformation and ρ unique. His axioms include weak order, independence axioms that in part yield the preceding representation of $\succ$*, and a continuity condition. Many other people (Fishburn, 1981) have developed alternative axiomatizations of (6) and closely-related representations.

Recent alternatives to Savage's subjective expected utility theory have been motivated by the empirical results cited in the preceding section and by Ellsberg's (1961) challenges to the traditional subjective probability model. Suppose an urn contains 30 red balls and 60 others that are black and yellow in an unknown proportion. One ball is to be drawn at random. Many people are observed to prefer a bet on *red* rather than *black*, and a bet on *black or yellow* rather than *red or yellow*. By the traditional model, the first preference gives $\rho(\text{red}) > \rho(\text{black})$ and the second gives $\rho(\text{black}) > \rho(\text{red})$.

Schmeidler (1984) axiomatizes a utility model that replaces the additive probability measure ρ in (6) by a monotone $[A \subset B \Rightarrow \rho(A) \leqslant \rho(B)]$ but not necessarily additive measure and argues that his model can accommodate Ellsberg's phenomena. A different model (Loomes and Sugden, 1982) uses additive ρ but accommodates other violations of independence and cyclic preferences.

Maximization of subjective expected utility is the core principle of Bayesian decision theory (Savage, 1954; Raiffa and Schlaifer, 1961; Winkler, 1972). This name, used in distinction to classical methods of statistical analysis pioneered by R.A. Fisher, Jerzy Neyman, Egon Pearson and Abraham Wald, recognizes the unabashed use of subjective probability and the revision of probabilities in light of new evidence by the basic formula of conditional probability known as Bayes's Theorem.

A typical problem in statistical decision theory is to decide which of several possible experiments, if any, to perform for the purpose of gathering additional information that will be used in a subsequent decision. In the Bayesian approach, the primary states that occasion the need for further information can be enriched to incorporate potential experimental outcomes in such a way that (6) refers to the entire decision process. The problem can then be decomposed, as is usually done in practice, to compute optimal subsequent decisions based on particular experiments and their possible outcomes. Decision functions for each experiment that map outcomes into best subsequent acts can then be compared to determine a best experiment. Various methods of analysis in the Bayesian mode are described and illustrated in Raiffa and Schlaifer (1961).

BIBLIOGRAPHY

Allais, M. and Hagen, O. (eds) 1979. *Expected Utility Hypotheses and the Allais Paradox.* Dordrecht: Reidel.

Arrow, K.J. 1974. *Essays in the Theory of Risk Bearing.* Amsterdam: North-Holland.

Bawa, V.S. 1982. Stochastic dominance: a research bibliography. *Management Science* 28, 698–712.

Bernoulli, D. 1738. Specimen theoriae novae de mensura sortis. *Commentarii Academiae Scientarium Imperalis Petropolitanae* 5, 175–92. Trans. L. Sommer, *Econometrica* 22, (1954), 23–36.

Chipman, J.S. 1973. The ordering of portfolios in terms of mean and variance. *Review of Economic Studies* 40, 167–90.

Ellsberg, D. 1961. Risk, ambiguity, and the Savage axioms. *Quarterly Journal of Economics* 75, 643–69.

Fishburn, P.C. 1970. *Utility Theory for Decision Making*. New York: Wiley.

Fishburn, P.C. 1973. *The Theory of Social Choice*. Princeton: Princeton University Press.

Fishburn, P.C. 1974. Lexicographic orders, utilities, and decision rules: a survey. *Management Science* 20, 1442–71.

Fishburn, P.C. 1981. Subjective expected utility: a review of normative theories. *Theory and Decision* 13, 139–99.

Fishburn, P.C. 1982a. *The Foundations of Expected Utility*. Dordrecht: Reidel.

Fishburn, P.C. 1982b. Nontransitive measurable utility. *Journal of Mathematical Psychology* 26, 31–67.

Fishburn, P.C. 1986. The axioms of subjective probability. *Statistical Science* 1, 335–45.

Hicks, J.R. and Allen, R.G.D. 1934. A reconsideration of the theory of value, I, II. *Economica* 1, 52–75, 196–219.

Houthakker, H.S. 1961. The present state of consumption theory. *Econometrica* 29, 704–40.

Hurwicz, L. and Richter, M.K. 1971. Revealed preference without demand continuity assumptions. In *Preferences, Utility, and Demand*, ed. J.S. Chipman, L. Hurwicz, M.K. Richter and H.F. Sonnenschein, New York: Harcourt Brace Jovanovich.

Kahneman, D. and Tversky, A. 1979. Prospect theory: an analysis of decision under risk. *Econometrica* 47, 263–91.

Libby, R. and Fishburn, P.C. 1977. Behavioural models of risk taking in business decisions: a survey and evaluation. *Journal of Accounting Research* 15, 272–92.

Loomes, G. and Sugden, R. 1982. Regret theory: an alternative theory of rational choice under uncertainty. *Economic Journal* 92, 805–24.

Luce, R.D. and Raiffa, H. 1957. *Games and Decisions*. New York: Wiley.

Machina, M.J. 1982. 'Expected utility' analysis without the independence axiom. *Econometrica* 50, 277–323.

Markowitz, H. 1959. *Portfolio Selection*. New York: Wiley.

Mas-Colell, A. 1974. An equilibrium existence theorem without complete or transitive preferences. *Journal of Mathematical Economics* 1, 237–46.

Nash, J. 1951. Non-cooperative games. *Annals of Mathematics* 54, 286–95.

Pratt, J.W. 1964. Risk aversion in the small and in the large. *Econometrica* 32, 122–36.

Raiffa, H. and Schlaifer, R. 1961. *Applied Statistical Decision Theory*. Boston: Division of Research, Graduate School of Business, Harvard University.

Ramsey, F.P. 1931. Truth and probability. In *The Foundations of Mathematics and other Logical Essays*, ed. R.B. Braithwaite, New York: Harcourt, Brace, Reprinted in *Studies in Subjective Probability*, ed. H.E. Kyburg and H.E. Smokler, New York: Wiley, 1964, 61–92.

Savage, L.J. 1954. *The Foundations of Statistics*. New York: Wiley. 2nd rev. edn, Dover Publications, 1972.

Schmeidler, D. 1984. Subjective probability and expected utility without additivity. Reprint no. 84, Institute for Mathematics and its Application, University of Minnesota.

Sen, A. 1977. Social choice theory: a re-examination. *Econometrica* 45, 53–89.

Shafer, W. and Sonnenschein, H. 1975. Equilibrium in abstract economies without ordered preferences. *Journal of Mathematical Economics* 2, 345–8.

Slovic, P. and Lichtenstein, S. 1983. Preference reversals: a broader perspective. *American Economic Review* 73, 596–605.

Sonnenschein, H.F. 1971. Demand theory without transitive preferences with applications to the theory of competitive equilibrium. In *Preferences, Utility and Demand*, ed. J.S. Chipman, L. Hurwicz, M.K. Richter and H.F. Sonnenschein. New York: Harcourt Brace Jovanovich, 215–23.

Stigler, G.J. 1950. The development of utility theory: I, II. *Journal of Political Economy* 58, 307–27, 373–96.

Tobin, J. 1965. The theory of portfolio selection. In *The Theory of Interest Rates*, ed. F.H. Hahn and F.P.R. Brechling, New York: Macmillan, 3–51.

Uzawa, H. 1960. Preference and rational choice in the theory of consumption. In *Mathematical Methods in the Social Sciences, 1959*, ed. K.J. Arrow, S. Karlin and P. Suppes, Stanford, California: Stanford University Press, 129–48.

von Neumann, J. and Morgenstern, O. 1944. *Theory of Games and Economic Behavior*. Princeton, NJ: Princeton University Press. 2nd edn, 1947; 3rd edn, 1953.

Whitmore, G.A. and Findlay, M.C. (eds) 1978. *Stochastic Dominance*. Lexington, Mass.: Heath.

Winkler, R.L. 1972. *An Introduction to Bayesian Inference and Decision*. New York: Holt, Rinehart and Winston.

Contributors

Maurice Allais Professor of Economics, Ecole Nationale Supérieure des Mines de Paris. Fellow, Econometric Society; Honorary Member, American Economic Association. 'The influence of the capital–output ratio on real national income', *Econometrica* (1962); 'Forgetfulness and interest', *Journal of Money, Credit and Banking* (1972); 'The so-called Allais paradox and rational decisions under uncertainty' in *Expected Utility Hypotheses and the Allais Paradox* (ed., with O. Hagen, 1979); 'The cardinal utility and its determination – hypotheses, methods and empirical evidence', *Theory and Decision* (1987); *L'Impôt sur le capital et la reforme monétaire* (1988).

Kenneth J. Arrow John Kenney Professor of Economics, Professor of Operations Research, Stanford University. Nobel Memorial Prize in Economic Science (1972). 'Le rôle des valeurs boursières pour la répartition la meilleure des risques', *Econometrie* (1953); 'Existence of equilibrium for a competitive economy', *Econometrica* (with G. Debreu, 1954); 'Uncertainty and the welfare economics of medical care', *American Economic Review* (1963); *Social Choice and Individual Values* (1963); *Essays in the Theory of Risk-Bearing* (1971).

R.D. Collison Black Emeritus Professor of Economics, Queen's University, Belfast. *Economic Thought and the Irish Question, 1817–1870* (1960); *Ideas in Economics* (ed., 1986); *The Marginal Revolution in Economics* (ed., with A.W. Coats and C.D. Goodwin, 1973); *The Economic Writings of Mountifort Longfield* (ed., 1971); *Papers and Correspondence of William Stanley Jevons* (ed., 7 vols, 1972–81).

C. Blackorby Professor, Centre for Operations Research and Econometrics, Belgium. *Duality, Separability and Functional Structure: theory and economic applications* (with Daniel Primont and R. Robert Russell, 1978).

Douglas H. Blair Associate Professor of Economics, Rutgers University. 'Impossibility theorems without collective rationality', *Journal of Economic Theory* (with G. Bordes, J. Kelly and K. Suzumura, 1976); 'On the ubiquity of strategic voting opportunities', *International Economic Review* (1981); 'Acyclic collective choice rules', *Econometrica* (with R. Pollak, 1982); 'Polychromatic acyclic tours in coloured multigraphs', *Mathematics of Operations Research* (with R. Pollak, 1983); 'Labour union objectives and collective bargaining', *Quarterly Journal of Economics* (1984); 'Unbuilding the voting rights and profit claims of common shares', *Journal of Political Economy* (1989).

Margaret Bray Reader in Economics, London School of Economics. 'Futures trading, rational expectations and the efficient markets hypothesis', *Econometrica* (1981); 'Learning, estimation, and the stability of rational expectations', *Journal of Economic Theory* (1982); 'Rational learning and rational expectations' (with D.M. Kreps) in *Arrow and the Ascent of Modern Economic Theory* (ed. G.R. Feiwal, 1987); 'Rational expectations equilibria, learning and model specification', *Econometrica* (with N.E. Savin, 1986); 'Convergence to rational expectations equilibria', *Individual Forecasting and Aggregate Outcomes* (ed. R. Frydman and E.S. Phelps, 1983); *Rational Expectations, Information and Asset Markets: An Introduction* (1985).

Larry G. Epstein Professor, Department of Economics, University of Toronto. 'Substitution, risk aversion and the temporal behavior of consumption and asset returns', *Econometrica* (with S. Zin, 1989); 'Risk aversion and asset prices', *Journal of Monetary Economics* (1988); 'A simple dynamic general equilibrium model', *Journal of Economic Theory* (1987); 'Decreasing risk aversion and mean variance analysis', *Econometrica* (1985); 'The rate of time preference and dynamic economic analysis', *Journal of Political Economy* (with A. Hynes, 1983); 'Stationary cardinal utility and optimal growth under uncertainty', *Journal of Economic Theory* (1983).

Peter C. Fishburn Distinguished Member of Technical Staff, Mathematical Studies Department, AT&T Bell Laboratories. Fellow, Econometric Society. *Decision and Value Theory* (1964); *Utility Theory for Decision Making* (1970); *The Theory of Social Choice* (1973); *Foundations of Expected Utility* (1982); *Interval Orders and Interval Graphs* (1985); *Nonlinear Preference and Utility Theory* (1988).

Xavier Freixas Professor, University of Toulon. 'Engel curves leading to the weak axiom in the aggregate', *Econometrica* (1987); 'Planning under incomplete information and the Ratchet effect', *Review of Economic Studies* (with R. Guesnerie and J. Tirole, 1985); 'Average cost pricing vs marginal cost pricing under moral hazard', *Journal of Public Economics* (with J.J. Lafont, 1985).

314

Giancarlo Gandolfo Professor of International Economics, Faculty of Economics and Commerce; Director of Graduate Studies, Department of Economics, University of Rome. *Mathematical Methods and Models in Economic Dynamics* (1971); *Qualitative Analysis and Econometric Estimation of Continuous Time Dynamic Models* (1981); *A Disequilibrium Model of Real and Financial Accumulation in an Open Economy: theory, empirical evidence, and policy simulations* (with P.C. Padoan, 1984); *International Economics I and II* (1987); 'The Italian continuous time model: theory and empirical results', *Economic Modelling* (with P.C. Padoan, 1989).

Irving John Good Distinguished Professor, Department of Statistics, Virginia Polytechnic Institute and State University. Fellow, International Statistical Institute; Member, American Academy of Arts and Sciences. *Good Thinking: the foundations of probability and its applications* (1983); *Probability and the Weighing of Evidence* (1950); *The Estimation of Probabilities: An Essay on Modern Bayesian Methods* (1965); 'The interface between statistics and philosophy of science', *Statistical Science* (1988); 'Weight of evidence: a brief survey', *Bayesian Statistics 2: proceedings of the second Valencia international meeting September 6/10 1983* (ed. J.M. Bernardo et al., 1985).

Ian Hacking Professor, Institute for the History and Philosophy of Science and Technology, University of Canada. Fellow, Royal Society of Canada. *Logic of Statistical Inference* (1965); *The Emergence of Probability* (1975); *Why does Language Matter to Philosophy* (1975); *Representing and Intervening* (1983); *The Taming of Chance* (1989).

Peter J. Hammond Professor of Economics, Stanford University. Fellow, Econometric Society; Guggenheim Fellow (1986–7). 'Markets as constraints: multilateral incentive compatibility in continuum economies', *Review of Economic Studies* (1987); 'Consequentialist foundations for expected utility', *Theory and Decision* (1988); 'Consequentialist social norms for public decisions' in *Social Choice and Public Decision Making: essays in honour of Kenneth J. Arrow Vol. I* (ed. W.P. Heller, R.M. Starr and D.A. Starrett, 1986); 'Project evaluation by potential tax reform', *Journal of Public Economics* (1986); 'Overlapping expectations and Hart's conditions for equilibrium in a securities model', *Journal of Economic Theory* (1983); 'Charity: altruism or cooperative egoism?' in *Altruism, Morality and Economic Theory* (ed. E.S. Phelps, 1975).

John C. Harsanyi Flood Research Professor in Business Administration; Professor of Economics, University of California. Fellow, Econometric Society, American Academy of Arts and Sciences. *Essays on Ethics, Social Behaviour, and Scientific Explanation* (1976); *Rational Behaviour and Bargaining Equilibrium in Games and Social Situations* (1977); *Papers in Game Theory* (1982); *A General Theory of Equilibrium Selection in Games* (with Reinhard Selten, 1988).

Paul William Humphreys Associate Professsor, University of Virginia. *The Chances of Explanation* (1989).

Edi Karni Professor, Department of Economics, Johns Hopkins University. 'Free competition and the optimal amount of fraud', *Journal of Law and Economics* (with M.R. Darby, 1973); 'On multivariate risk aversion', *Econometrica* (1979); 'On state dependent preferences and subjective probabilities', *Econometrica* (with D. Schmeidler and K. Vind, 1983); 'Risk aversion for state-dependent utility functions: measurement and applications', *International Economic Review* (1983); *Decision Making Under Uncertainty: the case of state dependent preferences* (1985); '"Preference reversal" and the observability of preferences by experimental methods', *Econometrica* (with Z. Safra, 1987).

Mordecai Kurz Professor of Economics, Stanford University. Fellow, Econometric Society; Guggenheim Fellow (1977–8). *Public Investment, the Rate of Return, and Optimal Fiscal Policy* (with K.J. Arrow, 1970); 'The general instability of a class of growth processes', *Review of Economic Studies* (1967); 'Equilibrium in finite sequence of markets with transaction cost', *Econometrica* (1974); 'Power and taxes in a multi-commodity economy', *Israel Journal of Mathematics* (with R. Aumann, 1977); 'Endogenous formation of coalitions', *Econometrica* (1983); 'Voting for public goods', *Review of Economic Studies* (with R. Aumann and A. Neyman, 1983).

Haim Levy Hebrew University and University of Florida. 'The efficiency analysis of choices involving risk', *Review of Economic Studies* (with G. Hanoch, 1969); 'International diversification of investment portfolios', *American Economic Review* (with M. Sarnat, 1970); 'Stochastic dominance, efficiency criteria and efficient portfolios: the multi-period case', *American Economic Review* (1973); 'The capital asset pricing model and the investment horizon', *Review of Economics and Statistics* (with D. Levhari, 1977); 'Equilibrium in an imperfect market: a constraint on the number of securities in the portfolio', *American Economic Review* (1978); 'Investment decision rules, diversification and investors' initial wealth', *Econometrica* (with Y. Kroll, 1978).

Dennis V. Lindley Formerly Professor of Statistics, University College, London. *Introduction to Probability and Statistics: from a Bayesian Viewpoint* (1965); *Bayesian Statistics: A Review* (1972); *Making Decisions* (1985); *New Cambridge Elementary Statistical Tables* (with W.F. Scott, 1984).

Mark Machina Professor, Department of Economics, University of California. *The Economic Theory of Individual Behavior Toward Risk: theory, evidence and new directions* (1987).

Peter Newman Professor of Economics, Johns Hopkins University. *Costs in Alternative Locations: The Clothing Industry* (with D.C. Hague, 1952);

'The erosion of Marshall's theory of value', *Quarterly Journal of Economics* (1960); *British Guiana: problems of cohesion in an immigrant society* (1964); *Malaria Eradication and Population Growth* (1965); 'Some properties of concave functions', *Journal of Economic Theory* (1969).

Jurg Neihans Professor of Economics, University of Bern. *The Theory of Money* (1978); *International Monetary Economics* (1984); *History of Economic Theory: classic contributions 1720–1980* (forthcoming).

Charles R. Plott Edward S. Harkness Professor of Economics and Political Science, California Institute of Technology. Fellow, Econometric Society, American Academy of Arts and Sciences; Guggenheim Fellow (1981–2). 'Rational choice in experimental markets', *Journal of Business* (1986); 'Dimensions of parallelism: some policy applications of experimental methods', *Laboratory Experimentation in Economics: six points of view* (ed. A.E. Roth, 1987); 'Laboratory experiments in economics: the implications of posted-price institutions', *Science* (1987); 'An experimental analysis of public goods provision mechanisms with and without unanimity', *Review of Economic Studies* (with J. Banks and D. Porter, 1988); 'Rational expectations and the aggregation of diverse information in laboratory security markets', *Econometrica* (with S. Sunder, forthcoming); 'An updated review of industrial organization applications of experimental methods', *Handbook of Industrial Organization* (ed. R. Schmalensee and R. Willig, forthcoming).

H. Polemarchakis Columbia University. 'On the desirability of a totally random monetary policy', *Journal of Economic Theory* (with L. Weiss, 1977); 'On the disaggregation of excess demand functions', *Econometrica* (with John Geanakoplos, 1980); 'Recovering cardinal utility', *Review of Economic Studies* (with P. Dybvig, 1981); 'We cannot disagree forever', *Journal of Economic Theory* (with J.D. Geanakoplos, 1982); 'Asset markets, general equilibrium and the neutrality of money', *Review of Economic Studies* (1984); 'Observability and optimality', *Journal of Mathematical Economics* (with J.D. Geanakoplos, 1988).

Murray N. Rothbard S.J. Hall Distinguished Professor of Economics, University of Nevada. Vice President for Academic Affairs, Ludwig von Mises Institute. *Man, Economy and State: a treatise on economic principles* (2 vols, 1962/70); *America's Great Depression* (1963); *Power and Market: government and the economy* (1970); *For a New Liberty* (1973); *Conceived in Liberty* (4 vols., 1975–9); *The Ethics of Liberty* (1982).

M. Rothschild Professor, University of Vienna. 'Increasing risk 1: a definition', *Journal of Economic Theory* (with J. Stiglitz, 1971); *Uncertainty in Economics* (ed. with Peter Diamond, 1978).

Zvi Safra Tel Aviv University. 'Manipulation by reallocating initial endowments', *Journal of Mathematical Economics* (1983); 'Existence of equilibrium for Walrasian endowment games', *Journal of Economic Theory* (1985); 'Risk aversion in the theory of expected utility with rank-dependent probabilities', *Journal of Economic Theory* (with Chew Soo Hong and Edi Karni, 1987); '"Preference reversal" and the observability of preferences by experimental methods', *Econometrica* (with Edi Karni, 1987); 'On the structure of non-manipulable equilibria', *Journal of Mathematical Economics* (1988); 'Efficient sets with and without the expected utility hypothesis', *Journal of Mathematical Economics* (with Itzhak Zilcha, forthcoming).

I. Richard Savage Professor of Statistics, Yale University.

David Schmeidler Tel-Aviv University. *Social Goals and Social Organization: essays in memory of Elisha Pazner* (ed., with L. Hurwicz and H. Sonnenschein, 1985).

Amartya K. Sen Drummond Professor of Political Economy, Oxford University; Lamont University Professor, Harvard University. President, Econometric Society 1984. *On Economic Inequality* (1973); *Poverty and Famines* (1981); *Resources, Value and Development* (1984); *Commodities and Capabilities* (1985); *On Ethics and Economics* (1987).

W. Shafer Professor, University of Bonn. *No Crisis: the implications of US dependence on Southern African strategic minerals* (1983).

Herbert A. Simon Professor of Computer Science and Psychology, Carnegie – Mellon University. Nobel Memorial Prize in Economics (1978); Distinguished Fellow, American Economic Association (1976). *Models of Man* (1957); *The Sciences of the Artificial* (1969); *Human Problem Solving* (with A. Newell, 1972); *Administrative Behavior* (1976); *Models of Discovery* (1977); *Models of Bounded Rationality* (2 Vols., 1982).

Peter Wakker Nijmegen Institute of Cognition and Information Technology. 'Agreeing probability measures for comparative probability structures', *Annals of Statistics* (1981); 'Cardinal coordinate independence for expected utility', *Journal of Mathematical Psychology* (1984); 'Nonexpected utility as aversion of information', *Journal of Behavioral Decision Making* (1988); *Additive Representations of Preferences, a new foundation of decision analysis* (1989).

Georg Henrik von Wright Research Professor, Academy of Finland. *A Treatise on Induction and Probability* (1951); *Logical Studies* (1956); *The Varieties of Goodness* (1963); *Norm and Action* (1963); *Explanation and Understanding* (1971); *Philosophical Papers I–III* (1983/4).

S.L. Zabell Department of Mathematics and Statistics, Northwestern University. 'Large deviations of the sample mean in general vector spaces', *Annals of Probability* (with R.R. Bahadur, 1979); 'W.E. Johnson's sufficientness postulate', *Annals of Statistics* (1982); 'What happened in Hazelwood: statistics, employment discrimination, and the 80% rule' (with P. Meier and J. Sacks), in *Statistics and the Law* (ed. M. DeGroot, S. Fienberg and J. Kadane, 1986).